FAR
ABOVE
RUBIES

VOLUME ONE

BY LYNDA COATS

A Jr. High & High School Unit Study
for Young Women

Volume I:
Units 1 - 10

DISCLAIMER

This new edition of Far Above Rubies was revised & updated in 2015.
Although the author and publisher have made every effort to ensure that the information in this book was correct at press time, the author and publisher do not assume and hereby disclaim any liability to any party for any loss, damage, or disruption caused by errors or omissions, whether such errors or omissions result from negligence, accident, or any other cause.

AUTHOR'S DEDICATION

This book is dedicated to my daughter Becky, the one for whom it was written.
She is living proof that this system works and can bring God's blessings to its users.
We also dedicate this to the glory of our Lord Jesus Christ, who made it possible and blessed its use.

FAR ABOVE RUBIES
VOLUME I

TABLE OF CONTENTS

FAR ABOVE RUBIES

VOLUME ONE

GUIDELINES FOR USING
Far Above Rubies
Proverbs 31:10-31

Far Above Rubies is designed to train girls of high school age to become the godly women our Lord wants them to be. It is based on Proverbs 31:10-31, and is designed to cover all subjects for a complete high school education, including many suggestions for expanding into specialized areas of interest.

Though the author has tried to provide a well-rounded curriculum useful for college preparatory purposes as well as offering a number of business and vocational skills, our primary goal is to help Christian young ladies develop their character and abilities for useful service to the Lord within the family setting. We hope to help maturing Christian girls under-stand the importance of homemaking as a full-time profession, even for a woman who may have another profession or occupation as well. This curriculum stresses the importance of a woman's making her family her number one Earthly priority in terms of time and emotional commitment, and of seeing this as her life calling from God.

In that context, we attempt to prepare a young woman for all the responsibilities of adult life. This requires a thorough well-rounded high school education, basic life skills, a variety of home-based business and vocational skills, and mastery of a wide range of house-hold and family-oriented tasks. The over-arching principle for all of this is to train the young lady to be a helper for her husband, nurturer of her children and keeper at home, all of which are Biblical priorities for women. College and job preparation is included, but it is only of secondary importance in the overall objectives of this study.

It is the heartfelt prayer of all those connected with the publication of this volume that the Lord would use it mightily to train Godly women to undertake the awesome task of rearing and nurturing the next generation of God's children. May their godly lives be used to bring great spiritual renewal to God's people and to richly bless all with whom they come in contact. Please join us in this prayer for your own family as you begin the adventure that is **Far Above Rubies.**

A Word from the Author

Far Above Rubies was not originally written to publish for sale. It is a product of our family's search for an appropriate course of study for our daughter Becky. When she turned twelve and had mastered all of her basic studies, we decided she was ready to begin high school. So, like most parents, my husband Lauren and I set off to find a curriculum for her. However, that proved to be much harder than we had expected.

Becky was a hands-on, activity-oriented learner — a combination of the learning styles described in this volume as The Builder and The Cooperator. She had always been taught with unit studies and other non-textbook methods, and we did not wish to change that. It seemed for a time, however, that we would have no choice. There were few options available for the upper grades at that time.

As we began to investigate materials that were out there, another problem arose. Since Becky had always felt called to be a home-working wife and homeschooling mom, we wanted a program that would encourage and prepare her for that life-styles. There were none. Everything we found, even from Christian publishers, was much more career-oriented than we wanted. There were some wonderful programs, but nothing that was right for Becky. We took the matter to the Lord, asking Him to lead us to the right material or help us modify one for her.

His answer was a shock to all of us and resulted in the volume you now hold in your hands. God, in His infinite wisdom, led me unmistakably to Proverbs 31, a passage I had always loved and tried to emulate. I began to look at it as the way to train Becky for her future calling, but still did not fathom the depths of God's plan.

At first, I thought I was to use Proverbs 31 as a Bible study on womanhood and the domestic calling to supplement (and perhaps, counteract) whatever prepared curriculum we would use for her. It was not until I began planning how to teach it, that God revealed the totality of His plan. He opened my mind and my heart to view the passage in a totally different way and to fully mine its riches for all areas of education.

Everything that Far Above Rubies has become has been due to His leading and the answer to the simple prayers of a pair of homeschool parents for their child. I take no credit for this work, but give all the glory to the One who truly made it happen. It is my prayer that He will use it as mightily in your family as He has in ours.

In His Love,
Lynda Coats

The Philosophies Behind Far Above Rubies

1.   **God created each of us as individuals.** Each person is a unique human being from the moment of conception, different from every other human being. This difference includes mental, emotional, and personality distinctives that impact how a person learns and what she will become. For this reason, **Far Above Rubies** was designed to be broad-based and flexible enough to meet a wide-range of educational needs and learning styles.

2.   **In their natural state, all human beings are sinners.** It is not enough to teach a student the difference between right and wrong. A moral, well-behaved sinner is still estranged from God. To have a right relationship with God, a person must repent of sin and be saved from it. It is up to Christian parents to teach this to their children and to pray for the Lord to make it real in their lives.

3.   **Salvation is in the blood of Jesus Christ and in no other.** We must lead our children to put their trust in the Lord Jesus and pray for their salvation, even as we train their minds and supply their physical needs. It is not possible to train' someone to become a Child of God (also known as being saved); that can only be done by God himself. We can only share the message, prepare the ground, and pray for the results, but we MUST do that. We should teach our children to walk in His truth, even before they understand it for themselves.

4.   **Our children belong to God.** They are given to us in sacred trust from God the creator for a relatively short time to bless our lives and give us a special ministry for God. We are responsible before Him for how we rear and train our children during the time they are in our homes.

5.   **God gave each child to specific parents for a reason.** Except for God, no one knows your child as well as you do or is as perfectly suited to teach him. When parents commit atrocities against their children, it is not parenthood or God's choice of parents that is faulty. Sin is the root cause of child abuse and neglect as well as all other evils. Leading parents into a right relationship with God through faith in Christ is the answer, not taking children from parents or forbidding parents to teach them.

6.   **Teaching is the domain of the parents, not of a school or any other entity.** Scripture is full of references to parents teaching and training their own children, but says nothing about schools or classrooms_ Scripture also abounds with evidence that it is the parents whom God holds responsible for the education and moral training of their children. Judging by Scripture, we must infer that this responsibility is still upon parents, even if the child attends school or is taught by someone else.

7.   **All education is religious.** All knowledge comes from God who is the author of it. Just as there can be no error in God's Word, there can also be no truth outside of its realms. Even those branches of education which are normally considered secular or morally-neutral, when we thoroughly investigate them, are found to center in and/or revolve around God, His creation, or His revealed word. We teach and learn either from this Biblical viewpoint or from a non-Biblical one.

8.   **Education is a natural part of life.** Notice the many times in Scripture when the Lord, in His earthly ministry or through the inspired writers, uses the everyday objects and affairs of life or nature to teach spiritual lessons. Everything with which we come in contact can teach us something. It is up to us as Christians to glean from those experiences all that the Lord has for us. As parents we are responsible to arrange our children's activities and environment to teach from them the things which are desirable and not the undesirable.

9.	**Teaching should be done in a natural way**. Deuteronomy 6:4-9 tells us how we should teach our children the things of God. it encourages us to tell them of these things throughout the day in everything that we do, and to diligently guide their education by example as well as instruction. As all of education is from God, this methodology can be applied to teaching all subjects and skills and is the pattern followed in this unit study manual.

10.	**Teaching should take a form that best meets the particular child's learning style and educational needs.** (See Learning Styles section elsewhere in this guide.) There are many activities in this unit study for each type of learner. The job of the parent/teacher is to help each student choose those items that best meet her individual needs, while including enough items designed for other learning styles to challenge her in areas of weakness and/or broaden her perspective.

11.	**Children should be immersed in Scripture.** It should be more than a school subject or something relegated to church or Sunday School. As parents we should open the Word of God to our children and train them to read it for themselves as soon as possible. As good as Bible stories, commentaries, dramatized audios, and Bible videos can be for teaching the stories and principles of the Bible, there is no substitute for reading or hearing the actual Word of God, word for word, in an accurate translation.

12.	**The purpose of teaching and parenting is to work ourselves out of a job.** It is the goal of all Christian education for parent/teachers to work as God's instruments in molding the little ones He gives us into mature, godly adults who are capable of replacing us in society in the future. As our children reach each new level of maturity, it behooves us parents to give them ever-increasing control over their own education within Biblical parameters.

13.	**Productivity is paramount for the servant of God.** It should be a part of every young person's education to learn the value of work and to be motivated to work heartily at whatever he does, realizing it is all for the Lord. As parents, we should encourage our young people to make good use of time in all circumstances and to be productive even in their spare time.

14.	**Young people after the age of about thirteen are ready to begin accepting adult responsibility.** For that reason, we should begin at that age to allow our children to make more and more of their own decisions. We are to counsel and guide, and we do still have veto power, if matters come to that, but it is important to let our daughters think through their own problems and exercise their own discernment rather than automatically solving their problems or telling them what to do.

15.	**No matter her age, every Christian woman belongs under the covering of her God-ordained head**. For an unmarried girl, this head is her father. For this reason, a daughter should live with or near and remain under the Spiritual leadership of her father until God gives her a husband. This is true whether or not the father is a Christian: Scripture is quite clear that God delights in leading the women who serve Him through even ungodly husbands and fathers. Women living without husbands or fathers should appeal to the elders of their church to be assigned to a spiritual head by them. This is God's plan for us as women.

16.	**Even a child has a place in God's family.** We should begin at a very early age to train our children to care about others and to serve the Christian community insofar as they can at each age. This curriculum offers many opportunities for service to others. It is part of the training of children to help them identify their own spiritual gifts and learn to use them for the glory of God.

Learning Styles

One of the most important steps in preparing to home school is determining the student's learning style. Everyone was created by God as a unique individual, and one way our individuality is expressed is in the variety of ways in which we best learn and/or work. Understanding the way in which a student learns best is a very important part of establishing and executing a successful program of home education. To make this a little easier, the many different variations of learning styles that exist can be catalogued into four basic types, which are described on the next two pages. These styles have been explored from many angles and given many names. The ones used here are our own and are guidelines only. You will find that **Far Above Rubies** has activities suitable to all learning styles. It is simply a matter of choosing those that best fit each student.

It is valuable to know how your daughter learns best, so you can help her choose those activities which will best meet her needs. It is unlikely that anyone will fit totally into any one of these categories, but knowing what type of learning comes easiest for your child allows you to make her schooling more efficient and easier for you and her. You are also better able to encourage her in those areas that don't come naturally and help strengthen her weaknesses. To that end, we offer these suggestions to be used as you see fit.

You will notice that each learning style has both positive and negative components. It is the job of the parent to make use of a student's positive traits while trying to alter his negative ones. If taught properly using the guidelines established for it, **Far Above Rubies** should offer a chance to do both those things. However, it is probably not advisable to teach the entire curriculum using only activities for any one particular style, as exposure to skills and activities which do not come naturally will strengthen your child's mental abilities and develop perseverance. Still, too much of that type pressure can result in discouragement. Be sensitive to the student's reaction as she works on different activities, and be prepared to intervene if the frustration level seems to get too high.

Characteristics of the Four Learning Styles

Type A — The Builder:

1. Learns best by that which she can do for herself

2. Prefers hands-on activities, (ie. projects, experiments)

3. Needs the freedom to be spontaneous

4. Learns best when allowed to explore a variety of activities

5. May need to change activities often,

6. Works without being pushed only on things she really enjoys

7. Sometimes needs guidance to stay on track

8. Does best with activities which are short in duration

9. Wants to be the center of attention in any group

10 Prefers non-structured activities

11.   Is best suited to a flexible schedule

12.   Especially enjoys music, art, athletics, and drama

13.   Will need help to develop responsibility

14.   Deals most effectively with that which can be demonstrated

15.   Learns skills more readily than information

16.   Will most likely enjoy a career in decorating, building trades, mechanics, visual arts, or hands-on technology

Type B — The Memorizer

1.   Learns by reading, answering questions, memorizing

2.   Prefers workbooks, word games, short answer quizzes

3.   Needs a well-organized day with no surprises

4.   Likes a consistent routine

5.   Has little trouble completing activities on time

6.   Does his work according to the rules, whatever they are

7.   Can easily follow preset plans on her own if well-explained

8.   Prefers for all lessons to be about the same length

9.   Seek approval of authority figures rather than popularity

10   Feels secure in a structured environment

11.   Likes all lessons in same order at the same time each day

12.   Especially enjoys math, spelling, geography, history facts

13.   Needs help to think or act creatively

14.   Works most effectively with things that can be memorized

15.   Is most interested in facts that can be neatly cataloged

16.   Will most likely enjoy a career in accounting, bookkeeping, auditing, law enforcement, management, clerical or office work, or government

Type C — The Questioner

1. Strives to understand why facts are true and how things work

2. Enjoys puzzles, brain teasers, and problem-solving

3. Like to plan own activities with minimum input from others

4. Prefers to vary routine as called for by specific projects

5. Usually prefers to stay with one project until it is done

6. Is self-motivated, often to the point of pushing herself

7. Prefers to do his own planning and work independently

8. Does extremely well with long-range projects

9. Tends to avoid group activities

10. Structures work environment to match current project

11. Varies schedule to match project and may lose track of time

12. Especially enjoys abstract math, sciences, technologies

13. Needs help to avoid becoming a "workaholic"

14. Deals most effectively with what can be empirically analyzed

15. Values learning and intelligence for their own sakes

16. Will most likely choose a career in engineering, analysis, applied science or technology

Type D — The Cooperator

1. Learns best concepts and ideas which have meaning for her

2. Enjoys creative projects and cooperative ventures

3. Works well in a loosely-organized environment

4. Sees routines as necessary evils and often ignores them

5. May move from one activity to another with no notice of time

6. Has a motivation level that varies with interest in lesson

7. Needs little supervision, but wants companionship at work

8. Cares less about length of project than type

9. Loves group activities, but hates conflict or criticism

10. Works best in casual environment with background music

11. Has little use for schedules

12. Enjoys creative writing, literature, languages, the study of other cultures, all performing arts

13. Needs help to get places on time and keep up with things

14. Deals more effectively with concepts and ideas than details

15. Sets high ideals for herself and society

16. Will most likely choose a career in the arts, health care, education, or other helping professions

The Six R's of Education

Most of us are probably familiar with the three r's', which is a popular phrase in spite of its misuse of spelling. We have an expanded version of this, which we believe defines all that makes up a quality education. Instead of three R's, we believe there are six. Specific ideas on how to teach each of these are included in the next section, and all are taught in **Far Above Rubies.**

1.   **Reading** — The ability to read a variety of material well and understand what is read is one of the major keys to real literacy. Many doors of opportunity are open to those who can read, and the well-read student will always benefit much from reading. Such a person can learn much and have many, valuable experiences between the pages of books and will enjoy the many good books in this unit. If your daughter has difficulty reading or is not on grade level, she may need some intensive tutoring in that area, perhaps including a phonics course or review, before beginning **Far Above Rubies** or concurrent with it. There are many good programs to teach reading and to improve skills in that area. The Appendix lists some specifically designed for older students and adults.

2.   **(W)riting** — It is crucial that a person be able to communicate her ideas in writing. Training for this includes, but is not limited to, penmanship, grammar, creative thinking, spelling, vocabulary, and composition in a wide variety of written work. If a student's poor penman-ship seems to hold her back in other areas of composition, there are several things that may ease the situation. Separate penmanship from creative writing by the use of typewriters, word processors, or tape recorders to do the initial composition. Often switching to another form of handwriting; e.g. Spencerian, Italic, etc. will improve legibility and confidence. Practice penmanship when content is not at issue by having her copy Scripture verses, grocery lists, items to be memorized, or similar things, while you let her write original compositions on the type-writer or computer or dictate them into a tape recorder. For other suggestions in this area, see "Supplemental Courses" in the appendix.

3.   **(A)rithmetic** — This can be broadened to include all aspects of math, including algebra, geometry, and more advanced math disciplines. It also includes business math, bookkeeping or accounting and consumer math. All math is best taught on the basis of need with immediate or near-immediate application. Many units suggest specific math courses to coincide with the unit. You will probably wish to supplement with additional math, using one of the books in the resource list on that topic.

4.   **Research** — For any student, gaining the ability to find for herself whatever information she might need to know is much more valuable than memorizing lists of names, dates, and other facts. Students should be introduced to dictionaries, encyclopedias, and libraries very early and should be given many opportunities to use card catalog systems, (online now) periodic guides, microfiche readers, and other research tools. It is also helpful to let them know what is the best source for finding which kind of information. There are ample projects in each unit of this curriculum that offer that type of training. It is important for the student to do as much of her own research, even locating the resources, as possible.

5.   **Responsibility** — This may be one of the most important goals most of us have for our children. If she has been given adequate training and opportunities, a young lady may already be quite responsible by the time she begins this course. Regrettably, however, most schools and curricula don't expect any more in this area from a 15 year-old than from a first grader. They `spoon-feed' material to the student, and urge teachers to explain everything thoroughly and monitor all work closely. Ideally, a high school student should be an apprentice adult, responsible for his own education as well as caring for herself and her own things in the home. If your

daughter is ready for this responsibility, she will be able to choose her own activities within a unit, make productive use of her time each day, and complete work on schedule without reminders. You should encourage her to do as much on her own as possible, but provide the supervision and guidance you deem necessary, decreasing it as you are able.

6.   **Righteousness** — The ultimate goal of all we teach our children is to develop godliness and lead them to a saving knowledge of Jesus Christ, who alone can give true righteousness. There is no greater ministry in our lives than to raise godly .adults to lead, train and nurture the next generation. This is both a privilege and a heavy responsibility, but God has promised to enable us with His power and bless our efforts. Bible study is important to this goal, as is examining all other studies in light of Scripture. Perhaps even more important is setting before our daughters a godly example of Christian living. Though mothers are the primary influence in this process, it is valuable for Dad to take as large a role as possible. As it is from their fathers that young women learn how to relate to a man, the input of a godly father is as great for a girl as for a boy, but it is not essential. God can meet any need in yours or your child's life. Rely on Him and let your daughter know that you do. Your relationship with the Lord may be as crucial in your daughter's life as any other single factor besides her own salvation.

BATHE ALL THAT YOU DO IN PRAYER AND GOD WILL BLESS IT.

To the Parents

Many parents approach unit studies with much fear and trembling, concerned that they are more work than other types of learning. This should not be the case with **Far Above Rubies**, as it is designed to be much more self-directed than most unit studies.. Since it is designed for young adults, the materials are written directly to the students, and students are not treated like young children. Instead, they are encouraged to take charge of their own education.

You, as the parents, should feel free to work with your students, monitor, and direct them as you see fit, and you should remain the final authorities in what and how the student is to study within this course. However, we recommend giving each young lady as much responsibility for and freedom in her own education as she can handle. Hopefully, this will increase as she progresses through the curriculum. We do recommend that all parents read through all sections of "To the Student" and other material in these guidelines so you will be better able to guide the students in these studies. This 'is especially important if the unit study is being used with children under fifteen or those who have done only traditional text-books in their past studies.

As with all unit studies, this course need not be pursued from start to finish in order. Nor should anyone attempt to do everything contained in it or in any unit of it. There is enough material in each unit to provide for every type of learning style and a wide choice of activities, much more than any one student will ever need. You are encouraged to work with your daughters to choose those items that are most appropriate to their learning styles, your family beliefs, and your educational goals for each student, being sure to adequately cover a variety of subject areas. It is important that neither you nor your students become slaves to this material, but rather let it work for you.

Each of the 20 units in the study (10 in Volume One and 10 in Volume Two) is based on one or more verses or portions of verses from Proverbs 31 and consists of activities related directly or indirectly to the target verse(s). These units are further divided into thematic mini-units, designed to give families an easy way to correlate lessons within a unit. Mini-units may be done totally separate from each other, combined in a number of ways, or skipped altogether.

Units and mini-units may be done in any order, or you may skip between units as you wish. It is even possible to work on one unit for one week (or more) switch to another, then another and so forth, going all the way through the book and covering some of each unit each semester or year and repeating the process each year.

Regardless of the order in which the units are approached, we suggest that you do work in all subjects from the same unit at one time to maintain the overall emphasis of the unit.

The author assumes that students who use this course of study already have a firm knowledge of basic math, a mastery of English grammar, and good reading ability. If you are using this with a student who lacks either of these, you may need to do additional work in those areas while using this curriculum. Suggestions of materials to use for that purpose can be found under the Supplementary Courses listing in the Appendix to this volume. Most families will wish to use a separate math course as well, particularly for algebra, geometry, or more advanced topics. Suggestions for those also are found in the Appendix.

Since this course is written for mature young people and is designed to produce well-trained Christian adults, it deals with some topics to which younger Christian children should not be exposed, including those which come under the general heading of "sex education". We believe these subjects should be taught only within the family and approached from each family's own religious and moral perspective. All resources suggested for use in relation to these topics are presented from a Christian moral viewpoint, but some may contain material with specific denominational or doctrinal leanings that might be unacceptable to certain families. **You are always free to substitute materials of your preference or to skip certain sections if you see fit.**

Other topics in this curriculum that may be controversial include millennial views, Sabbath observance, church government, secular psychology, mythology as literature, vegetarianism, and the use of alcohol. There are some resources recommended in some areas that are from secular sources, as we believe students of this age and maturity level need to begin to learn to glean truth and discern error in a variety of sources. No secular materials are used in areas of moral training or character development. Parents who do not wish their daughters to use secular material should advise them against those when they occur. We recognize differing opinions among sincere believers on all of these topics and try not to take a dogmatic stand on issues on which Biblical teaching seems to leave room for us to disagree.

This material also discusses abortion, evolution, the occult, and the New Age, but only from a Christian perspective. We do not present them as acceptable, but try to familiarize the student with each area so she can have a reasonable understanding of the issues if and when she is confronted by them. If you feel uncomfortable with having your daughter learn about any of the above topics, you can easily skip those activities. They are marked with an asterisk and are not essential to the remainder of the material.

Though designed as a complete high school curriculum, this study need not be used that way. It may be used to teach only certain topics or subject areas and combined with other studies in all areas. Each family should pursue this in the way they see fit and feel led of the Lord.

For the convenience of families teaching both boys and girls of this age, many activities here are coordinated with those in **Blessed is the Man**, the author's companion volume for boys. Parents interested in ordering that item may do so by contacting the homeschool supplier from which this one was purchased. In addition, a cross-reference of related mini-units from the two curricula is available in Volume Two of Far Above Rubies so lessons can be more easily made to dovetail.

This curriculum includes an extensive resource list for all materials referenced in any unit. You will notice that this guide is not done in bibliographical form, but as a more informal listing. We hope this will meet your needs.

Please note: These are suggested resources only – they are NOT requirements!

While the majority of these resources are easily accessible, some of the books, videos and audios suggested in these units may be out of print or difficult to locate. If you are not able to locate a specific resource, or if any of the suggested resources do not fit your family's personal beliefs, feel free to substitute a similar book, video, audio or online resource for the assignment you are working on. You may find ideas for appropriate substitutions by asking your curriculum provider or other home educators.

Remember, YOU are in control of both the assignments you choose to complete as you go through Far Above Rubies, AND the resources you use to complete each assignment. We encourage you to research and utilize comparable resources that you have found, as well as using these materials.

When to Start Using Far Above Rubies

Though **Far Above Rubies** is designed as a high school curriculum, we recommend starting at an earlier age than most students begin traditional high school courses. When your student has mastered the basics of language arts, reading and math at the elementary level, she can probably begin **Far Above Rubies** as a high school student. We recommend skipping junior high entirely, as these years are generally wasted anyway. Most, if not all, junior high courses are reviews of elementary school (which are not needed if that material really has been mastered) or they cover material that must be studied again in high school. We say, Why bother?'

Using Far Above Rubies with Different Ages

You will probably notice that many books suggested in **Far Above Rubies** are written at a lower reading level than high school, or even seventh grade. This is intentional and serves several purposes. First, it makes the material usable for younger students, siblings working together, those who have gaps in previous learning, and those with learning difficulties. In addition to that, many complex topics can be made simple enough for a child without losing any of their complexity and are thereby easier to understand for all. An advanced reading level does not necessarily imply a more thorough or better book. Parents should help their daughters choose the material and activities best suited for each of them.

To the Student

This material is designed to train you to work independently, making most of your own choices and doing your own research, etc. You are, however, expected to stay in close contact with your parents throughout this study, as they are responsible before God for your education. For this reason, they should have the final decision concerning what you are to study and how to go about it. They may also want input as to how you schedule your work, and will certainly need to be in on the keeping of records and granting of credits.

Before beginning this study, you may wish to briefly look over all the material in each unit to decide where you would like to start working. It is not necessary to do these units or mini-units in any particular order, but we do recommend starting with the **"Becoming a Virtuous Woman"** mini-unit, found in Unit 1, which is an introduction to the whole study. However, even that is up to you and your parents.

The **Graduation and Beyond** section of Unit 20 (in Volume Two) must be saved until last, as it is designed to offer a final evaluation of the course and your work in it. However, the mini-unit entitled Evaluation by Objective or Subjective Standards in this same unit involves the keeping of on-going records and should be studied early in your course. This mini-unit is an exception to the normal way of doing units, as many of the activities in it will necessarily be done at varying times during high school rather than as a unified whole. You will understand what this means when you have read through this mini-unit.

In all other units, you should choose activities in all subjects from within the same unit. You may combine mini-units within a unit, but most people find it easier to keep them more or less separate. You will find that there are some activities in some units that will take much longer than you will spend on the rest of that unit (e.g., reading through the entire Bible, or planting and growing various crops). In those instances, you should complete the other planned activities for the unit and carry those long-range projects over to the next unit rather than bogging down in one unit waiting to complete one thing.

DO NOT TRY TO COMPLETE ALL ACTIVITIES IN ANY ONE UNIT. This study is not designed to be used that way. Work with your parents to choose a reasonable number of activities in each of the subject areas so that you can cover each of the main lessons in each unit.

In planning how long a particular unit should take, it is important to remember that some units are much longer than others. Rather than trying to determine how many units to study per year, or how many weeks to spend on a unit, plan by credits. Divide the number of credits your state requires for graduation by the number of years in which you plan to complete this course. (Be sure to first subtract any credits you may have already earned in other schooling.) When you have earned the resulting number of credits, you have completed a year's worth of work. YOU DO NOT NEED TO BE A CERTAIN AGE OR IN "HIGH SCHOOL" TO START EARNING CREDITS. We agree with the many professional educators and others who believe that any student capable of high school work should be able to start doing it, regardless of her age.

The following pages will explain more of the specifics of how to use this material. Read it carefully and go over the material in To the Parents and other sections of the guide before you begin. You may wish to highlight or otherwise mark certain sections of this for easy reference in the future. May God bless you richly through this study.

INSTRUCTIONS FOR USING FAR ABOVE RUBIES

On the following pages, you will find directions for using this unit study. We recommend that both parents and students read it carefully before beginning and refer to it as needed throughout the course. While we have attempted to make these guidelines as comprehensive as possible, we realize no directions could possibly anticipate every situation every family may face. These are guidelines only and can be altered to fit your family.

School Subject Areas Covered in Far Above Rubies

All units in the Far Above Rubies curriculum include all of the following areas of study:

Bible and Christian Character - theology and Christian doctrine, personal Bible study, the use of concordances and commentaries, and the development of godly values and life-styles

Cultural Studies - U. S. and world history, geography, government, economics, law, sociology, philosophy, and other subjects normally considered social studies

Reading and Literature - the study of various literary styles, famous authors, literature from many parts of the world, poetry memorization, and lots of reading of good 'living' books, including biographies and historical fiction

Composition - handwriting, spelling, grammar, vocabulary development, research and related skills, as well as the ability to express one's thoughts in a wide variety of writing styles and formats

Math and Personal Finance - a review of arithmetic basics for those who need them, as well as activities in bookkeeping, accounting, statistics and graphing, consumer math, basic algebra and geometry, and some opportunities to study more advanced math for those who wish to do so

Science - all areas of biological, physical, environmental, and Earth science with opportunities ties to pursue various subcategories of those and suggestions for lab experience in each

Health and Physical Fitness - exercise and fitness activities, as well as general health education, disease prevention, first aid, and safety

Practical Arts - household maintenance, cooking, sewing and other domestic crafts, interior decorating, parenting skills, foreign languages, woodworking, business and vocational training, and other skills needed to operate as an independent adult in society

Decorative and Performing Arts - music, art, drama, both in performance and appreciation, and a wide array of methods and media for artistic expression

Understanding and Using the Number Codes

One of the first things you will notice when you open this study to any subject area of any unit is the columns of number along both sides of each page. These numbers are very important to your success with Far Above Rubies and are explained below.

Along the left side of each page are activity numbers like this:

01B54.C*

Each element of each number has a meaning as follows;

01 = the unit in which the activity is found (in this case Unit 1)
B = subject area category (in this case Bible)
54 = the order of the activity in its unit and category (#54 here)
C = the mini-unit in which this activity fits within its unit
* = these activities are especially appropriate for including younger children

These numbers will be useful in keeping records of what activities you have completed. However, it is not necessary that they be recorded this way if you or your parents prefer some other system.

The numbers in the right-hand column beside each activity designate the assigned points for that activity. The one-or-two letter code denotes the appropriate subject area for recording those points on a transcript. These codes are explained below and are suggestions only. You need not use this point system at all if you and your parents do not wish to do so for any reason.

Key To Credit Codes

A	Accounting & Bookkeeping	HM	Home Management
AA	Art Appreciation	IA	Industrial Arts
B	Bible & Christian Character	IM	Instrumental Music
BE	Business Education	L	Literature
BS	Building Skills	LH	Landscape Horticulture
CC	Clothing Construction/Care	LS	Life Skills
CD	Child Care & Development	M	Mathematics
CE	Economics	MA	Music Appreciation
CG	Government	MC	Musical Composition
CL	Law	NU	Nursing/ Medicine
CO	Computer Skills	PA	Practical Agriculture
CR	Practical Crafts	PH	Philosophy
CS	Sociology	PE	Physical Education
CT	Counseling and Guidance	RE	Recreation
DR	Dramatic Arts	SA	Safety Education
EC	English Composition	SB	Biology
EG	English Grammar/ Mechanics	SC	Chemistry
FL	Foreign Language	SE	Earth Science or Ecology
FN	Food and Nutrition	SP	Physical Science/Physics
G	Geography	ST	Scientific Technology
H	History	TE	Teacher Education
HA	Human Anatomy	VA	Visual Arts
HE	Health Education	VM	Vocal Music
HF	Home & Family Living	WW	Woodworking

Record Keeping, Credits, and Transcripts

A total of 135 points constitutes one high school credit. A credit may be earned in one single area or by combining two or more similar areas, e.g. grammar and composition, two types of science, etc. You and your parents may name credits other than these categories if you see fit, and points may be adjusted up or down at your parents' discretion.

In this context and throughout this study, the word "credit" refers to one complete school's year worth of work in a subject. In most states and private schools, these are re-corded as one credit per year. However, California and some other states record and require credits on a different basis. If you live in one of those states, please feel free to record the appropriate number of credits for your state's accounting system.

Points are largely based on Carnegie units, or the number of class hours needed to complete an activity. Modifications to this have been made to allow for the different pace of work in a homeschool setting or to assign more importance to certain projects. Still, some students will need more or less time than that allotted for some lessons. Parents simply adjust points accordingly, but extra points should not be given simply because a project takes longer. To do so, could reward dawdling or allow slow workers to earn points faster than others. More points should reflect higher levels of performance or effort, not just time spent.

Record Keeping

You will notice that this unit study includes a chart to be copied for each unit and used to check off when an activity is completed. These charts are also usable for recording points earned within each unit. They can be filled out as each activity is completed or done all at once at the end of the unit, filling in all activities included in that unit. All record sheets may be copied by an individual family for its own students without violation of copyright. It is important that all sheets be kept current as these provide a record by which parents can issue diplomas and parents or students can prepare transcripts.

You may wish to keep samples of the student's written work from each unit. We suggest doing this through the use of loose-leaf notebooks as explained in the How to Do It section of these guidelines. In addition to these, the units themselves suggest that some items be done in notebooks. None of these notebooks are necessary for completing the work or claiming credits. They are only one way of showing what the student has done.

In addition to these notebooks, you may want a folder or loose leaf notebook in which to file essays, reports and other written work. This is NOT mandatory, and no one should try to keep EVERYTHING completed during this course. We suggest only that it may be advantageous to have some of these materials in your files for future reference. If you are doing any or all of your written work on computer or word processor, saving the files on disk should be sufficient and will save storage space. Portfolios or scrapbooks can provide a way to keep calligraphy, artwork, musical compositions, and/or photographs of other projects.

Transcripts and Other Final Records

When the points you have earned in each unit have been tallied, you are ready to begin preparing your transcript, a copy of which is included in this manual. Having already deter-mined the credits you need to graduate, you will use the transcript to show that you have earned them. You will need to show the required credits as determined using the information in Using Credits for Graduation. If you have already done some high school work before beginning Far Above Rubies, you should already have some credits. Subtract those from the total credits required for your graduation to discover how you still need to earn.

Now you are ready to translate the accumulated points into credits and begin to fill out the actual transcript. Elsewhere in this book, you will find samples of three different types of transcript forms that can be used to total these credits. One of these forms should be filled in for each student, listing each subject in which she has earned a full credit or 1/2 credit, whether it was earned by accumulated points or given for one particular activity. Each time the total equals135, a credit in that subject area should be entered. Whenever you complete one of the activities that gives you 1/2 credit or more, that credit also should go directly into the transcript. It is important to keep track of those points that make up credits entered, so the same points will not be counted twice.

In some cases, a credit may include points in two or more related areas, rather than all in one. In this case, you may name the credit for any of the areas, or it can be given another name altogether. For example, if you have points in both human anatomy and health education, but not a full credit in either, you may combine the points and give a credit called Health and Human Anatomy. Combined points in those two subjects plus biology could make up a unit in life sciences if required or allowed.

You may want to wait until all units are completed before making combinations, as more points may later be earned in one or both subject areas, giving a credit in each as opposed to only one. This could be important, as many colleges are reluctant to accept more than one credit in some of these combined subjects, such as Government or U. S. History, where they might easily accept a credit in each of the original subjects.

Most school districts, colleges, etc., require multiple credits in some subjects, most notably English. These credits can be achieved by combining English grammar and mechanics, English composition, and literature into a general course called, simply, English. If you choose this option, you should claim a credit each time 135 points is reached, naming them English I, English II, etc. You may also choose to accumulate points in each of the individual subject areas and register separate credits for grammar, literature, etc. Either system will be accepted by most agencies to whom the transcript is submitted, but you may want to find out what your local public schools do and record your credits accordingly.

There are activities in Unit 20 (see Volume Two) which allow you to average your own grades, tally your own points and credits and complete your own transcript. It is not necessary, and may not be wise, to wait until the end of the curriculum for this. It can be worked on little by little as the credits are accumulated, and you will learn a valuable skill in the process.

If credits are needed in subjects other than those listed in this unit study, see if another topic may be similar enough to fulfill the requirement (e.g., government = political science or civics.) Students may also be able to meet some requirements by breaking a topic into its components (i. e. M into different types of math as appropriate; H into World History, U. S. History, Ancient History). Before breaking a topic apart, you should be sure that the items in each section really relate to that particular topic and that there are enough points of that type to constitute a credit.

Other than in English, you should not use general subject headings, such as Math, Science, or History on a transcript. Instead, you will want to name the courses things such as General Math, Consumer Math, General Science, Physical Science, U. S. History, World His-tory, or other specific topics. In English and other subjects where you need more than one credit, number them or differentiate in some other fashion (i.e. Spanish I, Spanish II, Beginning French, Advanced French). Never use the words "Language Arts" for a high school course. Most school systems relegate this to the lower grade levels, using English as the general term for high school courses.

All references to points and credits in this unit study are to be considered guidelines only. Parents should feel free to use their own system of tracking progress or to use our system according to their own discretion. Points may be changed in specific instances if parents fee l that the student has done an exceptional job with a particular activity, or if it has proven harder than expected. In some activities, points are not designated and should be given a value by parents, according to the amount of work that goes into the activity. In totaling points for credits, as in all other aspects of homeschooling, the parents are the final authority. You should always rely on their judgment and knowledge of you and trust them in making ALL decisions relating to your education.

Using Credits for Graduation

Most school systems and colleges require 20-24 credits in high school. It is up to you to ascertain what, if anything, your state and/or school district requires for home educators. This varies greatly from state to state, and sometimes even between local school districts in the same state.

In some areas, homeschoolers and/or those who operate as private or church schools are not bound by the requirements of the public schools at all. Local support groups, satellite or umbrella schools, or a homeschool legal advocacy group should be able to provide information and answer questions on that topic. If those options are not available, ask a local college for its requirements. These should be similar to those received by the average student in public schools in the area. That is also the guideline you will need to follow if you intend to attend college.

It may be wise to follow or closely approximate the credits expected in your state's public schools, even if you are not required to do so. Certificates of completion will be issued at a cost of $15 by the author upon receipt of parent's request and a signed affidavit of credits completed. For an additional $85 registration fee, students completing this course and submitting school records showing at least 24 total credits may receive a state-approved high school diplomas and official transcript of grades from Covenant Academy, a private church school in Montgomery, Alabama. To exercise either of these options, contact the author at:

Lynda Coats
PO Box 210026
Montgomery, AL 36121
email: FARauthor@aol.com

It is also acceptable in most states to make your own diploma and have it issued by parents or a homeschool support group.

HOW TO DO IT

This section of these guidelines is designed to help parents and students understand how to do specific activities that are called for in various FarAbove Rubies units that may be new to many of you. You may wish to read through them along with the other guidelines at the beginning of the course, or you may wait and refer to them as needed.

Notebooks Suggested for Far Above Rubies

Though some specific units call for booklets or notebooks for those units there are several notebooks the FAR student may want to keep throughout the entire course. These should be made in loose-leaf binders, preferably with pocket covers you can make yourself. These are optional but will add great value to your study and tie the lessons together. They can also serve as reference materials when younger siblings or friends are studying these topics, whether in FAR or with another course.

The following notebooks are suggested for materials in two or more units:

1.   Bible Study - to be used for taking notes on personal Bible reading, Bible study books or tapes, sermons or Biblical lectures; also use to collect copy and dictation work on Scriptures to be memorized.

2.   Personal Prayer Journal - not to be graded but to use for prayer requests and answers, meditations during devotions, self-examination, and other private communications with the Lord

3.   Formal Writing - samples (one or two per mini-unit) of essays, reports, book reviews, and articles on each area of study

4.   Creative Writing - a collection of short stories, plays, poems, and similar fictional and personal writings during this course

5.   School Journal - a brief summary of everything studied and learned during each day or week of the school year; can be done daily or weekly and should serve as documentation of the year for most purposes

6.   Vocabulary - to list and define all new words introduced in any studies in this unit with the intent of increasing the student's vocabulary

7.   The Human Body   reports on various organs and systems to be added as suggested in many different units

8.   Geography - reports on each country in the modern or ancient world to be written and added as that country is studied for the first time.

Making and Using Timelines

While not completely essential, timelines are a valuable device for helping students relate activities in history to one another. On a good timeline it is easy to see at a glance what happened in various parts of the world at different times, thus showing the relationship of various events to one another. Hence, a timeline must involve some way of placing events, people, movements, and developments throughout history on a continuum in relation to each other and cataloging them according to date (actual or approximate). How you do this is open to many interpretations.

Two books referenced repeatedly in this unit study, "Timetables of History" and Usborne's "World History Dates" offer excellent examples of the timeline concept. You can follow the pattern in either of these to make your own timeline. However, since your timeline will be an on-going process, you will want to construct it in some form that can be easily added to and changed. There are several methods for doing this.

Essentially, any timeline will need to include individual listings (on cards, cutouts, sheets of paper, or other formats) of historical events, people, movements, or developments to be included and a system for cataloging these by date. This can be done by drawing a physical line and attaching to it cards or papers bearing information about the events etc. However, that is not the only way to make a timeline. We have given several examples of timelines here, but you and your family may have other ideas. Please bear in mind that these are only suggestions. Feel free to use your imagination to design other methods for keeping your timeline as you see fit.

The simplest of timelines can be made using 3 x 5 or 4 x 6 index cards in an appropriate file box. Mark the dividers by century, beginning with Creation. For the earliest history, times will obviously be estimated, and time periods approximate. You may well start with a category like "Prior to 500 BC (or other date) ", for example. Each time a person, event, movement, nation or other happening is studied or discussed, the student should make a card showing the date(s) (beginning date for ongoing things, or beginning and ending dates for those that span multiple centuries). Each card should list the event, person, etc., the date or time period, and the area of the world. A small picture hand-drawn, or cut from an appropriate source, should illustrate each card. (Back issues of National Geographic or similar magazines can provide many of the needed pictures.) These cards would them be filed in their appropriate places in the file box. They can then be removed and lined up in order on a table or desk as needed to relate them to each other.

Another simple and popular method for keeping a timeline is to draw or print the line horizontally on continuous pages of a loose-leaf binder, writing in items and dates and adding pictures as needed. Pictures for this can also be cut out and pasted in, if you prefer. You could also use file cards as in the above suggestion, fastening them to the appropriate pages. This would allow you to easily record numerous items on the same page. One example of this method of timeline management in which much of the work is done for you is Bonnie Dettmer's "Book of the Centuries", published by Small Ventures. Contact the dealer from whom you purchased Far Above Rubies for more information on this item.

Many families prefer to display their timelines in their homes, adding a fun, educational element to their decor and keeping the time relationships ever apparent. This can be done in several ways, providing the family home has enough wall space to accommodate a long, horizontal strip of some type. A long hall or staircase wall is good for this, or you may run it around the top border of an entire room. It is also possible to place the time line on a shorter wall, with one or more centuries on each level, continuing, one under the other. Several homeschool companies publish and sell pre-printed timelines to be used this way. You would simply fill in the date and event, adding any desired personalization as you go.

You can create your own timeline wall display, using a roll of plain white shelf paper. To do this, you would prepare as long a strip of the paper as you can hang in a continuous path on your walls. On this paper, draw a long, continuous horizontal line, marking it with dates at appropriate intervals. You will probably not need to mark much more than centuries for the earliest years, with markings becoming more detailed as you proceed. The next step is to add the events, people, etc. While you may remove the timeline from the wall to draw and letter in each entry, this could cause damage over time. It would probably be easier to draw and letter on the paper while it remains on the wall or to use a separate sheet and glue it to the timeline later.

There are many other ways to display this timeline. Some families use sentence strips or pre-printed number lines or paper rulers (available at teacher supply stores) to which they add dates as desired. Items are then printed and illustrated on cards and attached to the line itself or the adjacent wall. One of our favorite timelines was created by stringing a clothesline around the perimeter of a room, just below the ceiling. Using clothespins and/or paper clips, we attached file cards (the larger size, due to the distance at which we were reading them) listing and illustrating events, etc. You might also attach sheets featuring the various timeline entries directly to the wall, simply placing them in order and leaving room for items to fall in between them but not putting up an actual printed line. In any of these displays, events occurring at the same time or overlapping each other can be placed above or below the line, even "stacking" several deep if needed.

Organizing Thoughts with Mind Mapping

Mind-mapping is a form of visual outlining or brainstorming. A mind-map consists of circles or boxes connected together in logical patterns, each level dividing the initial concept into smaller and more concise. Parts. They are similar to, but do not serve the same purpose as, flowcharts. Anything that can be outlined can be mind-mapped, often making the interrelationship of various components clearer.

To mind map, begin with a main idea or theme (in our example, we will use "homeschooling" in a circle in the center of a page. Then you would determine the main categories (Roman numerals in an outline) into which this theme would be divided (for our purposes, "advantages, challenges, methods, reasons", etc.) You can be as thorough here as you wish, but you will wish to allow for further breakdown of the topics (capital letters, Arabic numerals, etc.), as in an outline. You mind map might look similar to the one below:

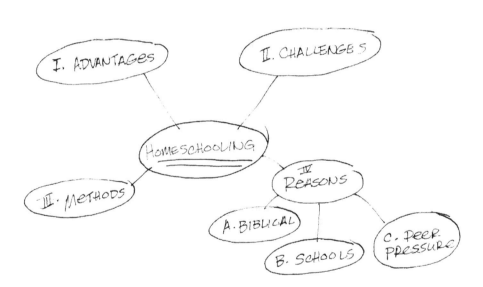

Using FAR for Chronological History

Those who wish to teach history in chronological order may do so by using the following list. You will notice that this pattern requires a shift from the general concept of completing all of one unit before going on to the next. Families may certainly do this if they feel the need to stress the chronology of the history as it is taught. Other families find that the use of timelines makes this type of chronological approach unnecessary. Use this as you see fit. Units or mini-units not listed here do not cover a specific time period and may be interspersed in any order.

WORLD HISTORY

TOPIC	UNIT #	MINI-UNIT TITLE
Creation	1	Creation and the Origin of the World We Know
Ancient History	1	The World of the Old Testament
Ancient Egypt	5	Ancient Egypt
Ancient Greece	7	Ancient Greeks: Founders of the Olympics
Roman Empire	7	Ancient Rome: Warriors of Great Strength
Middle Ages	14	The Middle Ages
Renaissance	12	Renaissance and Reformation
Reformation	12	Renaissance and Reformation
Age of Exploration	4	Explorers and the Age of Exploration
Industrial Revolution	9	The Industrial Revolution
World War I	10	The War to End All Wars (WW I)
Great Depression	10	The Great Depression
World War II	10	The Next Great War

UNITED STATES HISTORY
(Some World History categories do overlap)

Age of Exploration	4	Explorers and the Age of Exploration
Pre-Colonization	6	The First Americans
Colonial Period	13	The Founding of America
U. S. Independence	13	The U. S. Constitution and Political System
Westward Expansion	6	Westward Ho!
War between the States	5	The War Between the States and its Aftermath
Industrial Revolution	9	The Industrial Revolution
World War I	10	The War to End All Wars (WW I)
Great Depression	10	The Great Depression
World War II	10	The Next Great War

All units contain some history. Topics not listed here are covered incidentally in other units scattered throughout the course.

Essential Materials for this Course

This course cannot easily be studied without access to the following materials:

1. Bible - This can be any version, as long as it is a literal translation, not a paraphrase.

2. Concordance - Use one designed for the Bible translation you are using, if possible.

3. Dictionary - We recommend Webster's 1828 edition as well as a good modern one.

4. Encyclopedia - The library is close enough for these as they aren't used all the time; an on-line or CD reference system can take the place of this, if needed.

5. One or more hymnbooks or Christian songbooks and/or CD's or tapes of such songs - You may be able to borrow one from your church congregation.

6. English Grammar Handbook - We used a college-level one we found at a yard sale for 50 cents. This same book or a similar one will be available in any college bookstore and many general bookstores.

7. Writing style book - We recommend "Writer's Inc." or "Writing for College", but any similar book will do. This is not the same as a grammar handbook, and you will probably need both.

If you do not have any of these items, and cannot find them at your local library, you will need find a way to purchase them or borrow from someone. It would be very hard to accomplish the goals of Far Above Rubies without access to these materials.

Other Items Strongly Suggested

In addition to the items specifically referenced in the Resource Guide, you may find the following helpful throughout the course:

1. Bible commentaries
2. Field guides of birds and animals
3. Word processor or typewriter
4. MP3 device or CD player
5. Medical encyclopedia or health care book
6. General history texts
7. General and consumer math texts
8. Thesaurus
9. Guide for the writing of term papers
10. Classic poetry anthology
11. Extensive short story anthology
12. Anthology of Shakespeare's plays
13. Recent World Almanac
14. Assortment of classical music
15. Book or collection of prints of famous paintings

Some of the items listed above are specifically referenced in some units, but they may be helpful in many other places as well. It is advisable to keep each of these handy, if possible. Many of them are available in most public libraries, and that may be sufficient. You are urged to use the library or online resources whenever needed.

Downloadable Forms for use with Far Above Rubies

While you may use any recordkeeping system you wish in tracking your work with Far Above Rubies, we offer the following forms for you to use if you wish:

Lesson Plan Outline Form

Goal Planning Checksheet

Report Card

High School Cumulative Record Card

These forms may be downloaded at:

www.wholesomechildhood.com/FARforms/

Proverbs 31:10-31 KJV

☙

Who can find a virtuous woman? for her price is far above rubies.

The heart of her husband doth safely trust in her, so that he shall have no need of spoil.

She will do him good and not evil all the days of her life.

She seeketh wool, and flax, and worketh willingly with her hands.

She is like the merchants' ships; she bringeth her food from afar.

She riseth also while it is yet night, and giveth meat to her household, and a portion to her maidens.

She considereth a field, and buyeth it: with the fruit of her hands she planteth a vineyard.

She girdeth her loins with strength, and strengtheneth her arms.

She perceiveth that her merchandise is good: her candle goeth not out by night.

She layeth her hands to the spindle, and her hands hold the distaff.

She stretcheth out her hand to the poor; yea, she reacheth forth her hands to the needy.

She is not afraid of the snow for her household: for all her household are clothed with scarlet.

She maketh herself coverings of tapestry; her clothing is silk and purple.

Her husband is known in the gates, when he sitteth among the elders of the land.

She maketh fine linen, and selleth it; and delivereth girdles unto the merchant.

Strength and honour are her clothing; and she shall rejoice in time to come.

She openeth her mouth with wisdom; and in her tongue is the law of kindness.

She looketh well to the ways of her household, and eateth not the bread of idleness.

Her children arise up, and call her blessed; her husband also, and he praiseth her.

Many daughters have done virtuously, but thou excellest them all.

Favour is deceitful, and beauty is vain: but a woman that feareth the Lord, she shall be praised.

Give her of the fruit of her hands; and let her own works praise her in the gates.

☙

UNIT 1

A virtuous wife, who can find?
Her value is far above rubies.
Proverbs 31: 10

Overview

The verse on which this unit is based emphasizes the value of good Christian character, especially in a wife. Let us bear in mind that this entire passage is quoted from a godly mother's instructions to her son. This is what she considered to be important in the woman her son would marry. As a child of God, who will probably be called to become someone's wife someday, your job is to grow into this kind of woman. Your goal is to become a woman fit for a king, or the son of a King, as all believing men are.

It would seem that our first step in the process of becoming this kind of woman is to examine what kind of woman that should be. She is described in this passage with the word "virtuous", which you will investigate further in the study of this unit. You will quickly see that the Bible does not give one trait that constitutes virtue. Rather, it seems to be defined as a quality made up of many godly character traits. These traits and how to obtain them are the focus of this unit and, to a very large extent, all of *Far Above Rubies.*

In a very real sense, this Scripture verse is only an introduction to the remainder of Proverbs 31. The quality of "virtue", so highly praised here, is further developed throughout the entire passage. Bear this in mind as you work your way through the activities in this unit and its mini-units. It is for this reason that we highly recommend all students start with Unit One, though all other units may be done in any order.

Mini-Units

Mini-Units contained in this unit are:

A. Becoming a Virtuous Woman

B. Rocks, Rubies and Minerals

C. Creation and the Origin of the World We Know

D. The History of Old Testament Times

Each thematic mini-unit is described and designated with a letter of the alphabet in the following paragraphs. Individual activities designed for use in one particular mini-unit will be marked with those letters. (For further help with this, please refer to the explanation of mini-units in the Guidelines section of this unit study guide.)

Mini-Units

A. Becoming a Virtuous Woman

Though this mini-unit will highlight the primary theme of the unit, it does not preclude the discussion of this topic in other mini-units or activities related to it, since all units come together around this central theme. In the study of this mini-unit, you will examine the character traits that combine to produce the quality of virtue and how one obtains them. In this context, you will investigate the Beatitudes from the Sermon on the Mount and other Biblical teachings on the character traits that every Christian woman should nurture in her life.

After defining virtue, you will search for Scripture references on how one goes about obtaining it. In this quest, you will study the lives of many women from the Bible and throughout history, examining each of them by the standards of this passage, choosing those who are good role models for this verse. You will also sample Christian living and family life during different periods in history, helping you to understand the values of the Christian life which transcend culture and how culture may sometimes alter the life-style of even the godly. This unit also provides a look at other Scripture passages that lay out standards of behavior for the Christian. We will contrast the Biblical definition of "virtue" with the standards of "good' or "right" derived from other sources within society.

You will perform word studies in English and/or Hebrew on the actual meanings of the word "virtue" and all alternate translations of this word. You will examine and define all of the Fruit of the Spirit and write papers about them. Your studies will be enhanced by the reading of selected books in which the characters exhibit the traits that you are studying. This will include biographies, fictionalized biographies, historical fiction and classics.

After learning what virtue is, you will compute its value, using the mathematical formula given in this verse. You will also have an opportunity to calculate the value of the work a woman does at home even when she is not out in the work force, in hopes of seeing the importance of the stay-at-home wife and mother.

Another aspect of this topic involves the physical and emotional changes you will be undergoing as you become a woman. We will seek to help you understand these and adjust to them in a godly fashion. This section, more than any other in this unit, should be done in close cooperation with your mother.

B. Rocks, Rubies and Minerals

In order to understand how much King Lemuel's mother valued virtue, and how much God's Word seems to as well, you should study rubies and other gems. You will look at other Scripture references to various stones and minerals and investigate their uses and value in the time of the Old Testament. You will learn which stones, minerals, or metals had Spiritual significance to God's people at different times and what each signified.

You will learn how various gems and ores are produced within the Earth, discovered, polished and used. You will investigate the value of rubies and the relative values of other types of stones, minerals, and ores. This mini-unit also takes a look at the jewelry industry from the standpoint of both science and economics.

From examining the molecular structure of various gems and crystals, you will have the opportunity to launch into a study of atoms, molecules, and elements. From this beginning you will delve into rudimentary geology and some elemental chemistry. Students who wish to expand on these may use this study as a springboard for a full course in either subject.

Geometry is also introduced in relation to crystalline shapes. You and your parents may wish to expand this by going into a complete geometry course. If you are doing the course with a math text, you may prefer to skip all or most of the math in the unit.

C. Creation and the Origin of the World We Know

As the need for godliness and virtue begins with God the Creator and our relationship with Him, so will this mini-unit take us to that starting place. This is also the place where you will see the true beginnings of the processes we explained scientifically in the previous mini-unit. For those reasons, this is placed here rather than in another unit, though there are others in which it might seem to fit. Please feel free to move this or any other mini-unit around as you and your parents see fit.

In this section, you will study the Biblical account of God's Creation of the Universe and all that is in it. You will study the creation of Adam and Eve, and all mankind through them. Up against that, you will also be asked to look at other theories that claim to explain the origins of all these things. All ideas will be examined from God's Word and in light of real scientific evidence, much of which does abound on the side of Creation.

This study will take you into geology and topography as you learn about various Earth formations and how they speak of a powerful Creator. In this same context, we will also look at the flood told of in Genesis as an actual historical event, complete with geological evidences to prove it. You will see how this event altered the world of creation to bring about the conditions under which we now live. This could expand into a complete course in geology or Earth science if you desire.

D. History of Old Testament Times

This mini-unit uses the study of godly women in the Bible to introduce you to life during the time of the Old Testament, after the flood of Genesis. You will learn how people lived and especially the role and duties of women in the various cultures that arose during those years.

The unit will also cover the bigger picture of history during this time period, helping you understand what was going on in other parts of the world while the Bible was being written and the events in it were occurring. You will learn about, not only the Israelite nation, ancestors of our Lord Jesus, but also of other cultures and nations that developed when the world was divided at Babel and those that came along later. This will include, but is not restricted to Chaldea, Sumer, Assyria, Persia, Media, Phoenecia, Philistia. Ancient Egypt is not included here, as it is covered in Unit Five.

In exploring these nations and time periods, you will use Scripture and a variety of other material written by and about the people of the time. In addition to extensive reading , this mini-unit will involve you in various language arts skills, including book reports, hand-writing practice and improvement, and literary composition, You will be invited to write essays, poems, reports, stories and articles, as well as to summarize and outline reading material relating to the subject matter of the unit.

You will also learn to use tools of this time period and participate in some of the chores and crafts of the day. Music and art of and about the period will also be used heavily in this mini-unit.

BIBLE and CHRISTIAN CHARACTER

01B01.A	Study and memorize Proverbs 31:10 - 31.	B - 7
01B02.A	List all skills and character traits named in or reasonably inferred from Proverbs 31:10-31, breaking each into all of its component parts. Discuss with parents and/or consult commentaries so as not to miss anything. Save this list for use later in the unit. This describes the long-range goals of the study.	B- 1
01B03.A	Using a concordance for reference, make a chart showing one or more Scriptures that <u>command</u> or <u>teach</u> or <u>encourage</u> each skill or trait in 01B02. Read each of these passages.	B- 3
01B04.A	Choose one passage about each item above to memorize.	B - 5
01B05.A	Using a concordance or the book *All the Women of the Bible*, identify AND study a woman in the Scriptures who possessed each trait or skill on the list you made in #01B02.	B- 8
01B06.A	Study and memorize Matthew 5:3-11, that part of our Lord's teachings often called the Beatitudes and teaching the traits of a virtuous Christian.	B- 3
01B07.A	As you read through the entire New Testament, make a list of all women named there (or find such a list from one of the appropriate books in this unit's resource guide). Find, list, and read one or more Scripture passages about each woman that show whether or not her life-style and actions were godly. Make notes on your reading for use in a later project.	B- 10
01B08.A	From the lists of women you made in connection with this mini-unit, or the book All the Women of the Bible, list each woman the Scripture praises or holds up as a positive example. After reading about each in Scripture, make a mind map to show the qualities for which each woman is praised.	B - 5
01B09.A	Study *Christian Character: A Course for Training Young People* by Gary Maldaner, using it for your daily devotions or family Bible study time.	*B - 25*
01B10.A	Complete the *God's Priceless Woman* Bible study, alone, with your mother or in a group.	B - 26
01B11.A	Study the rules of behavior for women set forth in I Timothy 2. Discuss them with your mother or another Christian woman.	B - 1
01B12.B	Study Proverbs 31:10 using two or more commentaries to see how each interprets the word "rubies". Does this verse appear to be referring to rubies only or to all "precious" stones? Draw a mind map or chart to show your findings.	B - 1

BIBLE and CHRISTIAN CHARACTER

01B13.B   Examine the word translated here as "rubies" in the original   B - 1
Hebrew language to determine which of the possible meanings
suggested above is most likely implied from the actual word used.

01B14.B   Use a concordance to find and study all other Biblical references   B - 2
to rubies. List all qualities symbolized by or uses of the stone
mentioned in these verses.

01815.B   Use a concordance and/or Bible dictionary to look up all Scripture   B - 3
references to other gems or stones commonly considered
"precious."

01B16.B   Study all the Scripture references in the two previous activities   B - 2
and list on a chart those in which the gems or jewels are used in a
symbolic sense and those in which they are taken literally

01B17.B   From the above list of verses, list all items, objects or traits   B - 2
that are compared to gems or jewels, along with the appropriate
gem or jewel and be able to explain why each comparison is made.

01B18.B   Use a concordance to find all verses referring to gold, silver or   B - 1
other "precious" metals. Prepare a list of these as you did for gems
in activity #01B15.

01B19.B   Using the Scripture itself, as well as concordances, commentaries   B - 2
and other references, study the ephod of the Jewish priest, as
described in Exodus 29 and 38, and the symbolism of the jewels in
it.

01B20.B   From the above two lists, isolate and study all Scripture references   B - 1
to gems, jewels, and/or other "precious" stones that God ordained
for use in Hebrew worship. Study the passages to learn how each
gem or stone was used.

01B21.B   Study the building of the Tabernacle as recorded in Exodus   B - 2
25-27. List all gems, minerals, and/or metals mentioned there and
discuss with your parents the purposes for each.

01B22.B   Study God's instructions to Solomon for building the Temple.   B - 2
List and be prepared to discuss the variety of gemstones, jewels
and metals used.

01B23.B   Read Matthew 6: 19 - 21 as a reminder of what is really 'precious'   B - 1
to us in spite of the world's thinking, which is often to
the contrary.

01B24.B   Study Luke 12: 31 - 34, and compare it to the passage above.   B - 1
Learn and discuss how these verses relate to gems and minerals
and the mining of them.

BIBLE and CHRISTIAN CHARACTER

01B25.C	Study the creation account in chapters 1 & 2 of Genesis, paying close attention to the creation of Eve and the specific purpose for which God created her.	B - 1
01B26.C	From the passage above, make a chart dividing all creation into categories, based on the day of the creation week on which each was created. List as many different things as you can for each day.	B - 1
(01B27.C)	Read Job 37 and 38 and List all of God's works to which He calls Job's attention. List beside each item the day of Creation Week on which it was made.	B - 2
01B28.C	Memorize Genesis 1:1-5, the account of the first day of Creation.	. B - 2
01B29.C	Memorize Genesis 1: 6-8, which tells of the second day of Creation.	B - 1
01B30.C	Memorize Genesis 1: 9-13, which records the third day of Creation.	B - 2
01B31.C	Memorize Genesis 1:14-19, which tells of the fourth day of Creation.	B - 2
01B32.C	Memorize Genesis 1:20-23, an account of the fifth day of Creation.	B - 1
01B33.C	Memorize Genesis 1:24-31, which tells of the sixth Creation day.	B - 3
01B34.C	Read and memorize Genesis 2:1-3, which explains the establishment and purpose of the Sabbath as a day of rest.	B - 1
01B35.C	Use a concordance to find and study all Biblical references to the Sabbath. List on some kind of chart or poster, all laws, rules, and regulations given for Sabbath observance in Old Testament Israel and/or Judah, beginning from the giving of the Law and going into the time of Christ's earthly life.	B- 10
01B36.C	Using the same materials and format as above, list all New Testament references to the Sabbath and briefly paraphrase each. Prepare a chart showing which ones seem to support continued observance of the Sabbath and which seem to discourage it.	B- 10
01B37.C	Discuss your findings from the two activities above with your parents. Decide together whether you believe that Christians today should observe the Sabbath as it was done in Bible times. Defend your answer from Scripture, bearing in mind that sincere Christians disagree on this. Make decisions on it for yourself and your family only; don't try to judge others by it.	B - 3

BIBLE and CHRISTIAN CHARACTER

01B38.D	During this unit, you should begin to read through the entire Bible, reading 1-3 chapters per day. You may prefer to do this activity using *The Daily Bible*, or another version arranged chronologically. Either way, we recommend using a literal translation and not a paraphrase. You should continue these readings even when you move on to other units. Credit will be given only after the entire Bible has been read.	B - 1 credit when entire Bible is read.
01B39.D	As you read through the Old Testament, list each woman mentioned, with a verse to show whether her lifestyle and character were godly or ungodly.	B - 10
01B40.D	Instead of doing this as part of reading through the Bible, you may use the book *All the Women of the Bible* or another reference to find the names of women for your lists. You should still study each reference from the Bible itself.	B - 10
01B41.D	As you read the Old Testament history of God's people, make a chart showing all other nations mentioned and the book(s) in which they show up. Save this list for use in Cultural Studies in this mini-unit.	B - 8
01B42.D	If you are not reading through the Bible as part of this study, or if you prefer to complete this activity more quickly, use *Baker's Bible Atlas* or a similar reference to find nations to be studied. Look up all those nations in the concordance and read about them from the Scripture itself.	B- 10 *(not in addition to # 01B41.)* G - 2
011343.D	Use a concordance to identify and read all New Testament references to the nations listed above, and group them all by location, giving a word picture of what each nation was like.	B - 5
01B44.D	Read the books of Isaiah, Jeremiah, Ezekiel, and Daniel, using them to trace on some type of chart the progress and downfall of the Hebrew nations of Israel and Judah. Save to compare with secular accounts of the same time period and concurrent events in world history.	B - 6 H - 4
01B45.D	From the books above as well as Ezra, and Nehemiah, study and make a chart of the exile of God's people from their homeland, their years in captivity, and their eventual return. Show major events, locations, and people involved.	B - 1 H - 2
01B46.D	Study the book of Ruth and find out where it fits in Bible chronology.	B - 2
01B47.	Memorize one or more of the passages studied in the mini-unit.	B - 1 per 3 verses
01B48.	Read the chapter of Proverbs each day, that corresponds with that day's date.	B - 3 per week

BIBLE and CHRISTIAN CHARACTER

01B49.	Begin to keep a prayer journal, listing each day (or as the Lord brings to mind) prayer requests, needs in your spiritual life and things God is teaching you. Continue this throughout all units.	B - 2 per week
01B50.	Begin now and continue until done reading through the Bible at a rate of 3-4 chapters per day. If you use *The Daily Bible* or some other version designed specifically for that purpose, their daily readings will take you through the entire Bible in one year. You may follow a pattern of your own at a different rate if you like. Using a chronologically arranged Bible offers the added benefit of putting your reading in perspective as to time frame.	B - 1 credit when completed

CULTURAL STUDIES

01C01.A	Ask 6-8 Christian women the name of the one woman each looks up to as a role model and why. Study the life of each woman named, using books in the Reading section or any other resource. Concentrate on learning why each would be a good role model.	CS - 3 + B - 1
01C02.A	Using Christian magazines, biographies, web sites or other resources, study the lives of several prominent female authors, teachers, and leaders in the Christian community and compare their lifestyles to the Biblical ideal of virtue from Proverbs 31. Do you see areas where even these godly women fall short of God's standard? While you must not be judgmental about others' shortcomings, this exercise should make you aware of the need for all of us to be eternally vigilant about our spiritual growth, knowing that none of us can meet God's standard totally.	CS - B - I
01C03.A	Gathering information from magazines, Internet, books, or any other sources, study the wives of several prominent Christian leaders, comparing each to the ideal of Proverbs 31.	B - 2
01C04.A	Study your church's ruling documents to find its position on women in leadership. Find Scriptures to support or refute these teachings.	B - 1 B-I
01C05.A	Study the lives of women currently serving in public office in your nation, state, province or local area. Compare the lifestyle and character of each to the Biblical ideal of virtue as shown through your Bible study in this mini-unit.	H - 1 each
01C06.A	Using one of the history books listed in Reading and Literature for this mini-unit, list and study all women mentioned prominently therein.	H - '4 B - 2
01C07.A	Study the lives of women whose husbands are or have been political officials in your community, state, province, or nation. Compare each to the Biblical teaching on virtue and to Proverbs 31 in general.	CS - 2+

01C08.A	Using biographies, magazines and/or other sources, study the lives of other prominent women in various fields, comparing each to Biblical standards of virtue. Include any or all of these fields: military, politics, education entertainment, business/industry, and medicine.	CS - 3 + B - 1
01C09.A	Prepare timeline entries, as described in Guidelines, for major events in the lives of each of the women you studied in this mini-unit.	VA- 1 per 10 H - 1 per 10
01C10.A	Use *The Biblical Feasts, With Christ in the Biblical Feasts* or any similar book to study the Jewish holiday of Purim, which celebrates the acts of a virtuous woman.	B - 1 H - 1
01C11.A	Using any of the church history materials listed in the Reading and Literature section of this mini-unit, study how the role of women in the church has changed at different times in history. Compare each with Biblical references.	H - 2 B - 1
01C12.B	Study various uses made of gems, jewels and "precious" metals in the economy of your nation and the world. Use books on this from the Reading and Literature section, literature from jewelers or investment firms, and/or other resources.	CE - 1
01C13.B	Contact a financial institution to learn about the currency of your nation, how is it made and its value determined, and the metals on which it is based, if any.	CE - 1
01C14.B	Compare the currencies of various countries and learn how they relate to each other. Learn what it means when a currency is devalued.	CE - 1
01C15.B	Discuss with a jeweler financial counselor, or stockbroker (or study from other sources) the use of gold, silver, and other "precious" metals as investments.	CE - 1
01C16.B	Mark on a world map all countries that are major producers and/or exporters of gemstones and/or minerals. Identify in some way which mineral is plentiful in which countries.	CE - 1 G - 1
01C17.B	Study each of the countries listed in the previous activity to determine how gem and mineral deposits affect their economies and environment.	CE - 1 each country
01C18.B	Use a *World Almanac*, encyclopedia, or similar resource to learn basic geographic information about each of these countries.	G - 1 each country
01C19.B	Locate on a map all major mining areas in your country, using some symbol to designate each type.	G - 1

CULTURAL STUDIES

01C20.B	Study literature from both the mining industry (CE – 1, SE – 1) and environmental groups to determine the environmental impact of various kinds of mining and what steps are being (or can be) taken to minimize them.	
01C21.B	Study the geography of all states, provinces, or other regions (G - 1) in your country that contain major gemstone and/or other mineral deposits.	
01C22.B	Check your law library or other source for local and state (CL - 1+) laws regulating the mining or jewelry industry and study them.	
01C23.C	Research your state and/or local school district's policy (CL - 1+) regarding the teaching of creation and/or evolution in the public schools.	
01C24.C	Research any court cases that have been tried in your state with regard to the Creation - Evolution debate and their outcome. (A lawyer or law clerk can tell you how to go about doing this.)	CL - 1 H - 2
01C25.C	Read a true account of the Scopes trial, which dealt with the illegal teaching of evolution in a public school in the state of Tennessee. Discuss the ruling in that case with a Christian adult.	H- 1
01C26.C	Study the lives of Clarence Darrow and William Jennings Bryan, the attorneys on each side of the above court case.	L - 2 + H - 1
01C27.C	From the videos and audios listed in the Science section of this mini-unit, *How Should We Then Live*, and/or *The Biblical Basis for Modern Science*, make a list or mind map of concepts and ideas based on evolutionary theory but often accepted by Christians seemingly with little thought. Discuss how these assumptions affect the way we look at society, even outside the realm of science. Find and list beside each assumption Biblical answers to it provided by the sources in this unit.	SE - 1 *CS - 3* B - 5
01C28.C	After studying about the Scopes trial from encyclopedias or other resources, read or see the video of *Inherit the Wind*, a play about this trial. Compare it to the real life trial.	L - 3
01C29.C	Study the life of Charles Darwin, who was the father of the theory of evolution.	H 1
01C30.C	Make and illustrate timeline entries for the life of Charles Darwin. Include things other than his work on evolution.	VA - 1 per 10 H - 1 per 10
01C31.C	From Darwin's writings, identify the lands in which he traveled for his study of origins, and locate them on a map or globe.	G - 1 SE - 1

CULTURAL STUDIES

01C32.C	Use this opportunity to study basic geography of Australia and New Zealand, both of which figured prominently in Darwin's studies.	G - 1
01C33.D	Study the maps and other info in *Baker's Bible Atlas*, its study guide, or other map sources to locate all of the nations listed from your Scripture studies in this mini-unit and determine the names of the modern-day nation on each site.	G - 2
01C34.D	Use *Greenleaf Guide to The Old Testament* to give you a complete listing of all the lands of the Bible and read their description of each. Look up the Scripture reference for any you missed while working in the Bible section of this unit.	G - 2 B - 2
01C35.D	Read the first two chapters of *Streams of Civilization*, listing names and current locations of all countries mentioned there. Compare the list with that from Scripture and other sources.	H - 1 G - 1
01C36.D	Use the above resources, books in the Reading and Literature section, or other materials to study basic history of the ancient nation of Sumer.	H - 2
01C37.D	Use any or all of the resources listed elsewhere in this mini-unit or others of your choice to study the basic history of the nation of Assyria.	H - 2
01C38.D	Use the above resources or others to study the history of the Empire of Philistia and its best-known rulers.	H - 2
01C39.D	Use any available resources to study the lands and cities of the Biblical Canaanites.	H - 3
01C40.D	Use any of the resources mentioned in this mini-unit or others of your choice to learn basic historical facts about the Phoenicians and the lands of Tyre and Sidon.	H - 2
01C41.D	Study basic historical facts about the Babylonian Empire and its best-known rulers, using *Streams of Civilization* or another Christian resources.	H - 2
01C42.D	Use any of the above resources or others of your choice to study the basic history of the Medo-Persian Empire.	H - 10
01C43.D	Using *World History Dates, Timetables of History, Antiquities of the Jews, The Kingfisher History Encyclopedia*, or other sources, trace the history of each nation you listed in I-II Kings and/or I-II Chronicles. Compare on a chart as to time of founding and demise, number and power of rulers, level of mention in Scripture. Compare the study from these secular sources to that of the Bible and Christian sources.	H - 6

01C44.D	Listen to the first two CDs in *A Christian Survey of World History*, by R. J. Rushdooney and study all the nations discussed therein.	H - 6
01C45.D	Use any of the resources listed here or in the Reading and Literature section for this mini-unit to find and study as many as possible of the kings you listed from your Bible reading. Determine the dates of the reign of each king and make timeline entries (See Guidelines) for each one.	G - 12
01C46.D	Listen to & discuss units 2,4,5 and 6 of *What in the World is Going on Here?* and add new information to your notebook on each of the nations studied here.	*H - 4*
01C47.D	Study the geography of Palestine during Bible times and today by reading *Baker's Bible Atlas* and completing its study guide.	G - 10
01C48.D	Study the family life and role of women during Old Testament times using *The New Manners and Customs of Bible Times* or another book on that topic. Compare their plight in various nations and trace the changes over the years of the Old Testament.	CS - 2 H - 3
01C49.D	List and discuss ways that location, terrain, climate, and other geographical factors affected the activities of a diligent home-maker in Bible times. Save this list for a study in the Science section on how these can or have been overcome today.	G - 1
01050.D	Use *Chronology of the Bible* or *The Amazing Bible Timeline* to see when various Biblical women you studied probably lived and prepare timeline entries for the major ones.	VA- 1 per 10 H - 1 per 10
01051.D	Prepare timeline entries for the lives of all the other women you studied or read about in this unit.	VA- 1 per 10 H - 1 per 10
01052.	Using Usborne's *World History Dates, The Kingfisher History Encyclopedia, The Amazing Bible Timeline* or *Timetables of History,* find dates and prepare timeline entries (following instructions in Guidelines) for all important events and people in the history of each of the ancient nations studied in this mini-unit and their modern-day counterparts.	VA - 1 per 10 H - 1 per 10
01053.	Using the resources mentioned in the above activity, make timeline entries for each culture you studied in this mini-unit, their primary rulers, and major significant events in their history.	VA - 1 per 10 H - 1 per 10
01054.	Make timeline entries for major historical events mentioned in the books or videos used in this study.	VA - 1 per 10 H - 1 per 10

01055.	Use an encyclopedia or similar reference to study each country mentioned but not otherwise studied in this unit and take notes so you can write a brief report (1-2 pages) on each of them (see the Composition section). Keep these in a notebook for that purpose.	G - 1 each

READING AND LITERATURE

01R01.A	Read *Beautiful Girlhood* in either its original format or the revision by Karen Andreola and complete *The Beautiful Girlhood Companion* with your mother.	L - 2 B - 5
01R02.A	Read *Dear Princess*.	B - 3
01R03.A	Read any of the *Elsie Dinsmore* series or other Christian novels written for girls or young women and observe how characters follow or violate the Biblical standard of virtue as studied in this unit.	L — 3 per book B — 2 per book
01R04.A	Read *Little Women* and be prepared to document the personality and character differences between the four sisters. Show ways in which each exhibited one or more of the character traits studied in this unit. (If you prefer to do this in video, DO NOT USE THE WINONA RIDER VERSION MADE IN THE 1990's.)	L - 5 B - 1 *4/14/∞* *1933* *1949* *1978*
01R05.A	Read *Sense and Sensibility* or see a video of it and compare the three sisters as to personality and character traits. Pick specific quotes or passages to show examples of virtue in each of them.	L - 5 for book L - 2 for video
01R06.A	Read *Jane Eyre* and analyze her character and behavior in light of the Scriptures studied here.	R - 4 B - 1
01R07.A	Read *Wuthering Heights* and study the character traits of each of the women in it in light of the Bible's teaching on virtue.	R - 4 B - 1
01R08.A	Read other novels considered classics and compare each main female character to the Bible's standard of virtue.	R - 4 each B - 1 each
01R09.A	Read one or more of the vintage Christian 'romance' novels of an earlier era written by Grace Livingston Hill in which the heroines are godly, virtuous women who trust God for husbands with often surprising results. Analyze their behavior in light of the Biblical standard of virtue.	R - 4 each B - 1 each (up to 20 points total)
01R10.A	Read and memorize appropriate portions of William Bennett's *Book of Virtues* or *Children's Book of Virtues*, using it as part of your daily devotions.	B - 5 +

READING AND LITERATURE

0IR11.A	Read several articles from one or more Christian magazines about any of the character traits studied in this mini-unit. Analyze the articles in light of Scriptural standards and be prepared to write reviews or critiques of them.	B - 2 +
01R12.A	Read 3 - 7 biographies about godly women from history. Compare each to the Biblical standard of virtue.	H - 5 each
01R13.A	Read biographies of women who are or have been well-known or influential in the Christian church of our day. Compare their lives to the Biblical standard.	CS - 5each
01R14.A	Read *Alabaster Doves* and analyze each woman by Biblical standards of virtue.	CS - 4 B - 1
01R15.B	Read, from cover to cover, one or more of the trade journals of the jewelry industry.	SE - 1
01R16.B	Read one or more articles on gems, minerals or related topics in one of the journals of the U. S. Geological Survey, or the equivalent agency in your country.	SE - 1
01R17.B	Read the entire collection of pamphlets you received from various mining interests and environmental groups and contrast what they have to say.	SE - 1+
01R18.B	Read all of at least one issue of a hobby periodical devoted to rock collecting, jewelry making, gemology, or a related hobby.	SE - 1 OR IA - 1
01R19.B	Read Usborne's *Atoms and Molecules*.	Sc - 3
01R20.B	Memorize 10-15 lines of poetry on rubies.	L - 3
01R21.B	Read and memorize poems (10-15 lines each) about other "precious" stones.	L - 3 each
01R22.B	Read The Rare Jewel of Christian Contentment.	B - 7
01R23.B	Read one or more Christian or other wholesome novels set in a mining town or in some other way involving mining.	L - 5
01R24.B	Read one of more mystery novels involving theft or disappearance of jewels, gems, or gemstones.	L - 5
01R25.B	Read and discuss with a parent "The Necklace" by Guy de Maupassant.	L - 2
01R26.B	Read a Christian novel that in some way involves rubies or other gems.	L - 5
01R27.B	Read Usborne's *Rocks and Minerals*.	SE - 5
01R28.B	Read *Rubies and Sapphires* by Fred Ward.	SE - 6

READING AND LITERATURE

01R29.C	Read *Unlocking the Mystery of Creation* to help you develop a firm foundation before beginning the other materials in this mini-unit.	SE - 3 SB - 3
01R30.C	Read *Scientific Creationism*, to provide a background for the other material to be covered in this mini-unit.	SE - 5 SB - 5 B - 2
01R31.C	Read, alone, or with your family, *The Amazing Story of Creation*.	SB - 3
01R32.C	Read and study *Bone of Contention*.	SB - 3
01R33.C	Read *Creation Facts of Life*.	SB - 4
01R34.C	Read and discuss with a younger child *Dinosaurs by Design*, *D is for Dinosaurs* and/or other Christian children's books about these creatures.	SB I each TE - 1each
01R35.C	Study and use for reference in other work *Dinosaurs and the Bible* and/or *The Great Dinosaur Mystery* and the Bible.	SB - 3each B 1 each
01R36.C	Listen to Unit 1 of Disc 1 of *What in the World is Going on Here?* by Diana Waring, and take notes or discuss as appropriate.	H — 1 B - 1
01R37.C	To better understand what we must refute, study and discuss with parents Darwin's *Origin of Species,* which forms the basis of most evolutionary thought and theory. Find passages from Scripture or Christian works to refute each of his points.	SB - 10 + B - 5
01R38.C	Study *How Should We Then Live?* to help you understand how viewing man as a special being created in God's image should affect all areas of life. This can be in either book or video form.	B - 10
01R39. C	Read articles on evolution, the "Big Bang" theory and similar teachings from secular magazines. Search Scripture and Christian materials to refute these teachings.	SB - 2 or SE - 2 B - 2
01R40.C	Study the flood of Genesis and its ramifications by reading *The Genesis Flood*. Discuss it with your parents.	SE - 5 B - 5
01R41.C	Read *The Search for Noah's Ark* or watch the video of the same name.	B - 2 H - 3
01R42.D	Read Creation-based history of Bible times in *Adam and His Kin*.	H - 4
01R43.D	Read *The World that Perished*.	H - 5
01R44.D	Read *Genesis: Finding Our Roots*.	H - 4
01R45.D	Read one or more fictionalized biographies of Old Testament figures (see Appendix 1), checking each story with the Biblical account for accuracy.	H - 5

01R46.D*	To understand Old Testament times from a secular perspective, read *Antiquities of the Jews* by Josephus.	H - 25
01R47.D*	Read Usborne's *The First Civilizations*.	H - 3
01R48.D	Read Usborne's *Empires and Barbarians*.	H - 3
01R49.D	Read *Chronology of the Bible* to put all these events in perspective.	H - 4
01R50.D*	Read *History Begins at Sumer Enterprise: Thirty-Nine "Firsts" in Man's Recorded History* by Samuel Noah Kramer or some other book about this great early civilization.	H - 5
01R51.D*	Read any of the following books from the Time-Life series Lost Civilizations: *Sumer: Cities of Eden, Mesopotamia: the Mighty Kings* or *Persians: Masters of the Empire.*	H - 5
01R52.D	Read *Ah, Assyria: Studies in Assyrian History and Ancient Near East Historiography* or some other scholarly book about the Assyrians.	H - 5
01R53.D*	Read *The Ancient Near East* by Amelie Kuhrt and Eva Von.	H - 5
01R54.D	Carry this study into New Testament times by reading *The Jewish Wars* by Josephus.	H - 25
01R55.D	Read *Our Father Abraham: Jewish Roots of the Christian Faith*. Critique it from Scripture and discuss with your parents.	B - 5 H - 5
01R56.D	Read through *Celebrating Jesus in the Biblical Feasts: Discovering Their Significance to You as a Christian* to study the significance of Passover and other holy days established by God in the Old Testament and how they have changed over the years.	H - 3
01R57.	Read one or more historical novels set in one of the time periods studied in this unit.	H - 5 each
01R58.	Read one or more biographies of people studied in this mini-unit.	H - 5 each
01R59.	Read one book per week in addition to those given as assignments. Choose from those listed here or in the resource list or any others your parents approve.	L - 5 each
01R60.	Read any other appropriate books on the subject of the mini-unit you are studying.	5 pts. each in appropriate area

COMPOSITION

01W01.A — Define 'virtuous', 'noble', and 'godly', all sometimes used in Proverbs 31:10 and all synonyms for them. (Check a thesaurus for synonyms.) Write definitions in your vocabulary notebook (see Guidelines). Compare the modern definition of each with *Webster's 1828 dictionary*.

01W02.A — Write a DETAILED character sketch (1-2 pages) of one of the Biblical women you studied in this mini-unit. If you need help on how to do this, read the appropriate section in Writer's Inc..

EC - 1

01W03.A — Write a brief character analysis (2-3 lines) of each Biblical woman that you studied in this mini-unit, showing how she did or did not meet the Biblical standards of virtue.

EC - 1
per 6

01W04.A — Write a biographical sketch (2-4 pages) of one of the Biblical women you studied in this unit. Learn how this differs from a character sketch by reading about them in *Writer's Inc.* or a similar source.

EC - 2+

01W05.A — Write a brief report (2-3 paragraphs) on each of the modern-day women you studied in this unit.

EC - 1
per 3

01W06.A — Write a brief report (1-2 pages) on one or more of the historical women you studied.

EC - 1
each

01W07.A — Write a summary of your church organization's teachings and/ or rules with regard to the role of women. Analyze each part of these rules in light of Scripture, using the concordance to find appropriate passages. Include Scripture references.

EC - 1
B - 1

01W08.A — Write a complete description (1-2 pages) of the Christian woman you consider to be your role model or example, telling why you admire her.

EC - 1+

01W09.A — Write an essay on *The Biblical Role of Women in the Corporate Worship of the Church*, referencing specific Scriptures to support your beliefs.

EC - 2+

01W10.A — Write a newspaper ad that might be placed by a man looking for a godly wife, using the standards of Proverbs 31:10-31.

EC - 1

01W11.A — Using the lists you made in the Bible section of this mini-unit, write a job description for a godly wife based on the standards of Proverbs 31 and using the basic format used in industry.

EC - 1

01W12.A — Using the lists you made in the Bible section of this mini-unit, write a resume' for a woman who fits the Proverbs 31 ideal, relating each skill to an appropriate area of the job market. Use *Writer's Inc.* or a book on job hunting for help on this.

EC - 2

COMPOSITION

01W13.A	Write a diary (10-12 entries) as it may have been kept by one of the historical women studied in this mini-unit.	EC - 3	H 2
01W14.A	Write a formal term paper (5-8 pages) on one of the women you studied in this unit, using *Writing the Research Paper, Writer's Inc.*, or a similar book as a guide. Be sure to include footnotes, bibliography, etc.	EC - 25	
01W15.A	Write a speech to be given before an audience on "The Value of the Full-time Homemaker to Today's Family and Community".	EC - 5	
01W16.B	Write a Biblical exegesis on the use and significance of rubies and other "precious" stones in the Scripture.	EC - 2	B- 1
01W17.B	Write a comparative analogy using gems or "precious" stones as symbolic of some value or character trait. Do not copy from the Bible or other reading material.	EC - 2	
01W18.B	After talking with a jeweler or gemologist, analyze the qualities of gemstones that determine their value and write an essay or poem comparing each one to some desirable quality in a woman.	EC - 1+ each	
01W19.B	Prepare a 'prospectus' comparing various types of gems, jewels, and precious metals as potential investments.	EC - 2	
01W20.B	Write a report on the uses of gems and metals in the economy of your country.	EC - 2	
01W21.B	Write a report on the health benefits of a variety of minerals.	EC - 2+	
01W22.B	Write a short story on the discovery of ruby deposits and the opening of a mine. You may research and write the history of a real mine, or you may create a fictional one.	EC - 6	
01W23.B	Prepare a booklet on Gems and Minerals. Include types and descriptions of various gems; how they are made; the processes used for identification and appraisal; uses for various gems, mining methods; data on crystalline structure, etc. There should be at least one page for each gem and most minerals as well as general pages of introduction and other information that applies to all gems.	EC - 15 SE - 5 SC - 5	
01W24.B	Write a diary (minimum 20 entries) or first-person short story (minimum 1000 words) of a miner in whatever type of mine you prefer. Tell about his work and his life away from the job.	EC - 6+	
01W25.B	Prepare legal briefs for each side in a case that might be brought by environmentalists against a mining company.	EC - 2 CL - 1	
01W26.B	Define the word 'precious' and write an essay telling why many Christians object to the use of this word to describe gemstones, gold, silver, and other minerals or metals.	EC 1	

COMPOSITION

01W27.B	Write a description of the ephod of the Hebrew high priest as it might have impressed a young Israelite who was present the first time it was worn.	EC -	1
01W28.B	Write (and submit if possible) an article for a trade or hobby magazine about some hobby or occupation relating to gems, rocks, and/or minerals.	EC -	2+
01W29.B	Write a poem (at least 15 lines) about rubies or other gemstones, using them either literally or as symbols.	EC -	1- 2
01W30.B	Write a brief (1-2 pages) geographical report on each of the states, provinces, or other regions in your country where gems or minerals are mined commercially.	EC - each	1
01W31.C	For handwriting practice, copy Genesis 1:1-31, breaking it into the segments used for memorizing it.	EG - per hour	1
01W32.C	Practice writing Genesis 1 from dictation, breaking it into the same segments used for memorizing in the Bible and Christian Character section. Have someone read it while you write it, word for word with exact punctuation. If your family's beliefs allow, you may wish to use a modern Scripture translation for this activity.	EG - per hour	1
01W33.C	Write a Biblical refutation of one of the articles on evolution you read for this mini-unit. Use a journalistic style, as if for a newspaper or scientific journal.	EC -	3
01W34.C	Prepare a three-to-five-minute speech on "Evidences from Nature for the Biblical Creation", using not only Scripture but also scientific evidences.	EC SB **B**-2	-6 -2
01W35.C	Summarize your state and local laws with regard to the teaching of evolution and/or creation in the public schools.	CL-	2
01W36.C	Write a personification story about some animal or inanimate object of nature in which it tells the story of its own Creation. Use lots of description, telling what all was going on around it at the time and the other things that were being brought into existence on the same day.	EC - 25	
01W37.C	Write a letter to Charles Darwin, trying not only to refute his theory of origins but also to lead him to faith in the Lord.	EC- 1 **B**- 1	
01W38.C	Write an interview with either lawyer from the Scopes trial, asking pertinent questions, and answering as you think he would have.	EC - 3	
01W39.C	Watch and discuss *The Genesis 3D Movie*, due out by Summer 2016. Follow their progress and find out when and where the movie will be available at .genesismovie.com		

COMPOSITION

01W39.C   Write an extensive research paper (700-1000 words) on the subject: EC - 25
"Biblical Creation: More Than Just Science" in which you explore
how believing that man was created by God in His image affects the
way one looks at government, society and all of life. Use *Writer's
Inc.* or any other good writing resource to achieve proper format
and follow the appropriate steps for such a paper, including outline,
note cards, footnotes, and bibliography.

01W40. C   Take notes as you watch each of the creation science videos   EC - 2
listed in the science section of this mini-unit.

01W41. C   Prepare arguments for either side (or both sides) of a debate on   EC - 25
the topic "Resolved: Christians Today Should Still Observe the
Sabbath as A Day of Rest." Use Scripture verses, commentaries,
and other materials to research your position. If possible, team up
with another student to present this debate.

01W42.C   Write reviews of the creation science videos you watched in this unit.   EC - 2

01W43. C   Write a poem of praise to God for the magnificence of His   EC - 1+
creation or some particular part of it.

01W44. C   Write a Bible lesson on Creation to be taught to younger   EC - 10
children on their level.   B - 5

01W45.D   Write a television or radio news report on the Tower of Babel,   EC - 2
writing it as it might have been covered by a reporter present at   B - 1
the time.

01W46. D   Outline any or all of the Biblical books of history that you studied   EG - 3
in this mini-unit. If you have never learned to outline, read
about it and follow the instructions in *Writers Inc.* or a similar
writing handbook.

01W47.D   Instead of outlining the above books, summarize the contents of   EG   1
each chapter in one short paragraph. For help in learning to   per
summarize, consult *Writers Inc.* or another writing handbook.   chapter

01W48.D   For your Geography notebook (see Guidelines), write a brief   G   1
report (1- 2 pages) on each ancient nations mentioned in the Bible   EC -
studies of this mini-unit.

01W49.D   Use encyclopedias, the *World Almanac*, or other resources to   EC - 1
research and write a 1-2 page report for your geography notebook   G - 1
(see Guidelines) on the modem counterpart of each ancient
nation studied in this mini-unit.

01W50.D   Write a brief report on each king or ruler you studied in this   EC - 1
mini-unit.

COMPOSITION

01W51.D   Write a fictional story about an event that could have taken   EC   25
place in the life of one of the Biblical kings studied in this mini-unit. Set the tone and location as realistically as possible, and include some real events as well as things that may not have happened but were in keeping with traditions and lifestyle of the time.

01W52.D   Write fictional but realistic memoirs of one of the Biblical kings   EC - 25
you studied in this mini-unit.

01W53.D   Write 12-15 entries for a journal that might have been kept by   EC - 3
an Israelite in captivity in Babylon. Be sure to include: the captivity and march to Babylon, the stories told in the book of Daniel, their joy at being allowed to return to their homeland.

01W54.D   Write a short story set in some nation other than Israel or Judah   EC - 25
during Old Testament times.

01W55.D   Write a fictional short story in which one of the Old Testament   EC - 25
people you studied figures as a prominent character.

01W56.D   Write a newspaper report on the battle between David and Goliath   EC - 2
as it might have been written by a sports reporter of the day.

01W57.D   Write a first person story as though by Jonah after the conversion   EC - 10
of Nineveh. Include the actual events, his attitude at different times during them and what he learned from the experience.

01W58.   Define and put into your vocabulary notebook 10 new words per   EG - 1
week, using first those you have encountered in this mini-unit.   per week
Write all possible definitions and pronunciations for each.

01W59.   Learn to spell all the words that you put into your vocabulary   EG - 2
notebook during this mini-unit.   per week

01W60.   Using *Writers Inc., The College English Handbook*, or another   EG   -1
other grammar reference and a good dictionary, proofread and   per 4
correct grammar and spelling in all written work for this mini-unit.   pages

01W61.   Take notes as you listen to or watch any of the audio or videos   EC - 2
for this mini-unit. For help, consult the appropriate chapter   each
in Writers Inc. or another writing handbook.

01W62.   Use your notes to outline the lecture audios.   EC - 3
   each

01W63.   Use notes taken in the above activity to summarize and/or para-   EC - 1+
phrase one or more of the lectures or stories on the audios.

01W64.   Outline one or more of the nonfiction books used in this mini-   EG - 5
unit, following guidelines in *Writer's Inc.* or another writing   each
handbook.

COMPOSITION

01W65.	Write reviews, as if to be published in a periodical of some type, of any or all of the books read in this mini-unit.	EC - 1 each
01W66.	Write a brief report on any important person studied in this mini-unit.	EC - 2
01W67.	For handwriting practice, copy any Bible passage, poem or other material you are memorizing. Write it carefully as many times as you can in one hour.	EG - 1 per hour
01W68.	Use the material you are memorizing to write from dictation, being careful about spelling, punctuation, and other writing mechanics. To do this, have someone read the passage to you slowly while you write it, word for word.	EG - 1 per hour
01W69.	As an alternative to cursive writing, learn Spencerian or Italic calligraphy using books in the resource list or other materials.	VA – 1 per Hour (or 1 credit for complete course)
01W70.	Keep a journal of each day's school activities throughout the curriculum. If done well, this journal can serve as a documentation of your school year.	EC - 2 per week
01W71.	Write a news article on each of the field trips you took in this mini-unit.	EC - 2 each
01W72.	Write a thank you note to the organizer, guide, and/ or supervisor of any field trip you took for this mini-unit.	EC - 1 each

MATH & PERSONAL ECONOMICS

01M01.A	Make a line or bar graph showing the number and percentage of women of different ages in the work force of your country, using census or similar data.	M - 5
01M02.A	Prepare a graph to compare the number of mothers in the work force in different years in your country.	M - 5
01M03.A	Use the data collected above to make a graph showing the percentages of children of different ages whose mothers work outside the home on a full-time basis.	M - 5
01M04.A	Using current census figures or other available data, make a graph to illustrate the number of moms in the work force full-time, part-time and not at all.	M- 5
01M05.A	From figures in the above activities and other appropriate data, compute the mean and median incomes of women in the work force of your nation in various decades. Compare on a graph of your choice.	M - 7

MATH & PERSONAL ECONOMICS

01M06.A	List all jobs done by a godly wife/mother in her home. Use the average hourly pay and estimated time spent in each job to compute her weekly earnings if she were paid for her work in the home. Add all jobs during the week and multiply by 52 to get the annual value to her family of her work in the home. (Due to overlap, total hours worked may be more than actual hours in a week.) Compare this value to the mean and median incomes of women in the work force to see where a woman would be more productive.	M-	3

01M07.A	From your figures in the above activity, find what percentage of the average homemaker's (or your own mother's) time (out of 168 hours in a week) is spent in each chore or activity on the above list. (Since some jobs overlap, it is possible for the total to exceed 100%.)	M -	1

01M08.A	Show the above information in ratios and/or proportions as appropriate.	M -	1

01M09.A	Make a pie graph using the above data to show what percentage of a wife's/mother's time is spent in which of her duties.	M-	5

01M10.B	Using data from a bank or currency exchange, perform all calculations to compare the currency of each of the countries studied in this unit with that your own.	M-	2

01M11.B	Ask a jeweler for (or find online) the current per carat value of rubies and how to convert carats to pounds and kilograms. Multiply cost per carat by your weight in carats to calculate your value if you are, indeed, "worth more than rubies" as the Proverbs 31 woman would be.	M-	2

01M12.B	Calculate and graph the per carat value of 8-10 different gemstones.	M-	5

01M13.B	Study the "karat" used to measure gold and make a graph to show a comparison between the percentages of pure gold contained in items of varying "karats".	M-	3

01M14.B	Identify the geometric shape of each type of crystal studied and learn the formulas for perimeter, area and volume of each.	M -	3

01M15.B	Further investigate geometric shapes by playing the game "Oh, Euclid".	M -	1 each time

01M16.B	If you plan to take a plane geometry course, this is the part of the study in which it would fit. Use a text from the resource list or any other one you and your parents choose.	1 credit in Geometry

01M17.B	Complete "Geometry: The Beauty of Numbers" from Old-Fashioned Crafts. (Find them at www.mugginsmath.com)	M - 20	

01M18.C   Use the genealogical lists found in Genesis 5 and Matthew 1 to   M - 1
determine the approximate age of the Earth, by adding together the
ages given and the lengths of time between Creation and things for
which we know the date.

01M19.C   From reference books of various kinds, compute what scientists   M - 2
believe to have been the relative sizes of the various types of
dinosaurs. Use this data for or drawing constructing dinosaurs to
scale in the Science section of this mini-unit.

01M20.C   Prepare some type of graph to show relative sizes of dinosaurs   M - 5
as determined in the above activity.

01M21.C   Gather data on numbers of known species of each of the kinds   M - 2
of animals created on the fifth day of Creation. Calculate ratios and
proportions to show the relationships between these species.

01M22.C   Gather data on numbers of species of each type of animal created   M - 2
on the sixth day. Calculate ratios and proportions to show the
relationships between these species.

01M23.C   Convert Biblical dimensions for the ark into English and metric   M- 2
measures. Then compute the complete surface area of it and its total
interior volume.

01M24.D   Use available resources to find or estimate the highest-known   M - 1
population of each ancient culture studied in this mini-unit.

01M25.D   Using any available sources to gather data, prepare a graph   M - 5
comparing the populations of various ancient nations at five
different specified times in history.

01M26.D   Use the genealogical lists found in Genesis 5 and Matthew 1 to   M - 3
compute the number of years between Creation and the flood,   VA -
the flood and the tower of Babel, the tower and Abram's departure   each
from Haran, Abram's travels and the exodus from Egypt,   H - 1
the exodus and the exile into Babylon, the return from exile and   each
the birth of Christ. Put each of these events on the timeline.

01M27.D   Using the genealogy lists of Genesis 5 and other resources, calculate   M - 1
the approximate population of the Earth at the time of the flood
and the tower of Babel.

01M28.D   Prepare a bar graph showing relative ages at death of selected   M - 5
people from the genealogy in Genesis 5.

01M29. D   Use maps from *Baker's Bible Atlas* and its study guide or other   M - 6
sources to determine the sizes of various countries mentioned
in the Old Testament and draw a pictograph to show relationship
between those sizes.

01M30.D   Prepare a graph of your choice to compare the sizes of various   M - 5
Biblical countries with their modern-day counterparts.

| 01M31. | Use data from the graphs made in this unit to practice proportions and ratios. | M - 1 |
| 01M32. | Use data from the graphs in this unit to review per cent, decimals, and/or fractions. | M - 1 |

SCIENCE

01S01.A	Investigate secular psychology's definition of 'virtue' or 'character' and compare it to the Scriptural standard.	CS - 1
01S02.A	Compare and contrast Freudian, Rogerian, and Skinnerian psychology or counseling and study how each would determine right or wrong, good or evil. Learn from this why a Christian cannot get her ideas of virtue from either of these systems.	CS - 3
01S03.A	From *Competent to Counsel* and/or other writings of Jay Adams, learn about nouthetic counseling and how its approach differs from that of secular psychology and counseling.	CS- 5
01S04.A	Study any of the above types of psychology or counseling as thoroughly as you and your parents see fit.	1 credit in Psychology for a complete course
01S05.A	As virtue relates to moral purity, study the purity of your drinking water and the process used to purify it. What elements or chemicals cannot be completely removed? How is this analogous to sin in your life?	SE - 1 SP - 1
01S06.A	Visit the water purifying plant in your area to see firsthand how this is done.	SP - 2
01S07.A	Consult a water purification specialist about the various filtering processes consumers can use in their own homes to further purify drinking water after it has come from the pipes.	SP - 2
01S08.A	Attend a home demonstration of a water purifying system.	SP - 2
01S09.A	Study common household air pollutants and various methods of air purification.	SE - 1
01S10.A	Study the construction and material used in HEPA filters and why they are so effective for filtering air pollutants.	SP - 2
01S11.A	Learn about the "purifying " process used to draw pure metal out of ore.	SP - 2
01S12.B	Examine other properties of the various "precious" metals valued highly in our culture. Compare their luster, hardness, weight, and other properties.	SE - 4

01S13.B	Research and list the scientific names of as many naturally-occurring gems as possible.	SE - 2
01S14.B	Research each stone listed above to determine its rarity, relative value, common locations for deposits, methods of mining and/or production, and uses.	SE - 2 SP - 1
01S15.B	Examine various synthetic or 'salted' gems and the process by which they are made.	SP - 2
01S16.B	Study and complete all activities in the "Task-Oriented Physical Science" (TOPS) unit on Rocks and Minerals.	SP - 2
01S17.B	Using a commercial kit or the directions from www.kidzworld.com/article/26598-make-your-own-crystals, grow your own crystals from various substances and watch them develop. Investigate each type under a microscope, comparing shape and size of the individual crystals.	SC - 3
01S18.B	Identify crystalline structures of several common and 'precious' gemstones you identified elsewhere in this mini-unit and the various types of bonding in them.	SC - 3
01S19.B	Use Usborne's *Essential Chemistry* or other resources to investigate the formation, makeup and bonding of crystals.	SC - 3
01S20.B	Use the study of crystals to learn about atoms and molecules in general and to learn to identify various molecules by appearance and formula, using the recommended Usborne book, *Essential Chemistry* or a similar one.	SC - 10
01S21.B	In the context of gems, crystals and molecular bonding, use the "Friendly Chemistry" kit with all of its projects to investigate and learn the Periodic Table of Elements and other basic chemical principles in a fun, hands-on manner.	SC - 20 +
01S22.B	Use any of the recommended sources in this mini-unit to study minerals and to learn which minerals are also elements.	SC - 3
01S23.B	Use a wall chart or other source to learn to read the Periodic Table of Elements.	SC - 2
01S24.B	Instead of individual activities 01S18-01S23, take a complete chemistry course, using Usborne's *Dictionary of Chemistry, Essential Chemistry, Apologia Chemistry,* the "Friendly Chemistry" kit or some similar resource. (If you do this, do not count any of the above-listed activities in addition.)	SC - 1 credit
01S25.B	Study various methods of mining gems, metal ore and other minerals and the effect of each on the environment.	SE - 1 SP - 1
01S26.B	Tour a commercial metal or mineral mine or ore processing facility and learn how it operates.	SP - 2

SCIENCE

01S27.B	Tour a commercial ruby or other gemstone mine in operation.	SP - 3
01S28.B	Tour a jewelry manufacturing facility to see how gems are cut, polished, and set into jewelry.	SP - 2
01S29. C	Watch the video series "The World that Perished: Evidence of the Global Flood of Genesis".	SE - 2
01S30.C	Study the Creation Resource Foundation's audio or video seminar on "Unlocking the Mysteries of Creation".	SB - 5 SE - 5 B- 5
01S31.C	Expand "Unlocking the Mysteries of Creation" into a full credit by completing all work in the accompanying text and workbook.	1 credit in Creation Science
01S32.C	Watch, take notes on, and discuss with parents any or all of the videos in the *Origins: How the World Came to Be* series by Dr. A. E. Wilder-Smith. Individual titles are: "Origins of the Universe"; "The Earth, A Young Planet"?; "The Origin of Life"; "The Origin of Species"; "The Origin of Mankind"; and "The Fossil Record".	SE - 10 SB - 10
01S33.C	Conduct a thorough study of dinosaurs, using books recommended here, in the Reading and Literature section and/or the Resource Guide or other Christian materials. You may combine activities 01S34 - 01S36 to do this one. However, you should not take credit for those and this one.	SB - 25
01S34.C	Relate the book of Job to Creation by studying *Dinosaurs: Those Terrible Lizards*.	SB 5
01S35.C	Attend and take good notes at an "Answers in Genesis" seminar.	SE - 20 SP - 20
01S36.C	In lieu of attending a seminar, watch and complete the study guide for the complete Answers in Genesis video series.	S E - 25 SB - 25
01S37.C	After reading *What Really Happened to the Dinosaurs* and/ or other books on that subject, reconstruct, using charts or dioramas, the events leading to their apparent extinction. Show how (or if) you believe it was impacted by the cataclysm (flood) of Noah's day.	SB - 5 SE - 5
01S38.C	Watch other Creation videos by the Institute for Creation Research, Moody Press, or others. Take notes on each one and discuss with parents.	SB -leach SE -leach
01S39.C	At this stage in life, it may be wise to study the theory of evolution as it is taught in most secular schools and colleges, along with the Biblical evidences to refute it. You may use any secular biology book to study it along with material from Master Books or Institute for Creation Research to refute it.	SE - 25 B - 10

SCIENCE

01S40. C	Investigate the "Big Bang" and other 'scientific' theories that admit that the world and the universe had a definite time of beginning but do not acknowledge a Supreme Creator. Look for Christian materials to refute these theories.	SE - 10 B - 3
01S41.C	Use any of the suggested books to study the dinosaurs and what may have happened to them. Be sure this is done from a Christian perspective.	SB -2
01S42.C	Watch the *Grand Canyon: Monument to Catastrophe* video for an introduction to the geology of the Biblical Flood.	SE - 2
01S43.C	Locate and study canyons, mountains, gorges, caves, and/or other geological formations in or near your area and examine them as evidences of the Flood (cataclysm) described in Genesis. Explore these on your own if allowed to do so.	SE -2 +
01344. C	Take a guided tour of one or more caverns, caves or similar geological formations.	SE - 3
01S45.C	Using materials from the Geological Survey or other sources, study geologic faults, tectonic plates, and underground fissures of all types. Investigate what part those may have played in creating the changes that occurred during the Flood of Genesis.	SE - 10
01S46.C	Study volcanoes and volcanic action. Determine what part, if any, this may have played in the Flood of Noah's time.	SE - 3
01S47.C	Tour the site of any modern or ancient volcanic activity and examine its effects on the surrounding landscape.	SE -2
01S48.C	Study whirlpools and tidal waves, both used by God in creating the cataclysm.	SE -3
01S49.C	Investigate other geological structures of the earth that were created by the cataclysm of Noah's time.	SE -5
01S50.D	From resources named in this unit or others, study the Hanging Gardens of Babylon and determine how they could have been built using only materials and technology known to exist at that time.	SP - 5 H -1
01S51.D	From resources named elsewhere in this unit or others of your choice, study the engineering feat that was the known as the Great Lighthouse and determine how it could have been built using only materials and technology known to exist at that time	SP - 5 H-1
01S52.D	From resources named elsewhere in this unit or others of your choice, study any of the other engineering feats known as the Seven Wonders of the Ancient World and determine how each could have been built using only materials and technology known to exist at that time. (The Pyramids are covered in Unit 5 with the Egyptians, so you might want to skip them here.)	SP - 5 each H - 1 each

SCIENCE

01S53.D	Study the Seven Wonders of the World and other technological feats of Old Testament times in the book *The Ancient Engineers*. Draw parallels between each item there and similar technology of today.	SP - 10
01S54.D	Use any of the suggested resources to examine the technology that provided running water and indoor plumbing for some societies of the Old Testament era.	SP - 2
01S55.D	Study the processes by which homes and other buildings were heated and cooled in various cultures during this time period.	SP - 2
01S56.D	Study the forms of indoor lighting used during Bible times and the fuels for them.	SP - 2
01S57.D	Study the various methods and fuels used in cooking by the women of that day.	SP - 2
01S58.D	Investigate utensils used in the home of Old Testament times, learning how each was made and used.	SP - 2
01S59.D	Investigate tools of Old Testament times, learning how each was made and used.	SP - 2
01S61.D	Investigate the weapons and other military equipment used by the armies of Old Testament times, learning how each was made and used.	SP - 3
01S62.D	From books and other resources on the topic, learn how archaeologists locate and unearth. ruins of ancient cultures.	SP - 2 H -2
01S63.D	From an archaeological journal or some similar resource, study the processes used for dating artifacts.	SP - 3
01S64.D	Talk with an archaeologist or museum curator to learn how they preserve and restore artifacts from their digs.	SP - 2
01S65.D	If you wish to get into this on a larger scale, you may take a complete course in archeology at a local college, or through college at home.	1 credit in Archeology

HEALTH & PHYSICAL FITNESS

01H01.A	Study and discuss with your mother *Preparing for Adolescence*, a guide on the path toward Christian womanhood.	HE - 5
01H02.A	Study about becoming a woman in *Almost Twelve*, even if you are already 12 or over.	HE - 2
01H03.A	Discuss with your mother the changes your body has begun and/or will be going through as you become an adult woman.	HA - 1

HEALTH & PHYSICAL FITNESS

01H04.A   Study the hormones that will affect your body as you change   HA - 2
from a child to a woman. Learn the medical effects these can have
on you.

01H05.A   Investigate common herbal and nutritional remedies for PMS,   HE - 2
cramps, and other hormone-related problems in women.

01H06.A   Read and discuss with your mother *The Care and Keeping of You*   HE - 2
a book on basic changes in puberty and how to deal with them.

01H07.A   If your mother believes you are ready, read and discuss with her   HE - 2
The Care and Keeping of You 2: The Body Book for Older Girls.

01H08.B   Study the use of gems and crystals in surgery and medical   SP - 1
technology.

01H09.B   Study and make a booklet about "minerals" needed for a   HE - 10
healthy body and the foods that contain them.

01H10.B   Study specific disorders caused by lack or overabundance of   HE - 2
certain of the above "minerals".

01H11.B   Study the commonly-recognized methods for prevention and   HE - 2
treatment of disorders and/or deficiencies related to minerals as
studied in the above activity.

01H12.B   Analyze your family's meals for one week to discover the levels   HE - 2
of needed minerals you are getting. Alter or supplement your
meals to correct any shortages.

01H13.B   Study the various natural and synthetic mineral supplements   HE - 3
available to you and compare them.

01H14. C   Examine human anatomy and physiology and list as many examples   HA - 3
as you can of ways the human body takes care of itself. These are
seen by many as evidences of the special Creation of man in God's
image.

01H15.C   From a study of Genesis 2 and 3, determine why bodies created   B - 1
so perfectly get sick and die.

01H16.C   Study *The Whole Foods Book, The Herbal Bible*, or any good   HE - 5
book on natural healing to see how God's creation includes all those
things we need to care for our health.

01H17.C   Use one of the health books recommended in the above activity   HE- 2
or another of your choice to learn about natural treatments and/
or medications commonly available and recommended for any
chronic ailments that affect members of your family.

01H18.D   Study leprosy, which was rampant in Bible times, to learn   HE - 1
how it is caused or contracted and the symptoms of it.

01H19.D	Study the medical treatments now available for leprosy. Discover why it is no longer as common or deadly as it was.	HE - 1
01H2O.D	Study the kosher laws of the Old Testament and learn how they coincide or conflict with current teachings on healthy eating, especially in the areas of calories, fat, and cholesterol.	B - 2 HE - 2
01H21.D	Learn the specific human health problems that are impacted by the eating of pork, shellfish, and scavenger animals like catfish; all of which were prohibited to the Old Testament Jews.	HE - 2
01H22.D	Study deafness and ways that modern science can enhance or restore hearing, something that could only be done by "supernatural" miracle in the Bible times.	HE- 3
01H23.D	Study the medicinal properties of "essential oils", many of which have been known and widely-used in Old Testament time and were later a part of the ritual healing of the New Testament church.	HE - 2

PRACTICAL ARTS

01P01.A	If you are not actively involved in having your own regular quiet time for devotions, work with a parent to start one.	B - 1
01P02.A	Learn how to keep a prayer journal and begin one of your own, following directions in the FAR Guidelines for Students or any other resource.	EC - 1 B - 1
01P03.A	Analyze your life in light of the Scriptures studied in this mini-unit and begin working and praying for improvement in the areas that need it.	B - 1
01P04.A	Prepare a lesson for younger children on the Beatitudes, trying to put them into language little ones will understand.	B - 1 TE - 2
01P05.A	Use the Bible lesson you prepared in the previous activity as the cornerstone of a complete lesson and teach it to a Sunday School class or other group. Include games, play activities, appropriate songs, audiovisual aids, and/or a craft to help children remember the lesson.	TE - 4
01P06.A	Create a poster or bulletin board display to teach young children about the Beatitudes or another passage on virtue. If you are going to teach a lesson on them as well, this can support it.	VA - 2 TE - I
01P07.A	Give before an audience your speech on "The Value of a Full-time Homemaker in Today's World."	DR - 3
01P08.A	Build your own water purifying system and install it in your home or some other location.	IA - 3 +

01P09.A	Build and install your own air purifier.	IA - 2+
01P10.A	Build a web site to share with other young ladies what you have learned about virtue and purity.	BE -2+
01P11.A	Learn to use, clean and change the filter in any air or water purifier you may already have in your home.	HM - 1
01P12.B	Learn how to test 'precious' stones for purity and how purity affects their value.	IA - 1 SE - 1

next summer

01P13.B	Try your hand at ruby mining in one of the mines open for tourists in the Nantahala River valley of North Carolina (in the US) or any other place these may be found.	IA - 2
01P14.B	Learn to cut and polish the various gemstones you studied in this mini-unit.	CR - 3
01P15.B	Get a geological map of your state or locality and learn what minerals and/or gems are available there.	SE - 1 G - I
01P16.B	Learn from a jeweler how to measure, weigh, and appraise gems.	BE - I
01P17.B	Watch a jeweler set stones into rings or other jewelry and get him to instruct you in doing it.	CR - 2 +
01P18.B	Learn the proper way to clean and care for gold and silver jewelry and decorative items as well as the jewels that are often set in them.	HM - 1
01P19.B	After analyzing the mineral content of your typical family meals, institute any changes within your family's diet needed to achieve proper mineral consumption.	FN - 2
01P20.B	Secure a rock polisher and use it to produce beauty from common rocks, mineral ore and/or gemstones.	CR - 2
01P21.B	Use "Gem Hunters' Kit" to mine and identify real gems, displaying them in the tray provided.	SE - 3
01P22.B	Learn to polish and clean various types of finished jewelry. Compare to the processes used for rock polishing,	HM - 1
01P23.B	Make a batch of rock candy, using a recipe or the general directions for growing crystals using sugar.	FN - 2
01P24.C	From the U. S. Geological Survey or your country's equivalent, obtain and learn to use a seven-mile map for the study of geological features in your local area.	G - 1 SE - 1

PRACTICAL ARTS

01P25.C   Create an original game or play activity to be used to help a   TE - 4
           young child learn about Creation. It could center on what was
           created on each of the six days, on helping the child memorize
           related Scriptures, or on any other aspect of Biblical Creation.

01P26.C   Use your study on Creation week from the Science and Bible   TE - 3 +
           and Christian Character sections to teach a Sunday School or
           Bible club class for young children on that topic. Include the Bible
           lesson you wrote for the Composition section, the mural you
           created for the Decorative and Performing Arts section and/or
           other visual aids, games, and one or more craft projects for the
           children to complete.

01P27.C   Try your hand at spelunking to explore some of the geological   PE - 3 +
           formations created by the flood.

01P28.C   Try rock climbing or rappelling as another way to investigate the   PE - 3 +
           geology of your area.

01P29.C   To experience and learn about the process by which scientists   SE - 2
           collect and attempt to put together various parts of what appear
           to be dinosaur skeletons, use "Restoration Kits" to find and restore
           your own fossils.

01P30.C   Build one or more wooden dinosaur models from the kits sold   CR - 2
           for that purpose.

01P31.C   To duplicate the process used by scientists in their fossil restoration,   CR - 2
           take parts from several of the above dinosaur model kits,   SE - 2
           as if they were bones found together in a dig. Try to determine how
           they fit together to create some type of being. Bear in mind that
           paleontologists have created entire species of creatures from less
           than this.

01P32.C   Volunteer to help in a science or natural history museum to   SE - 2
           learn how fossils and similar exhibits are prepared for display   H- 2
           and maintained once they are there.

01P33.D   Using information from *The First Civilizations: History of*   CR - 2 +
           Everyday Things, reproduce and learn to use various household   H - 2
           tools and utensils used in Old Testament times.

01P34.D   Using one of the reference books in this unit, design and make   CC - 3
           costumes like those worn during the time of the Old Testament   each
           and wear them for your feast day celebrations.

01P35.D   If you have not previously done so, use this mini-unit to learn   G - 1
           to read ancient maps and correlate them to modern ones.

01P36.D   Use a good Jewish cookbook and learn to cook one or more   FN - 2
           kosher dishes not normally served in your home. Do all the   each
           work from scratch.

PRACTICAL ARTS

01P37.D	Prepare and serve a traditional dinner for Rosh Hashanah, Yom Kippur or another of the holy days celebrated by the Israelites of the Old Testament. (Purim and Passover are covered in other units and should be skipped here.) You will find help for this in any of the books on Biblical holidays suggested in the Reading and Literature section of this unit.	FN - 3 B - 1
01P38.D	Prepare appropriate centerpieces or other decorations to be used for one of the holidays of the Old Testament Jews.	CR - 2 +
01P39.D	Build a 'booth' typical of those used for the Feast of Tabernacles in Old Testament times and live in it with your family for a few days.	CR - 3 B - 1
01P40.D*	With your parents' permission, attend a Feast Day celebration at a local Messianic congregation or Jewish synagogue. Note the differences, if any, between the way they celebrate and the Biblical instructions for that holiday.	B- 2
01P41.D	Use this opportunity to learn to read and/ or speak Hebrew. You may use one of the courses listed here, search for an Internet web site, or attend a Hebrew course at a seminary, Bible college or Jewish synagogue.	1 credit for complete course or parental discretion
01P42.	If you don't already know how to create and use a computer database, you may wish to learn in this mini-unit so you can use the skill in later units of this study.	CO - 5
01P43.	Create and maintain a database to assist you as appropriate in this mini-unit.	CO - 2
01P44.	Type all written work using a computer.	CO -leach paper
01P45.	If needed for computer work, take a class, follow a computerized, written or video tutorial, or complete a correspondence course in keyboarding, typing, and/or word processing.	BE-V2 credit in Keyboard-ing
01P46.	Create a computer web site to display what you have learned and done in this mini-unit.	CO - 2
01P47.	Frame and/or mat one or more of the pictures or posters you drew or otherwise created in Decorative and Performing Arts for this mini-unit.	CR - 2
01P48.	Make your own costumes for any performances you chose to do in the Decorative and Performing Arts section of this mini-unit	CC - 5 each
01P49.	Make your own puppets for the puppet show in this mini-unit.	CR - 3 +

DECORATIVE & PERFORMING ARTS

DECORATIVE & PERFORMING ARTS

01A01.A	Prepare a poster or bulletin using drawing, painting, collage, or other desired medium to display the variety of activities performed by a virtuous full time homemaker.	VA- 1
01A02.A	Use calligraphy in your choice of style to design a poster of Proverbs 31:10-31.	VA - 2 +
01A03.A	Use the art medium of your choice to illustrate the poster you made in the above activity. You can include not only your original painting or drawing, but also tracing, or collage.	VA - 1
01A04.A	Prepare and perform for an audience a dramatized song, creative dance routine, pantomime, musical dramatization, or other presentation based on Proverbs 31:10-31.	DR - 5
01A05.A	Set Proverbs 31: 10-31 to music, using an existing tune, learning to play it as you go.	MC - 3
01A06.A	Compose an original tune for singing the verses of Proverbs 31: 10-31.	MC - 5
01A07.A	Learn to play your composition for Proverbs 31:10-31 on your instrument.	VM - 2
01A08.A	Listen to a large number of songs (25-30) of different types about the values taught in this mini-unit. If possible and acceptable to your family, include both Christian and secular, modern and ancient, as well as a good international mix. Compare each of the songs to the Biblical standard of virtue.	MA - 2 B - 1
01A09.B	Illustrate each chapter, report or section of the booklet on gems and minerals you created in the Composition section.	VA -
01A10.B	Create a decorative display using gems and/or rocks, polished or unpolished, as a focal point.	VA - 1
01A11.B	Create a rock garden in a dish and decorate as you desire.	VA - 1
01A12.B	Paint a face, animal or other decoration on a smooth, flat rock and shellac it to use or give as a paperweight.	VA - 2
01A13.B	Create and perform a skit or monologue about a prospector who finds a really valuable claim.	DR — 10
01A14.B	Draw. paint, or finger paint a poster design based on a collection of geometric shapes like those found in crystalline structures.	VA - 1
01A15.C	Prepare a chalk talk or other illustrated lesson on Creation to be taught to young children.	TE - 2 VA - 1
01A16.C	Set to music one or more poems about Creation, using original or existing tunes.	MC - 5
01A17.C	Using the medium of your choice, create a mural showing the six days of Creation and what God wrought on each.	VA - 2 +

DECORATIVE & PERFORMING ARTS

01A18.C	Practice and learn to sing well enough to perform for an audience "This is My Father's World", "How Great Thou Art," or another song exalting God specifically as Creator.	VM - 3 each
01A19.C	Learn to play one or more of the above songs on the musical instrument of your choice and perform before an audience.	IM - 3 each
01A20.C	Compose an original tune to set the poem you wrote in the Composition section of this mini-unit to music.	MC - 5
01A21.D	Make a room box or diorama of a typical home in one of the studied nations during Bible times.	VA -
01A22.D	Paint a high quality picture (suitable for framing) of any one of the Seven Wonders of the Ancient World.	VA - 5
01A23.D	Design and create a historically correct paper doll wardrobe like one that Queen Esther might have worn.	VA - 5 H 1
01A24.D	Create a miniature replica of the tabernacle as described in the Old Testament, including all furnishings.	VA - 3
01A25.D	Use sugar cubes, Legos. or a some other type of building media to create a replica of one of the Seven Wonders of the World studied in this mini-unit.	VA - 3 +
01A26.D	Draw, paint, or otherwise create a mural depicting a day in the life of a godly homemaker in one of the time periods studied.	VA - 2+
01A27.D	Visit an art gallery and view paintings of family life from different time periods in the parts of the world known in the Old Testament times. Look for a variety of styles and media.	AA - 2
01A28.	Use calligraphy to create a poster of one of the Scripture verses or poems you memorized in this mini-unit.	VA - 2
01A29.	Illustrate your calligraphy of verses or poems.	VA - 1
01A30.	Create and produce a puppet show about one of the people or events studied in this unit.	DR 10
01A31.	Perform a skit or monologue based on one of the stories, diaries, or memoirs you wrote in the Composition section of this mini-unit.	DR - 10 +
01A32.	Use your artistic talents to illustrate one of the short stories you wrote in the Composition section of this mini-unit.	VA - 3
01A33.	Draw pictures of each field trip in this unit.	VA - 1 each
01A34.	Produce, direct, and/or perform in the cast of a play you wrote for this unit or one adapted from a story you wrote for this unit.	DR - 50

UNIT 2

The heart of her husband safely trusts in her;
he will have no lack of gain.
She does him good and not evil
all the days of her life.
Proverbs 31:11-12

Overview

This intent of this Scripture passage is to continue pointing out the importance of choosing a wife carefully. The King's mother wants him to see how important being able to trust his wife is. For that reason, this unit will strive to teach and inspire you, the student, to develop the traits that make one worthy of trust. In this context, you will study the concepts of dependability, loyalty, honesty, and submission to authority as taught in Scripture. You will learn about making wise choices, exercising good stewardship, and being a good manager of resources, all things that can help your husband "gain" from your efforts.

Within this unit, you will examine the God-ordained place of man and woman within the marriage and their respective responsibilities. You will look at attitudes they are to have toward each other and with others outside their union. You will see how a commitment to husband and marriage branches out to include; keeping hurts and problems within the family, being a good example in public, boosting your husband's reputation within the community, all ways a woman can to do her husband "good and not evil" all the days of her life.

You will examine all aspects of marriage, including physical intimacy and procreation. You and your parents are encouraged to discuss these topics and determine how they wish you to proceed with this study in a way which suits the values and beliefs of your family. We believe this must, of necessity, include the study of male and female anatomy and the physiology of sexual intercourse. We attempt to recommend resources which treat these topics from a Christian perspective whenever possible and suggest that you consult your parents before making any substitutions in this area.

This unit and the passage on which it is based puts a handle on the God- ordained system of government and order within the family and the family's correct role within the church and community. We will investigate the many realms in which civil governments tend to operate and seek to determine which of these areas should be the jurisdiction of the family and/or the church as outlined in Scripture. You will compare family life-styles in different cultures and at different times in history, and look at famous women in history who did their husbands "good and not evil."

You will examine the Christian family as part of the Lord's Church, and the proper role of women in the organized church congregation. Not to be neglected is the rightful extent to which a godly woman can or should be involved in the community beyond her home, and how she can help her husband by doing so. Some of these concepts and activities will also be covered in other units. Use each activity only one place or the other, not both.

Mini-Units

Mini-Units contained in this unit are:

A. God's Plan for Romance

B. Human Sexuality

C. The Role of a Trustworthy Wife

D. Managing Personal and Family Finances

Each thematic mini-unit is described and designated with a letter of the alphabet in the following paragraphs. Individual activities designed for use in one particular mini-unit will be marked with those letters. (For further help with this, please refer to the explanation of mini-units in the Guidelines section of this unit study guide.)

A. God's Plan for Romance

In order for her husband's heart to trust in his wife, the marriage must be built on mutual trust in each other and God. Building this kind of a marriage starts long before a couple says their vows. For that reason, we begin this unit at the same point. This mini-unit is devoted to helping you discover God's plan for finding you a mate, and to avoid things that might short-circuit that. In here, you will study dating, courtship and other approaches to romance, examining each in light of Scripture to find the route to God's blessing.

You will read books and listen to tapes on courtship and dating, but this unit is not entirely about that. There will also be ample opportunity to discuss and learn ways to spend your young adult single years in service to the Lord, waiting on Him for guidance into romance. This will encourage you to avoid the pitfalls often caused by anxiety over whether or when one will marry.

You will look at examples of how Biblical couples came to marry one another, looking for a pattern to follow in your own life. The marriage and "mating" customs of other cultures will also be explored for a broader understanding of this topic, always comparing each to our standard, the Scriptures. You will also be able to read writing by and about couples who have followed this Biblical pattern and wish to share their experiences.

B. Human Sexuality

This mini-unit could be described as "sex education", and must be saved until your parents feel you are ready for it. As this is an area of life that is very important for every young person who would be godly, we have tried to be frank and thorough without being unnecessarily graphic. The activities in this mini-unit do approach everything from a distinctly Christian perspective. We will examine all areas of sexuality and sexual behavior in light of God's Word and His design for purity in marriage. In addition to extensive Scripture study on this and related topics, you will be given opportunity to read godly counsel from a number of famous and not-so-famous Christian teachers and scholars, most of whom are sharing from their own experience as well as God's Word.

In this mini-unit you will also study the anatomical and physiological aspects of sexual intercourse and human reproduction. Though the processes of childbirth and the development of children is specifically covered in a later unit, there will be some overlap here as you study this process from conception to labor. This will not be handled in depth here, but is more thoroughly covered in unit 18. Some of the activities here are also used in other units and may in studied in whichever place you prefer. However, no one activity should be counted for credit points more than once.

In addition to learning about both male and female reproductive systems and primary and the secondary sex characteristics of each, you will come to understand the processes of sexual intimacy between husband and wife and the proper venue for it. In this mini-unit, you also will cover various forms of sexual misconduct and perversions, not to glorify such things, but to help you see God's attitude toward them and why they must be avoided at all costs. These will include pornography, homosexuality, fornication and adultery, all condemned by the Scriptures and not to be practiced by God's people. As with all parts of this particular mini-unit, you should pursue this only in close contact with your parents when they believe you are ready for it. We don't wish to soil your conscience by familiarity but to heighten it by knowledge of the evil that lurks around us all.

With societal attitudes in most of the world what they are, we feel it is important that this unit deal with consequences of irresponsible actions in the area of sexuality. The most serious of these is abortion, often seen as the ideal solution to an unwanted pregnancy. This we will deal with only slightly here, since it is covered more thoroughly later, as is pregnancy itself. We will also look at AIDS and other sexually transmitted diseases, learning treatment for those already stricken, as well as prevention techniques. We do not want to neglect the moral, social, or emotional consequences of illicit sexual behavior as well.

C. The Role of a Trustworthy Wife

In this mini-unit, you will study marriage and the roles and duties of each of the marriage partners. We will touch on the sanctity of marriage, the Bible's view of divorce, but these are all covered more thoroughly in Unit 19. Here we are content to help you see the importance of fidelity in marriage, in spite of the world's view to the contrary. You will learn how a wife who can be trusted must, first be faithful to her marriage vows and chaste in all her relationships. This mini-unit will include a study of the marriage vows themselves and the permanence of marriage in God's eyes.

In addition to remaining married and being faithful to her marriage partner, the godly wife has many other responsibilities to her husband. You will learn what these are and how to fulfill them as you study this mini-unit. You will discover, for example, the many ways in which a woman can be a "help" to her husband, encouraging him and helping him grow in the Lord through being willing to let God lead her through her husband.

We will, of course learn all about submission and the Bible's command to women concerning it. You may be surprised to discover that God's plan for marriage and submission to the husband in that setting is not the evil subservience many people of this day and age believe. You will see how God put that relationship in place for the protection of both man and woman from their natural weaknesses. You will also see how God honors women who follow Him without violating the trust or commands of the most ungodly of husbands.

After studying the wife's role in the family and her proper relationship to and attitude toward her husband, you will examine various traits that make any person trustworthy and how to develop them in your own life. In addition to the obvious areas of honesty and keeping one's word, you will also look at diligence, time management, accepting responsibility, being able to work without supervision, productivity, and making good use of resources. All of these are ways in which a husband needs to count on his wife. You will learn how to cultivate them to grow more and better in this area of your life.

In addition to investigating the above traits and duties on a personal level, you will look at their effect on society. What are some areas in which whether or not others can be trusted affects our day to day lives? How would our society be different if everyone was trustworthy? How would that alter our laws and government? These and other questions will be answered during your studies of this mini-unit.

D. Money Management

This mini-unit is about money and the proper way to use it. In it, you will learn about spending wisely, saving for the future, and tithing to the Lord. You will explore how to man-age your money by making budgets and balancing checkbooks. By the end of this mini-unit, we hope you will be able to handle your own finances, including completing your own income tax returns and caring for your own investments. These will also be covered here.

Budgeting, investing, and balancing checkbooks are only a part of how a trustworthy wife can guard and increase the spendable income of her husband. Careful shopping, con-sumer awareness, and other methods by which a stay-at-home wife may increase the family's income and/or decrease expenses are also covered in this mini-unit. Here you will learn to become a wise and frugal shopper, and to "make do" with what you have whenever possible. We will study or review decimals, per cents, and interest rates and how to read contracts. Practical arts include financial management skills, sewing, home management, and clothing care, all of which can help your husband in a financial manner.

This mini-unit will also teach you about the banking and financial industry in your country and the world. You will see how banks manage your money and how the Federal Reserve (or similar agency in countries other than the U.S.) is set up to help manage banks. You will learn about various types of accounts and what each does for you as well as other services offered by banks and the fees charged for them. This will include learning about installment loans, credit cards and mortgages, although these are also covered in a later unit. Do not take points for the exact same activity more than once.

BIBLE & CHRISTIAN CHARACTER

02B01.A	Use concordance to find, look up and study all Scripture references to the words "date" or "dating", or any synonym of either word and to the words "court", "courting", or "courtship". Discuss this activity, its results, and the conclusions drawn from them with one or both of your parents.	B-	2
02B02.A	Look up all Bible references to marriage that use the phrase "give in marriage" or some variation of it. Discuss with a parent what you think that means.	B-	2
02B03.A	Look up the love story of Isaac and Rebekah in Genesis 24 to see and example of God's plan for romance and marriage, paying special attention to verses 57, 58, and 67. How does this alter your opinion of the parent-arranged marriages of Bible times?	B-	1

02B04.A	Look up in your concordance and study "betrothed", "betrothal", and "espoused" (a synonym). Read all references found to determine what a Biblical "betrothal" actually should be. (Hint: It is not the same thing we call engagement.)	B - 2
02B05.A	Listen to Jonathan Lindvall's audio #317, "The Great Romance: The Ultimate Purpose" which puts betrothal in the context of the "marriage of the lamb" of whom we, the redeemed Church, are the betrothed bride.	B - 2
02B06.A	Read and complete the study guide for *Why True Love Waits*.	B - 5
02B07.A	Complete the entire lesson series in the *True Love Project* including workbook.	B -10, HA - 2
02B08.A	After reading one or more of the Scripture passages here and the books suggested in Reading and Literature, discuss them with your parents to help establish (or have them explain previously-established) family policy on dating or courtship.	B- 1
02B09 .A	Attend one of Joshua Harris' seminars on romance or listen to his audios on that subject.	B- 3
02B10.A	Read the *Song of Solomon*, remembering that this couple was in an arranged marriage. How does that knowledge alter your preconceived notion of arranged marriages?	B- 3
02B11.B	Read *Quest for Love: True stories of Passion and Purity* by Elisabeth Elliot and discuss it in light of the Scriptures in this unit.	R - 2
02B12.B	Read Deuteronomy 22:22-30 and discuss it with your parents.	B- 1
02B13.B	Look up and study all Biblical passages using the word 'fornication' or any synonym of it.	B- 2
02B14.B	Use the concordance to find and study all Biblical references to sexual relations, paying attention to the kinds that are approved and the kinds that are not. (Bear in mind that the KJV uses the word 'know' or 'knew' and the phrase 'uncover the nakedness' to denote this.)	B- 3
02B15.B	Study Leviticus 18 and list all sinful sexual relationships named there. If you read from the KJV or NKJV, consult a commentary to find the meaning of the term "uncover the nakedness of."	B- 1 B- 2
02B16.B	Read Numbers 5:12-31 and discuss it with your parents. In what ways does your own society attempt to prove or disprove claims of adultery?	B- 1

02B17.B	Read Deuteronomy 22: 4 and discuss it with a parent, using a commentary to help you understand its meaning.	B - 3
02B18.B	Look up, read, and study all other Scriptural references to adultery.	B - 2
02B19.B	Listen to and take notes on the audio "Moral Purity Before a Holy God" from Pilgrim Tape Ministry.	B - 1
02B20.B	Read Romans 1, and discuss with a parent what it teaches about sexual immorality.	B - 2
02B21.B	Read the story of the adulterous woman in John 8:3-11. In light of the other Scriptures in this mini-unit, do you believe Jesus was excusing what she did, changing the God-given death sentence for adultery, or trying to make some other point in this encounter? Discuss and be prepared to write about all these options.	B - 1
02B22.B	Study the references to adultery in Jesus' Sermon on the Mount (Matthew 5:27-32) and discuss this with a parent.	B - 1
02B23.C	Read Ephesians 5:22-24 and discuss with an adult its teachings about the role of a wife in marriage.	B - 1
02B24.C	Read God's instructions to wives in I Peter 3 and discuss it with a parent.	B - 5
02B25.C	Use a concordance to find all other Scriptures that relate to the duties of wives or the marital relationship. Study these carefully.	B - 3
02B26.C	Read Genesis, chapters 1-3 to understand the effects of the Fall upon the family.	B - 1
02B27.C	Study all Biblical references to Aquila and Priscilla and try to describe their relationship.	B - 1
02B28.C	Read Acts 5: 1 - 11 as an example of when a wife should not obey her husband. Discuss this with your mother or another godly wife.	B - 1
02B29.C	Complete *The Challenges of Christian Womanhood* interactive Bible study series. (This may be hard to find but is worth the search.)	B- 8
02B30.C	Complete the Bible study on "Faithfulness" for the Navigators Fruit of the Spirit series. Discuss it with your parents.	B — 10
02B31.C	Look at all passages in Proverbs that use the word trust and determine what is the object of the trust in each passage. How does this one differ from all the others. What do you believe is the significance of this?	B - 3

BIBLE & CHRISTIAN CHARACTER

02B32.C	Study Matthew 5: 33 - 37 and explain how it relates to the topic of this mini-unit.	B -	1
02B33.C	In a concordance, look up the words trustworthy', 'faithful', and all synonyms of either. Count and list the number of verses that refer to this character trait. Save list for later use.	B -	2
02B34.C	Study the references from the above activity to find different ways in which one may prove to be trustworthy. Build a mind map showing your thoughts on this.	B -	3
02B35.C	Read Psalm 15 and explain how it relates to this topic, paying special attention to verse 4.	B -	1
02B36.C	Study the Biblical accounts of Jezebel and Delilah, two women who were curses, not blessings, to their husbands. Determine where each went wrong and why. Contrast their motivations and attitudes toward their husbands to see that even women who truly care about their men can end up doing them evil.	B -	3
02B37.D	Study Jesus' instructions to the rich, young ruler in Matthew 19:16-22. Discuss why you think Jesus gave him those particular directions. Do you think He would say the same thing to all of those who are wealthy in the world's eyes?	B-	2
02B38.D	Study Christ's teachings about wealth and financial gain in other verses of Matthew 19. What would this say to you as a wife and helper to your husband?	B-	2
02B39 D	Study Christ's teachings on wealth and prosperity in Matthew 6: 19 - 34.	B -	2
02B40.D	Study Matthew 25:14-29, and explain how it applies to your own life in the area of personal finances. Discuss with your parents how you and your family can be like the good servant in your own lives.	B -	1
02B41.D	Study all other Scriptural references to tithing and determine what you believe to be the Bible's position on this and how you as a wife could help your husband implement it while not taking over or usurping his authority in the family.	B-	3
02B42.D	Study and memorize Malachi 3:10-13 and discuss with a parent how it would affect you as wife and mother in the future.	B -	1
02B43.D	Study all Biblical commands about stewardship and investigate the full meaning of the word. Mind map about the various ways stewardship could be improved within your own family.	B-	3
02B44.D	Do a word study on 'contentment' as used in Scripture and discuss with a parent what part this would play in a wife's doing her husband good and not evil.	B-	2

02B45.D	Read and memorize Luke 12:22-31 and discuss its relationship to the topic of this mini-unit.	B - 2
02B46.	Memorize one or more of the passages studied in the mini-unit.	B - 1 per 3 verses
02B47.	Read through the book of Proverbs each month, reading the chapter to coincide with each date.	B - 3 per week
02B48.	Continue reading through the Bible at a rate of 1-5 chapters per day. If you use *The Daily Bible* or some other version designed specifically for that purpose, their daily readings will take you through the entire Bible in one year. You may follow a pattern of your own at a different rate if you like. Using a chronologically arranged Bible offers the added benefit of putting your reading in perspective as to time frame.	B - 1 credit when completed; no partial credit
02B49.	Begin (or continue) a prayer journal, listing each day (or as the Lord brings to mind) prayer requests, needs in your spiritual life and things God is teaching you. Continue this throughout all units.	B - 3 per week

CULTURAL STUDIES

02C01.A	Research your own family's history to discover how various ancestors met and came to love each other. Make notes on this for use in further studies later.	H- 5+
02C02.A	Study the history of betrothal, beginning with the Biblical Jews, and see how it has spread to other areas, died out in some areas, and been changed over the years.	H - 3 B- 2
02C03.A	Study the history of courtship, dating, and other forms of romance in your country. Read articles from women's periodicals in different decades to see how this has changed over the last three generations.	H - 5
02C04.A	Study marriage and courtship in other countries to present in a report or booklet as directed in the Composition section.	H - 5 CS - 10
02C05.A	From the above studies, take a closer look at countries where most marriages are arranged. Compare the rates of divorce, spousal abuse, runaway spouses and suicide among upper and middle classes of those countries. Compare totals and percentages of each to those in the U. S. Do you believe any of the differences can be traced to marriage customs?	CS - 10
02C06.A	Interview a couple who have been in an arranged marriage for five or more years (look for people from the Middle East or Eastern Europe where such marriages are common). Ask how and when they met, what input they had in choosing each other, who arranged the marriage, how they felt about it at the time, how they feel now, whether they will arrange marriages for their children.	CS - 3

CULTURAL STUDIES

02C07.A	Study the traditional Hebrew betrothal ceremony and how it has been altered over the years within their own religion and culture.	H - 2
02C08.A	From an Orthodox Jewish website, synagogue or some other source, study the actual wording of the Covenant of Betrothal. How does this differ from marriage vows? From engagement in your culture?	CS — 2
02C09.A	Study the vows used in the marriage ceremony as conducted in your church, and look for the Scriptural significance of each. Compare them to the betrothal covenant in the above exercise.	CS - 1 B - 1
02C10.A	Interview a Justice of the Peace, a Roman Catholic priest, a Jewish rabbi, and one or more evangelical pastors asking what they require before marrying a couple and why.	CS - 5 B - 2
02C11.B*	Study the laws of your state regarding common law marriage and unmarried cohabitation to see what rights and/or obligations each partner has under the law. Do you believe such an arrangement is considered a marriage in God's eyes, and if so under what conditions? Support your answer from Scripture.	CL - 5
02C12.B*	Study the societal changes in attitude toward sex and sexuality that have taken place in your country during the lifetime of your own parents. Research and discuss the effects of these changes on other aspects of society.	CS - 3
02C 1 3.B	Study laws regarding pornography in your nation, state/province, or locality.	CL - 3
02C14.B*	Study local and state rape laws and how they are enforced.	CL - 3
02C15.B*	Investigate the legal concept of "date rape" and laws involving it. Compare this to the rules of sexual conduct set out for Israel in Deuteronomy 22:22-29, to see the Biblical way of dealing with this issue.	CL - 3 B- 1
02C16.B*	Study the economic and societal impact of AIDS and other sexually-transmitted diseases. Look at medical costs; changes in the way first aid, CPR, and other medical treatments are administered, attitudes toward sexual promiscuity, as well as other things that may come to mind.	CS - 3 CE - 3 HE - 2
02C17.B	Study the most recent statistics on illegitimate births in your country and the economic impact they make on your national, state and/or local government.	CE - 5
02C18.B*	Study the forms of government and private social services and funds given to unwed mothers. Do you believe this encourages premarital sexual intimacy? Discuss your thoughts with a parent.	CS - 3

CULTURAL STUDIES

02C19.B	Study the section on Self-Government in *God and Government*. Discuss with a parent how a widespread, thorough understanding of this topic would impact the societal problems of sexual promiscuity and its consequences	CS - 2 CG - 2 B - 1
02C20.C	Look at the lives, roles, and structure of typical families in different countries and time periods. Compare on some type of poster or chart.	CS - 3 H - 2
02C21.C	Listen to and take notes on all the audios in the series, *The Shaping of the Christian Family,* written by Elisabeth Elliott as a true account of her own childhood family.	B- 6
02C22.C	Study the section on Family Government in *God and Government*. Compare each family studied in this mini-unit to the standards set here and in Scripture.	CG - 3
02C23.C	Spend a minimum of 2 hours on Ancestry.com tracking your family tree to learn about your own family history. It is free to start, but there will be a fee later. Do NOT sign up for anything without your parents' permission.	H - 2 each time
02C24.C	Study the lives of Narcissa Whitman, Elisabeth Elliot, Edith Schaeffer, Ruth Graham, and other Christian wives who were Biblical 'help meets' to their husbands in Christian ministry.	H - I each
02C25.C	Briefly study the lives of all the First Ladies of your nation, noting especially the ways each "did her husband good". Be prepared to explain which ones you believe did or did not fill the Biblical role of a wife.	H- 10
02C26.C	Study the women's liberation movement of the 1960's and 70's and determine how it altered the woman's role in the family. Did this in any way change God's plan for women?	H - 1 CS - 2
02C27.C	Study the American temperance movement of the 1800's and decide whether the women leading it were examples of this passage.	H - 2
02C28.C	Study the women's suffrage movement in the U. S. (or your own country, if applicable) and determine whether the women leading it were examples of women in whom their husbands could trust.	H - 2
02C29.C	Study and discuss the rising popularity of prenuptial agreements. Examine several samples of these or the actual ones done by real couples What does this say to you about trust between marriage partners?	CS - 2
02C30.D	Analyze the history of the security industry and determine to what extent it is based on lack of trust within society.	CS - 1 H - 1
02C31.D	Study tort law in your state and determine how it reflects man's inability to trust one another.	CL 2

CULTURAL STUDIES

02C32.D	Briefly examine contract law in your state, looking for provisions that specifically reflect people's lack of trust of each other.	CL - 2
02C33.D	Talk with a bank employee to learn how banks earn money from the deposits of their customers and the difference in the way they handle checking and savings accounts. Discuss why some accounts give interest and some do not and why interest amounts vary.	CE - 2
02C34.D	Learn about the various kinds of bank accounts offered by your own bank and other financial institutions and the differences between them.	CE - 2
02C35.D	Study the Federal Reserve Bank and the United States banking system.	CE - 3
02C36.D	Discuss with a real estate agent or loan officer to learn the procedure to follow in applying for a mortgage or similar loan and all the factors that have to be considered by the financial institution in deciding whether to grant it.	CE - 3
02C37.D	Tour all departments of a large commercial bank and/ or credit union and learn what each department does and how it works.	CE - 2
02C38.D	Collect consumer information on loans and credit from your State's Office of Consumer Affairs or any financial institution. Study this material as well as statements, applications and other literature from credit card providers to learn about credit cards and the credit industry.	CE - 3
02C39.	Use encyclopedias or other references to study all countries mentioned in this unit.	G - 2 each
02C40.	Locate on a map or globe all countries studied or mentioned in this unit.	G - 1
02C41.	Locate on a map and study the geography of all cities or municipalities and states or provinces studied in this unit.	G - 2
02C42.	Use books listed elsewhere in this unit, Usborne's *World History Dates, The Kingfisher History Encyclopedia,* or any other reference books to make timeline entries for all people, movements, and/or events you studied in this unit.	VA - 1 ea. H - 1 ea.
02C43.	Make timeline entries for major events in the lives of each of the authors whose works were read in this unit.	VA - 1 ea. H - 1 ea.
02C44.	Make timeline entries for other famous people who lived in the time period being studied.	VA - 1 ea. H - 1 ea.
02C45.	Make timeline entries for all inventions and/or discoveries studied in this unit and major events in the lives of their inventors.	VA - 1 ea. H - 1 ea.

CULTURAL STUDIES

02C46.	Make timeline cards for all major events and/or people mentioned in books read or studied in this unit but not included elsewhere.	VA - 1 ea. H - 1 each
02C47.	Study the homeland of each author, inventor, or artist whose works were used or studied in this unit.	G - 1 each

READING AND LITERATURE

02R01.A	Read *I Kissed Dating Goodbye*, and/or the DVD of the same name, which expands on the book. Then read *Boy Meets Girl: Say Hello to Courtship*, which is a follow-up to the previous book.	R – 5, B - 2
02R02.A	Read *Her Hand in Marriage* for the same topic from another perspective.	B - 5
02R03.A	Read *Dating with Integrity* for a differing viewpoint on this issue.	CS - 5
02R04.A	Read the Christian novel *The Courtship of Sarah McLean* and/or its counterpart, *Jeff McLean: His Courtship*.	L - 5
02R05.A	Read the book *A Good Man is Hard to Find – Unless God is the Head of your Search Committee*, then read *Before You Meet Prince Charming*. Compare the two books in writing or discuss with your mother or other Christian adult.	R- 5 B – 2
02R06.A	Read *Waiting for Her Isaac*, a novel about Biblical courtship.	L - 5
02R07.A	Read *The Art of Choosing Your Love*.	HF - 5
02R08.A	Read the true account of the courtship, betrothal, and marriage of Jeff and Danielle Myers in their book, *Of Knights and Fair Maidens*.	HP - 5
02R09.A	Read novels by Grace Livingston Hill, Janette Oke or others featuring courtship or another form of parental involvement in youthful romance. Discuss with your parents the romances in these novels and their relation to the reality of your life.	- 5 each
02R10.A	Read Shakespeare's *Romeo and Juliet* and discuss with your parents the disaster brought about when these young people tried to usurp the God-given authority of their parents.	L- 4
02R11.B	Research with your mother medical information about biological changes you will encounter as you grow into a woman. Discuss this freely with your mother, keeping it in a Biblical perspective.	HE - 5
02R12.B	Another book of the same type but more unisex in its approach is *Preparing for Adolescence*. Read this aloud and discuss it with a parent.	HE - 4
02R13.B	Read *Passion and Purity* by Elisabeth Elliott and discuss it with your parents.	B - 5

READING AND LITERATURE

02R14.B	Read Josh McDowell's *Why Wait?* series.	B - 5 each
02R15.B	Read *What Every Christian Should Know about AIDS* or another well-researched book on this topic from a Christian perspective.	HE - 5
02R16.B*	Use a library Guide to Periodical Literature to find and read several magazine articles about sexual morality at different times during the last two decades. Note changes of attitude among the general population about activities and things God calls sin.	CS- 3+
02R 17.B	Read articles in Christian magazines about sexual morality. Compare and contrast these to the ones in the previous activity.	CS - 2
02R18.B	Read *Letters to Karen* by Charlie Shedd.	B - 5
02R19.B	Read and discuss with your mother *Facing the Facts: Truth about Sex and You.*	HE - 5
02R20.C	Study *The Christian Family*, by Larry Christenson, looking up all relevant Scripture passages and taking notes on the role of the Christian wife it describes.	HF - 5
02R21.C	Read *Christian Living in the Home*.	HF- 5
02R22.C	Read and outline *Creative Counterpart*.	HF- 7
02R23.C	Read *Straight Talk to Men and Their Wives*.	HF - 5
02R24.C	Read biographies of any American First Ladies and pay special attention to the relationship each had with her husband and her level of involvement in his job or his political career.	H - 5 each
02R25.C	Read a biography of Carrie Nation and/or any other women instrumental in the U. S. Temperance Movement. Discuss traits and actions that show whether or not each was a trustworthy wife. Did she exhibit a Biblical attitude toward the role of a wife?	H - 5 each
02R26.C	Read a biography of Susan B. Anthony, leader of the suffragettes. Discuss with your mother whether or not she seems to have been a woman in whom her husband could trust whole-heartedly. Did she show a Biblical attitude toward the role of wife?	H - 5
02R27.C	Read Lois Henderson's fictional biography of Abigail, a Biblical wife who could be trusted to do 'good and not evil' for her husband, even in spite of his own foolishness and without his knowledge.	B 4
02R28.C	Read Lois Henderson's fictionalized biography of Aquila and Priscilla.	B - 4

READING AND LITERATURE

02R29.C	Read 3 - 5 wholesome novels about family life, analyzing the family's relationships from a Biblical perspective. Include books that are specifically Christian perspective and others approved by your parents.	L - 5 each
02R30.C	Read biographies of any other women studied in this mini-unit. Compare each to the ideal of this passage.	H - 5 each
02R31.C	Read *Christy* by Catherine Marshall, paying close attention to the traits that made her trustworthy.	L- 5
02R32.C	Study Shakespeare's *Macbeth* paying special attention to how Lady Macbeth's "help" for her husband really did him evil.	L - 4
02R33.C	Study *The Taming of the Shrew.* Compare the couple's personalities and their relationship at the beginning and the end, contrasting both to the Biblical ideal.	L- 4
02R34.D	Read *More than Enough* by Dave Ramsey.	R - 3
02R35.D	Read any of the *Tightwad Gazette* books.	CE - 4 ea.
02R36.D	Read *How to Live on Practically Nothing and Have Plenty.*	CE - 5
02R37.D	Read *Big Ideas, Small Budget.*	CE - 5
02R38.D	Read *Miserly Moms.*	CE - 5
02R39.D	Read other books on frugal living.	HM - 5
02R40.D	Read *Whatever Happened to Penny Candy?*	CE - 4
02R41.D	Read any book by Larry Burkett on personal money management.	CE - 5 ea.
02R42.D	Read any of Ron Blue's books on finances.	CE - 5 ea.
02R43.	Read one or more historical novels set in one of the time periods studied in this unit.	H - 5 each
02R44.	Read biographies of people studied or mentioned in this unit.	H - 5 each
02R45.	Read one book per week over and above those you are doing as assignments in this study. Choose from those in our resource list, or use any book your parents approve.	L- 5 each
02R46.	Read any other appropriate books on the subject of the unit you are studying.	L- 5 each

COMPOSITION

02W01.A Define 'dating', courtship', engagement' and 'betrothal' in your EC - 2
      notebook and write an essay to contrast and compare them.

02W02.A Write an extensive term paper (15-20 pages) entitled "God's Plan EC - 35
      for Romance and Marriage". Support all statements from Scripture
      and use 3-5 other references as well. Include footnotes and
      thorough bibliography.

02W03.A Prepare arguments for either side (or both) of a debate on "Parents EC - 10
      Should Help Choose Their Daughter's Life Mate."

02W04.A In an essay entitled "To Date or Not to Date" share what you EC - 3
      believe to be the wise, and Biblical, answer to this dilemma of
      young people in every generation.

02W05.A Write a short story, set in any time period you wish, in which EC- 15
      courtship and/or betrothal plays a prominent role.

02W06.A Write a letter to a younger girl, explaining the proper role for EC - 2
      the young lady in the Biblical process of finding a husband. (Hint:
      Girls do not court)

02W07.A Using resources in this unit and what you learned from them, EC - 3
      write an essay entitled, "Betrothal and Engagement — Are They the
      Same?" Support all statements and conclusions from Scripture.

02W08.A Write a diary or journal as Rebekah might have kept before her EC - 3+
      marriage to Isaac. Begin when Abraham's servant showed up in
      her town, and end after she and Isaac were married.

02W09.A Rewrite *Romeo and Juliet* as you believe it would have happened EC - 30
      if Juliet had put herself under her father's leadership in the area of
      romance. Be sure to include a happy ending.

02W10.A Write a letter to your parents to share your feelings about 'courtship' EC - 3
      and 'betrothal'. If you have questions, ask them in the letter. If
      you have misgivings, express them. If you strongly want your
      parents to change their position on this issue, tell them your
      opinion and reasons. Support all statements with Scripture,
      statistics, and/or other data. Be prepared to discuss your letter with
      your parents after they receive it. Whatever their reaction, do your
      best to remain respectful and submissive.

02W11.A Write a Biblical betrothal covenant as you might use for your EC - 1
      own ceremony when the time comes. Be sure to include the
      elements of commitment to one another and the Lord before
      witnesses.

COMPOSITION

02W12.B   Write a journal (10-12 entries) that may have been kept by Eve,   EC - 4
starting at her Creation and including her relationship with Adam,
their sin and its punishment, the conception and birth of her first
child and other things as you wish. Write not only events but also
feelings as she would have experienced them with no prior
knowledge of any of it.

02W13.B   Define 'adultery', fornication', 'harlotry', and 'intercourse' into   EG - 1
your vocabulary notebook. Use a thesaurus to look up all
synonyms for each word, and add those to the notebook too.

02W14.B   Paraphrase in modern English the Song of Solomon or any   EC - 1 per
chapters thereof.   chapter

02W15.B*   Write the arguments on either side of a debate on "Man-made   EC - 10
Birth Control is a Violation of God's Will." Support all statements
from Scripture.

02W16.B   Describe in writing women's secondary sex characteristics that   EC - 1
come with puberty.

02W17.B   Write an essay or poem about what being a woman means to   EC - 2
you.

02W18.B*   Write an analysis of societal trends in attitude toward sexual   EC - 3
immorality as seen in the magazine articles you read.

02W19.B*   Write an analysis of all taws of your state/province or nation   EC - 2
that concern sodomy and/or other sexual perversions
condemned in Romans 1 and other Scripture passages.

02W20.B   Write a report on the female reproductive system and each of   EC - 1
the organs in it. Be factual, but not overly graphic. Put this   each
into a notebook labeled "The Human Body" and be prepared
to add additional material to it in other units.

02W21.B   Write a report on the male reproductive system and its organs   EC - 1
and add it to the notebook on "The Human Body". Stay factual   each
but not graphic.

02W22. C   Write an extensive research paper on the Biblical role of a wife   EC - 35
and her responsibilities toward her husband. Include note cards,
footnotes and a bibliography, and follow the format as taught in
Writer's Inc., Writing the Research Paper, or some similar book.
Support conclusions with Scripture.

02W23.C   Write an essay on "What It Means to Be a Help Meet".   EC - 2
Support all statements with Scripture references.

02W24.C   Read several articles from women's magazines on topics   EC - 2
related to marriage and family life and write an essay analyzing
each in light of Scripture.

COMPOSITION

02W25.C   Write a play or short story about a Christian family in some other time period. Create one or more problems that were common to their day but not to ours, and show how they work together, within their own roles, to solve the problems using principles that are common to all believers. Demonstrate the woman as a wife who could be trusted to do her husband good and not evil.   EC - 15

02W26.C   Write a report (2-3 pages) on the Women's Liberation Movement and how it changed family life in the United States and/or your country, if not U. S.   EC - 2

02W27.C   After studying the topic in Health and Fitness in this mini-unit, write a paper to explain how having a good wife can improve a man's health and lengthen his life span.   EC - 2

02W28.C   Write a letter that might have been sent by a man away on business to his trusted wife in a time prior to telephones, telegraph, and e-mail. It should include directions for things he needs her to do and express his confidence that she will do them well.   EC - 1

02W29.C   Write an essay on the old saying "behind every successful man is a supportive woman". Tell whether you consider it true or false and why, supporting your arguments and conclusion from Scripture.   EC - 2

02W30.C   Write a short story about the life of Samson and Delilah as it might have been if she had been a godly wife.   EC - 15

02W31.C   Write an essay on what you believe it means to trust someone fully.   EC - 2

02W32.C   Research the word of 'audit' to learn what it is, how it is conducted, and what its purposes are. Write a paper explaining how the need for audits relates to being untrustworthy.   EC - 1

02W33.C   Write a character sketch of the type of person you would trust.   EC - 1

02W34.D   Compare in writing the various kinds of checking and savings accounts offered by your bank, giving the rates of interest, benefits and requirements of each.   EC - 1

02W35.D   List and/or mind map ways a wife can increase the financial position of her husband without working outside her home. Write one or more paragraphs to explain each idea and how one could start doing it.   EC - 2

02W36.D   Interview several Christian husbands and use their thoughts to write an essay about the importance of a wife's contentment to a husband's sense of well-being.   EC - 5

COMPOSITION

02W37.D	Write a humorous skit or monologue in which a woman learns how to save money in ways that she never has before.	EC - 5
02W38.D	Write an analysis of the saying, "Use it up; wear it out; make it do or do without." Explain how this relates to a wife as caretaker of family finances.	EC - 2
02W39.D	After reading several of them, write a prospectus for one or more of the specific investment opportunities you investigated for your family.	EC - 1
02W40.D	Write a brochure or flyer advertising the various services available at your bank.	EC - 1
02W41.D	Compare in writing the rules of operation, criteria, security, and rate of return for specialty banks, credit unions, and full service banks.	EC- 1
02W42.	Define and put into your vocabulary notebook 10 new words per week, using first those you encountered in your studies. For each, write all common definitions and pronunciations.	EG - 1 per week
02W43.	Learn to spell all the words in your vocabulary notebook for this unit.	EG - 2 per week
02W44.	Using *Writers Inc.,* the *College English Handbook*, or another grammar reference, proofread and correct all written work for this unit.	EG- 1 per 5 pages
02W45.	Use a good dictionary to proofread all written work in this unit and correct it for errors in spelling.	EG - 1 per 5 pages
02W46.	Keep a journal of each day's school projects throughout the entire curriculum. If done well, this journal can serve as official documentation of your school year to meet legal requirements in many states.	EG - 2 per week
02W47.	As you listen to any of the suggested tapes in this unit, take notes on them.	EG - 2 ea.
02W48.	Use your notes to outline, summarize, and/or discuss the audios as requested.	EC 1 ea.
02W49.	Outline one or more of the nonfiction books used in this unit.	EG - 3 ea.
02W50.	Instead of, or in addition to, outlining the books studied here, write reviews of them, as might be published in a periodical of some type.	EC - 1 ea.
02W51.	Write a brief report on any important person studied in this unit.	EC - 2 ea.
02W52.	Use any Scripture passage, poem or other material you are memorizing to copy for handwriting practice.	EG - 1 per hour

COMPOSITION

02W53.	Use the same material to write from dictation, being careful about spelling, punctuation, etc. Have someone read the passage to you slowly while you write it.	EG - 1 per hour
02W54.	As an alternative to cursive writing, try Italic or Spencerian calligraphy, using books in the resource list.	VA - 1 per hour
02W55.	Write a news article on each of the field trips you took in this unit.	EC - 2 ea.
02W56.	Write a thank you note to the organizer, supervisor, and/or guide of any field trip you took for this unit.	EC - 1 ea.
02W57.	Write summaries of any or all of the books read in this unit.	EC - 1 ea.
02W58.	Write reports on any or all of the women studied in the unit.	EC - 1 ea.
02W59.	Write one book report per week on a book approved by parents Use a variety of approaches, including any or all of those listed in the Appendix.	EC - 2 ea.

MATHEMATICS AND PERSONAL FINANCE

02M01.A	Collect data and plot on a graph to show the correlation, if any, between length of engagement and likelihood of divorce. Repeat with only first marriages.	M - 7
02M02.A	Using statistics from the Cultural Studies section, compare on a graph rates of divorce, suicide, spousal neglect, runaway spouses, and similar problems among members of the upper and middle classes in countries with arranged marriages and those where people "fall in love" before they choose to marry.	M - 7
02M03.A	Prepare a graph showing the ratio and/or proportion of divorces to marriages in various time periods of your country's history. Correlate these in some way to methods of finding a mate that were most common in each time period.	M - 5
02M04.A	Gather statistics within your community for a certain period and determine the average age of couples at marriage. Do it again using only first marriages.	M- 1
02M05.A	Collect data to calculate and plot on a graph the correlation, if any, between probability of divorce and ages of couple at time of marriage. Use one-year increments only. Repeat with only first marriages.	M - 5
02M06.B	Make a graph to show the rise and/or decline in births to unwed mothers in your country during each of the last ten years.	M - 5

MATHEMATICS AND PERSONAL FINANCE

02M07.B	Prepare a graph to show the growth of sex education classes in the same country during the same time period.	M - 5
02M08.B	Correlate, in whatever way you like, the data from the two activities above to show any relationship between them.	M - 2
02M09.B	Prepare some type of graph showing reported cases of sexually-transmitted diseases over the last decade, and the correlation between that and the abundance and growth of secular, `sex education' classes in public schools.	M - 5
02M10.B	Collect data from your state Department of Human Resources or similar agency on the cost to the taxpayer of supporting one out-of-wedlock child for a year and the number of such children being supported. Chart these figures over a ten-year period.	M - 3
02M11.B	After obtaining a copy of the current budget for your local school board and individual schools in your district, calculate the cost of sex education classes and how much could be saved if they were discontinued.	M- 1
02M12.C	For a look at one concrete way women can do their husbands good, compile and analyze insurance data on number, percentage, and seriousness of traffic accidents, alcoholism, drug addictions, and other health problems for single and married men of the same age groups. Notice those that are significantly lower for husbands.	M- 1
02M13.C	Compile and study police statistics on crime rates of single and married men of the same or similar ages. Express in terms of ratio and/or proportions. What do you believe is the significance of these findings?	M - 2
02M14.C	Study and plot the difference in average life expectancy of married and single men of the same ages. Explain what you believe is the reason that married men live longer.	M - 1
02M15.C	Collect data from your insurance company on accident and traffic violation averages among married and unmarried men and how this affects their insurance rates. Calculate the percentage of savings given to married men on average.	M - 1
02M16.C	Study auditing, the process whereby companies and agencies can check their financial records for error or fraud.	CE - 1
02M17.C	In order to prepare for auditing, you may need to do a quick study of accounting principles and procedures in Accounting Made Easy or a similar resource	M - '/2 credit
02M18.C	Should you wish to go deeper into accounting at this time, you can do a complete accounting course, using any standard text-book.	M - 1 credit for complete course

02M19.D	Study and use as much as possible the Financial Management Calendar available from your county Agricultural Extension Office.	CE - 5
02M20.D	Study *Surviving the Money Jungle* and/ or *Get a Grip on Your Money* financial management course, completing all activities satisfactorily.	CE - 1/2 credit
02M21.D	Using real income and expenses prepare a workable budget for your own family.	M - 3
02M22.D	Prepare your family's income tax return, including schedule A.	M - 3
02M23.D	Keep a record of your savings from coupon shopping and compile them statistically.	M - 2 per month
02M24.D	Study or review math operations using decimals (money) and per cents, all of which relate to finances.	M - 2
02M25.D	Study interest rates and learn to compute simple and compound interest.	M- 1
02M26.D	Study your homeowner's or renter's insurance policy and determine if you think the money spent on premiums is good stewardship. Do you think having insurance indicates a failure to trust God, or is it God's way of protecting our assets?	CE - 2
02M27.	Continue to review basic math as needed.	M - 1 per hour
02M28.	Use data from any of the graphs you make or study in this mini-unit to practice calculating per cent, ratio and proportion.	M - 1 per Hour
02M29.	Attend or study the DVD of *Financial Peace University* by Dave Ramsey.	M - 20

SCIENCE

02S01.A	Study the 'courting' and mating rituals of a variety of birds and other creatures. Try to observe them, noticing what part is played by which gender.	SB - 1
02S02.A	Observe the mating rituals of a variety of mammals, noting the role played by each.	SB - 1
02S03.A	Analyze the differences and similarities between animal mating rituals and the dating practices of your society.	SB - 1 CS - 1
02S04.A	Study the causes of halitosis, a severe problem for those who are dating, and how good dental hygiene can reduce it.	HE - 1
02S05.A	Study the various products used to fight bad breath and whiten teeth, of primary importance to the dating crowd. Learn which chemicals are contained in which products and which are most effective.	CS - 1

SCIENCE

02S06.B*	Using any good anatomy book, study the human reproductive system, both male and female.	HA - 2
02S07.B*	Complete the coloring pages of both male and female reproductive organs in *Gray's Anatomy Coloring Book*.	HA - 2
02S08.B	Study menstruation and its purpose.	HE - 1
02S09.B	Study the physiological processes by which conception takes place.	HA - 2
02S10.B	Study the Endocrine System, with emphasis on the hormones related to sexuality.	HA- 2
01S11.B	Study the growth of body hair, which usually begins at puberty, and the different patterns it takes in men and women.	HA- 1
01S12.B	Investigate the primary reasons women in your culture shave their legs (if they do) and discuss with your mother if and when she believes you are ready to do so.	CS - 1
01S13.C	Use periodicals and other materials to research physical differences between men and women that are not directly related to genitalia. Note specific strengths of each gender and how these fit the roles to which God has called them within the family.	HA - 2
01S14.C	Using the above procedures, note the different mental strengths, weaknesses and abilities of each gender. Relate these to the requirements of the roles to which God has called each within the family.	HA - 1
01S15.C	Study the equipment and procedures used to administer the polygraph (lie detector) test, which would not be needed if people could be trusted.	SP - 1
01516.C	Examine the construction and functioning of various types of home systems we use to protect ourselves from the dishonest among us.	SP - 2
01S17.C	Study the construction and functioning of various personal security devices (mace sprays, body alarms, etc.) used for protection from robbery, mugging and assault.	SP - 2
01S18.C	Look at the different forms of theft-protection we have available to us for our automobiles and learn the principles on which each works.	SP - 2
01S19.D	Study the construction of safes and safe deposit boxes and the materials from which they are usually made.	SP- 1
01S20.D	Study the materials used to build and lock bank vaults.	SP - 1
01S21.D	Study the scientific processes involved in the printing of paper money and the precautions taken to prevent forgeries.	SP - 1

SCIENCE

01S22.D	Study the materials, equipment and processes used for the coinage of money in your country.	SP - 1
01S23.D	Study the system of magnetic encryption used on your personal checks and the computer equipment used to read it. Find out how this protects your funds from going to the wrong account.	SP - 1
01S24.D	Study the operation of various small and large appliances and what is required to keep them operating properly and efficiently.	SP - 1
01S25.D	Study the energy ratings of electric appliances and learn how they are measured.	SP - 1

HEALTH AND PHYSICAL FITNESS

02H01.A	Study mononucleosis, known as the kissing disease and often passed by common dating activities. Note other ways it can be contracted.	HE - 1
02H02.A	Study acne and other skin disorders that are so troubling to young people on the dating roller coaster of always needing to look their best for their dates.	HE- 1
02H03.A	Study common pharmaceutical remedies for acne, eczema, and similar skin problems.	HE - 1
02H04.A	Research natural remedies for acne, eczema and other skin disorders. Compare their advantages and disadvantages with those of regular medications.	HE - 1
02H05.A	Study dental hygiene and its importance to health and attractiveness to the opposite sex.	HE - 1
02H06.A	Study the reasons young people often get braces on their teeth, types of braces that can be used, and why young people who are dating especially hate to wear them.	HE - 1
02H07.B*	Study the Christian sexuality course *What's the Big Deal?* or a similar program of Christ-centered sex education.	1/2 credit in Human Sexuality for the complete course
02H08.B*	Learn about sexually-transmitted diseases and the necessity of abstinence and monogamy in preventing them.	HE - 2
02H09.B	Study the causes and prevention of AIDS from a Christian perspective using books in the Reading and Literature section.	HE - 2 +

HEALTH AND PHYSICAL FITNESS

02H10.B	Use medical literature or other material to study the health problems associated with menstrual periods and remedies for them.	HE - I
02H11.B	Watch the video *Feminine Hygiene and You* and discuss it with your mother.	HE - 1
02H12.B	Use medical literature or other material to study menopause and the health problems often associated with it.	HE - 1
02H13.B	Research the various medications that are often prescribed for 'female problems' and the natural alternatives to them.	HE - 1
02H14.C	Study health problems most common in men and investigate possible steps a wife might take to prevent or alleviate each.	HE- 1
02H15.C	Study life expectancy data from medical personnel and/or insurance companies to determine why happily married men normally live longer than those who divorce early or never marry. Discuss how this relates to a wife's doing her husband good and not evil.	HE - 1
02H16.C	Study the common causes of death in married and single men and see which are less in married men because of the influence or care of their wives.	HE - 1
02H17.C*	Study erectile dysfunction, which can be a major problem in some marriages, and ways to treat it at home in private.	HE - 1
02H18.C*	Study the various drugs and medical procedures that are being ing used to treat erectile dysfunction.	HE - 1
02H19.C*	Study various forms of birth control to learn how each operates and at what point in the conception process it works. Discuss with your mother your family's beliefs about the acceptability of any or all methods of birth control. (This is entirely a decision that belongs within the family.)	HE - 2 B - 1
02H20.C	Study cholesterol, especially the bad' kind, which is generally much higher in men than in women.	HE- 1
02H21.D	Learn about baking soda and other common household products hat can replace expense health or hygiene items and save your family money.	HE - 1
02H22.D	Use the *Physician's Desk Reference* (PDR) to research all the medications members of your family are currently taking and the generic equivalents of them to see how much you can save your family by using the cheaper versions.	HE - 1
02H23.D	Study the *Physician's Desk Reference* (PDR) and/or a medical encyclopedia or talk with your doctor or pharmacist to find out if specific brands of any of the above medications have properties that make them worth the extra price difference in your family's particular case.	HE- 1

HEALTH AND PHYSICAL FITNESS

| 02H24.D | Investigate all natural alternatives to the above medications and the cost differences, not only in actual price of the product but including the cost of doctor visits necessary for the prescriptions and the cost of treating any common side-effects from the drugs. | HE - 1 |
| 02H25.D | Read food labels to determine the difference in quality among various brands of the same food and the importance of buying the most nutritious, even if it is not the least expensive. | HE - 2 |

PRACTICAL ARTS

02P01.A	After studying Joshua Harris' book, listed in the Reading and Literature section of this mini-unit, mind map ways in which you need to prepare yourself to be a good wife for your future husband. Set up a plan to begin doing that.	HF - 2 B - 2
02P02.A	Discuss your feelings about youthful romance with your parents and develop a plan to prepare for handling it as a family when the time comes. Enlist your parents' help in guiding you to know when you are ready for this step.	HF - 1
02P03.A	Start a club or group for young people who are taking the same path to romance that you and your family have chosen. Set up rules for who can join and/or attend, based on a commitment to this life-style. Publicize it through churches, homeschool groups, etc.	CS - 5
02P04.A	Plan social activities for your group to do that will help everyone get to know each other without the usual pressure to date or 'pair off'.	RE - 2 + each
02P05.A	Plan and institute one or more service projects in which your club or church youth group can serve others, while learning and growing together.	CS - 2 each
02P06.A	Alone or with others in your club, build a website on the topic of "God's Plan for Romance" or a similar topic, helping other young people to see the benefits of this lifestyle.	CO - 2 +
02P07.B	Examine various 'feminine hygiene' napkins and tampons and get your mother to teach you how to use them and which is best for you.	HE - 1
02P08.B	Learn how to get blood and similar stains out of clothing.	HM - 1
02P09.B	Learn how to perform internal feminine cleansing and the right products to use.	HE - 1
02P10.B	Put together or participate in some type of anti-pornography campaign in your own community.	CS - 3

PRACTICAL ARTS

02P11.B	Talk with your mother about the shaving of legs and when you should start. Then, get her to show you how it is done.	HE- I
02P12.C	Create an original needlework project illustrating some aspect of husband/wife relationships or extolling the value of a good wife. Give as a wedding gift or save for your hope chest.	HM - 4 VA 1
02P13.C	Learn to sew one or more items of men's clothing.	CC- 5 +
02P14.C	Learn the proper way to clean and care for suits, lined trousers, ties, and other clothing worn predominately by men.	HM - 2
02P15.C	Learn how to iron a man's dress shirt and slacks.	HM- 1
02P16.C	Audit the books of a real or imaginary small business.	BE - 5
02P17.C	Watch someone administer a lie detector test and find out how it is done, or learn about it on www.howstuffworks.com	SP- 1
02P18.C	Learn how to reduce cholesterol in your family's diet while still providing the same tasty meals.	FN - 2
02P19.D	Prepare and use a simple coupon file.	HM - 2
02P20.D	Working from the current shopping list, sort and organize appropriate coupons for a particular grocery shopping trip.	HM - I
02P21.D	Shop for your family's groceries for one full week, (or pay period, if other than weekly), doing everything from making the list to putting away the groceries. Compare prices and use coupons when advantageous. (This can be done up to ten times, with a record kept of coupon savings, amount spent, etc., each time)	FN- I HM - 1 CE - 1
02P22.D	Prepare and keep up a home financial file.	CE - 2
02P23.D	Learn to write checks and balance a checkbook.	CE - 1
02P24.D	Assist your parents in price comparison when shopping for an appliance or other major item.	CE - 1
02P25.D	Prepare a basic joint income tax return, including itemized deductions, and learn what records to keep for that purpose.	CE - 2 M - 1
02P26.	Type any or all papers written during the study of this unit.	BE - 1 per hr
02P27.	Make your own puppets for any puppet show you do in this unit.	CR - 3 +
02P28.	Design and sew your own costumes for any play you present in this unit.	CC - 5 each
02P29.	Use a variety of lettering styles to make the posters required for any exhibits or displays in this unit.	VA - 1 each

PRACTICAL ARTS

02P30.	Use your computer to make posters, signs or other graphics for your exhibits or displays.	CO - 1

DECORATIVE AND PERFORMING ARTS

02A01.A	Direct or act in a play based on the short story you wrote about a courtship in the Composition section of this mini-unit.	DR - 50
02A02.A	Produce a puppet show about the 'courtship' of Isaac and Rebekah, doing everything yourself.	DR - 10
02A03.A	Make a card for a bride-to-be or a betrothed couple using the ideas taught in this unit.	VA- 1
02A04.A	Watch a live performance of *Romeo and Juliet* and analyze their relationship from a Biblical perspective.	DR- 3
02A05.B	Make a greeting card from a woman to her husband or betrothed, using calligraphy and verses from Song of Solomon.	VA - 2
02A06.B	Illustrate a card with original artwork.	VA - 1
02A07.B	Set one or more chapters of Song of Solomon to music with an original tune.	MC - 3
02A08.B	Tour an art gallery and observe a wide variety of classic paintings of people, both full body and facial only, and notice how a skilled artist can put the characteristics of masculinity or femininity on canvas without nudity or skimpy clothing.	AA- 2
02A09.B*	Create and perform with your family or other FAR students a monologue or skit in which a Christian young person comes into sexual temptation and uses Scriptural knowledge to avoid it. After the skit, discuss the mistake that allowed the person to be in such a situation.	DR - 10
02A10.C	Write and produce a play or puppet show on the lives of Aquila and Priscilla, Abraham and Sarah, or another Biblical couple who exemplified these verses.	DR- 50 for show DR - 10 for puppets
02A11.C	Watch a live performance of *Macbeth* paying close attention to how Lady Macbeth, while trying to better her husband's state actually contributed to his downfall. She was totally loyal. Where did she go wrong? Discuss this with others who saw the play.	DR - 3
02A12.C	Prepare a mural using your choice of media, to show the various ways in which a person can be trustworthy.	VA - 2
02A13.C	Using pictures cut from magazines, brochures, etc., create a collage of the activities a trusted wife might perform on behalf of her husband. Calligraphy or print attractively the verse for this unit across the collage.	VA - 1

DECORATIVE AND PERFORMING ARTS

02A14.C	Create a humorous skit about the suffragettes, showing the inappropriate nature of their methods, no matter how lofty their goals.	DR- 10
02A15.C	Examine words to a large variety of songs about wives and/or marriage. Make a list of and listen to several samples of different types of music with words that encourage and support marriage and wifely responsibility.	MA- 2
02A16.C	If you play an instrument, learn to play one or more of the above songs.	IM - 3
02A17.D	Create and illustrate a brochure to advertise the services of your bank.	VA - 1
02A18.D	Decorate a cloth or plastic pouch or heavy-duty envelope to make a storage pouch for coupons when you shop.	VA - 1
02A19.D	Prepare and perform a humorous monologue or skit in which a wife has to find a way to solve money problems.	DR -10
02A20.D	Draw the best possible illustrations of unusual possessions for the home inventory you created in the Practical Arts section of this mini-unit.	VA 1 +
02A21.D	Plan and perform a role-playing skit about the importance of budgeting.	DR - 10
02A22.D	Draw original illustrations to make into a coloring book on banking for young children.	VA - 5
02A23.D	Plan and perform a puppet show designed to teach young children about banks and what they can do for you.	DR - 10
02A24.	Draw pictures of any field trips you took in this mini-unit.	VA - 1
02A25.	Use drawing, painting and graphic arts to create displays and make posters as called for in this study.	VA - 1 each
02A26.	Illustrate one or more of the poems you studied or memorized for this unit.	VA - 1 each
02A27.	Set one or more of this unit's poems to music, using an original tune.	MC - 3 each
02A28.	Set one or more of the Scripture passages in this unit to music, using a tune you wrote for the purpose.	MC - 2 each

UNIT 3

She seeks wool and flax and works
with her hands in delight.
Proverbs 31:13

Overview

In this verse, the King's mother stresses the importance of diligence and care in the work of a godly wife. She urges her son to look at the quality and effort a woman puts into what she does as one of the measures of a godly wife. We have chosen not to make a separate mini-unit of either of these qualities but have interspersed Scripture about them throughout all the mini-units as seemed appropriate. As you study the academics in this unit, keep in mind the emphasis on diligence and productivity and quality of ingredients.

This unit allows you to explore the Biblical concept of God as our Shepherd and the proper relationship of the sheep to the Master. You will have the opportunity to examine this with a wide variety of Scriptures, including the beautiful Psalms of David written when he was a shepherd, and parables on this topic from Jesus, the Good Shepherd. You will be asked to compare these Scriptures to real sheep and shepherds now and at various times in history.

Expanding beyond sheep, this unit includes a more complete study of animals in general, both domesticated and wild. You will learn of their life-styles, efforts to domesticate them and their usefulness to man, always keeping in mind that they are all creations of God.

What the godly woman of King Lemuel's day did personally with her hands has grown into a massive multinational industry, which you will examine here. This will include cottage industries such as this woman was doing, but will also look at a much broader picture of the field known as textiles. You will study the history and origins of fibers, fabrics and textiles. You will learn about the development of the textile industry and those who have worked in it.

Mini-Units

Mini-Units contained in this unit are:

    A. The Good Shepherd and His Sheep

    B. Breeding and Raising of Livestock

    C. The Beasts of the Field

    D. Fabrics, Textiles and the Textile Industry

Each thematic mini-unit is described and designated with a letter of the alphabet in the following paragraphs. Individual activities designed for use in one particular mini-unit will be marked with those letters. (For further help with this, please refer to the explanation of mini-units in the Guidelines section of this unit study guide.)

Mini-Units

A. The Good Shepherd and His Sheep

As this Scripture verse refers to wool, it seemed good to us to begin with the sheep who are its source and are often used as symbols of God's relationship to His people. You will examine a wide range of verses about sheep, both in the literal sense and as symbols of spiritual truths. You will read about Biblical shepherds who were called and used by God for other things.

This mini-unit will include a study of the anatomy and physiology of sheep and the various species available. You will investigate the differences between domesticated and wild species as well as the care of domesticated varieties. This will include an opportunity to learn about breeding and raising the animals.

You will study the daily life of the shepherd in a variety of cultures and time periods, from the Old Testament until today. In the process, you will see the growth of sheep-raising as an industry and its demise in many areas today. This will, of course, lead you to an understanding of the changes technology has brought to all of rural life. The economics of sheep-raising will also be examined, both from the standpoint of the individual in the business to the national and worldwide economic impact of the industry.

B. Breeding and Raising of Other Livestock

For the purpose of this unit, livestock is defined as animals generally kept and raised for the purpose of food or work. This will include but is not totally restricted to those animals referred to generically in Scripture as 'cattle' — all four-footed, hoofed mammals whose meat might be used as food

You will investigate the livestock raised in various countries and their uses, making special note of which ones are raised in your own area. You will learn the anatomy and physiology of each of the primary species and the type of care each needs in a domesticated situation. You will examine the steps necessary for the care and breeding of various domestic animals and how they are used and marketed. You will also study the economic impact of the industry as a whole and various branches of it.

This mini-unit will include a chance to look at the various species of these animals that are not fully domesticated, if at all, and to compare them with others of their family. You will investigate the advisability of domestication for those animals. You may be in for a few surprises when you begin to look at this in light of God's word, not what the environmentalists tell us.

C. The Beasts of the Field

This is the denotation used by Scripture for all other four-footed or upright animals not included under cattle. It does not include bugs, worms, most reptiles, etc., as they are called 'creeping things'. This unit exists primarily to tie up loose ends and give you a complete education in the area of animals. Thus we will also include any of these 'creeping things, and/ or birds not covered in other units.

You will learn about the taxonomy of animals as first created by the Linnaeus and compare it to the pattern found in Scripture. This should give you a chance to see God's plan in the creation of so many animals and their relationship to each other.

This mini-unit covers the anatomy and physiology of many of these species, especially those known as mammals, and general information applicable to large groups. You will learn about the food chain and about animal life cycles, as well as how they breed, reproduce, and crossbreed. You will have opportunity to study endangered species and attempts to save them, possibly arriving at some surprising solutions.

D. Fabrics, Textiles and the Textile Industry

In this mini-unit, we have expanded the verse beyond a young woman doing her own needlework to study the vast, multinational textile industry. This will include the growing of flax and cotton and the difficulties associated with each. We will investigate the various chemical and physical processes that take place to produce a certain fabric from its parent fiber as well as the chemical production of synthetic fabrics.

This unit offers a wide range of suggested reading and composition activities related to any or all of the topics covered herein. The unit's mathematics, likewise, is related to the topics of farming and textiles. We will continue to work with graphs, per cent, ratio, and proportion, as well as figuring total output of various phases of the textile industry. We will work with price comparisons as well.

BIBLE AND CHRISTIAN CHARACTER

03B01.A	Study and memorize John 10: 1 - 18.	B - 6
03B02.A	Study and memorize Psalm 23 (if you have not already done so.)	B - 2
03B03.A	Study and memorize Psalm 100.	B - 2
03B04.A	Look up and study all other Psalms that refer to us as God's sheep or Him as our shepherd.	B - 2
03B05.A	Memorize one or more Psalms about sheep and the Shepherd other than those named in previous activities.	B - 1 per 3 verses
03B06.B	Study all other Psalms David wrote while he was a shepherd.	B - 2
03B07.A	Study Matthew 18 and relate to parents or others how confronting a fellow Christian about his/her sin can be seen as rescuing a lost sheep.	B - 1
03B08.A	Use concordance to find and study other Scripture passages that use sheep in a symbolic sense.	B - 3
03B09.A	Use a concordance to investigate Scripture verses that explain the role of sheep in Old Testament Hebrew worship.	B - 2
03B10.A	Study the Book of Hebrews and mind map about it to learn why the need to sacrifice sheep in Old Testament worship ended with the death of Christ and why He is called the Lamb of God.	B - 3

BIBLE AND CHRISTIAN CHARACTER

03B11.B   Study Matthew 25:31-46. From whatever you can learn about   B - 1
the nature of sheep and goats, try to determine why our Lord
referred to His children as one and the unbelievers as the other.

03B12.B   Read Genesis 4, which contains the first known account of   B - 1
animal husbandry.

03B13.B   Study the lives of Jacob, Joseph, Moses, and David and the   B - 2
part sheep and/or shepherding played in each of them.

03B14.B   Study the parting of Abram and Lot and the part their 'herdsmen'   B - 1
played in that.

03B15.B   Look up and study the lives of all shepherds or herdsmen in   B - 3
Scripture.

03B16.B   Use the concordance to find and study all Biblical references   B - 1
to "cattle", and make a list of all animals you can think of that
seem to fit that category. (HINT: This term includes all
mammals considered livestock in any part of the world.)

03B17.B   Study all Scriptural references to goats. Document each reference   B - 2
as to where it fits in the following categories: raising live
animals, sacrifice, symbolism, or food.

03B18.B   Look up in a concordance and study all references to each of   B - 3
the other animals (besides sheep and goats) from the above
list of things the Bible considers 'cattle'.

03B19.B   From the book *All the People of the Bible*, or some similar   B - 2
resource, study all other important people of the Bible who
made their living in jobs related to livestock.

03B20.C   Read Genesis 1:24-31 and discuss the relationship this passage   B - 1
establishes between God and man and between man and
the various animals.   What is our responsibility toward the
animals?

03B21.C   Read the story of Noah's departure from the ark in Genesis   B - 1
8:15-9:15 and mind map or discuss with your parents how
this changed the previous relationship between man and the
animals.

03B22.C   Study God's 'taxonomy' of the animal kingdom in Deuteronomy   B - 1
14:4-20 and prepare a list of the various divisions into which
He groups animals. This will be used for other activities later.

03B23.C   Read God's discussion of the animals He created in Job 38:39   B - 1
& 39:30. Add any new categories to the above list, studying
each to see where it fits.

BIBLE AND CHRISTIAN CHARACTER

03B24.C	Read Job 40 and 41, adding to the above list all animals mentioned there. Save this list for later activities in science.	B	1
03B25.C	Use the concordance to look up and study all Scripture references to each of the animals on the list you made in activities 03B22-03B24.	B - 2	
03B26.D	Use a concordance to find and read all Scripture references to wool or sheep shearing.	B - 1+	
03B27.D	Use a concordance to find and read all Scripture references to flax and other fiber crops and/or the fabrics made from them.	B - 1	
03828.D	Use *Beggar to King: All the Occupations of the Bible*, or any similar resource to identify textile-related occupations of Bible times. Then look up an example of each in the Scripture itself.	B - 2 H 1	
03B29.	Meditate on and memorize one or more of the passages studied in the unit.	B 1 per 3 verses	
03B30.	Read through the book of Proverbs each month, reading the chapter to coincide with each date.	B - 3 per week	
03B31.	Continue reading through the Bible at a rate of 1-5 chapters per day. If you use *The Daily Bible* or some other version designed specifically for that purpose, their daily readings will take you through the entire Bible in one year. You may follow a a pattern of your own at a different rate if you like. Using a chronologically arranged Bible offers the added benefit of putting your reading in perspective as to time frame.	B - 1 credit when completed; no partial credit	
03B32.	Continue (or begin) to keep your prayer journal, listing each day (or as the Lord brings to mind) prayer requests, needs in your spiritual life and things God is teaching you. Continue this throughout all units.	B - 3 per week	

CULTURAL STUDIES

03C01.A	Study the importance of sheep in the history and culture of Israel and its neighbors during Bible times.	H - 2	
03C02.A	Study the importance of sheep-raising in that same part of the world today.	CE - 1	
03C03.A	Study the life-style and work of a shepherd in Palestine and the surrounding areas during Biblical times and now. Contrast and compare them.	H - 1 CS - 1	
03C04.A	Study the life of shepherds in various parts of the world at different times in history, using any material of your choice.	CS - 1	

CULTURAL STUDIES

03C05.A	From Scripture, Jewish history, and other sources, study the religious significance of sheep to Biblical Israel. Research a variety of resources to determine if other religions use sheep in a similar fashion.	B - 1 CS - 1
03C06.A	From the book, *Celebrating Jesus in the Biblical Feasts: Discovering Their Significance to You as a Christian*, study the Biblical holiday of Passover & the importance of the lamb in it.	B - 1
03C07.A	Study the changes that have been made to the feast of Passover in modern times, and the reasons given by the Jews for them. To what extent do these changes alter God's original purpose for the Feast Day?	H- 1
03C08.A	Using *Celebrating Jesus in The Biblical Feasts* or similar resources, study the importance of sheep in the Hebrew celebration of Yom Kippur.	B - 1
03C09.A	Study the book of Hebrews to see why the traditional observances of these two holidays and their spiritual meanings are no longer appropriate for the Christian.	B - 3
03C10.A	Study *Celebrating Jesus in the Biblical Feasts* and mind map how these feast days can be celebrated by us without negating Jesus as the Messiah.	B - 2
03C11.B	Use encyclopedias or other references to identify and mark on a world map all countries that are major growers and/or exporters of sheep (or sheep products).	CE - 1
03C12.B	Use encyclopedias or other references to identify and mark on a world map all countries that are major producers and/or exporters of cattle or cattle products.	CE or G - 1
03C13.B	Use encyclopedias or other references to identify and mark on a world map all countries that are major growers and/or exporters of poultry, and poultry products.	CE or G - 1
03C14.B	Use encyclopedias or other references to identify and mark on a world map all countries that are major producers and/or exporters of hogs or products from them.	CE or G - 1
03C15.B	Investigate the raising, export and economic impact of other domesticated animals considered livestock by other cultures. Be sure to include: camel, elephant, burro, reindeer, water buffalo, yak, and any others you can discover.	CE - 2
03C16.B	Study the economic impact of the livestock industry in your country.	CE- 1
03C17.B	Study the economic impact on your own state or local area of animal husbandry in any of its forms.	CE- 1

CULTURAL STUDIES

03C18.B	Study the history of animal husbandry and the various developments in the process of animal breeding in your own country and others.	H - 1
03C19.B	Study the impact made on animal husbandry by the domestication of dogs, horses, oxen, and other service animals.	H- 1
03C20.B	Study the uses of working dogs around the world. Compare how they are used and their impact on the societies involved, economically, socially, and otherwise.	CS - 1
03C21.C	Study the history of the dog as a pet or companion animal.	H - 1
03C22.C	Study the history of the cat as a pet or companion animal.	H - 1
03C23.C	Study wild or exotic animals that are often kept as pets and determine the impact their domestication seems to have had on their proliferation.	CS - 1
03C24.C	Study the network of zoos in your country and how they provide for the continuation of species they have in residence.	CS - 1
03C25.C	Study endangered species of the world and where the various known examples are now. Plot these on a map.	SB - 1
03C26.C	From their own literature, study the structure and goals of the World Wildlife Fund and its various national affiliates.	CS - 1
03C27.C	Study your national and state/provincial wildlife conservation agencies.	CO - 1
03C28.C	Talk with a representative of one of the above agencies about his job and how he perceives it as helping his country or state/province.	CS - 1
03C29.C	From the above agencies, your lawmaking body or other sources, learn about the hunting and fishing laws of your state/province.	CL- 1
03C30.C	Study other laws relating to animal conservation in your nation, state or province.	CL - 2
03C31.D	Prepare a chart of different fabrics and the ways in which they have been used at different times in history.	H - 2
03C32.D	Use any available resources to identify and mark on an appropriate map the areas in your state/province and nation that grow cotton, flax or silk or produce any of the corresponding fabrics. Designate each of these by a different and add to the wool map above, if you made one.	CE or G - 1

CULTURAL STUDIES

03C33.D	Use encyclopedias and/or other resources to identify all nations or other geographic regions that are major producers or exporters of wool, flax, cotton or silk, in any form, or any item made from any of these. Locate these on a world map, designating each export with a different symbol. If you did a sheep export map in mini-unit A, you may just add these to it.	CE or G - 2
03C34.D	Make a chart of some type to compare the types and qualities of textiles produced and used in different countries.	CS - 2
03C35.D	Study the invention of the cotton gin and its impact on the textile Industry.	H - 1
03C36.D.	Study the lives and work of Whitney, Daniel Pratt, Elias Howe and others who built the textile industry through their discoveries or inventions.	H 1 each
03C37.D	Study the history of cotton to discover where its use in textiles originated.	H 1
03C38.D	Investigate the economic impact of the textile industry in your state, province or region.	CE - 1
03C39.D	Study the role of cotton and the cotton gin in the development of the plantation system and slavery in the U. S. South.	H- 1
03C40.D	Study the history of the textile industry in various countries, including the abuses of workers for which it once was notorious and evidences of worker abuse today.	H - 3
03C41.D	Study the role of the textile industry in fueling the Industrial Revolution.	H - I
03C42.	Use Usborne's *World History Dates, The Kingfisher History Encyclopedia,* or *Timetables of History* to further study and determine the dates surrounding people and events studied in this unit to prepare timeline entries.	VA - 1 H -1
03C43.	Using any or all of the resources mentioned herein, create timeline entries (following the instructions in Guidelines) for all important people and events in the history of each of the ancient nations studied in this unit and their modern-day counterparts.	VA - 1 H -1
03C44.	Make timeline entries for all authors, inventors, artists, composers or others whose works were read, studied or discussed during this unit.	VA 1 H -1
03C45.	Make timeline entries for major historical events mentioned in the books or videos used in this study but not already in your timeline.	VA - 1 H -1
03C46.	Locate on a map or globe all countries studied or mentioned in this unit.	G - 1

CULTURAL STUDIES

03C47.	Locate on a map and study the geography of all cities or municipalities and states or provinces studied in this unit.	G - 1
03C48.	Use an encyclopedia, *World Almanac* or appropriate websites to study the geography & culture of each country mentioned in this unit that you have not studied previously. Take notes on your studies so you can write a brief report (1-2 pages) on each of them in the Composition section.	G - 1
03C49.	Make timeline cards for all other major events and/or people mentioned in books read or studied in this unit.	VA - 1 H - 1
03C50.	Study the homeland of each author, inventor, or artist whose works were used or studied in this unit	G - 1 each

READING AND LITERATURE

03R01.A	Read *A Shepherd Looks at Psalm 23*.	B - 4
03R02.A	Read *Lessons from a Sheep Dog*.	B - 4
03R03.A	Read and memorize 15 - 20 lines of poetry about sheep or shepherds.	B - 3
03R04.A	Read the fictionalized biography David about the shepherd king and writer of many of the Psalms.	B - 5
03R05.A	Read *David the King*, another version of the same thing.	B - 5
03R06.A	Read any other biography of a Biblical or historical shepherd.	H - 5
03R07.A	Read one or more historical novels set on a sheep ranch or in which sheep figure prominently.	H - 5
03R08.B	Read *Charlotte's Web* and share it with a young child.	L - 3
03R09.B	Read *Black Beauty, National Velvet, The Black Stallion, Misty of Chincoteague* or other books about horses.	L - 4 each
03R10.B	Read one or more novels about cattle or set in a cattle ranching area.	H - 5
03R11.B	Read biographies of famous people who grew up on ranches, spent part of their lives working on ranches or owned one. Among these could be: Sandra Day O'Connor, Ronald Reagan, William F. Cody, Lyndon Johnson and many others.	L - 3
03R12.B	Read one or more issues of your local cattleman's trade magazine newsletter or online website, paying close attention to articles describing the lifestyle of the cattleman.	CS - 2
03R13.B	Read one or more issues of trade magazines (in print or online) for other livestock-related industries.	CS - 2 each

READING AND LITERATURE

03R14.B	Read and study 3-5 4-H publications on various animal husbandry projects.	SB - 2
03R15.B	Read *All Creatures Great and Small* or other collections of James Herriot's stories based on his life and as a country veterinarian caring mostly for livestock.	L- 5 each
03R16.C	Read *Lassie Come Home, Lad - A Dog*, and/or similar novels about dogs.	L - 4 each
03R17.C	Read *Where the Red Fern Grows*.	L- 5
03R18.C	Read *Call of the Wild* and/or *White Fang* or other novels about working dogs.	L - 5
03R19.C	Read and share with a younger child, Rudyard Kipling's *The Jungle Book*. Do not watch the movie (cartoon or other version) instead of reading the book, but you may do both and compare them.	L- 5
03R20.C	Read and/or watch as a movie *Born Free*.	L- 4
03R21.C	Read a biography of P. T. Barnum, Gunther Gebel-Williams or any other famous circus animal trainer.	L - 4
03R22.C	Read or watch a video of *The Lion the Witch and the Wardrobe* and/or any of the other books in The Chronicles of Narnia series.	L - 4 each book L - 2 each video
03R23.C	Read *Bambi, Watership Down*, and/or other novels in which wildlife are personified	L-5 each
03R24.C	Read *The Yearling* about a boy's experience with an animal he came to love.	L- 4
03R25.D	Read biographies of Eli Whitney, Daniel Pratt and other scientists or inventors whose work had a major impact on the textile industry.	H - 5 each
03R26.D	Read one or more historical novels set in the U. S. antebellum South in which cotton plays a major role.	L or H - 4 each
03R27.D	Read one or more novels in which flax or linen or its production played a major role.	L - 4 each
03R28.D	Read one or more novels about or touching on any other aspect of the textile industry.	L - 4 each
03R29.D	Read care instruction booklets put out by the county extension office and/or the manufacturers for several different fabrics. Compare the care required for each fabric	HM - 5
03R30.D	Read biographies of the men who founded and made money in textile manufacturing companies.	H - 4 each

READING AND LITERATURE

03R31.D	Read one or more novels set in any country heavily involved in the textile industry.	L- 5 each
03R32.	Read Christian or other wholesome novels set in the time period under study in any particular mini-unit.	H - 5 each
03R33.	Read suitable novels set in any of the countries or cultures studied in this unit.	L- 5 each
03R34.	Read short stories written in or by people from one or more of the countries you have studied in this unit.	L or H - 1 each
03R35.	Read other works by any authors studied in this unit.	L - 4 each

COMPOSITION

03W01.A	For handwriting practice, copy the analogy of the Good Shepherd from John 10 once a day for as long as it takes you to memorize it.	EG - 1 per hour
03W02.A	Rewrite the story of the above passage from the standpoint of the sheep.	EC - 1
03W03.A	Copy Psalm 23 for handwriting practice once per day for a week.	EG - 1 per hour
03W04.A	Write a Psalm of your own, praising God for some aspect of His Creation or some attribute of Himself.	EC - 2
03W05.A	Write an essay on what it means for us to be the sheep with Jesus as our shepherd.	EC - 2
03W06.A	Write a report on the uses and significance of sheep in the religious worship of Old Testament Israelites.	EC - 3
03W07.A	Write a paper describing the origin and significance of the Passover and how God instructed His people to commemorate it. Compare and contrast that to the celebration of the Passover as observed by the Jews today	EC - 1 B - 1 CS - 1
03W08.A	Write a scholarly report on the Jewish Passover custom of the empty chair. Explain the religious significance of that chair and whether or not it should be used in Christian commemorations of Passover.	EC - 2 B - 1
03W09.A	Write an essay on "Jesus, the Lamb of God", explaining what that phrase must have meant to the Jews of New Testament times. Support all statements from Scripture.	EC - 1 B - 1
03W10.B	Write an essay explaining the 'scapegoat" used in the Jewish celebration of the Day of Atonement. Tell from Scripture what its purpose was and why we as Christians should not make this part of our observance of this day.	EC - 2

COMPOSITION

03W11.B	Write a short story featuring a goat, cow, pig or other livestock animal as the main character. This can be realistic or with animals having human traits like speech.	EC -10
03W12.B	After studying the physiology and life patterns of sheep and goats in the Science section, write an exegesis of Matthew 25:31-46, explaining what natural characteristics of sheep and goats would cause the Lord to choose each to represent the class of people He did.	EC - 1 B - 1 SB-1
03W13.B	Write a journal as may have been made by a shepherd watching his flocks near Bethlehem on the night that Jesus was born. Record not only what he saw that night, but also his thoughts and feelings about it then and at several intervals later. Make at least three one-page entries.	EC- 1
03W14.B	Write a short story set on a ranch raising some type of food animal.	EC-10
03W15.B	Write a market report on the livestock industry in your state/province, including such facts as the types of animals raised, area(s) of the state or province primarily involved, the economic impact on those area(s) and the state/province as a whole, and any other facts you consider important.	EC- 2
03W16.B	Write a series of letters as might have been sent home by a cowboy on one of the cattle drives of early U. S. History.(Minimum of 3 letters and about six handwritten pages).	EC-2
03W17.B	Using 4-H and/or extension service materials and other resources, write a how-to manual (10 - 12 typewritten, double-spaced pages) on the breeding, raising and care of some particular livestock breed.	EC - 5 PA - 5
03W18.C	After researching each thoroughly, write brief science reports (1-2 handwritten pages) on several different animals from each endangered species list. For each species, include facts about its anatomy, characteristics, feeding habits, mating rituals, habitat and reasons for becoming endangered. Compile these into a booklet on this topic.	EC - 1
03W19.C	Write a short story featuring a personified wild animal as the main character.	EC-10
03W20.C	After interviewing a game warden or other wildlife conservation officer, write a detailed (2 - 3 double-spaced, typed pages) job description for his/her occupation.	EC- 1
03W21.C	Write an owner's manual (5-6 typewritten, double-spaced pages) on the care of an animal you have had or would like to have as a pet. Be thorough, including such things as where it will live, what it eats, when and how to feed it, if and when it should be exercised or played with, and treatment and prevention of any ailments or diseases to which it may be prone.	EC - 3 SB-2

COMPOSITION

03W22.C	Write a play or puppet show to teach younger children about hunting/ fishing safety and/or wildlife conservation.	EC- 10 +
03W23.C	Write a short story in which hunting, fishing or nature study involving animals plays a major role.	EC- 10+
03W24.C	Write a simple legal brief, summarizing the wildlife conservation laws of your nation, state or province.	EC - 2
03W25.C	Write a formal essay on the Biblical position with regard to the killing and eating of animals. Support all statements with Scripture references.	EC - 2
03W26.C	Prepare debate arguments for either side of the topic, "Resolved: The Best Way to Restore Endangered Species is by Domesticating Them." Support every statement with statistics or other data.	EC - 10 each side
03W27.D	Write reports on Eli Whitney, Daniel Pratt or other industrialists whose work directly influenced the textile industry.	EC- 1 each
03W28.D	List and define in vocabulary notebook the names of the various types of fabrics you discovered in your trip to the store.	EG - 1 per 10 words
03W29.D	Prepare a brief outline of the history of the textile industry in your country.	EG - 2
03W30.D	Write thorough, detailed descriptions (1-3 pages each) of the growing and harvesting of cotton, flax and/or other plants used in making fabric. Put these into a notebook labeled FABRICS, which will be added to in other activities in this and other units.	EC- 1 each
03W31.D	Write separate reports (1-3 handwritten pages each) on the production of thread and/or fabric from wool, flax, cotton, silk and any other fibers you have studied. Add these to the booklet on FABRICS.	EC - 1 each
03W32.D	Write a detailed description (1-2 pages) of the processes used in the tanning of hides to produce leather, both as it was done prior to industrialization and the method used in the leather industry today. Add this to your FABRICS booklet.	EC - 1 each
03W33.D	Write separate reports (1-3 pages) on the production and uses of acetate, nylon, rayon, polyester, and other man-made fabrics. Add to FABRICS notebook.	EC - 1 each
03W34.	As you read the Bible each day, keep a spiritual journal, taking notes on your readings and their applications in your life. Add prayer requests and answers as well as insights God may give you.	EC - 3 per week

COMPOSITION

03W35.	Define and put into your vocabulary notebook 10 new words per week, using first those you encountered in your studies. For each, write all common definitions and pronunciations.	EG - 1 per week
03W36.	Learn to spell all the words in your vocabulary notebook for this unit.	EG - 2 per 10 words
03W37.	Using *Writers Inc.*, the *College English Handbook*, or another grammar reference, proofread and correct all written work for this unit.	EG - 1 per 5 pages
03W38.	Use a good dictionary to proofread all written work in this unit and correct it for errors in spelling.	EG - 1 per 5 pages
03W39.	Keep a journal of each day's school projects throughout the entire curriculum. If done well, this journal can serve as official documentation of your school year to meet legal requirements in many states.	EG - 2 per week
03W40.	As you attend worship services or hear them on radio, TV, or audios, take notes on the sermons.	EG - 1 each
03W41.	As you watch videos and/or listen to audios take notes on them.	EG - 3 each
03W42.	Use your notes to outline, summarize, and/or discuss the sermons as requested.	EC or EG - 1 each
03W43.	Use your notes to write a synopsis or summary of each audio and/or video used in this mini-unit.	EC - 1 each
03W44.	Outline one or more of the nonfiction books used in this unit.	EG – 5 each
03W45.	Instead of, or in addition to, outlining the books studied here, write reviews of them, as might be published in a periodical of some type.	EC - 1 each
03W46.	Use any Scripture passage, poem or other material you are memorizing to copy for handwriting practice.	EG - 1 per hour
03W47.	Use the Scripture verses, poems and other material you are trying to memorize to write from dictation. Have someone read the passage to you slowly while you write it, being careful about correct spelling, punctuation, etc. If your beliefs allow, you may want to use a modern Bible translation for this exercise.	EG 1 per hour
03W48.	As an alternative to cursive writing, try Italic or Spencerian calligraphy, using books in the resource list.	VA- 1 per hour
03W49.	Write a news article on each of the field trips you took in this unit.	EC - 2 each

COMPOSITION

03W50.	Write a thank you note to the organizer, supervisor, and/ or guide of any field trip you took for this unit.	EC - 2 each
03W51.	Write summaries or synopses of any or all of the books read in this unit.	EC - 1 ea.
03W52.	Write a report on one or more of the people you studied in this unit.	EC - 1 ea.
03W53.	Write one book report per week on a book included in this unit or another approved by parents. Use a variety of approaches, including any or all of those listed in the Appendix.	EG - 1 per hour
03W54.	Write a brief (1-2 pages) report on each country studied in this unit. Put each of them into your geography notebook.	EG - 1 per hour
03W55.	Write reviews of any or all of the videos in this unit, as if done by a movie critic.	VA- 1 per hour
03W56.	Write a character sketch of one or more of the men and women studied in this unit.	EC - 2 each
03W57.	Write a thorough exegesis of any of the Bible chapters studied in this unit.	EC - 1 each
03W58.	Write a review of each play you watched or read for this unit.	EC - 1 each

MATHEMATICS AND PERSONAL FINANCE

03M01.A	After finding the average size of sheepfolds in Old Testament Israel and the average number of sheep in a flock, calculate the space allowed to each sheep in the fold.	H - 1 M - 1
03M02.A	Contact the county extension office and/or other livestock experts to find the amount of pasture space recommended for each head of sheep to be grazed there. Have one of a parent, sibling, or friend design 10-12 pastures in a variety of shapes and sizes for which you must compute the area and the number of sheep each will support, based on the above data.	PA - 1 M- 1
03M03.A	Use the shapes in the above activity to practice and/or review converting between square feet, square yards, square miles, and acres and their equivalents in the metric system.	M - 1
03M04.A	If needed at this time, use a workbook or text to review formulae for finding the area of various regular polygons.	M - 5 +
03M05.A	Using figures from within the industry, determine how much wool the average sheep will produce each year, how much thread that will make once spun, and how much of different types of cloth can be woven from it. Use this data to calculate the number of sheep needed to provide enough wool for making a given garment or other item of a given size.	M - 2

MATHEMATICS AND PERSONAL FINANCE

| 03M06.A | Prepare a pictograph to show wool exports from various countries of the world. | M - 5 |

| 03M07.A | Translate the above graph on wool exports into a pie graph, showing the top ten producers with all others listed together. | M - 5 |

| 03M08.B | Write a financial analysis of the cost of raising sheep, goats, and cattle. Compare amount of land and feed needed, yield of milk and other salable products, amount of care needed, market value for both buying and selling. Prepare all this data in a statistical format. | M - 2 / A - 2 |

| 03M09.B | Prepare a bar graph or pictograph to show the relative numbers of cows, sheep, goats, pigs, ratites, and/or other types of livestock being raised commercially in your state or local area. | M - 5 |

| 03M10.B | Use the data from your graph to compute the ratio of each type of livestock to all the others and to the total number. Express in terms of proportions and percentages. | M - 1 |

| 03M11.B | Convert the above data into a pie graph. | M - 5 |

| 03M12.B | Investigate the livestock futures market and learn how futures are determined. Plot the statistics for one week on a line graph. | CE - 1 / M - 5 |

| 03M13.B | Prepare graphs of your choice to compare the numbers of various kinds of livestock being raised commercially in various countries, one graph for each type (7-10 countries per graph). | M   5 each |

| 03M14.C | Using data provided by conservation groups or other sources, prepare a pictograph showing known populations of 5-7 endangered species. | M - 5 |

| 03M15.C | Prepare a line graph comparing the apparent population growth for endangered animals under surveillance and census in the wild and the same breeds in captivity in zoos, etc. | M - 5 |

| 03M16.C | Prepare an appropriate graph of your choosing to compare the length of hunting seasons in various states/provinces. | M - 5 |

| 03M17.C | Make a pictograph or bar graph to show relative legal limits for hunting various animals in your state or province. | M - 5 |

| 03M18.C | Make a graph to compare periods of gestation among various animals studied in this unit. | M - 5 |

| 03M19.C | Make a graph to compare average birth weights and growth rates of the animals used for the last activity. | M - 5 |

| 03M20.D | Prepare a bar graph showing production of flax by various nations and regions. | M - 5 |

03M21.D	Make a pie graph showing the above information in terms of percentages of world flax production, showing at least the top five producers.	M - 5
03M22.D	Prepare a bar graph showing the production and/or exportation of cotton by various nations and regions.	M - 5
03M23.D	Make a pie graph showing the above information in terms of percentages of world cotton production, showing at least the top five producers.	M - 5
03M24.D	Prepare a bar graph showing production of silk by various nations and regions.	M - 5
03M25.D	Make a pie graph showing the above information in terms of percentages of world silk production by each of the top five producers.	M - 5
03M26.D	Investigate the fluctuations of cotton, wool, and flax prices on the commodities market of your area over a given time period. Chart this data on a line graph.	CE - 1 M - 5
03M27.D	Using figures from the above activities determine the gross income a farmer could make from any given amount of a specified product at a given time. Work out several of examples of this, and calculate which of the fiber crops would have the best yield and/ or be most profitable in today's market.	M- 1
03M28.	Use data from any of the above graphs to practice making and solving problems using percent, ratio, and proportion,	M - 1 per hour
03M29.	Continue to review basic math as needed.	M - 1 per hour

SCIENCE

03S01.A	Study the scientific innovations and inventions that have changed the lives of sheepherders in various parts of the world. Notice particularly the areas of communication, transportation, and the processing of wool and other products.	ST - 1
03S02.A	Study the construction of a sheepfold now and at different times in history. Discuss how they were built in different times and places and the variety of materials used. Investigate to determine reasons for the differences.	ST - 1
03S03.A	Study the makeup and uses of barbed wire and how it's invention changed the life of shepherds and other livestock owners and workers.	SP - 1
03S04.A	Visit a sheep farm at shearing time to see how the wool is collected and processed.	PA - 1

SCIENCE

03S05.A	If available in your community, attend a sheep-shearing festival or demonstration and learn as much as you can about all the different activities and items featured there. (If your area does not have a significant sheep population to support a shearing festival, check out a local Renaissance Festival or Highland Games Exhibition. Those often feature sheep shearing contests and/or demonstrations.)	CS - 1 PA - 1
03S06.A	Study the various types of shears and other equipment used for shearing sheep. Learn how each is made, how it works, what it does to/ for the sheep or the wool, and any other uses for it.	ST - 1
03S07.A	Study the common diseases of sheep and other hazards to their health.	SB - 1
03S08.A	Study the prevention and treatment of each of the disorders listed above.	SB - 1
03S09.A	Study the mating, gestation, and birthing characteristics of sheep.	SB 1
03S10.A	Study the anatomy and physiology of sheep.	SB - 1
03S11.A	Study the various species of sheep and how they differ from each other. Determine which one you would prefer to raise and why.	SB - 1
03S12.A	Study the predators that commonly like to feed on sheep and can make a shepherd's life miserable.	SB -1
03S13.A	Study the process of cloning, which has been successful on sheep, among other creatures.	SB - 1
03S14.B	Study various breeds of cattle and the attributes of each.	SB - 1
03S15.B	Study the anatomy of the cow, drawing an illustration of the major organs.	SB - 2
03S16.B	Study the common diseases of cattle and the prevention and treatment of each.	SB - 1
03S17.B	Study the anatomy and physiology of the pig.	SB - 1
03S18.B	If appropriate to the remainder of your studies, dissect a fetal pig, available from most science supply houses.	SB - 2
03S19.B	Study the common diseases of pigs and their prevention and treatment.	SB - 1
03S20.B	Study the anatomy and physiology of various kinds of poultry and compare them on some type of chart or report.	SB - 3

SCIENCE

03S21.B	Study the common diseases of poultry and the prevention and treatment of each.	SB - 1
03S22.B	Study the anatomy and physiology of various ratites and compare hem on some type of chart or report.	SB - 1
03S23.B	Study the common diseases of ratites and the prevention and treatment of each.	SB - 1
03S24.B	Tour a meat or poultry packing and/or processing plant and study the various equipment you find in operation there.	ST - 2
03S25.B	Tour a dairy's milk processing plant and learn about the various equipment and procedures being used there.	ST- 2
03S26.B	Tour an egg processing facility.	ST- 1
03S27.B	Study artificial insemination and why many livestock producers prefer it.	SB - 1
03S28.B	Learn about genetics and the process of selective breeding often used in the livestock industry.	SB - 2
03S29.C	Tour behind the scenes of a zoo or wildlife park and learn how various wild animals are bred and their offspring delivered.	SB − 3
03S30.C	Study the anatomy and physiology of the dog and ailments common to it.	SB - 1
03S31.C	Study the anatomy and physiology of cats and ailments common to them.	SB - 1
03S32.C	Study the anatomy and physiology of one example of each other class of mammals.	SB - 5
03S33.C	Study the basic characteristics of reptiles and amphibians and any examples of either that might be of a size and type to be included in 'beasts of the field' as opposed to those the Bible refers to as 'creeping things'.	SB - 2
03S34.C	If you feel the need for and are not morally opposed to animal dissections, you may wish to do some in connection with this unit. The most common mammals available for dissection are cats and fetal pigs, which may be ordered from any of several different school supply houses, complete with all directions and supplies needed.	SB - 2 each
03S35.C	Instead of buying animals to dissect, you may want to use game animals you plan to dress for eating. Simply open up the internal organs and investigate them before separating the body parts for carving and processing or storing.	SB - 2 each

SCIENCE

03S36.C   Another way to learn about dissections is to watch a dissection   SB - 2
            video from one of the companies that sells them (see Resource   each
            Guide for names and addresses).

03S37.C   Instead of the biology activities in this and the previous mini-   SB - 1
            unit, you may take a full course in zoology or animal biology   credit
            using materials from the resource guide.

03S38.C   Study the life-style, habitat, feeding habits, general characteristics   SB - 2
            and mating habits of wildlife commonly hunted in
            your area.

03S39.C   Study the animals on the endangered species list of your local   SB - 3
            zoo or wildlife conservation agency. Learn where each is found
            in the wild and whatever you can about their habitats,
            characteristics, feeding habits and mating rituals. Discuss with a
            knowledgeable adult what this information tells you about how
            the animal became endangered and how we can best help
            increase its numbers.

03S40.C   Study the animal taxonomy of Linnaeus, dividing each animal   SB - 3
            into its appropriate phylum, class, genus and species. Note
            those phyla and classes whose members could rightly bear
            the designation as beasts of the field" and the categories into
            which they are grouped.

03S41.C   Make some type of poster, bulletin board, or other visual display   SB - 3
            showing all animal phyla and one representative sample
            of each using either pictures or some type of 3-D models.

03S42.C   Compare the taxonomy above with that found in Deuteronomy   SB - 3
            14. Designate each Biblical animal from the lists you made in
            the Bible and Christian Character section into a place in
            each system.

03S43.D   Study wool production from sheep to finished garment and   SP - 3
            prepare a flow chart to illustrate it.

03S44.D   Study cotton farming and the production of cotton fabric. Prepare   PA - 1
            a poster or flow chart tracing cotton from plant to fabric   SP - 2
            as you did for wool in #03S43.

03S45. D   Observe planting, cultivation, harvesting, and baling of cotton   PA - 1 per
            and learn how and where it grows best.   hour

03S46.D   Tour a cotton gin, observe the processes, ask questions and   ST   -2
            take notes.

03S47.D   Prepare a poster or flowchart to illustrate the production of   SP - 3
            linen from plant to fabric as you did in activity #03S43 and
            #03544.

03S48.D   Tour a flax farm and/or talk to a farmer about how flax is   PA - 2
            grown and harvested.

SCIENCE

03S49.D	Draw a poster or flow chart to show the processes used in the production of silk, beginning with the hatching of the larvae and ending with silk cloth.	SP - 2 SB - 1
03S50.D	Examine the chemical and physical properties of various fabrics by subjecting each to moisture, fire, boiling, temperature extremes, and chemicals like bleach. Pull out a few fibers and examine them under a microscope. Record results and compare.	SC - 4
03S51.D	Study various fabrics with regard to use-related properties such as density, weight, tightness of weave, warmth, sheen, etc., to determine what fabrics are best suited for what purposes.	SP - 2
03S52.D	Study or review the basics of organic chemistry as it relates to the various natural and/or man-made fibers used for textiles.	SC - 2
03S53.D	Investigate and report on how various synthetic fabrics are made.	SC - 2
03S54.D	Study and catalog the flammability of various fabrics and fabric finishes.	SC - 1
03S55.D	Study the processes used to make fabrics flame retardant, using using *The 'New' Way Things Work* or howstuffworks.com.	SC- 1
03S56.D	Study the various machinery used in the processing of fabrics and learn how each operates, using *The 'New' Way Things Work* or howstuffworks.com.	SP- 2
03S57.D	Tour a textile plant and learn the various processes and equipment involved in creating yarn, fabric, and completed garments.	SP- 3

HEALTH AND PHYSICAL FITNESS

03H01.A	Study health hazards that might be commonly associated with sheep raising.	HE - 1
03H02.A	Study the health benefits of the outdoor life of a shepherd.	HE - 1
03H03.A	Study the basic health needs of mankind as those things which God, our Good Shepherd, provides for His children.	HE - 1
03H04.A	Compare the bedside manner of a good doctor to that of a kind shepherd caring for a sick or injured sheep.	CS - 1
03H05.B	Study the relative nutrient and fat content of meat from various of livestock.	FN - 1
03H06.B	Study the health effects to the end consumer of the hormones often used in commercial meat production.	HE - 1
03H07.B	Study the advantages and disadvantages of meat in the diet.	FN 1

HEALTH AND PHYSICAL FITNESS

03H08.B   Study trichinosis and other diseases people can get from   HE- I
improperly processed meat.

03H09.B   Study cholesterol, which comes only from meat fat, and it's   FN - 1
hazards and benefits for the human body.

03H10.B   Learn about diseases of cattle and other livestock that can be   HE - 1
passed to humans through consuming meat or milk. Explore
how your country attempts to control each of these and the
recommended treatment for those who do contract them.

03H11.C   Study rabies, which can be contracted only through contact   HE - 2
with an infected animal. Learn about the effects of the disease
on humans and how it is treated.

03H12.C   Study cat scratch fever and its treatment.   HE - 1

03H13.C   Study rabbit fever and learn how it is contracted, diagnosed   HE - 1
and treated.

03H14.C   Study bubonic plague, which was believed to have been caused   HE - 1
by cats. Learn the real cause and why is it is very rare today.

03H15.C   Study fleas, licks, lice, mites, and other parasites humans can   HE - 2
get from common companion animals or wildlife. Learn about
their life cycles and how to eradicate each type before and
after the human host has been infested.

03H16.D   Study dermatitis and other conditions that might occur in   HE - 1
reaction to contact with certain fabrics by an allergic person.

03H17.D   Study the skin and proper care of it, including the treatment   HE - 1
of rashes and/or itching such as could be caused by contact
with certain fabrics.

03H18.D   Learn about the various chemical finishes sometimes used in   Sc - 1
clothing and the effects each may have on conditions of the
skin.

03H19.D   Learn about different weights and weaves of fabrics and which   CC - 1
ones offer more protection from various kinds of weather.

PRACTICAL ARTS

03P01.A   Learn to properly brush and groom sheep.   PA - 1

03P02.A   Learn to work with and command a sheep dog in actually herding   PA - 3
the sheep.

03P03.A   Try your hand at shearing one entire sheep.   PA- 1

PRACTICAL ARTS

03P04.A	Work on a sheep farm as an employee or a volunteer to learn all aspects of raising and caring for sheep.	PA- 1 per hour up to 20
03P05.A	Instead of learning to care for someone else's sheep, raise one of your own, beginning as soon after birth as possible and using 4-H materials to help you.	PA- 25+
03P06.A	Prepare a flannelgraph or other visual aid to teach a young child about Jesus as the Good Shepherd.	TE - 2
03P07.A	Spend several hours working or observing on a sheep farm to learn as much as you can about the nature of sheep. Apply that knowledge for a better understanding of what it means for us to be the "sheep" of God's pasture and similar Scripture references.	SB - 5 B - 1
03P08.B	Spend several hours over the period of a week observing and/or working with goats, learning as much as you can about their nature. Apply this knowledge to help you understand Christ's reference to unbelievers as 'goats' in Matthew 25.	SB - 5 B - 1
03P09.B	Tour a cattle ranch or other livestock- raising facility.	PA - 2
03P10.B	Attend the birth of a calf, lamb or other livestock offspring.	SB - 3
03P11.B	Tour a dairy farm and learn to milk a cow and/or goat.	PA- 1
03P12.B	Learn and use the processes by which one can pasteurize milk at home.	FN - 1
03P13.B	Observe and/or work on a ratite or poultry farm, learning the procedures of caring for the animals and the various equipment used to do it.	PA - 3 SP - 3
03P14.B	Learn to clean and dress freshly-killed chicken or other poultry.	FN - 2
03P15.B	Learn and practice safe meat handling techniques.	FN - 2
03P16.B	Breed, raise and sell chickens, rabbits or other small livestock.	PA- 25 each type
03P17.B	Learn to properly butcher and/or carve beef and pork roasts and other meats.	FN - 1
03P18.C	If you live in an area where it seems needed or appropriate and have a family who approves, take a licensed hunter safety course.	1/2 credit in Hunter Safety
03P19.C	If you and your family are so inclined, learn to hunt one or more types of wildlife.	RE - 5
03P20.C	Learn to clean and dress any wildlife you or members of your family hunt.	FN - 3

PRACTICAL ARTS

03P21. C   Volunteer to work with a wildlife rescue team and learn how they restore abandoned wild babies or injured wildlife to a healthy life in the wild.   SE - 1 per hour

03P22.C   Volunteer at a humane shelter to exercise, feed or otherwise care for the various domesticated animals brought in there.   RE 1 per hour

03P23.C   Work or volunteer in a veterinary clinic, learning to care for and groom animals.   SB - 1 per hour

03P24.C   Volunteer to work at the zoo, helping with baby animals in its nursery, helping care for sick or injured animals, or just tending to the daily needs of any of the animals. Take advantage of this opportunity to learn as much as you can about a wide variety of animals, especially those not native to your country.   SB - 1 per hour

03P25.D   Collect and mount samples of various types of fabrics. Label each with name, fiber content, origin, recommended uses, and care needed.   CC - 3

03P26.D   Visit a fabric store and list all the fabrics they carry that are made wholly or in part from wool, flax, or cotton. Note the differences and similarities of each type of related fabrics. Ask for swatches or small samples of all the different types available.   CC - 2

03P27.D   Visit a clothing store to see the variety of fabrics used for different types of clothing. Compare the texture and weight of natural and synthetic fibers and choose those for different uses. Compare prices of natural garments, synthetics and blends, and woven fabrics to knits. Record in some way for FABRICS notebook.   CC - 3

03P28.D   Learn the appropriate fabrics for various uses and make pages in your FABRICS booklet to show that, using the samples you collected at the fabric store and pictures of garments or other things that could appropriately be made from each. Show only one fabric per page.   CC - 3

03P29.D   Become competent in doing your family's laundry, sorting by color and fabric type and learning to care for each fabric needs.   HM - 1

03P30. D   Use fabrics of various weights and textures to make a texture ball for an infant or toddler. Cut several swatches into circles ovals, or hexagons of uniform size sew them together in such a pattern as to make a ball, positioning fabrics of very different textures together. Before sewing the last seam, fill the ball with soft cotton or polyester quilt batting.   CR - 2

03P31.D   Plan a wardrobe for each season for a person living a certain life-style in a particular climate.   CC - 2

03P32.   If you don't already know how to create and use a computer database, you may wish to learn in this mini-unit so you can use the skill in later units of this study.   CO - 6

PRACTICAL ARTS

| 03P33. | Create and maintain a database to assist you as appropriate in this mini-unit. | CO - 2+ |

| 03P34. | Type all written work with a typewriter or word processor. If you do not know how to type, now is the time to learn. | BE - 1 per 4 pages |

| 03P35. | If needed, take a class, follow a computerized, written or video tutorial, or a correspondence course in typing, keyboarding, and/or word processing. | 1/2 credit in Typing or Keyboarding |

| 03P36. | Frame and mat one or more of the pictures or posters you drew or created in the Decorative and Performing Arts section of this mini-unit. | CR - 2 each |

| 03P37. | Make your own costumes for any performances you chose to do in the Decorative and Performing Arts section of this mini-unit or plays you wrote in the Composition section. | CC - 5 + each |

| 03P38. | Create a computer website to display what you have learned in this unit. | CO - 3+ |

DECORATIVE AND PERFORMING ARTS

| 03A01.A | Learn to sing any of the many musical versions of Psalm 23. | VM - 3 |

| 03A02.A | Set one or more of the other Psalms studied in this unit to original tunes. | MC - 5 |

| 03A03.A | Learn to sing well enough to perform in public "Savior, Like a Shepherd Lead Us", and/or other Christian songs about Jesus as the Shepherd. | VM - 3 each |

| 03A04.A | Learn to play any or all of the above songs on a musical instrument. | IM - 3 each |

| 03A05.A | Make a poster or plaque of Psalm 23 using your best calligraphy and original illustrations. | VA - 2 |

| 03A06.A | Draw or paint your own illustration of one of the Psalms of David. | VA - 1+ each |

| 03A07.A | Draw or paint a pastoral scene showing sheep and the shepherd. | VA - 2 |

| 03A08.B | Tour an art exhibit and look for paintings of sheep, cattle, or other livestock in pastures or farm scenes. Study each work and its artist. Compare time periods and styles. | AA - 2 |

| 03A09.B | Draw or paint a farm or ranch scene, showing one or more types of livestock. | VA - 2 |

| 03A10.B | Find and listen to a variety of songs about sheep, shepherds, cowboys or other elements of the livestock industry. Compare styles and messages. | MA- 2+ |

DECORATIVE AND PERFORMING ARTS

03A11.B	Learn to sing some of the old cowboy songs from the days of open ranges, roundups, and cattle drives.	VM - 2 each
03A12.B	Draw a series of 4-6 cartoons to tell a story or teach a lesson about the livestock industry.	VA - 5+
03A13.B	From the book *How to Draw Animals* or a similar volume, practice until you can draw well a variety of animals that would be considered livestock.	VA- 3+
03A14.C	Use any good art instruction book to learn to draw well a variety of wildlife.	VA - 3+
03A15.C	Draw a mural of a zoo, circus, jungle, savannah or other locale featuring several different types of wildlife in natural or contrived environments.	VA - 3
03A16.C	Learn to play "Baby Elephant Walk," the theme to "Born Free," any of the music from "The Lion King", and/or another tune relating to the animals in this mini-unit.	IM - 3 each
03A17.C	Tour a museum or gallery exhibit of wildlife paintings and/or sketches.	AA- 2
03A18. C	Instead of a drawing, create a collage of varied species of wildlife, using your creative talent to arrange the cutouts in an attractive pattern. Using your best calligraphy or careful block lettering, entitle it "The Beasts of the Field."	VA - 2
03A19.D	Glue or sew together swatches, scraps, and samples of various fabrics to make a picture or collage.	VA - 2+
03A20.D	Paint pictures of your choice on velvet or similar fabric. Frame and hang.	VA - 4
03A21.D	Create your own designs to decorate T-shirts or other clothing.	VA- 2
03A22.D	Tour an exhibit of fabric arts and notice the varied types and styles of work. Discuss with a parent.	AA 2
03A23.D	Study and learn to make molas.	CR - 3
03A24.	Draw pictures of any field trips you took in this mini-unit.	VA- 1+ ea
03A25.	Use drawing, painting and graphic arts to create displays and make posters as called for in this study.	VA - 1 ea.
03A26.	Illustrate one or more of the poems you studied or memorized for this unit.	VA - 1 ea.
03A27.	Set one or more of this unit's poems to music, using an original or existing tune.	VA 1 ea.
03A28.	Set one or more of the Scripture verses in this unit to music, using a tune you wrote for the purpose.	MC - 5 ea.

UNIT 4

She is like merchant ships; she brings her food from afar.
Proverbs 31:14

Overview

This verse extols the virtues of careful shopping and looking for quality in purchasing. The issue is not so much they she goes far away to get her food, but that she will if necessary to get the best value. In essence, she is a bargain hunter and will go to extra trouble to find good deals on the things her family needs.

In this unit, you will learn how to shop for food and what type of products provide the best values. You will also study the food industry, with emphasis on how food is procured and distributed. This will include lessons in supply and demand, as well as other factors that influence price.

In addition to learning these traits and concepts, this unit introduces you to travel, trade and exploration, a study that will encompass all time periods, areas of the world, and major modes of transportation. This will, of course, include an investigation of the time period commonly known as the Age of Exploration and the explorers who made major discoveries during and leading up to that time.

The emphasis on ocean travel will also serve as an introduction to the world of oceans and ocean life. We have also chosen this unit on travel to highlight animal and bird migrations, which will introduce a study of birds as a whole. Map reading and writing skills have been included here as well.

Mini-Units

Mini-Units contained in this unit are:

    A. Food Production and Distribution

    B. Trade, Travel and Transportation

    C. The Age of Exploration

    D. Oceans and Ocean Life

Each thematic mini-unit is described and designated with a letter of the alphabet in the following paragraphs. Individual activities designed for use in one particular mini-unit will be marked with those letters. (For further help with this, please refer to the explanation of mini-units in the Guidelines section of this unit study guide.)

Mini-Units

A. Food Production and Distribution

In this unit, you will learn about the commercial production and distribution of food. This is not the elementary concept of "where food comes from" but a more thorough look at how it gets from one place to the other. This will include the origins and cultivation of various foods, concentrating on the animal or plant origins, its earliest known uses, and the geographic regions in which each grows most plentifully. You will investigate the uses of various herbs and spices in a variety of ethnic foods and reasons for each developing where it did.

You will then examine the processes by which various foods are harvested, processed, packaged and shipped by commercial operations. This will be accomplished through reading, studying web sites, interviews with those in this field, and the touring of such facilities. You will compare various methods of commercial processing and storage on the basis of both health and economic considerations. You will look at food additives and the purposes they serve, as well as the negative side-effects some of them have.

This unit will also allow you to enter into the world of marketplace economics and distribution. Here you will learn about supply and demand and the natural market fluctuations that causes. You will examine various programs that attempt to regulate or control prices of food items, thus doing away with the true free enterprise system. This will be discussed more thoroughly in a later unit, so it will not be studied extensively here.

The final aspect of this unit is the part of the consumer in the process of food distribution. You will learn how you can become a knowledgeable and careful food shopper through price comparison, brand name flexibility, and other "tricks of the trade". You will also learn what you, the consumer, can do to influence the prices of the products you buy. You will learn about different methods of preservation and storage of large quantities of food in the home, thereby enabling you to stock up when prices are best.

B. Trade, Travel and Transportation

In this unit, you will look more closely than in Unit One at the lives and travels of Old Testament patriarchs as well as the New Testament apostles and missionaries. You will also study ancient seafarers, early native peoples of the Western Hemisphere, nomads throughout history, and other important travelers, ending with the astronauts of the twentieth century.

This mini-unit includes a look at common modes of travel throughout history and around the world, beginning with animals commonly ridden or used as beasts of burden. As this is also covered in the mini-unit on livestock in unit 3, there will be some overlap with it. As usual in these cases, use the activities listed birth places in whichever unit you prefer. Do not count the same thing twice.

You will examine how various man-made modes of transportation came into being and how they operate. This will include many unusual, localized forms of transportation as well as those that are more in the mainstream. You will study the history of travel and the equipment used by modern-day pilots of sea and air.

To facilitate your own travel and its study, you will learn the basics of cartography, map reading, and world geography, including an investigation of other peoples and cultures. This is the unit in which you should begin to study a second language, if you wish to do so. Immigration and customs laws will also enter the picture here in relation to travel across national boundaries. This emphasis on travel skills will also include learning to use the Internet for making travel plans, providing maps of your route, and enjoying virtual travel to places you may never actually get to go.

Mini-Units

You will investigate the literature, art, and music of a wide variety of countries, learning about their culture from their writings and artistic expressions. Among American and British authors, your reading for this mini-unit will center on works by writers who wrote extensively about other parts of the world to which they had traveled or about travel itself. These will include both true accounts of travels and novels featuring travel by such authors as Jack London, Robert Louis Stevenson, Thor Heyerdahl, Ernest Hemmingway, and James A. Michener.

You will study the nomadic life and the types of people who live it. Particular examples of this include the Ishmaelites and the Bedouins of ancient history and some original American peoples (Native Americans). Others to be studied might be the gypsies of Europe and a wide variety of refugees and displaced persons throughout history who have been forced to travel through harsh living conditions in their homelands.

Though the Crusades involved much travel and led to many of the later explorations, they will not be covered here. The relative sizes of mini-units has led us to put it in the section on the Middle Ages instead. If you prefer to study them with this unit, please feel free to do so.

C: The Age of Exploration

This mini-unit centers on the time period known as the Age of Exploration, which started in close conjunction with the Renaissance and Reformation. However, you will study important explorers of earlier times as well, especially those whose discoveries led to further explorations with highly significant results. You will then study all later Explorers who discovered new worlds or routes to old ones, as well as those who made other important discoveries or conquests in "the new world" or the "new frontier" of space. In the area of explorers, we have included the Vikings and Marco Polo, who preceded the Age of Exploration but did much to set the stage for it.

Your literature will include mythology and stories from early civilizations that sparked the imagination and led people to seek adventure in new lands. We have especially concentrated on Norse, Anglo-Saxon, and other nomadic or seafaring cultures, leaving the Greeks and Romans for the units specifically devoted to their cultures.

As this is written in the United States, by someone from there, this section and most of the history after this time period, centers on North America. This is not out of any sense of this continent being more important than others, but rather in the interest of time and effort. Most students using this are North American, so it seems only natural that they should study their own history in more depth than any other. Therefore, this is where we have devoted the bulk of our time and space. Families in other countries are encouraged to add their own nations' history as appropriate, either to supplement or replace this.

D. Oceans and Ocean Life

As most of the explorers traveled the oceans to accomplish their discoveries, it seems logical to study oceans in this unit. For that reason, this mini-unit is devoted to the study of water, sea life, and the ocean floor. You will learn about tectonic plates, and other undersea formations and how they affect the climate of the world. You will study the scientific causes of tides and their effect on climate and weather.

One basic part of this unit is to study about the various oceans of the world, locating each of them on maps or globes. We will take a look at ocean navigation and the importance of ocean travel to international trade, overlapping slightly into our study of ocean-going exploration in mini-unit C. This will include a study of various ocean-going vessels and the commerce they allow, which meshes well and might overlap with mini-unit B on travel.

Mini-Units

A unit on oceans would be incomplete without a study of the water itself and the organisms that live in it. These range from tiny algae and protozoans to the giant marine mammals which are often considered fish by many people. We will look at the biological makeup and life cycles of these creatures and their significance in relation to man. This will include at least a cursory look at the fishing, shrimping and general seafood industry. Coral, sponges and similar creatures will be investigated with relation to the formations they create and leave for others to enjoy.

BIBLE AND CHRISTIAN CHARACTER

04B01.A	Study God's miraculous provision of food in Luke 9:10 -17.	B-1
04B02.A	Study Mark 8:1-9 and determine if you believe this is the same incident or a different one. Give reasons for your answer.	B-1
04B03.A	Study Matthew 14:14-21 and compare it to the two passages above.	B-1
04B04.A	Study God's miraculous provision of food for the prophet Elijah as told in 1 Kings 17:1-16.	B-1
04B05.A	Study Yahweh's (Jehovah's) provision of manna for the children of Israel during the Exodus.	B-1
04B06.B	Read in Genesis 12-14 of the travels of Abram (Abraham).	B-1
04B07.B	Study the travels of Jacob to and from his father's homeland in Genesis 28 and 31.	B-2
04B08.B	Study the account of Jacob's ladder in Genesis 28, and discuss it with a parent or other adult.	B-1
04B09.B	Study the exile of God's people as told in the books of Daniel and Esther and their return from it in Ezra and Nehemiah.	B-6
04B10.B	Study the travels of the apostle Paul as told in the book of Acts.	B-6
04B11.B	Use a concordance to find and study all other Biblical references to travel.	B-3
04B12.C	Look up and study all Scripture references to the Phoenicians, probably the first nation to send out extensive explorations.	B-2
04B13.C	Read and memorize Psalm 107:23-30.	B-3
04B14.C	Study Bible references to the seafaring towns of Tyre and Sidon.	B-3
04B15.C	Look up in concordance and study in Bible all references to ships.	B-5
04B16.C	Look up and study all Biblical references to seafaring or seafarers.	B-2

BIBLE AND CHRISTIAN CHARACTER

04B17.D	Study the book of Jonah in which the Lord God used the sea, waves and a marine creature to discipline one of His servants.	B-3
04B18.D	Study the event recounted in Matthew 8 in which the Lord Jesus exercised his authority over the wind and the waves. Notice the response of his disciples to this revelation of his power.	B-1
04519.D	Study Psalm 65, which emphasizes this power over the waves, and all of Creation.	B-2
04B20.D	Study Psalm 107: 23 - 32, for yet another account of God's power over the forces of the sea (meaning oceans and similar large bodies of water.)	B-1
04B21.D	Read the description of "Leviathan" from Job 41, and determine what name we now use for this marine animal.	B-1
04B22.D	Use a concordance to look up and study all other Scripture passages that refer to 'seas" or 'the sea'.	B-3
04B23.	Memorize one or more of the passages studied in the mini-unit.	5-1 per 3 verses
04B24.	Read through the book of Proverbs each month, reading the chapter to coincide with each date.	B-10 per month
04B25.	Continue reading through the Bible at a rate of 1-5 chapters per day. If you use *The Daily Bible* or some other version designed specifically for that purpose, their daily readings will take you through the entire Bible in one year. You may follow a pattern of your own at a different rate if you like. Using a chronologically arranged Bible offers the added benefit of putting your reading in perspective as to time frame.	B-1 CREDIT When completed No partial credit
04B26.	Continue to keep your prayer journal, listing each day (or as the Lord brings to mind) prayer requests, needs in your spiritual life and things God is teaching you. Continue this throughout all units.	B-2 per week

CULTURAL STUDIES

04C01.A	Study the grocery industry and how they decide which items to sell and how those items are acquired, shipped and sold.	CE-2
04C02.A	Interview members of several different food co-ops to better understand how they operate, what makes each one unique, and the advantages and disadvantages of being in one.	CE-1
04C03.A	Investigate a warehouse grocery chain and see how they differ and resemble both a coop and a retail store.	CE-1

CULTURAL STUDIES

04C04.A	Contact your local grange or farmers' cooperative and see how uniting for the common good benefits the food producer and self-sufficient family farm as well as the consumer. Investigate the people they serve, the products they carry, and the services they offer.	CE-2
04C05.A	Contact Archer-Daniels-Midland (ADM), Beatrice, or another food conglomerate to learn how they operate and how their operation has impacted the production and availability of food to the general public.	CE-1
04C06.A	While inventorying the food items in your kitchen, as suggested in the Practical Arts section of this mini-unit, read the product labels to learn where each product originated. List on a chart and mark on a world map each country of origin.	G-1
04C07.A	Use a *World Almanac* or encyclopedia to study the country from which each of the food items in your pantry originated.	G- 1 each
04C08.A	Research the food items on your inventory list to find what other countries produce and/or export significant quantities of each these items or any of their components. Mark each on a map, using the same designation as above.	G-3
04C09.A	Using the *World Almanac* or similar resource, look up and study the countries on the list in the previous activity.	G- 1 each
04C10.A	Go through cookbooks and find dishes that are common to each of the countries from which the spices you have are exported. Study the common ingredients and learn which ones grow well in which countries.	CS-2 G-1
04C11.A	Study the U. S. Food and Drug Administration and/or similar agencies in other countries and how they regulate the sale and distribution of food.	CG-1
04C12.A	Study the laws of your country that relate to food processing or packaging.	CL-2
04C13.A	Study the role of the United States Department of Agriculture (or its equivalent in your country) in the regulation of food products.	CG-1
04C14.A	Study any laws or regulations your state may have concerning food products coming into it from other areas.	CL-1
04C15.A	Play the "Spices of the World" game and memorize the sources of the common spices as introduced in that game.	G-1 per time 10 MAX.
04C16.A	Use periodicals, political treatises, info from the National Archives, or history textbooks to learn about the use of food as a weapon of war and/or a tool of foreign policy throughout history.	CG-2 H-2

CULTURAL STUDIES

04C17.A	Study the ministry of Feed the Children, Second Harvest, and other groups devoted to providing food for hungry people from the leftovers or castoffs of grocery stores and other businesses.	CS-2
04C18.B	Using your choice of research materials, trace the history of trade and transport of goods from the earliest Bible times until today. Record major developments in each area on some type of chart, poster or report. Note the part played by traders in the early spread of Christianity.	H-5
04C19.B	Use *Baker's Bible Atlas* and other maps to trace all of the Biblical journeys studied in the Bible and Christian Character section of this mini-unit. Compare the two versions of the map, identifying both current and ancient names of each city, country, and other political entity or geographic feature traversed or passed on these travels.	B-1 each journey G-1 each journey
04C20.B	Use any available resources to study each city or area included on any of the Biblical travels in this mini-unit, whether or not it still exists. For each city, learn: history of its founding, all past names, country in which located, current form of government, current economic system, and special points of interest.	G-1 each
04C21.B	Study thoroughly the sections in *Baker's Bible Atlas* and its study guide that relate to any areas involved in the Biblical travels of this mini-unit. Study maps and globes from various periods of history to see what other names various nations have used and how their borders have changed.	G-4
04C22.B	Learn about latitude, longitude, and meridians and how to read them on a map or globe.	G-1
04C23.B	Study the continents of the world and what countries are located on each by playing the Aristoplay game "Where in the World?"	G-2 ea. time 28 MAX.
04C24.B	Play Global Pursuit, On Assignment, or other National Geographic board games to increase your knowledge of geography.	G-2 each time Max. of 20 times per game
04C25.B	Play the computer game "Where in the World is Carmen San Diego?"	G-2 each time Max. of 20 times
04C26.B	Study the role of consulates and embassies in international relations and travel. If possible, visit a consular office or embassy and discuss with employees how they promote travel to and from that country and help those traveling to your country from there. If you cannot visit, try a virtual tour online.	CG-3
04C27.B	Study your country's immigration service and the laws, regulations, and policies under which it works. If possible, tour or take a virtual tour online. (These are often located in major airports or may be close to the consulate or embassy.)	CG-2
04C28.B	Study patterns of immigration in your nation's history, charting trends in new residents from specific countries.	H-3

CULTURAL STUDIES

| 04C29.B | Tour a customs office (located at major seaports, airports, and national borders) to learn about your country's import and export laws, quotas, tariffs, and duties. | CG-2 |

| 04C30.B | Interview an importer/exporter about the daily operation of the business, applicable laws and regulations and common problems relating to international trade. | CE-2 |

| 04C31.B | Use Usborne's *Invention and Discovery* or some similar book to study the history of transportation and learn when various modes of it were invented and/or perfected. Prepare timeline entries to show this data. | H-2 |

| 04C32.B | Research the highway system of your country, including its history, the agencies and regulations governing it, and the economics of its operation. | H-1 CS-1 |

| 04C33.B | Study the history and impact (economic and social) of the railroad in your country. | CS-1 H-1 |

| 04C34.B | Study laws and agencies that regulate air travel within, into and out of your country. | CL-1 H-1 |

| 04C35.B | Tour a major airport and study the jobs of various workers there, including air traffic controllers and other regulatory personnel. | CL-1 |

| 04C36.B | Study ancient and modern trade routes through various parts of the world and trace them on map. As you study explorers later in this unit, bear in mind that many of them undertook their travels to broaden these trade routes or find new ones. | CS-2 |

| 04C37.C | Use *Baker's Bible Atlas* and its study guide to learn about the culture and explorations of the Phoenicians, Bible time explorers. | H-2 |

| 04C38.C | Study the travels of the Vikings and mark the primary routes they used and major discoveries made by them on a map. | H-1 |

| 04C39.C | Study the lives of Eric the Red, Leif the Lucky, and other Viking explorers using books recommended in the Reading and Literature section or any other resources. | H-3 |

| 04C40.C | Use any of the books from the Reading and Literature section to study the culture and lifestyle of the Vikings. | H-4 |

| 04C41.C | Use encyclopedias or similar resources to study the countries of Scandinavia, once the homeland of the Vikings. | H-5 |

| 04C42.C | Using *Streams of Civilization* or other resources, study Marco Polo, Prince Philip, and other pre-Columbian European explorers who found new lands or new routes to known ones while searching for more efficient trade routes. | G-5 |

CULTURAL STUDIES

04C43.C	Use encyclopedias or similar resources to study all countries through which Marco Polo traveled, including his homeland.	H-1 each
04C44.C	On a map or globe, trace all four voyages of Columbus and identify all the places where his ships landed with both their ancient and current names.	G-1 each
04C45.C	Study all original documents contained in the Jackdaws portfolio on Christopher Columbus and compare them with various biographies of the man, using those in the Reading and Literature section or others.	G-1
04C46.C	Watch a video of the movie *1492*, and compare it to Columbus' life as told in his biography and/or original writings.	H-5
04C47.C	Study the voyages of circumnavigation undertaken by Magellan, Cook, and Drake using some or all of the suggested books from the next section or other resources of your choice.	H-3
04C48.C	Use *Atlas of North American Exploration* or a similar reference to trace the routes of all the explorers discussed in the books used in this mini-unit.	H-5
04C49.C	Study the first tape of *America: The First 350 Years*, which deals with the early explorations of the New World.	G-1 H-1
04C50.C	Study and complete the activities in the Good Apple workbook *Explorers.*	H-2
04C51.C	Read all appropriate chapters in *Streams of Civilization* for an overview of the lives and travels of all major figures of what was known as the Age of Exploration.	H-5
04C52.C	Use materials referenced here or others to investigate the political situation in Europe during the Age of Exploration and how it impacted explorers and their explorations.	H-2
04C53.C	Study the native country and sponsoring nation of each explorer in the unit.	H-1
04C54.D	Locate on a map or globe, each of the world's oceans. Outline their coasts with a marker, noticing that they all connect to each other at one or more places.	G-1 each
04C55.D	In an encyclopedia or other synoptic reference, study each of the oceans of the world, comparing and contrasting them on some type of chart or poster.	G-1
04C56.D	Identify and mark on a world map, all gulfs, seas, sounds, and other bodies of open, salt water smaller than oceans.	G-1
04C57.D	Using a synoptic reference, study each of the maritime bodies of water other than oceans, listed in the previous activities.	G-1

CULTURAL STUDIES

04C58.D	Investigate the economics of commercial fishing and seafood industry in your state or province and your nation as a whole.	G-1 each
04C59.D	Study the laws affecting the maritime shipping industry in your country and the international treaties regarding it.	CE-1
04C60.D	From a synoptic reference, study the history of the merchant marine industry in your country and the world, paying special attention to ways in which it has changed and improved the ability to ship goods quickly and efficiently.	CL-2
04C61.D	Investigate the degree to which your country's economy depends on the availability of efficient, low-cost maritime shipping.	H-2
04C62.D	From appropriate books in the Reading and Literature section and/or other chosen materials, learn about the part of the world once known as the Barbary Coast, haven for pirates who preyed on merchant ships of Europe and the Americas.	CE-2
04C63.D	Tour a merchant ship, fully loaded and ready to sail. Interview its captain and/or crew to learn about life on board and the ports of call to which it is going.	H-1 G-1
04C64.D	Tour a major seaport facility, paying careful attention to the number of ships there and their countries of registry and the type of cargo each is carrying.	H-1 CG-1
04C65.D	Tour a navy or Coast Guard vessel. Talk to one or more crew-men about their individual jobs and their life aboard ship.	CE-2 Or CS-2
04C66.D	Study the history of the maritime services of the United States (Navy, Marines, and Coast Guard), and the duties of each. (Those in other countries may study their own marine services if preferred.)	CS-2
04C67.D	Study historical accounts of the sinking of the Titanic and determine all possible ways that it could have been prevented..	CS-2
04C68.D	Tour a luxury liner, examining amenities offered at the various cabin levels. If you cannot take a physical tour, take a virtual one on the website of any major cruise line.	CS-2
04C69.D	Accompany your parents or another adult on a cruise with at least three ports of call. Follow your route on a map, marking it appropriately. In each port, take a sight-seeing excursion to learn more about the areas to which you travel. Attend all onboard video or lecture sessions dealing with the various ports of call and what is available to do there.	Parents Discretion Depending on how much you learn
04C70.	Use encyclopedias or other synoptic references to study all countries mentioned in this mini-unit.	H-2
04C71.	Use books listed elsewhere in this mini-unit, Usborne's *World History Dates, The Kingfisher History Encyclopedia,* or any other reference books to make timeline entries for all people, movements, and/or events you've studied in this mini-unit.	G-1 each

CULTURAL STUDIES

04C72.   Make timeline entries for major events in the lives of each of the authors whose works were read in this mini-unit.   VA-1 each / H- 1each

04C73.   Make timeline entries for other famous people who lived in the time period being studied.   VA-1 each / H-1 each

04C74.   Make timeline entries for all inventions and/or discoveries studied in this mini-unit and major events in the lives of their inventors.   VA-1 each / H-1 each

04C75.   Make timeline cards for all major events and/or people mentioned in books read or studied in this mini-unit but not included elsewhere.   VA-1 each / H- 1each

04C76.   Locate on a map or globe all countries studied or mentioned in this mini-unit.   G-1

04C77.   Locate on a map and study the geography of all states, cities and/or municipalities studied in this mini-unit.   G-1

04C78.   Locate on the U. S. map any or all states studied in this mini-unit.   G-1

04C79.   Study the homeland of each author, inventor, or artist whose works were used or studied in this mini-unit.   G-1 each

04C80.   Prepare a timeline card for each person, culture, and event studied in this unit.   VA-1 each / H-1 each

READING AND LITERATURE

04R01.A   Read pamphlets on various brands and forms of foods to determine which are best for your family.   FN-2

04R02.A   Read cookbooks from different countries to find recipes for using and/or preparing foods native to each country.   FN-2 / CS-2

04R03.A   Read novels in which the growing of food crops or other aspects of food production figure prominently.   L-5

04R04.A   Memorize 20 - 25 lines of poetry glorifying some type of food.   L-5

04R05.A   Read 3-5 articles each in several periodicals devoted to the food industry. (You can find out about these by asking people in that profession.) Discuss or present the information in these with/for your parents.   FN-2

04R06.A   Read novels centered in one of the countries from which foods your family eats originate as listed by you in this mini-unit's Cultural Studies section.   L-5 each

READING AND LITERATURE

04R07.A	Read biographies of Cyrus McCormick and other inventors whose inventions helped to make commercial food production, processing, preservation and distribution safer and/or more efficient. (You can find their names in Usborne's *Invention and Discovery* and/or similar resources.)	H-5 each
04R08.A	Read books relating to the history of food production and commercial distribution.	H-5 each
04R09.A	Read one or more how-to books on home food preservation.	FN-5 each
04R10.B	Memorize 80 - 100 lines of poetry about some form of travel.	L-20
04R11.B	Read a variety of poetry (200-300 lines) from different parts of the world. Compare style and content.	L-3
04R12.B*	Read 8-10 short stories written by people from other countries. Compare the writing styles of different authors and cultures.	L-5
04R13.B	Peruse visitors' brochures and other materials published by various countries to learn more about them.	G-1
04R14.B	Read novels written by Robert Louis Stevenson about his travels and the places he went or set in those locations.	L-5 each book
04R15.B*	Read one or more novels involving the railroad or its construction.	H-5 each
04R16.B	Read the Sower series (or other) biography of the Wright Brothers.	H-4
04R17.B	Read *Around the World in Eighty Days*.	L-5
04R18.B	Read other novels or short stories about flight or airplanes.	L-5 each book
04R19.B	Read one or more novels by Jack London and/or others who traveled extensively and wrote about their experiences.	L-5 each
04R20.B*	Read one or more short stories based on the life of American immigrants in the late 19' and early 20th centuries.	H-5 each
04R21.B	Read biographies of famous people who immigrated to the land where they later became famous.	H-5 each
04R22.C*	Study samples of Norse mythology and discuss it. Be aware that these myths describe the religious beliefs that made the early Vikings what they were and that Leif Erikson was one of the first Norsemen to become a Christian.	H-3+
04R23.C	Read the original (translated, of course) writings of Leif Erikson in *American Original Documents* from the Harvard Classics series.	H-5
04R24.C	Read the chapters dealing with early exploration of North America in *The Light and the Glory*.	H-3

READING AND LITERATURE

04R25.C	Read *Columbus and Cortez: Conquerors for Christ* and/or *Columbus: the Last Crusader* or other Christian biographies of this great explorer.	H-5 each
04R26.C	Read original documents (translated) written by Christopher Columbus and found in American Original Documents from Harvard Classics series.	H-2
04R27.C	Read biographies of Magellan, Cook. Drake, and any other explorers studied in this mini-unit.	H-5 each
04R28.C	Read *The Sea Hawk* or other novels written about the Age of Exploration.	L-5 each
04R29.C*	Read *Search for the Blue Nile*, a journal of the exploration of the Nile River that finally discovered its source. (Parents should be aware that this book contains some rather graphic descriptions of native life that may not be appropriate for some girls.)	H-6
04R30.C	Read biographies and/or journals of those who explored other areas of the world after the end of the Age of Exploration. Some to include are: Admiral Byrd, Sir Richard Burton (not the actor), Commodore Perry, Amundsen, Stanley and Livingston,	H-5 each
04R31.C	Read Usborne's *Explorers: Columbus to Armstrong*.	H-4
04R32.D	Read *Kon Tiki*.	L-5
04R33.D	Read *Two Years Before the Mast*.	L-5
04R34.D	Read *Treasure Island* and/or *Kidnapped*.	L-5 each
04R35.D	Read *The Old Man and the Sea*.	L-5
04R36.D	Read other novels about the sea or seafaring.	L-5 each
04R37.D	Read and discuss "The Ancient Mariner".	L-2
04R38.D	Memorize 30-40 lines of poetry related to the sea, seafaring, or sea life.	L-8
04R39.D	Read *The Sinking of the Titanic and other Sea Disasters*, written the same year the great tragedy occurred and filled with testimony from eyewitnesses to it.	H-6
04R40.D	Read *Riding with the Dolphins*, from the Equinox Guide series	SB-3
04R41.D	Read *Meeting the Whales*, from the Equinox Guide series.	SB-3
04R42.D	Read Usborne's *Ocean Life*, or a similar book on the same topic.	SB-3
04R43.D	Read one or more novels about whales, dolphins, and other ocean life.	SB-S each
04R44.	Read one or more biographies of any of the men or women studied in this mini-unit.	SB-5 each

READING AND LITERATURE

04R45.	Read Christian or other wholesome novels set in the time period or culture under study in any particular mini-unit.	H-5 each
04R46.	Read novels set in any of the countries or cultures studied in this mini-unit.	H-5 each
04R47.	Read short stories written in or by people from one or more of the countries you have studied in this mini-unit.	L-5 each
04R48.	Read other works by authors studied in this unit.	G-1 each

COMPOSITION

04W01.A	Write a report on one or more of the countries that are major sources of export for the spices or foods studied in this unit.	G-2 each
04W02.A	Write a first person account of the feeding of the five thousand from one of those in the crowd.	B-1
04W03.A	Write a thorough analysis of Matthew 14:14-21, Mark 8:1-9 and Luke 9:10-17. Compare and contrast the three passages and explain whether you think they describe the same event and why.	B-1 EC-1
04W04.A	Write a print advertisement for one particular food product or brand, extolling its virtues over similar products or brands.	EC-1
04W05.A	Write a television or radio commercial for a food or brand of foodstuffs.	EC-1
04W06.A	Write a recruiting brochure of the food coop you studied, explaining the way it operates and how it can save members money.	EC-1
04W07.A	Write a news report on the grocery industry, revealing some of the facts you learned about it as if they were late-breaking news stories.	EC-2
04W08.A	Write a fictional story set in an open-air food market of Bible times.	EC-10
04W09.A	Write a report as if for a scientific journal on a "brand-new" invention guaranteed to revolutionize the growing and distribution of food. Choose any invention in the history of the food industry and write as it would have been viewed when it was brand new.	H-1 EC-2
04W10.B	Write a transcript of an imaginary interview with Paul, Abraham, Jacob, or another Bible traveler.	EC-1 B-1
04W11.B	Write reports on any or all of the countries or cities included in the travels of one or more of the Biblical personages studied in this unit, being sure to include their Biblical history and any name changes.	G-1 each

COMPOSITION

04W12.B	Write a diary or journal as might have been kept by an Israelite during the Exodus, the Exile, or the return from exile.	EC-5
04W13.B	Write a report of either of the above travels or one of the events involved in it as it might have been done by a news reporter of that day.	EC-2
04W14.B	Interview an ambassador or consular officer from a foreign nation (or someone on his/her staff) about their country and its immigration laws as well as the purpose served by their office as it relates to immigration and travel. Write the results into a newspaper report.	EC-4
04W15.B	Write a story or play about a family migrating to America around 1900. Try to be historically accurate about conditions in the country they left, travel conditions, and the life they found when they arrived.	EC-10
04W16.B	Write a travel brochure to attract foreign visitors to your country or one you studied in this unit.	EC-1 G-1
04W17.B	Write a travelers' health bulletin warning of various health hazards in particular countries and with travel in general.	EC-1 HE-1
04W18.B	Write a poem about traveling or one of the places you would like to visit.	EC-3
04W19.B	Write a paper comparing and contrasting various commonly-available forms of public transportation.	EC-2
04W20.B	Write 3 to 5 letters a sailor might have written home from various ports of call on one of the ancient trade routes.	EC-2
04W21.C	Write an original poem about the sea or seafaring.	EC-1
04W22.C	Write an article a news correspondent might have written while covering the first voyage of Columbus.	EC-1
04W23.C	Choose one explorer of the "New World " and write an essay analyzing the "morality" of his dealings with the natives, after reading at least two biographies of him and some of his own writings as well, from either *The Light and the Glory* or Harvard Classics' *American Original Documents*.	EC-3
04W24.C	Write a speech that might have been given by a native chief as he welcomed Columbus or another explorer to his land.	EC-2
04W25.C	Write a one-page report on any or all of the explorers studied in this unit.	EC-1
04W26.C	Write an extensive formal term paper on the life, travels, and discoveries of one of the explorers studied in this unit.	EC-1
04W27.C.	Write a report for your geography notebook about the home-land and the sponsoring country of each explorer studied.	G-2 each

COMPOSITION

04W28.C	Write a first person story or journal of a crew member of an explorer in this unit.	H-10 EC-10
04W29.D	Write a script for an interview with an oceanographer, whether you actually get to interview one or have to research the answers yourself. Ask about the duties and goals of the job as well as details on the study of oceanography.	EC-3
04W30.D	Write a journal of an ocean voyage to a real or imaginary destination at a time period of your choice.	EC-3
04W31. D	Write a detailed research paper on one of the classes (or phyla) of ocean animals studied in this unit. Use one of the guides to writing term papers and follow all procedures for a serious, formal paper (minimum 10-12 pages, typed.)	EC-25
04W32.D	Write a brief report on each animal or class of animal studied in this unit.	EC-2 each
04W33.D	Write a first-person short story (at least 10-12 typewritten pages) about life in a submarine or bathyscaphe beneath the sea.	EC-20
04W34.D	Write a fantasy or personification story or play about the life of one or more ocean creatures in which a sea creature is a main character.	EC-20
04W35.D	Prepare a notebook on "Oceans of the Deep". In it, write reports on each of the oceans from both geographic and scientific viewpoints. Write a synopsis of the history of marine travel and exploration. Define, describe, and analyze the various features of the ocean floor in a separate report for each ocean. Include reports on a representative sample of sea life.	EC-25 SE-15 SB-10
04W36.D	Write a 2-3 paragraph report on each animal phylum, genus, and or family that is primarily made up of ocean dwellers. Write a separate report on one example of each group.	EC-1 each
04W37.	As you read the Bible each day, keep a spiritual journal, taking notes on your readings and their applications in your life. Add prayer requests and answers as well as insights God may give you.	B-3 per week
04W38.	Use the Scripture passages in this unit to practice dictation. Have someone else read them aloud while you copy them, word for word, careful to use exact punctuation. If your beliefs allow, you may want to use a modern Bible translation for this exercise.	EG-1 per week Five times
04W39.	Write a report (1-2 pages) on one or more of the people you studied in this unit.	EC-2 each
04W40.	Write a brief (1-2 pages) report on each country studied in this unit. Put all of these into your geography notebook.	G-1 each

COMPOSITION

04W41.	As you attend worship services or hear them on radio, TV, or audios, take notes on the sermons.	EG-1 each
04W42.	As you watch videos and/or listen to audios recommended in this unit, take notes on them.	EG-1 each
04W43.	Use your notes to write a synopsis or summary of each audio and/or video used in this unit.	EC-1 each
04W44.	Write reviews of any or all of the videos in this unit, as if done by a movie critic.	EC-1 each
04W45.	Write a character sketch of one or more of the men and women studied in this unit.	EC-2 each
04W46.	Write a brief (1-2 paragraphs) report on each field trip taken in this unit.	EC-2 each
04W47.	Add one page to your school journal each day as explained in the Guidelines in the front section of this unit study book.	EC-3 per week
04W48.	Write book reports on any or all of the novels or biographies you read in this unit.	EC-2 each
04W49.	Outline one or more of the nonfiction books read in this unit.	EG-3+ each
04W50.	Write summaries and/or synopses of any books read in this unit.	EC-1 each
04W51.	Write a thorough exegesis of any of the Bible chapters studied in this unit.	EC-1 each
04W52.	Put ten or more new words from your studies each week into your vocabulary notebook along with their definitions, pronunciation marks, and syllables.	EG-1 per week
04W53.	Learn to spell all words added to your vocabulary notebook each week.	EG-2 per week
04W54.	Write a review of each play you read or watched (live or on video) for this unit.	EC-2 each
04W55.	Use any good contemporary dictionary to proofread and correct spelling in all written work. (No pts. for automatic spell checker.)	EG-1 per 10 pages

MATHEMATICS AND PERSONAL FINANCE

04M01.A	Use nutrition and size information from food labels to learn ratio, proportion, and percent. For example, using the number of grams of a nutrient provided by a food product and the percentage of RDA, calculate what is considered to be the RDA of that nutrient. You could also divide the total grams in a serving of something by the grams in a particular nutrient to see how much of the item is made up of that nutrient	M-1
04M02.A	Prepare a line graph comparing the nutritive value of various brands of particular food.	M-5

MATHEMATICS AND PERSONAL FINANCE

04M03.A   Use nutritional information to plan theoretical meals for one   FN-2
day that will provide   100% RDA of all essential nutrients,
selecting the brands with the best ratings.

04M04.A.   Compare prices on different size packages of the same   M-1
product and determine which gives the lowest price per unit.

04M05.A   Compare prices on various foods listed in store sale circulars   M-1
to decide where to shop for each item on a particular grocery list.

04M06.A   Use advertisements and coupons to find the best price to buy   M-2
groceries for three meals giving 100% of a day's nutritional needs
at the lowest possible price. Try this several times, trying to
improve on total cost per meal per person each time. (Use only
items members of your family will eat.)

04M07.A   Keep track of and graph as appropriate your own savings in   M-5
various food categories through use of coupons, rebates, etc.

04M08.B   Check and compare fares for various modes of travel to the   M-6
same destination. Show findings in a graph and as ratios or
proportions. Do this for several (at least 8 - 10) different
destinations.

04M09.B   Find the distance between your point of origin and each of the   M-1
above destinations and do the calculations needed to find the
average cost per mile on each form of transportation. Show this
information and the relationship between the various pieces of
data on some type of graph.

04M10.B   Use the mathematical formula for finding distance traveled (D   M-2
= r x t) to calculate how long a trip to the same destination will take
on different modes of transportation, given the average speed of
each. (Do this for 10-15 different locations before taking the
assigned points.)

04M11.B   Given the Earth's radius, find its diameter, circumference, surface   M-1
area, and volume.

04M12.B   Use the study of the Earth's geography to learn how to   M-3
compute circumference, radius, diameter, area and volume of
circles, ellipsoids, and spheres and to memorize the formulae
for finding them.

04M13.B   Learn to use nautical units of measure.   M-1

04M14.B   Use any available resources to determine and calculate the   M-5
dimensions of each of the continents and make a scale map of
them.

04M15.C   Use atlas or other source to find the distances traveled by   M-5
various explorers on their voyages and compare them on a
graph of your choice.

MATHEMATICS AND PERSONAL FINANCE

04M16.C   Use the information from the above activity and other resources   M-1
to make various calculations of distance, time, and rate (D/T = R)
with relation to each voyage of each explorer.

04M17.C   Use the above totals to compute the average distance traveled   M-1
on each of the voyages of each explorer who made more than one,
and the total distance of all voyages for each explorer.

04M18.C   Find the cost of each of the voyages of Columbus and compute   M-2
it in today's dollars.   Convert to the currencies of Italy (his home
country) and Spain (his sponsor) at today's rates of exchange.

04M19.C   At the current market rate of gold, calculate how much gold   M-1
Columbus would have had to bring back to Spain to cover the cost
of each trip to the New World.

04M20.C   Study the calculations and formulae used in early navigation,   SP-5
as explained in the book *Christopher Columbus: How He Did It.*

04M21.C   Using your own figures for distances and the best available   M-1
data on times of the voyages, calculate the average speed of each
voyage and of all of them combined.

04M22.C   Given measurements of each explorers' ships, and the sizes of   M-1
their crews, compute the space allotted to each man.

04M23. D   Figure the area of each of the world's oceans and the total   M-1
area of all of them, expressing it in square miles, square
kilometers, and acres.

04M24.D   Prepare a graph showing the area of each ocean and of all of   M-5
them.

04M25.D   Plot a graph to show the relative sizes of all the oceans and   M-5
continents.

04M26.D   Prepare to build a scale model of a saltwater aquarium by   M-5
determining the average size of various marine creatures and how
much space and water each needs to be comfortable. From these
figures, calculate the size of aquarium you need for the models you
will use (or the size of each model you will need for the aquarium
you already have, if any).

04M27.D   To go in with your study of ocean travel, try your hand at the   M-1 each
math game Pirates and Plunder. Play regularly until you master   time
the concepts.

04M28.   Use information from any or all of the graphs you have made   M-2
to practice making and solving problems with percent, ratio,
and proportion.

04M29.   Continue to brush up on basic math as needed.   M-1

SCIENCE

SCIENCE

04S01.A   Investigate your kitchen cupboards and list all spices and seasonings   FN-2
used in your home. Find out where and how each
grows; what part of the plant it is; how it is cultivated and/or
gathered; and the processing it undergoes for household use.
Record these findings in a notebook or some other format.

04S02.A   Find out how other favorite food products are grown and how   SE-1
they are processed, shipped, and marketed.

04S03.A   Tour an herb or spice garden to learn how the many varieties   PA-1
grow.

04S04.A   Tour a cannery and learn what processes are involved in canning   PA-2
of various foods, or take a virtual online tour.

04S05.A   Tour another type of commercial food packing plant and observe   IA-2
the various steps in the processes they use, or take a virtual online tour.

04S06.A   Tour a major port to see how foods are shipped and stored in   CS-2
transit, or take a virtual online tour.

04S07.A   Tour the food transport and storage area of a train yard,   CS-2
including grain elevators if possible, and have someone explain
the equipment and processes used to preserve the grain and
other foods in transit, or take a virtual online tour.

04S08.A   Visit the warehouse of a grocery chain or food distributor to   CS-2
see they handle the various food products to preserve quality.

04S09.A   Study the process of refrigeration and various chemical   FN-2
refrigerants.

04S10.A   Use material from the U. S. Department of Agriculture or   SP-2
County Extension Service to study food safety during
commercial handling, processing, and shipping.

04S11.A   Through your county extension service or local farmers' groups,   FN-2
find out what food items grow abundantly in your area and
why they do so well there. Learn how each is cultivated, grown,
and harvested.

04S12.B   Study aviation, aerodynamics, and flight, learning the principles   FN-1
of what makes things fly and the various power sources   SB-1
available for flight.

04S 13.B   Examine and learn how an automobile engine works and how   SP-4
it differs from an airplane engine.

04S14.B   Study the history of man's attempts at flight from the earliest   SP-4
time until now and try to determine why each one did or did
not work.

04S15.B   Study gliders and other types of planes without engines.   SP-1

04S16.B   Study blimps, dirigibles, and other types of "lighter-than-air   SP-2
ships" and the principles on which they are based.

SCIENCE

04S17.B	Compare and contrast prop and jet airplane engines.	SP-1
04S18.B	Tour the air traffic control tower of your local airport and learn what instruments they use and how each works.	SP-2
04S19.B	Study the rudder of a ship and how it works.	SP-1
04S20.B	Study the various types of motors used on boats and ships.	SP-2
04S21.B	Study sonar, radar and other modern technological navigational tools used by planes and ships today that were not available to the early explorers.	SP-3
04S22.B	Tour a major seaport to observe different types of ships and the cargoes they carry. Study the differences between them and how each operates.	SP-4
04S23.B	Tour one or more types of oceangoing merchant vessels.	CS-2
04S24.B	Study the locomotive as it has developed through history and learn how the engines work. Compare them to automobile, airplane and jet engines.	SP-3
04S25.C	Learn about the principles on which sailing vessels operate and how they can increase or decrease speed. Compare modern sailing vessels with those of the early explorers.	SP-2
04S26.C	Study various theories about the shape of the world that were held at different times in history, noting that many believed in a round Earth long before Columbus.	SE-1 H-1
04S27.C	Study the tools and techniques used in navigation during the Age of Exploration and how they have changed over the years.	SP-2
04S28.C	Study the principles behind the compass and how it was used in navigation during the Age of Exploration.	SP-1
04S29.C	Expand your study of the compass to learn about magnetism and gravity, using Usborne's *Kids Kit* on magnets or any books on that topic in the Reading and Literature section.	SP-3
04S30.C	Study the sextant, the principles behind it, and how it was used in navigation.	SP-1
04S31.C	Study a good textbook or the "Power Squadron" course on celestial navigation, the method used by Columbus and his contemporaries.	CREDIT
04S32.C	In order to become proficient at celestial navigation, learn to identify constellations and find them in the night sky.	SE-3
04S33.C	Tour an online planetarium and learn about the location of various constellations.	SE-3

SCIENCE

04S34.C	Study the development of spyglasses and telescopes from the primitive ones used by the early explorers to the myriad types available today.	SP-1 H-1
04S35.D	Study the contents of seawater and the processes by which it can be purified and desalinated to use for drinking and other purposes.	SE-1 SP-1
04S36.D	Study the phylum Mollusca, most of which are sea creatures.	SB-3
04S37.D	Study the phylum Crustacea, most of which are also ocean dwellers.	SB-3
04S38.D	Study the many varieties of saltwater fish and the basic traits they all share.	SB-3
04S39.D	Study coral and sponges.	SB-2
04S40.D	Study dolphins, porpoises, and whales.	SB-3
04S41.D	Study seals, manatees, walruses, and sea lions, contrasting and comparing them.	SB-3
04S42.D	Tour a saltwater aquarium where you can visit these animals.	SB-2
04S43.D	Study algae, kelp, and other marine plants.	SE-1
04S44.D	Study ocean currents and the effect they have on climate.	SE-1
04S45.D	Study the relationship of the moon on tides and currents of the oceans.	SB-2+
04S46.D	Tour a marine biology lab, talk with the biologists there and/or sit in on a lab session.	SB-2+
04S47.D	Instead of the biology-related activities in this unit, take a course in marine biology, using a textbook, correspondence course, or online program.	SB-1 CREDIT

HEALTH AND FITNESS

04H01.A	Study the medicinal and therapeutic uses of herbs and other natural foods.	HE-2
04H02.A	Learn about the health benefits (and/or dangers) of various methods of storing and preserving foods and how each method keeps food safe for shipping and storage.	HE-2
04H03.A	Use material from the U. S. Department of Agriculture or the county Extension Service to study food-borne diseases and the safe food handling rules that help prevent them.	HE-1
04H04.A	Learn about the shelf life of various food products and how long they can safely be stored before use.	HE-2

HEALTH AND FITNESS

04H05.A	Study the nutrients needed by the human body and which foods provide which ones.	HE-3
04H06.A	Investigate the purity and safety of various vitamin and food supplements on the market. Try to determine which, if any, your family should take.	HE-1
04H07.B	Study the causes, symptoms, treatment, and prevention of motion-related illnesses.	HE-1
04H08.B	Learn and try to apply all safety rules for various forms of travel and to avoid the health hazards associated with each.	PS-2
04H09.B	Study the effectiveness and proper use of automobile and air-plane seat belts.	PS-1
04H10.B	Investigate and compare various children's car seats and other motion restraints used for travel.	PS-2
04H11.B	Study the phenomenon that causes ear-popping in travel at high altitudes. Learn how to prevent this problem.	HE-1
04H12.B	Study jet lag and the physical problems that stem from it. Learn how to prevent, minimize, or overcome each of these.	HE-1
04H13.C	Study rickets, a disease common to sailors during the time of the early explorers. Find out the causes, prevention, and types of treatment used then and now.	HE-2
04H14.C	Study scurvy, another ailment common to explorers and their crews. Learn what caused it and how it was treated and prevented then and now.	HE-2
04H15.C	Study modern equipment and processes that have been so effective in the prevention of the above diseases that they are almost unknown today.	HE-2
04H16.C	Study various tropical diseases that were first contracted by Europeans during the Age of Exploration.	HE-2
04H17.C	Study seasickness and the remedies for it that would have been available to the early explorers. Contrast to today's cures for it.	HE-1
04H18.D	Study the diseases that may be carried by sea animals and contracted by humans from handling or eating them incorrectly.	HE-1
04H19.D	Study the possibility and frequency of allergies to various types of seafood.	HE-1
04H20.D	Study the dangers of bends and other ailments that plague divers.	HE-1
04H21.D	Learn about the stings of jellyfish, men-of-war, stingrays, or other stinging sea creatures and how each can be treated.	SB-1

HEALTH AND FITNESS

04H22.D	Learn the nutritional value of iodine, a resource found in abundance in the salt water of oceans.	FN-1
04H23.D	Learn about the nutritional value of various kinds of seaweed and the commercial foods that are made from it.	FN-1

PRACTICAL ARTS

04P01.A	Shop for your family's groceries for one week, making menu plans beforehand, checking for sales, using a list, and redeeming coupons.	FN - 3 HM - 2
04P02.A	Learn to read grocery labels and compare the nutritive value of similar products and of different brands of the same item.	FN - 1
04P03.A	Visit a farmer's market or food co-op. View products offered, compare prices, and talk with vendors to learn how shopping there works and who is eligible to use it.	HM - 2
04P04.A	Buy and prepare a full meal from products grown in your area and sold locally at the farmer's market or roadside stands.	FN - 3
04P05.A	Using pamphlets from your county's Agricultural Extension Service or other available materials, learn to can one or more fruits or acidic vegetables by the water bath method.	FN - 3 each type
04P06.A	Using above sources for instructions, make and can one or more kinds of jam, jelly, or preserves,	FN - 3 each type
04P07.A	Can one or more vegetables, using a pressure canner and info from one of the above sources.	FN - 3 each type
04P08.A	Prepare one or more types of fruit or vegetable for freezer storage.	FN - 3 each type
04P09.A	Dry one or more fruits, using a dehydrator, the oven, or natural processes found in the above resources or *Back to Basics*.	FN - 3 each type
04P10.A	Instead of activities 04P05 - 04P09, take a class in food preservation through 4-H, the extension service, or a local junior college or continuing education program.	FN - V2 credit
04P11.A	Learn to handle, serve, and store various foods properly for maximum flavor and health benefits.	FN - 1
04P12.A	Take a class in food safety through 4-H, County Extension Service, or other agency.	FN - 20
04P13.B	Experience for yourself as many of the types of public transportation as possible, learning how to ride each safely.	LS - 2 each
04P14.B	Learn to pack for a trip in the most efficient manner, using as few bags as possible.	LS - 2

PRACTICAL ARTS

04P15.B	Apply for and get a passport.	LS - 2
04P16.B	Go through all the steps of applying for a visa to a country you would like to visit, whether or not you actually go there.	CG - 2
04P17.B	Put together model kits of one or more boats, trains, planes, or cars from various periods of history.	CR - 2 each
04P18.B	Instead of traditional plastic model kits, build various types of vehicles using Construx, KNEX Fisher Technics, or similar materials.	CR - 2 each
04P19.B	Learn to read maps, globes, and navigational charts.	G - 2
04P20.B	If you are old enough to do so legally in your state, learn to drive a car and get your driver's license.	LS - 25
04P21.B	Take a course in driver's education or defensive driving, studying at home with your parents or in whatever classes are available in your area.	2l/credit in Driver's Education
04P22.B	If your interests lie in that area, take a course in flying and become a pilot.	1 credit in Aviation for complete course
04P23.B	To tie in with travel, learn a classical or modern foreign language at this time, if you plan to include it in your studies. Use any method or material of your choice.	1 credit for complete course
04P24.B	Use Usborne's *How to Draw Maps and Charts* to learn the skills needed to make a map of any location.	G - 2
04P25.B	Learn to use the map-making software available from Rand McNally or other sources or from www.mapquest.com or another website.	CO - 2
04P26.C	Make a compass, using only items available in the 16th century.	CR - 2
04P27.C	Learn how to find your way from place to place with only a compass as the early explorers had to do.	LS - 1
04P28.C	Learn to use a sextant as used by the early explorers.	LS - 1
04P29.C	If you have access to a sailboat, learn to sail it correctly.	RE -15
04P30.C	Learn to hoist, lower, and maintain your boat's sails.	RE - 5
04P31.C	Learn how to navigate and tell directions by sun and moon as early explorers did.	LS - 2
04P32.C	Learn to operate the ship-to-shore radio and/or other communication equipment on your boat.	LS - 1
04P33.C	Learn to identify various constellations and to navigate by them.	SE - 2
04P34.C	Follow the information in *Everything Kids Science Experiment Book* or similar books and build a crude spyglass or telescope of the type and size used by the early explorers.	CR - 3

PRACTICAL ARTS

04P35.D	Take a motor boating safety course through your state parks, conservation, or transportation department or the U. S. Army Corps of Engineers.	1/2 credit in Boating for complete course
04P36.D	Learn how to rescue a person from a capsized or sinking boat without risk of getting pulled under the water yourself.	PS - 2
04P37.D	Take a course in water safety and/or lifesaving through the Red Cross, YMCA, or similar group.	1/2 credit for complete course
(04P38. D)	Take a course in CPR (used to rescue drowning victims) through the Red Cross or some similar organization and earn your certificate.	HE - 25 points
04P39.D	Take a deep-sea fishing trip and try catching something.	RE - 5
04P40.D	Learn snorkeling or scuba diving.	PE - 10
04P41.D	If you live in or visit an area where it is possible, try crabbing or shrimping.	RE - 3
(04P42.D)	Learn to clean fish and various types of seafood.	FN 2
04P43.D	Learn various ways to cook fish and seafood.	FN - 3 +
04P44.D	Fill and maintain (for at least six months) a saltwater aquarium in your home.	SB - 5
(04P45.D)	Collect a variety of seashells and use them in a creative way in your home decor.	VA - 2
04P46.	Take a course or tutorial in computer literacy or computer science and use the computer for word processing and doing research for papers in this unit.	21/credit for complete course
(04P47.)	Use a computer or typewriter to type papers written for this mini unit.	BE - 1 per 4 pages
04P48.	Frame and/or mat and hang one or more of the pictures you painted or drew in the Decorative and Performing Arts section.	CR - 2
04P49.	Design and make your own costumes for any or all of the plays or skits in this unit.	CC - 5 +
(04P50.)	Build your own puppet stage for your puppet performances.	WW - 3 +
(04P51.)	Create and make several puppets for use in the shows you wrote.	CR - 5

Sunday School

DECORATIVE AND PERFORMING ARTS

04A01.A	Prepare a collage of food labels to create an attractive design or picture.	VA - 1
(04A02.A)	Sketch a still life featuring various processed food products.	VA- 2

DECORATIVE AND PERFORMING ARTS

04A03.A	Use your choice of media to paint a still life featuring fruits, vegetables, or other natural food products.	VA- 3 +
04A04.A	Create a mosaic trivet by arranging dried peas, beans, corn, and/or other grains into a design and gluing them to a square or circle of thin plywood or paneling or corrugated cardboard.	CR - 2
04A05.A	Draw illustrations for the print advertisement that you wrote in the Composition section.	VA - 1
04A06.A	Perform and record the television or radio commercial that you wrote in the Composition section.	DR - 2
04A07.A	Illustrate the food coop recruiting brochure that you wrote in the Composition section.	VA - 2
04A08.B	Write lyrics and music for one or more songs about sailing or travel in general.	MC - 5 each
04A09.B	Listen to and discuss the style and theme of one or more songs from or about each of the countries studied in this unit.	MA- 5
04A10.B	Learn to play on the instrument of your choice one or more songs from other nations.	IM - 3
04A11.B	Listen to and translate one or more songs written in the second language you are learning.	FL - 2 each
04A12.B	Learn to sing one or more songs in the second language you are learning.	FL - 3 each
04A13.B	View artwork from a wide variety of countries and compare the themes and styles of the work.	AA - 3
04A14.B	Draw or use cutouts to create a mural featuring a wide variety of modes of transportation, current and historic.	VA - 2
04A15.B	Use your artistic ability to illustrate the travel brochure that you wrote in the Composition section.	VA - 2
04A16.B	Create a poster of the travel poem you wrote in the Composition section, copying it in calligraphy and illustrating it with your choice of artwork.	VA - 2
04A17.C*	Watch and/or listen to *The Ring of the Nibelung*, an opera based on Norse (Viking) mythology.	MA - 7
04A18.C	Illustrate the original poem about the sea or seafaring that you wrote in the Composition section.	VA - 1
04A19.C	Draw a mural to illustrate various parts of the news article covering the first voyage of Columbus that you wrote in the Composition section.	VA - 1
04A20.C	Listen to and discuss a variety of seafaring songs that may have been popular with the Explorers.	MA - 2

DECORATIVE AND PERFORMING ARTS

04A21. C — Using the techniques in *How to Draw Ships and Boats* or any similar book, and pictures of ships from the correct time period, draw what you believe the Nina, the Pinta, and the Santa Maria looked like.　　VA - 4 / H - 2

04A22.C — Draw illustrations that could have been used for Columbus' dairy or the diary of one of the other explorers you studied.　　VA - 2 / H - 2

04A23.C — Build models (from kits) of a variety of sailboats, old and modern.　　CR - 3

04A24.D — Create a mural or wall scene made from pictures of different types of ships you have learned about in this unit.　　VA - 3

04A25.D — Paint an attractive seascape (on canvas, large enough for hanging).　　VA - 5

04A26.D — Listen to and critique several seafaring songs from various time periods. Vary the types of music selected.　　MA - 3

04A27.D — Learn the words and how to sing one or more seafaring songs from various time periods. If you do more than one, try to vary the types of music selected.　　VM - 3 each

04A28.D — Learn to play on your instrument one or more of the seafaring songs used elsewhere in this section.　　IM - 3 each

04A29.D — Draw sketches to illustrate your booklet on ocean life, one picture for each creature included.　　VA - 1 for every 2

04A30.D — Study artwork displays that include ocean creatures.　　AA - 2

04A31.D — Draw or otherwise create a mural of undersea life.　　VA - 3

04A32. — Draw pictures of any field trips you took in this unit.　　VA - 1 each

04A33. — Use drawing, painting and graphic arts to create displays and make posters as called for in this study.　　VA - 1 + each

04A34. — Illustrate one or more of the poems you studied or memorized for this unit.　　VA - 1 each

04A35. — Set one or more of this unit's poems to music, using an original tune.　　MC - 5

04A36. — Set one or more of the Scripture passages in this unit to music, using a tune you wrote for the purpose.　　MC - 5

04A37. — Perform one or more of the plays or skits you wrote in the Composition section.　　DR - 20

UNIT 5

She rises while it is yet night and gives food to her family and a portion for her maidens.

Proverbs 31:15

Overview

While this unit speaks specifically of the task of preparing food for her family, the character traits it teaches are much broader than that. The activity described here requires diligence, organization, and creativity on the part of this woman. This is a woman who is ready to do whatever needs to be done at any time. She stays one step ahead of her family, which we all know is sometimes hard to do She is also able to guide and supervise well those within her domain, be they hired help or children. Since these traits are looked at in other units as well, we will not devote a mini-unit to studying them. However, it is wise to be conscious of these traits while learning the academic and practical skills that are included here.

These practical skills include meal planning, cooking, and food service and presentation on the plate and the table. This is the outstanding point for which this woman is noted in this verse. She plans meals ahead of time and knows what she is serving and when, as well as how it is to be served. It is obvious from the context that she knows how to cook and what foods are good choices for her family. This is what you will be learning in this unit as the basis for other studies.

As with other units, this unit also lends itself to several other themes, mostly relating to the mention of "maidens". In the time of its writing, these maidens, were probably slaves, which will lead us to look at the Bible's teachings about slavery and servitude. We will attempt to understand why the Bible appears to permit something that seems so evil. We will also look at other societies that practiced slavery and examine what was different about them. This will, of course, include a study of slavery in the United States, and various outgrowths from it, including the abolition movement and the War Between the States. In the course of this study, you will examine other causes of this war and the beliefs of both sides about it.

Mini-Units

Mini-Units contained in this unit are:

    A. Food and Nutrition

    B. The Institution of Slavery

    C. Ancient Egypt

    D. The War Between the States and its Aftermath

Mini-Units

Each thematic mini-unit is described and designated with a letter of the alphabet in the following paragraphs. Individual activities designed for use in one particular mini-unit will be marked with those letters. (For further help with this, please refer to the explanation of mini-units in the Guidelines section of this unit study guide.)

A. Food and Nutrition

In this mini-unit, you will study nutrition, meal planning, and cooking of food. You will consider the nutritional needs of your family and learn to plan nutritious, attractive meals to meet those needs. This will include studying vitamins, minerals, etc. and food sources of them.

You will also learn to prepare various foods for optimum nutrition and taste appeal. This means learning to cook a variety of dishes and develop other skills in food service, hospitality and entertaining. You will also examine techniques for counting and controlling calories, fat, cholesterol and other things we need to restrict in our diets. We will study positive and negative claims made in these areas and seek evidence to substantiate or refute them.

In this area, you will learn about the anatomy and physiology of digestion (including the roles played by the endocrine and excretory systems) whereby the body is able to use the nutrients in food. We will look at diseases and disorders of the digestive tract, eating disorders, and food-related allergies or illnesses and their treatment and prevention. In this context, we will learn about bacteria and other microscopic organisms, both harmful and benevolent, and how to control them in cooked and uncooked food. We will take a look at nursing practices used for combating the above ailments. Opportunity is given for more detailed study in the field of nursing.

B. The Institution of Slavery

In this unit, you will look at slavery and bondage throughout history, both officially legal and 'under the table' types. In this list, we will include indentured servitude, slavery for debts, and other forms of voluntary or involuntary unpaid service to a master.

You will be asked to investigate slavery as it existed in the ancient world, comparing the way it was handled in various nations. This will include an in-depth study of slaves and slavery in the Bible. We will study verses about the treatment of slaves, and commands to slaves on how to behave toward their masters. You will be encouraged to learn why the Bible even permitted slavery at all, rather than demanding that all slaves be freed by all who be-came Christians.

You will read biographies, historical fiction and original writings of those who were slaves, those who kept slaves, and those who tried to help free slaves. Some of the things you will read in this context may surprise you. Be sure to keep an open mind and let the Scriptures speak to you without preconceptions.

The other main topic covered within the context of slavery is the various antislavery movements that have flourished at different times in history. You will learn about their leaders, how they happened, and what effect they had on the reality of slavery. You will be offered the chance to read biographies of many of these people and study the movements they founded.

Mini-Units

C. Ancient Egypt

The study of slavery seems a perfect place to include a unit on Ancient Egypt, the land in which God's chosen people were enslaved for so many years. You will begin to learn about this great and mighty land through the story of Joseph, son of Jacob, who was sold into slavery there and rose to a position of national prominence. You will read his story and all related passages from the Scripture and supplement it with studies from other resources.

You will examine the geographic features of the nation of Egypt and its current and ancient boundaries, using a variety of maps and a Bible atlas. You will learn about the races and ethnic groups of people that make up its population and how they have related to each other over the years. You will discover how the terrain and climate made the Egyptians what they became.

The most important aspect of your study of ancient Egypt is their culture. You will examine all aspects of it, paying special attention to ways in which the early Egyptians influenced the rest of the world, even up to our own day. You will look at archaeological finds and other evidences of the glorious past of this North African nation.

D. The War Between the States and its Aftermath

Since it was connected with slavery in the minds of so many, this seems to be the obvious place to study this war. You will investigate the true causes of the war, which are many and may be quite surprising, and the real impact of slavery on the whole nation. You will learn why so many devout Christians cast their lot with the South even though they did not have slaves or advocate slavery and why many Christians felt called of God to own slaves.

In studying the war and the period in which it occurred, you will read writings of several famous people of that time, including sermons by some of the most godly men in U. S. history, who could be found in both camps. You will read novels and biographies about people and places on both sides of that war, including a number of slaves and former slaves who put on uniforms and went to fight for what they believed — on both sides.

Your study of the actual war will include learning about the states that made up the Confederacy and the Union, and which states remained (or tried to remain) neutral. You will study battles and strategy and what finally won the war. This will include some detailed study of major battles and campaigns and the men who waged them.

This unit will end with a study of life at the end of the war, especially in the South. You will study the assassination of President Lincoln, the impeachment of his successor, and the laws of Reconstruction passed by a vengeful Congress against what they knew to have been the wishes of the nation's fallen leader. Through biographies and historical, you will see what life was like in the South during the time known as Reconstruction and how events during that time contributed to racial unrest for generations.

BIBLE AND CHRISTIAN CHARACTER

05B01.A	Study God's provision of food for Adam and Eve in the Garden of Eden as told in Genesis 1:29-30 and the expansion of it given in Genesis 2:15-17. Discuss with an adult why you think these two passages are so different.	B-1
05B02.A	Read and discuss the commands and provisions God gave Noah upon his return to dry land from the ark in Genesis 9: 1-5. How does this differ from the previous command to Adam?	B-1
05B03.A	Study the above passages in at least two different commentaries and try to determine why God made the change in what man was allowed to eat.	B-1
05B04.A	Use a concordance to look up and study all other passages that might support or refute the belief that the Bible calls us to be vegetarians.	B-2
05B05.A	Study Genesis 25 and Genesis 27 to see the significance of food in the lives of Jacob and Esau.	B-1
05B06.A	Read Genesis 42 - 45 to see how God used food to bring about much in the life of Joseph and his family.	B-2
05B07.A	Use concordance to find and study other passages in which food plays a major part.	B-3
05B08.A	Study the lists from Leviticus 11, 17, and 19 of foods the Old Testament Israelites were forbidden by God to eat.	B-2
05B09.A	Look up and study other 'laws" or commands of the Old Testament with regard to food.	B-2
05B10.A	Read Acts 10 and discuss with a Christian adult its full meaning and how (or if) it affects the laws of eating you studied.	B-1
05B11.A	Read the book of Hebrews and discuss how or if the teachings there alter the kosher laws of the Old Testament.	B-5
05B12.B	Read the story of Hagar in Genesis 16 and 21, noticing that Scripture makes no reference to slavery being wrong. Nor does it censure Abram for having a slave or for taking her as his wife. Discuss that seeming contradiction with your parents.	B-1
05B13.B	Study the Bible's commands regarding slavery in Leviticus 25:35-55. Take special note of the importance of the Jubilee year and how it made slavery among the Israelites different from that practiced by any other culture.	B-1
05B14.B	Study all other Biblical laws in Leviticus and Deuteronomy governing the taking and treatment of slaves.	B-3

BIBLE AND CHRISTIAN CHARACTER

05B15.B	Study all New Testament commands regarding slaves or their masters.	B-2
05B16.B	Read and paraphrase the book of Philemon.	B-2
05B17.B	Identify and list all other slaves mentioned by name in the Bible. Read their stories and learn about them.	B-2
05B18.B	Use a Bible dictionary, concordance, and/or other resource to find and read all other Bible references to slavery.	B-5
05B19.B	Study Daniel's captivity in exile. Contrast and compare it to examples of slavery in other verses.	B-4
05B20.B	Learn to share the gospel with others from the standpoint of being freed from slavery to sin.	B-1
05B21.C	Study Joseph's life as a slave in Egypt and his rise to power.	B-2
05B22.C	Study Joseph's reactions to circumstances at various stages in his life, measuring spiritual growth at each step, especially in his attitude toward his own brothers.	B-2
05B23.C	Watch the Genesis Project video *Joseph* and compare it to the Bible's account of his life.	B-3
05B24.C	Study the slavery of the Israelites in Egypt and God's deliverance of them in the book of Exodus.	B-5
05B25.C	Continue to follow the flight of the Israelites from Egypt in the books of Numbers and Deuteronomy.	B-10
05B26.C	Study the life of Moses, who was raised in the Pharaoh's household in Egypt.	B-2+
05B27.C	Watch the video *Moses* by the Genesis Project and compare it to the Biblical account of his life.	B-2
05B28.C	Watch a video of Cecile B. DeMille's *The Ten Commandments* and compare it to the real Biblical account of the life of Moses and the exodus of the people of Israel from Egypt.	B-4
05B29.C	Watch the video *Prince of Egypt* and compare it to the above movie and to the Biblical account.	B-2
05B30.C	Read Matthew chapter 2 to determine the place of Egypt in the life of Jesus. Discuss the relationship of this with the Exodus of the Israelites in the Old Testament.	B-1
05B31.C	Use a concordance to find and study all other Biblical references to Egypt.	B-5

BIBLE AND CHRISTIAN CHARACTER

05B32.D	Study the I Chronicles 12:1-22 account of the repudiation of Saul as king and acceptance of David by the tribe of Judah and some from Benjamin. Why do you think this passage was instrumental in leading Christians in the U. S. South to advocate secession from the Union.	B-2
05B33.D	Read and study all Bible passages quoted or used in sermons and/or writings of abolitionists to advocate or justify going to war over slavery.	B-2
05B34.D	Read Luke 11:17, which was quoted by Abraham Lincoln as reason to force the seceded states back into the Union. Read the entire passage, verses 14-26 to see if you believe this was a proper use of that verse.	B-1
05B35.D	Study Matthew 5, that urges Christians to be peacemakers, and explain what you believe this means. Keep this verse in mind as you read about the Quakers (Friends), Amish, and Mennonites, all of whom opposed slavery but considered it wrong to take up arms or fight a war for ANY cause.	B-1
05B36.D	Find and read other Scripture passages that might tend to support the pacifist views of groups such as those mentioned in the previous activity. Discuss with your parents and/or pastor.	B-4
05B37. D	Read the book of Joshua, in which God Himself sent His people directly into war for a cause He had mapped out for them. As you read, make note of all such instances, and discuss them later with your parents. Determine how these can be explained in light the many Scriptures that seem to urge peacemaking.	B-5
051338.D	Look up and study passages in the New Testament in which the Christian life is compared to a soldier fighting (or preparing for) a battle. In what way does this use of soldiers and wars symbols of godliness seem contradictory to the verses you studied in the last three activities? Discuss with a parent.	B-2
05B39.D	Look up in concordance and study all passages in which the Lord Jesus had amicable dealings with soldiers. In light of His teachings on peacemaking, why do you suppose He did not confront these men as sinners or tell them to leave their profession and seek another.	B-1
05B40. D	Verify from the Scripture any other verses used in writings suggested in the Reading and Literature sections of this mini-unit.	B- leach
05B41.	Memorize one or more of the passages studied in the mini-unit.	B- leach
05B42.	Read through the book of Proverbs each month, reading the chapter to coincide with each date.	B - 10 each time

BIBLE AND CHRISTIAN CHARACTER

05B43.   Continue reading through the Bible at a rate of 1-5 chapters per day. If you use *The Daily Bible* or another version designed for that purpose, following their assigned daily readings will take you through the entire Bible in one year. You may follow a pattern of your own at a different rate if you like.   B-1 credit when completed

CULTURAL STUDIES

05C01.A   Study the food preparation, recipes and dining customs of various countries and compare them.   CS-3+

05C02.A   Contact a synagogue or rabbi to learn how Old Testament dietary laws are practiced among Orthodox or Conservative Jews today. Compare your diet to see what you eat that is forbidden under these laws. If you prefer, you may look up this information online.   B-1

05C03.A   From *How They Lived in Bible Times, Manners and Customs of the Bible* or a similar resource, plan a week of meals the Proverbs 31 woman might have cooked for her family. Bear in mind the lack of refrigeration, the difficulty of transporting goods from other places, and the primitive cooking methods and equipment.   *B-2* H-2 HM-2

05C04.A   Study a good book or online resource on international customs to determine which foods you commonly eat would be considered vulgar or sinful in other cultures. (Some examples are pork, beef, shellfish. Find several others and discover where and why each is forbidden?)   HM-1 H-1

05C05.A   Find examples of countries or cultures in which things you would never eat are considered normal fare or delicacies.   H-2

05C06.A   Study the history of food preservation and the invention of the equipment and utensils now used in it.   CS-1

05C07.A   Tour a museum display of cooking utensils used in various periods of history, paying attention to how items used for the same purpose have changed over the years.   HM-2

05C08.A   Study the various social uses of food and meals in different cultures and periods in history.   CS-1

05C09.A   Visit a gourmet or imported food shop and take a look at all the varieties of foods that are not common in your country, and especially any that you may never have seen before. If this isn't available where you live, check out online catalogs of such things.   HM-2

05C10.A   Visit a gourmet or specialty kitchen shop and examine equipment that is unfamiliar. You can also search online. Research these items to find out where each originates and how it is used there.   HM-2

CULTURAL STUDIES

05C11.A* Study the use of wine and similar alcoholic beverages in a   B-1
variety of countries. Discuss with your parents why this seems CS-2
acceptable, even among Christians and for children in some
cultures and not in others.

05C12.B Listen to and discuss with your parents audios # 5 - 8 of *World* H-5
History: A Christian Survey, dealing with time periods when slavery
and feudalism were common.

05C13.B Using *Streams of Civilization,* another Christian world history H-5
text or resources listed in other sections of this mini-unit, trace the
development of slavery from Bible times until it was abolished in
the United States in the 1860's.

05C14.B Study feudalism in the Middle Ages and compare the life of a H-3
serf to that of a slave in Biblical times and in the American South
of the 1700-1800's.

05C15.B In Biblical Israel, a man could sell himself into slavery to pay H-2
his debts. The British of earlier centuries dealt with that problem
through the debtor's prison. Study about this institution and
compare life there to that of a slave in Biblical times or in England
or America in the heyday of slavery there.

05C16.B Study the founding of the U. S. state of Georgia and its H-2
connection to the debtors' prison system.

05C17.B Study the founding of Australia and its use as a penal colony. H-2
How does this differ from slavery?

05C18.B Study indentured service as instituted in England and its colonies. H-1
Compare and contrast to slavery of Bible times and of England
and early America.

05C19.B Using Clarence Carson's U. S. History series, the Jackdaws H-5
portfolio "Slavery in the United States", or other resources, study
the history of slavery in the U. S. Mark on a map all states and
territories that allowed slavery at some time in their history.

05C20.B Identify, mark on a map, and study all countries other than H-4
the U. S. or Great Britain that were heavily involved in slave
holding or the slave trade at some points in their history.

05C21.B Study the economic impact of the slave trade on each of the CE-5
countries above.

05C22.B Study all laws, rules and court decisions in your country related H-2
to slavery. Compare to Biblical slavery laws found in the passages
studied in Bible and Christian Character. (For U. S.
citizens, be sure to include the Dred Scot decision, the Missouri
Compromise, and the Fugitive Slave Act, all of which helped fuel
opposition to slavery in your country prior to the War Between the
States.)

CULTURAL STUDIES

05C23.B	Study the Underground Railroad network established to help runaway slaves escape from the United States into Canada and freedom. Learn about the methods used and the 'conductors' who made it work.	H-2
05C24.B	Learn about the "freedom trains" (actually boats) financed by certain Southerners (of the U.S.) to send slaves to freedom in Africa. Learn about the motives of those who financed and ran this and how the slaves fared when they arrived in the land they named Liberia.	B-2
05C25.B	Study the lives of George Washington Carver, Booker T. Washington and other former slaves from the U. S. South who made important contributions to their nation during the Reconstruction Era.	H-3
05C26.B	Tour Tuskegee University, Hampton University or another institution of higher education started by and for freed slaves during the Reconstruction period. You can find much help about this online, but the actual tours will be even better.	CS-2
05C27.B	Study and compare the abolitionist movements (H-4) in Great Britain and the United States.	H-4
05C28.B	Examine periodicals and other sources to learn about areas of the world in which some form of slavery still exists.	CS-2
05C29.C	Study Greenleaf's *Guide to Ancient Egypt*, doing only those activities that appeal to you and your parents and taking points based on the amount of work done.	H-parents discretion
05C30.C	Read the *Streams of Civilization* chapter on Ancient Egypt.	H-1
05C31.C	Study the history of the pharaohs and other leaders of Egypt.	H-1
05C32.C	Use *Baker's Bible Atlas* and the Rod and Staff study guide for it to study the geography of ancient Egypt.	B-1 G-3
05C33.C	Study the geography of Egypt and its surrounding area as it is today. Compare to the ancient Egyptian Empire in size and power.	G-1
05C34.C	Learn about the gods of the Egyptians so you will better understand the significance of the plagues God brought against them in the book of Exodus.	H-2
05C35.C	Investigate the Egyptian beliefs and burial customs that resulted in the elaborate pyramids of Egypt and the practice of mummification of the dead.	H-3
05C36.C	Study the history of efforts to excavate the tombs of the pharaohs in the pyramids of Egypt.	H-2

CULTURAL STUDIES

05037.C	Study the use of hieroglyphics and the discovery of the Rosetta Stone that helped archaeologists learn to decipher them.	H-2
05038.C	Study the various pharaohs covered in the books in the Reading and Literature section of this mini-unit and place each of them on the timeline.	H-5
05C39.C	Study life in Egypt today and compare to that of Old Testament times.	H-1 G-1
05C40.C	Study the history and current location and life-style of the Copts, the true descendants of the ancient Egyptians.	H-2
05C41.D	Study the War Between the States from *America: The First 350 Years* or other Christian sources and list factors other than slavery, that contributed to the start of the War.	H-5
05C42.D	Mark on a US map those states that fought on each side in this war, heavily embattled border states, those that remained neutral and those that were not states at the time.	H-1
05C43.D	Study all original documents in the Jackdaws portfolio of The Civil War.	H-7
05C44.D	Study the lives of famous political leaders who served the U.S. or the Confederacy just before and/or during the War Between the States. Include Davis and Lincoln, and lawmakers, cabinet members and others.	H-5
05C45.D	Play the "Civil War Game" by Educational Materials Associates to learn about major battles of this war.	H-5
05C46.D	Mark on a U. S. map the sites of major battles of the War Between the States, designating by color the winner of each.	H-3
05C47.D	From your own research, identify the major military leaders and commanders of each side in the War Between the States. Study the life and military career of each, before, during, and after the War.	H-2each
05C48.D	Watch the Ken Burns video series *The Civil War*, take notes on it, try to verify the information in it from other sources and discuss the findings.	H-2
05C49.D	Study the lives and teachings of wen-known, outspoken preachers on both sides of the War Between the States.	H-2
05C50.D	Tour one or more battlefields, museums, or other historic sites connected with the War Between the States.	H-2
05C51.D	Read the original document of the Emancipation Proclamation in its entirety. Determine and discuss with parents or others which slaves were actually freed by the signing of that document.	H-1

CULTURAL STUDIES

05C52.D	Using the same materials you used in your study of the War Between the States, study the period immediately following it known as Reconstruction. Discuss or mind map on these questions: What was the purpose of the laws that created this situation? Did they accomplish their purpose?	H-2
05C53.D	From the political speeches and writings of Abraham Lincoln, decide how you believe Reconstruction would have been handled differently if he had lived to implement it.	H-2
05C54.D	Study the assassination of Lincoln and the controversies that surrounded it.	
05C55.D	Study the impeachment of Andrew Johnson and the reasons for it, both real and alleged. Determine and discuss how this impeachment affected Johnson's ability and effectiveness as President thereafter.	H - 2
05C56.	Make timeline cards for all major events mentioned or studied in this unit.	VA-leach H- leach
05C57.	Make timeline entries for the major events in the lives of each of the authors, inventors, or artists mentioned or read in this mini-unit.	VA-leach H- leach
05C58.	Make timeline entries for each person, movements and / or event studied in this mini-unit.	VA-leach H- leach
05C59.	Use material studied for this mini-unit as well as Usborne's *World History Dates, Kingfisher History Encyclopedia, Timetables of History* and/or similar reference books to find the information needed for making timeline entries for all the people, movements, and events studied in this mini-unit.	H-1 VA-1
05C60.	Use Usborne's *World History Dates, Kingfisher History Encyclopedia, Timetables of History* or a similar book to identify and make timeline entries for other important events during each time period studied in this mini-unit.	H-1 VA-1
05C61.	Make timeline entries for all inventions and/or discoveries studied in this mini-unit and all major events in the lives of their inventors.	H-1 VA-1
05C62.	Use encyclopedias or other references to study all countries mentioned in any context within this mini-unit.	G-2
05C63.	Locate on a map or globe each country studied in this mini-unit.	G-3
05C64.	Locate on a map of the world and/or your country and study the geography of all cities and municipalities you studied in this mini-unit.	G-2

CULTURAL STUDIES

| 05C65. | Locate on a U. S. map all states mentioned or studied in this unit. | G-1 |
| 05C66. | Study the geography of the home country of each author, inventor, or artist whose works were used or studied in this mini-unit. | G-2 each |

READING AND LITERATURE

05R01.A	Read all sections of *The Hidden Art of Homemaking* that deal with cooking or serving food.	HM-3
05R02.A	Read the cooking and nutrition sections of *How to Live on Practically Nothing and Have Plenty*.	HM-1
05R03.A	Read assorted Foods and Nutrition project literature from 4-H and the Agricultural Extension Service.	HM-1
05R04.A	Read *Food, Fitness, and Health* from Usborne.	HE-3
05R05.A	Read *Once a Month Cooking* and discuss with your mother to decide if this method is for your family.	HM-6
05R06.A	Read and study *Homemade Health,* and discuss with your mother what portion (if any) of it she wants you to implement in your home,	HE-6
05R07.A	Read all non-recipe sections of *The Whole Foods Cookbook* or another book on the advantages of eating whole, natural foods.	HE-3
05R08.A	Read *Recipes for Life, The Art of Life,* and all other non-recipe sections of Hearth and Home by Karey Swan.	HM-3
05R09.A	Read *Eat Well, Live Well,* concentrating on the non-recipe sections but looking over recipes as well.	HE-3
05R10.B	Read Lois Henderson's Bible-based biographies of Hagar and/ or Miriam, both of whom were slaves for part of their lives.	L-5
05R11.B	Read *Twice Freed,* the Bible-based biography of Onesimus, friend of Paul and slave of Philemon.	L-5
05R12.B	Read *Up From Slavery*, the autobiography of Booker T. Washington.	L-5
05R13.B	Read biographies of Sojourner Truth, George Washington Carver and/or other slaves who went on to become famous after Emancipation.	B-4each
05R14.B	Read a biography of Harriet Tubman and/ or one or more other `conductors' of the Underground Railroad.	H - 5

READING AND LITERATURE

05R15.B*	Read and discuss *Roots* or watch the mini-series on video.	H - 6
05R16.B	Read *Devil on the Deck*, the biography of John Newton, converted slave trader who became a dynamic pastor, totally sold out as a slave to the Lord Jesus Christ.	H - 8
05R17.B	Read *Little Dorritt* or see the six-hour video about life in debtors' prison.	H - 5
05R18.B	Read *My Folks Don't Want Me to Talk about Slavery*, or *Before Freedom: When I Just Can Remember*, both of which are anthologies of reminiscences by former slaves given just 60-80 years after the War Between the States.	L - 6
05R19.B	Read biographies of well-known leaders of the abolitionists in (H - 5) the United States or elsewhere, including any or all of the following as well as others: Henry Ward Beecher, Harriet Beecher Stowe, William Wilburforce.	H-5each
05R20.C	For a quick overview of ancient Egypt, read Usborne's condensed version of *The Egyptians* from the Hotshots series.	H-5
05R21.C	Read Usborne's *Pharaohs and Pyramids* to get a more detailed look at these two aspects of ancient Egypt.	H-2
05R22.C	Read Usborne's *The Egyptian Echo* written as if it were a newspaper or magazine of ancient Egypt.	H-3
05R23.C	Study the Dorling Kindersley book *Ancient Egyptians* for a more thorough study of this culture.	H-5
05R24.C	For a Biblical perspective on this, read *Pharaohs and Kings: A Biblical Quest* by David Rohl.	H-5 B-2
05R25.C	Read *Into the Mummy's Tomb*, a real-life account of the discovery and excavation of the tomb of King Tut.	H-5
05R26.C	Read Usborne's *Archaeology*, to learn more about this fascinating text.	H-4
05R27.C	Read **The Golden Goblet**, a fictional story of a young boy in Ancient Egypt.	L-5
05R28.C	Read *The Cat of Bubastes* by G. A. Henty, a novel about ancient Egypt.	L - 5
05R29.D*	Read *Uncle Tom's Cabin*, a fictional book that played a major role in igniting American sympathies toward the Union cause in the War Between the States.	H - 6
05R30.D	Read sermons, essays, and other writings of the abolitionists that contributed to starting the War Between the States.	H - 1 each B - 1 each

READING AND LITERATURE

05R31.D   Read one or more books of collected sermons from Thornwall, B - 5 each
paying close attention to those in which he gave Biblical
grounds for secession. Decide whether or not you agree with his
interpretation of the passages.

05R32.D   After watching the Ken Burns video *The Civil War*, read and compare H - 5 each
pare to it *Facts the Historians Leave Out*. Many people believe
this may be the single most significant book on the topic of this war.
HIGHLY RECOMMENDED

05R33.D   Read one or more biographies of the military leaders of H - 5 each
the War Between the States, being sure to include Robert E. Lee
and Stonewall Jackson, both of whom were strong Christians.
Videos may be substituted if they are factual.

05R34.D   Read *Christ in the Camp* to get a look at the great H - 8
Spiritual revival within the Confederate army during the War
Between the States, proof that the Lord used even the awful
war to bring men to saving faith in Him.

05R35.D   Read *Killer Angels* and compare it to the movie H - 5
Gettysburg, which was based on it and to original archived
accounts of the battle.

05R36.D   Read *Mrs. Robert E. Lee*, by Rose Mortimer Ellzey MacDonald. H - 5

05R37.D   Read a biography and/or memoirs of Abraham Lincoln, or H - 5 book
watch the Arts and Entertainment network's biography of him, H - 2 video
available on video

05R38.D   Read a biography of Jefferson Davis and/or his memoirs, or H - 5 book
watch the Arts & Entertainment network's video of his life. H - 2 video

05R39.D   Read *Red Badge of Courage* and discuss it with your parents L - 5
or give a presentation on it for your family.

05R40.D   Study the poem "John Brown's Body" and memorize 100 or L - 20
more lines of it.

05R41.D   Read one or more of the books in Bruce Catton's famous series H - 5each
on the War Between the States.

05R42.D*   Read *Gone with the Wind*, by Margaret Mitchell for an accurate L - 7
view of life in the Confederacy and during Reconstruction in the
postwar South.

05R43.D   Read the book *Black Confederates* to understand why some H - 5
slaves and free blacks chose to fight for the South during the
War Between the States.

05R44.   Read one or more historical novels set in one of the time periods H 5each
studied in this unit.

05R45.	Read biographies of other people you studied in this mini-unit.	H - 5each
05R46.	Read at least one book per week in addition to those assigned in this or any other section of this study. Choose from those listed here or in the resource list or any others your parents might approve.	L - 5each
05R47.	Read any other appropriate books on the subject of the mini-unit you are studying.	L - 5each

COMPOSITION

05W01.A	Write an essay on "The Importance of Good Nutrition for Good Health".	HE 2
05W02.A	Prepare Biblical arguments for both sides of a debate on the topic: "Resolved: God's People are Called to be Vegetarians" or "Resolved: The Eating of Meat is Harmful to Our Health".	EC - 5 HM - 4 HE - 4
05W03.A	Write a well-researched essay to answer the question: "Are Christians Bound by Old Testament Kosher Laws?" Support all statements from Scripture.	CE - 3 HM - 3
05W04.A	Prepare a how-to-cook manual to be used by a younger child. Include in it basic information on how to measure, substitutions you can use when a product is not available, definitions of cooking terms, food safety rules, and simple directions for general dishes (i. e., quick breads, cooked puddings, etc.) Add 3 - 5 pages each of recipes for salads, soups, entrees, vegetables, breads, and desserts that are easy enough for young children to make with little or no supervision. End with tips for serving food and storing any leftovers.	HE - 5 B - 5 EC - 5
05W05.A	Prepare a booklet on nutrition, devoting one or more pages to each major nutrient and one or more foods providing that nutrient. Also include common nutrition deficiencies and food-related diseases, giving symptoms, severity, and treatment. The last section to include should cover dangers from food, like cholesterol, caffeine, sugar, chemical additives, and artificial sweeteners.	EC - 2 B - 1
05W06.A	Write a demonstration speech (complete with directions for demonstrating) on how to cook some particular dish.	HE - 6 EC - 6
05W07.A	Write a nutrition brochure to be distributed to children on the advantages and disadvantages of sugar and the various artificial sweeteners.	EC - 2
05W08.A	Write a story in which someone learns to cook and/or eat food of another type or culture and is able to build friendships or minister to someone through that.	EC - 10

COMPOSITION

05W09.A   Research and write a report (1 - 2 pages) on one of the   EC - 2
unusual utensils you found in a museum or kitchen store.
Describe it for those who have never seen it and explain how,
when, and where it was used. Tell what utensils are used in your
own time and area for the same purpose.

05W10.A   For handwriting practice in this unit, copy your family's favorite   HM- 1
recipes, with complete cooking instructions, onto 3 x 5
or 5 x 7 file cards to begin your own recipe box for your hope
chest.

05W11.A   Write a report on the human digestive, endocrine, and excretory   HA - 5
systems and the component parts of each. Write about a   EC - 10
page on each system itself, 1/2 to 1 page one each of the organs
involved, and 1 or more pages on each disorder of the system that
you studied (with remedies). Keep this in your notebook on the
HUMAN BODY, to which you will add other reports throughout
the unit study as other systems are studied.

05W12.A   Write a news report on some aspect of nutritional health, like   EC - 2
cholesterol, food allergies, diabetes.

05W13.B   Write an essay to compare and contrast slavery as practiced   H - 2
by Old Testament Hebrews and that in the U. S., Britain, and/
or Canada in the 1700's and 1800's.

05W14.B   Write a research paper (6-7 typed pages) comparing the institution   EC - 5
of slavery as sanctioned in the Old Testament with that   B - 1
practiced in the U.S. in the 19th century as well as with the
practices of indenture, feudalism, and debtor's prison.

05W15.B   Write a letter that might have been left behind by a slave   H - 1
leaving on the Underground Railroad. Explain his/her reasons   EC - 2
for leaving, how much (s)he will miss those left behind, the fears
she has of dangers on the trip.

05W16.B   Write reports on two or more of the 'conductors' of the   H - 2 each
Underground Railroad.

05W17.B   After reading *The Debate is Over* and/or other abolitionist   EC - 3
literature, paraphrase it to relate to the abortion issue of today.

05W18.B   Write a geography report (2-3 pages) on Australia to go in your   G - 2
GEOGRAPHY notebook begun in other units.

05W19.B   Write a report for your GEOGRAPHY notebook on the nation   G - 1
of Liberia.

05W20.B   Write a short story set in Australia during the time it was a   G - 5
penal colony. Work that fact into the story somehow.   EC - 5

05W21.B   Write a fictional story of a slave who gained his/her freedom   H-3
at the conclusion of the War Between the States.   EC-3

COMPOSITION

05W22.B	Prepare a Bible-based reaction to the Supreme Court's ruling in the Dred Scott decision. Use Deuteronomy 23:15, and/or other appropriate passages.	H-1 B-1
05W23.B	Write a first person story of Joseph's life in Egypt. Fill in events that may have occurred during the times for which the Bible is silent. Try to capture his feeling at the time of each major turning point mentioned in Scripture.	B-1 EC-1
05W24.B	Write an evangelistic tract (3-5 pages) from the standpoint of Jesus rescuing us from slavery to sin.	B-3 EC-5
05W25.C	Write a first person short story about a Hebrew slave leaving Egypt with Moses and Aaron in the Biblical Exodus.	EC-5 B-3
05W26.C	Write an imaginary dream and an interpretation that Joseph might have given for it.	EC-2
05W27.C	Write a play or puppet show set in ancient Egypt.	EC-4
05W28.C	Write (8-10) entries for a journal kept by Aaron during the events recorded in the book of Exodus.	B-2 EC-3
05W29.C	Write a scientific report explaining in detail the processes that go into the excavation of a pyramid and the dating and cataloging of artifacts uncovered there.	EC-4
05W30.C	Write reports on any of the pharaohs you studied by name.	EC- 1 each
05W31.C	Write a geography report on the nation of Egypt and add it to your GEOGRAPHY notebook.	EC-1
05W32.C	Write a brief (2-3 page) history of the Copts, the true descendants of the ancient Egyptians and one of the earliest Gentile cultures to be highly Christianized. Explain what happened to their culture and where their remnant is today.	EC-2 H-1
05W33.C	Write a news article (1 - 2 pages) as might have been done by a reporter of the day watching the Israelites leave Egypt and/or walk across the Red Sea on dry land.	EC-1
05W34.C	Write step-by-step instructions explaining the mummification process used by the early Egyptians.	SB-1 EC-1 H-1
05W35.D	Using passages studied in Bible and Christian Character in this mini-unit, write an analysis of the Biblical basis for secession.	EC-1 H-1 B-1
05W36.D	Write a detailed character sketch for one or more of the Christians who were prominent in the War Between the States.	EC- 1 each
05W37.D	Write a brief report on each of the military leaders studied in this unit.	EC- 1 each

COMPOSITION

05W38.D	Write a short story centered around one or more of the battles or other events you studied in this mini-unit.	EC-5 H-5
05W39.D	Prepare 8-10 (minimum) diary or journal entries for a wife or mother waiting for her loved one to return from the war. Recount her sorrow at watching him leave home, the widespread frustration at the lack of good communications with the front lines, the fear she tried to fight each time a list of battle casualties was distributed, her relief at not finding his name there, the eagerness with which she awaits word from him. Add her reminiscences of better times with him and prayers for the future.	EC-5
05W40.D	Write an "eyewitness" account of one or more of the major battles of this war, as if written by a war correspondent traveling with one of the armies.	EC-1each
05W41.D	Write letters that might have been sent home by men on opposite sides of important battles, doing one for each side in each instance.	EC-1each
05W42.D	Write a report on the assassination of President Lincoln as it might have been reported in a newspaper of the day.	EC-2 H-1
05W43.D	Write legal arguments to be presented by each side in the impeachment trial of Andrew Johnson.	EC-10
05W44.D	Write an essay on "Reconstruction Under Lincoln" in which you explain how you think it would have been different if he had not been killed.	EC-3
05W45.	Using *Writers Inc., College English Handbook*, or other grammar reference, proofread and correct all written work for this mini-unit.	EG-1 per 5 pages
05W46.	Use a good dictionary to proofread and correct spelling in all written work for this mini-unit.	EC-1 per paper
05W47.	Keep a journal of each day's school activities throughout the entire study. If done well, this journal can serve as documentation of your school year.	EC-2 per week
05W48.	As you listen to any of the suggested audios or watch the videos in this mini-unit, take notes on what you hear and/or see.	EG-1 or 2 each
05W49.	Use your notes to outline, summarize, and/or discuss the audios and videos as requested.	EC-1 each
05W50.	Outline one or more of the nonfiction books used in this mini-unit.	EG-3 each
05W51.	Instead of, or in addition to, outlining the books studied here, write reviews of them, as might be published in a periodical of some type.	EC-2 each

COMPOSITION

05W52.	Write a brief report on any important person studied in this unit.	EC-2 each
05W53.	Use Scripture passages, poems or other memory work to copy for practice in handwriting.	EG-1 per hour
05W54.	Use the same material to write from dictation, being careful about spelling, punctuation, etc. Have someone read the passage to you slowly while you write it.	EG-1 per hour
05W55.	As an alternative to cursive writing, try Italic or Spencerian calligraphy using books in the resource list.	1 credit in calligraphy for complete course
05W56.	Write a news article on each of the field trips you took in this mini-unit.	EC-2each
05W57.	Write a thank you note to the organizer, supervisor, and/or guide of any field trip you took for this mini-unit.	EC-1each
05W58.	Write summaries of any or all of the books read in this unit.	EC-2each
05W59.	Write reports on any or all of the women studied in the mini-unit.	EC-2each
05W60.	Write one book report per week on a book related to this unit or another approved by your parents. Use a variety of approaches, including any or all of the ones listed in the Appendix.	E-2 each
05W61.	Define and put into your vocabulary notebook 10 new words per week, using first those you have encountered in your studies. Write definitions and mark proper pronunciations.	EC-5 week
05W62.	Learn to spell all the words in your vocabulary notebook for this mini-unit.	EC-1 per week

MATHEMATICS AND PERSONAL FINANCE

05M01.A	As you make your menu plans, use the nutrition information on labels and your own knowledge of fresh ingredients to plan daily menus that provide 100% of the USDA daily recommendations for the 10 most important vitamins and minerals.	HE-3
05M02.A	Using charts from USDA, doctors, County Extension Agents, or other reliable sources, determine the appropriate amount of each major nutrient needed for optimum health for all members of your family. Notice how widely the amounts vary by product.	HE-2

MATHEMATICS AND PERSONAL FINANCE

| 05M03.A | Graph the above nutritional information to show the relative amounts of each needed by each person. | M-5 |

| 05M04.A | Use the data on the above graph to make per cent, ratio, and proportion problems for younger siblings or friends to solve. Work them yourself, so you will be sure you know the answer, | M-5 |

| 05M05.A | Tally costs of all meals you cook for one week. Try to plan menus containing the required amount (or more) of all of the necessary nutrients at a lower than average per person cost. | M-2 |

| 05M06. A | Use your basic math and algebra skills to alter sizes and portions of your recipes as needed. | Parent's Discretion |

| 05M07.A | Compare and chart on a bar graph the differences in prices of regular, low-fat, low-sodium, low-sugar, and/or organic versions of the same food, using at least 10 different examples. | M-4 |

| 05M08.B | Using statistics from history books and/or data from your archives department and such, make a bar graph or pictograph showing the population of the U. S. in several different years of the 1800's, comparing the numbers of free citizens and slaves in each year. | M-5 |

| 05M09.B | Perform calculations to show the data from #05M08 as percentages, ratios and proportions. | M-2 |

| 05M10.B | Calculate the percentage of the people in each U. S. state or territory who were slaves in each of several years before 1864. | M-10 |

| 05M11.B | From census records or other archival data, determine the number of slaves in each state and U. S. territory in several different years prior to 1861 and show increase or decrease on a line graph. You may be surprised to see how many slaves were in some Northern states even as the War Between the States began. | M-2 |

| 05M12.B | Make a pie graph to show data collected or calculated in the two previous activities. | M-4 |

| 05M13.C | Using a scale map of the ancient world, compute the largest total area ever covered by the Egyptian Empire. | M-4 |

| 05M14.C | Use the same map as in the previous activity to measure the distance between Goshen, where the Hebrews lived as slaves, and the Promised Land of Canaan. At average walking speed (which you must determine), calculate how long it would have taken the Hebrews to travel that distance if they had gone straight there. | M-1 |

MATHEMATICS AND PERSONAL FINANCE

05M15.C   Using the population numbers given in Exodus and at the   M-1
census in Numbers and a distance of one foot between people
determine how far the line of Hebrews would reach if they all
marched single file, two-by-two, by fives, by tens, and in rows
of one hundred. Calculate in feet, yards, miles, meters, and
kilometers.

05M16.C   At the average walking speed you used in #05M14 determine   M-2
how long from the time the first one left it would take all of the
Israelites in the Exodus to get out of Egypt if they left one at a
time in a single line. How long would it take the same group
to cross the Red Sea in the same way?

05M17.C   Using available data on sizes of various pyramids, calculate   M-1
and build a scale model of one or more of them, using sugar
cubes or other material of your choice.

05M18.D   Compile data on the numbers of casualties suffered by each   M-2
side in several major battles of the War Between the States
and calculate various relationships between them.

05M19.D   Make a graph of your choice to show the above data on   M-5
battle casualties.

05M20.D   Use state and federal archival data to determine the population   M-5
of the states in the Union and in the Confederacy in 1961.
Compare sizes of the individual states and the respective
nations on a graph of your choice and creation.

05M21.D   Use the resources named above to find the number of men in   M-5
each army at the start and end of the war. Make a graph to
compare the sizes of the two armies and show the percentage
of each nation's population that served in its military.

05M22.   Use data from any or all of the above graphs to practice   M-5
making and solving problems using percent, ratio, and proportion.

05M23.   Continue to brush up on basic math as needed and suggested   M-5
by activities in this unit.

SCIENCE

05S01.A   Study the anatomy and physiology of the human digestive
system.

05S02.A   Study the anatomy and working of the teeth, gums, and tongue,
using cross-section pictures or a cutaway model.

05S03.A   Study enzymes, hormones, and other "juices" that play a part
in digestion and the organs that produce them.

SCIENCE

05S04.A	Study the excretory system, how it works, and its connection to digestion.	HA-1
05S05.A	Study the digestive systems of one of more animals representative of a genus or class, using actual dissection, a plastic cutaway model, videos, or transparencies.	SB-2each
05S06.A	Learn about the chemical processes involved in digestion and the chemical makeup of the various digestive juices.	SC-1
05S07.A	Experiment to observe the effect of saliva on various food substances.	HA-1
05S08.A	Subject a variety of foods to common chemical tests for salt, sugar, acidity, etc., and record your findings on some type of chart or in your nutrition notebook.	SC-1
05S09.A	Study the effects of varying temperatures, humidity, and other environmental factors on the quality, safety, and taste of various food products.	HE-3
05S10.A	Study the life cycles of various bacteria, fungi, and other organisms that affect food and may cause illness.	SB-2
05S11.B	Study the work of former slave George Washington Carver with peanuts and sweet potatoes. Try to duplicate his work and produce usable products.	PA-5
05S12.B	Tour a plant that produces peanut oil, peanut butter or some other common peanut product. Notice the methods and equipment used in this endeavor and learn how each one works.	PA-2
05S13.B	Study the growth and propagation of the peanut and other legumes and the areas and conditions in which they grow best.	SB-1
05S14.B	Tour a peanut farm during harvest time to learn how these legumes are grown and harvested.	SE-1
05S15.B	Study the nonfood uses for peanut oil and other peanut by-products.	HM-1
05S16.B	George Washington Carver discovered uses for all parts of the peanut plant, even the hulls and stems. Investigate how these are used today and what purpose they serve.	PA-1
05S17.B	Study the soil replenishment properties of the peanut and other legumes.	SB-3
05S18.B	Study the common parasites, pests, and diseases that attack the peanut plant.	SB-4
05S19.B	Study the nutritional value of the peanut in all its edible forms.	SB-2

SCIENCE

05S20. C	Use "The Pyramid Explorer's Kit" to learn about the science of archaeology, the work of archaeologists on Egypt's pyramids, and what they have been able to discover about them.	SP- 3
05S21.C	Study any of the books under the Reading and Literature section and/or other archaeological evidence explaining the pyramids and how they were built.	SP-1 H-1
05S22.C	Investigate the tools and utensils used in and outside the homes of ancient Egypt.	SP-2
05S23. C	Given the tools and materials of the time, try to determine how the pyramids were constructed. Explain and defend your beliefs orally or in writing. Build or draw a model, diagram, or picture to illustrate and explain your theory.	SP-2
05S24.C	Investigate the irrigation methods used by the Egyptians then and now to grow crops out of the desert that is their homeland.	SP-1
05S25.C	Use resources of your choice to study the flora and fauna common to a desert such as covers and surrounds much of Egypt.	SE-2
05S26.C	Watch one or more books good science videos on deserts and the various life forms that call them home. Try films by National Geographic or Moody Science.	SE-1
05S27.C	Study the procedures and materials used in the mummification process in ancient Egypt.	SC-3
05S28.C	Study the modern processes used for embalming and compare them to the Egyptian form of mummification.	SC - 3
05S29.D	Study the Gatling Gun, an early type of automatic weapon first used in the War Between the States.	SP - 1
05S30.D	Study other weapons available to the soldiers of the War Between the States. Learn how each operated and compare them to their modern-day counterparts.	SP - 3 H - 1
05S31.D	Study the telegraph, which was a valuable tool for the armies in the War Between the States. Learn how this device is built and the principles on which it operates.	SP - 1
05S32.D	Study various materials that might have been used to build various components of the telegraph. Determine what properties of the materials chosen were most important to the final outcome.	SF' - 1
05S33.D	Mind map about the importance of the telegraph at this time and why it is no longer widely used. Include in your mind map the various modern communication equipment that made the telegraph obsolete.	H-2

SCIENCE

05S34.D	At this time you may study, as in-depth as you wish, any or all of the communication advances you listed in the above activity.	H - 1 SP - 2
05S35.D	Investigate the hot air balloon and its use in the War Between the States. Learn how they are made, how they operate, and why the military found them useful.	SP - 1 H - 1
05S36. D	Following directions in The Backyard Scientist or another book of science experiments, build a small hot air balloon and propel it as far as you can.	SP - 4
05S37.D	Take a ride in a real hot air balloon, helping with the launch and landing in so far as possible.	RE - 3

HEALTH AND PHYSICAL FITNESS

05H01.A	Study diseases and disorders of the digestive system and the proper treatment for them. Be sure to include ulcers, gastritis, hiatal hernia, heartburn, as well as others.	HE-2
05H02.A	Learn about all types of dental ailments and diseases and their causes.	HE-1
05H03.A	Discuss your dental records with your dentist and find out what they show him.	HE-1
05H04.A	Tour a dental office and lab and learn how a dentist and his staff do their work and what equipment they use.	HE-2
05H05.A	Learn about food allergies and intolerance and how to identify them.	HE-1
05H06.A	Study other health problems connected with specific foods or types of foods. Learn their symptoms, prevention, and treatment.	HE-2
05H07.A	Study a complete nutrition course using any good textbook or material from 4-H, county extension office or other sources.	HE or FN-30
05H08.A	Study and compare the pros and cons of saccharin, sugar, honey, aspartame, and powdered fructose as sweeteners.	FN-2
05H09.A	Prepare a poster on the nutritional pyramid. For each food group show main nutrients offered, amounts, and primary sources. Include your own drawings or cutout pictures of foods that are examples of each category.	FN-3
05H10.A	Study positive and negative health effects of caffeine, tannin, and other natural or artificial stimulants.	FN-1

HEALTH AND PHYSICAL FITNESS

05H11.A   Compare various sources of nutrients needed by the body and   FN-3
learn to choose those low in fat, cholesterol, sodium and/or
calories, as prescribed for any members of your family.

05H12.A   Study cholesterol, its effect on your health, and methods of   HE-1
controlling it

05H13.A   Study vitamin and food supplements and decide which are   HE-2
best to meet specific nutritional needs of your family.

05H14.A   Investigate prescription drugs taken by members of your family   SC-1
for any type of digestive disorder or food reaction. Learn   HE-1
what the medications contain and what risks, if any, they pose.

05H15.A   Study vegetarian sources of protein and amino acids using   FN-1
Home Made Health or some similar resource.

05H16.A   Study food safety and the prevention of food poisoning.   HE-1

05H17.B   Study the illnesses often contracted on the slave ships and   HE-4
trace them to their causes. How many were natural results of
crowded and unsanitary conditions? What new, strange (to them)
illnesses did slaves contract because their systems were not
prepared for certain aspects of life in their new land?

05H18.B   Of the illnesses detailed in the previous activity, learn which   HE-3
ones are still common today and how they are currently treated.

05H19.B   From the books listed in this unit or others on the topic period,   HE-3
study the medical care available to slaves in the United States.

05H20.B   From the book, *From Calabar to Carter's Grove*, list all specific
illnesses or injuries mentioned and how they were treated.   H-3

05H2 1.B   Compare the medical care given these actual slaves in that
book (activity # 05H18) to the normal medical practices of the   H-2
day, both for slaves (as discovered in activity # 05H17) and for   HE-3
the general population.

05H22.B   Compare the treatment of illnesses discovered in activities
05H17-05H21 with the way similar ailments are treated today.   H-2
What new drugs and/or procedures are available and
how have they changed things?

05H23.B   Compare the medical care of African slaves in North America   HE-5
to that of slaves in other times and places.   H-2

05H24.B   Examine the medical care available in Western Africa in the   H-3
1700's-1800's. Compare to that offered American slaves in the
same period.

05H25.B   As most slaves we will study extensively in this unit were African,   HE-2
this is a good time to study sickle-cell anemia and other diseases
that solely or primarily strike those of African descent. Research
each disease to learn its causes, symptoms, and methods of
treatment and prevention.

HEALTH AND PHYSICAL FITNESS

05H26.C	Use books already suggested in this unit or others on life in ancient Egypt to study treatments used in that culture for injuries of various sorts.	HE-3
05H27.C	Study diseases prevalent among early Egyptians and the treatment used for them, then and now.	H-2
05H28.C	The Egyptian midwives were praised in Exodus 1 as heroines who saved the lives of many Hebrew babies. The same Scripture passage mentions the use of a "birthing stool". Study this tool and its use in labor and delivery then and now.	HE-2
05H29.C	Use this opportunity to study the history of midwifery if you do not do so in Unit 18.	H-2
05H30.C	Study the medical procedures that are employed in the mummification process and determine what uses any of them might have on live people.	HE-3
05H31.C	It is believed that the ancient Egyptians began the practice of shaving the armpits. Study the health and hygiene principles behind this.	HE-1
05H32.C	Study the health and hygiene value of shaving facial hair and/ or that on any other body parts. is this a health consideration of strictly a matter of appearance? If it does affect health, explain how.	HE-1
05H33.C	Investigate antiperspirants and deodorants (first used by the ancient Egyptians) to learn what ingredients they all share, how they differ from each other, and which one is most effective for you.	SC-2
05H34.C	While you are on the subject, use this chance to study creams, waxes, and other depilatory tools and methods used in our society today. Learn the pros and cons of each.	SC-2
05H35.D	Study dysentery, which was very prevalent among soldiers on both sides during the War Between the States, and its treatment , then and now.	HE-1
05H36.D	Study the anesthetics and pain killers that were available for use during the War Between the States.	HE-2
05H37.D	In a history of medicine, study the strides made in nursing and bedside care during the war you are studying in this unit.	H-2
05H38.D	Study skin-grafting, often used nowadays for victims of burns and explosions, like many of the soldiers injured in this war.	HE-2
05H39.D	Study the development of reconstructive surgery, which could have prevented scarring for many war-injured soldiers had it been available at that time.	H-1
05H40.D	Investigate the current uses of "plastic" surgery and deter- mine which are not truly health-related.	HE-3

HEALTH AND PHYSICAL FITNESS

05H41.D	Study the medical practice of amputations, which were common among soldiers wounded in the War Between the States. Study how the procedure has changed over the years.	HE-2
05H42.D	Study the causes of gangrene and blood poisoning, the two most common causes for the loss of limbs during the time studied, and how they affect the body.	HE-1
05H43.D	Learn how can gangrene and blood poisoning can be prevented or treated before amputation of the affected limb is necessary? Learn which, if any, of these methods were available at the time of the war studied in this unit	H-3
05H44.D	Study the processes by which mangled or severed body parts can be restored and the history of this medical advancement that would have been so helpful during the War Between the States but was not available until much later.	1-1E-2
05H45.D	Investigate the use of artificial limbs and the history of their development, tracing the changes made in them over the years.	HE-3
05H46.D	Tour a factory that makes prosthetic limbs and learn how they are manufactured.	HE-2
05H47.D	Tour a rehabilitation clinic where patients are being fitted with prosthetics and/or taught how to use them.	HE-2

PRACTICAL ARTS

05P01.A	Make felt cutouts, transparency overlays, cutaway diagrams or other visual aids to teach younger children what you have learned about the digestive and excretory systems.	HE-2
05P02.A	Learn to test yourself and family members for blood glucose levels, high blood pressure, and other danger signs of food-related illness you can easily monitor at home.	HE-1
05P03.A	Analyze the nutritional value of all the meals your family eats over the course of a few days. Look for ways to add nutritional value and cut down on fats, sugar, and other negatives consumed.	FN-5
05P04.A	Complete the entire "Cooking School" series by Usborne. This consists of the following books: *Cooking for Beginners, Cakes and Cookies for Beginners, Pasta and Pizza for Beginners,* and *Vegetarian Cooking for Beginners.*	FN-20
05P05.A	Attend a Southern Living Cooking School.	FN- 6
05P06.A	Plan and prepare all of your family's meals every day for at least one full week, working to balance all meals nutritionally and staying within a given budget.	FN- 5 each day
05P07.A	Prepare casseroles, one-dish dinners, and/or other appropriate meals to share with sick or bereaved friends and their families.	FN-5

HEALTH AND PHYSICAL FITNESS

05P08.A	Prepare for yourself a scrapbook or card file of healthy, inexpensive recipes you can make and know your family will enjoy. Add to it as you go through this entire unit study.	HM-1
05P09.A	Learn several methods of presenting a variety of foods in an appealing, eye-catching manner.	HM-leach
05P10.A	Instead of card files or a cookbook, turn your recipe collection into a database on your computer.	CO-3+
05P11.A	Learn to cook a variety of new dishes low in sugar, cholesterol, fats, salt, etc.	FN-3+
05P12.A	Alter some of your family's favorite recipes to make them healthier by eliminating or minimizing fat, cholesterol, sugar, etc.	FN- leach
05P13.A	Learn to cook as many different types of food as possible, concentrating on those you know your family particularly enjoys.	FN- leach
05P14.A	Plan and arrange appealing table settings and decorations for several different types of meals and occasions.	HM-2
05P15.A	Make a tablecloth or place mat set and use it in one of your table arrangements.	HM-2
05P16.A	Make napkins and napkin rings to go with the tablecloth or place mats you made.	VA-1
05P17.A	Prepare an attractive meal tray with decorations for a sickbed patient or an invalid.	HM-2
05P18.A	Tour the kitchen of a hospital, prison, or other institution, talk with the dietitian in charge and observe the facility in operation.	HM-1
05P19.A	Help cook and/or clean in a commercial, church, or other institutional kitchen.	HM-2
05P20.A	Learn to decorate cakes, candies, etc.	FN-3
05P21.B	From your studies of the everyday lives of the slaves in North America, try to learn some of the games they played together to entertain themselves after work and when the weather was bad. Learn to play one or more of them with family or friends.	RE- 2
05P22.B	Teach one or more of the games used by slaves in the American South to your friends or a group of younger children.	TE-2+
05P23.B	Teach a group of children to sing some of the songs, now known as spirituals, popular with the African slaves in North America.	TE-1&YM-1 per song
05P24.B	Prepare an anti-abortion flyer or brochure using paraphrased arguments from the 19th century abolitionists in the United. States. Do all typesetting and design work yourself.	EC-2 BE-2
05P25.B	Distribute your anti-abortion flyers to crisis pregnancy centers, churches, schools, or other places you and your parents considers appropriate.	Parent's Discretion

PRACTICAL ARTS

05P26.B	With parental permission, join an on-site protest at an abortion clinic and distribute your flyers to potential patients there. DO NOT TRY TO DO THIS BY YOURSELF.	Parent's Discretion
05P27.B	Prepare and give as a speech a courtroom argument for a hypothetical appeal of the Dred Scott Decision, using as a foundation the paper you wrote on that topic in the Composition section.	EC-2 CL-2
05P28.B	Study and learn to speak and/or write the language of one of the African nations whose people were brought to North America as slaves.	FL-1/ 2CREDIT
05P29.B	After studying the work of G. W. Carver with peanuts, plant and attempt to grow them.	PA-5
05P30.B	Take part in or observe a peanut harvest on a commercial peanut farm.	PA-2
05P31.B	Work in a peanut processing plant to learn how the peanuts are sorted, graded, hulled, and prepared to be sold in various forms. Note the difference in processing for those that will be sold directly to consumers and the ones to be used as ingredients in other products.	IA-1 per hour
05P32.B	Prepare peanuts several different ways for eating, comparing the flavor and fat content of each. Try to include: boiling, dry roasting, steaming, baking in oil, and honey-roasting.	FN-2
05P33.B	Make your own peanut butter from peanuts you grew. You may buy raw peanuts to complete this if you did not grow any.	FN-2
05P34.B	Learn to make at least one dish (not a snack) using peanuts as one of the ingredients.	FN —1
05P35.B	Observe for a full day or work in a peanut butter factory to see how the commercial process varies from making it yourself.	IA-3+
05P36.C	Tour an archaeological dig and observe the work going on there.	H-4
05P37.C	Participate in whatever way you are able in an archaeological excavation.	H- 1per hour
05P38.C	If you are unable to take part in a real "dig", use "Ancient Egypt Explorer's Kit" to excavate and restore the artifacts buried therein.	H-2
05P39.C	Volunteer in a museum and learn how to best handle ancient artifacts so they will be most carefully preserved.	H-1 per hour
05P40.C	Using Usborne's *Fun with Hieroglyphs* or another resource, learn to read and write hieroglyphics.	H-5 CR-5
05P41.C	Make your own papyrus scrolls, writing your own message in hieroglyphs	
05P42.C	Use patterns and materials in "Ancient Egypt Explorer's Kit", World Book's *Make it Work: Ancient Egypt*, or any other resource to make one or more authentic Egyptian garments of this period. In so far as possible, try to use only supplies and techniques available at the time in question.	CC-3+ each

PRACTICAL ARTS

05P43.C	Make and learn to play the Egyptian game of "Senet", using directions and game pieces found in "Egyptian Treasure Chest".	RE-2
05P44.C	Teach a younger child to play "Senet".	TE-2+
05P45.C	Put together the intricate model of an Egyptian Funeral Boat contained in the kit of that name from the British Museum.	VA-2
05P46.C	Assist a younger sibling or friend in making any or all of the projects in *Make History: Ancient Egypt*.	TE- 1each
05P47.D	If your parents will allow it, find someone who has a muzzle-loading gun and practice loading and firing it.	PS-1 H-1
05P48.D	Learn to pitch a tent of the type soldiers on both sides lived in during the War Between the States.	RE-2
05P49.D	Use this opportunity to learn to cook over an open fire, outside and/or in a fireplace.	RE-2 per meal
05P50.D	Using a cookbook from the time period, learn to cook one or more dishes that were popular in that day.	FN-1 each H - 1 each
05P51.D	Make a basic telegraph system and practice sending messages on it.	CR - 3
05P52.D	Learn Morse Code to send messages on your model telegraph.	H - 1
05P53.D	If you have not done so in any other unit, learn to quilt, one of the ways women of both the Union and the Confederacy occupied their time and helped the troops, and make a quilt.	HM - 20+
05P54.D	Use your War Between the States study as a chance to learn how to access information in your state's archives.	BE - 1
05P55.D	Attend a reenactment of the War Between the States or other event of that period. Learn about what life was really like at that time and how to do the chores and crafts of the time.	H - 2 +
05P56.D	Put together your own costume for this time period, using only the materials and sewing techniques that would have been common to that time period.	CC - 4 each
05P57.D	Participate in a reenactment of the War Between the States or another event that took place during that time period.	H - 4+
05P58.	Type any or all papers written during the study of this unit.	BE- 1 every 4 pages
05P59.	Make your own puppets for any puppet show you write and/ or present in this mini-unit.	CR-5
05P60.	Design and sew your own costumes for any play you present in this unit.	CC-5+
05P61.	Present before an audience any speeches written for the Composition section of this unit.	DR-1 each

DECORATIVE AND PERFORMING ARTS

05A01.A	Draw onto transparencies and color with highlighters each of the organs studied in this mini-unit. Prepare in order as overlays and use to demonstrate what you have learned.	VA-2 HA-3
05A02.A	Draw a life-size outline shape of a human being. (Tracing around someone's clothed body is the easiest way to do this.) and fill in the organs you studied in this mini-unit, either drawing them directly onto the paper or making cutouts and fastening them where they belong.	VA-1 HA-2
05A03.A	Color and study in *Gray's Anatomy Coloring Book* all organs and systems studied in this mini-unit.	VA-1 HA-1
05A04.A	Use calligraphy, drawing or other graphic arts to make tray cards to go with meals for hospital or nursing home patients.	VA-1
05A05.A	Use any form of lettering and graphics and/or decorative artwork to create place cards for a special family dinner.	VA-1
05A06.A	Design and draw pictures of your choice to be laminated for use as place mats on your table.	VA-2
05A07.A	Learn to create floral and other suitable centerpieces for a variety of table settings.	HM-2
05A08.A	Make a collage or mosaic picture using whole or cut food labels.	VA-1
05A09.A	Make a picture or design using beans, pasta, rice or other dried food items.	VA-3
05A10.B	Tour an exhibit of paintings by Grandma Moses that depict, in her own primitive style, the lives of the Negro slaves and their descendants.	AA-2
05A11.B	Listen to and analyze several spirituals and other songs popularized by the slaves of the American South.	MA-3
05Al2.B	Learn to sing some of the above songs.	VM-2each
05A13. B	Learn to play some of the above songs on an instrument.	IM-2each
05A14.B	Study the combat dance of the Brazilian slaves of the 19th century and learn to perform it.	MA-2
05A15.C	Use sugar cubes or some type of small blocks to build a model of the pyramids.	VA-2
05A16.C	Color the preprinted papyrus sheet images of Queen Cleopatra, Queen Nefertiti, and Ramses II, all available from Greenleaf Press	VA-2
05A17.C	Build Usborne's *Make this Egyptian Temple*.	VA-5
05A18.C	Build Usborne's *Make This Egyptian Mummy*.	VA-4

DECORATIVE AND PERFORMING ARTS

| 05A19.C | Create a chart or poster using real or made up hieroglyphs as found in the pyramids. | VA-3 |

| 05A20.C | Complete Bellerophon's *Queen Nefertiti* coloring book. | VA-3 |

| 05A21.C | Color all the pages in *A Coloring Book of Ancient Egypt*, also by Bellerophon. | VA-3 |

| 05A22.C | Use the hieroglyphic rubber stamps to create a mural or collage. | VA-2 |

| 05A23.C | Watch a live performance of the play *Joseph and the Technicolor Dream Coat*. | DR-3 |

| 05A24.C | Direct or participate as a cast member in *Joseph and the Technicolor Dream Coat* or a similar play. | DR-1/2 CREDIT |

| 05A25.D | Learn to sing all verses of "The Battle Hymn of the Republic" the rallying song of the Union army. | VM-2 |

| 05A26.D | From *America Alive* or another book of historic songs, learn one or more other songs that were popular with soldiers in that war. | VM-2 each |

| 05A27.D | Learn to play one or more of the songs you learned to sing in this mini-unit. | IM-3each |

| 05A28.D | Set any section of Benet's book-length poem *John Brown's Body* to music, using an original tune. | MC-3+ |

| 05A29.D | Illustrate with your own drawings any or all of the narrative segments of Benet's poem. | VA-2+ |

| 05A30.D | See a production of any play about this time period in the United States. | DR - 2 |

| 05A31.D | Produce, direct, and/or act in *The Last Curtain* or another one-act play about Lincoln or another important figure in the War Between the States. | DR - 30+ |

| 05A32.D | By searching archives and/or the Internet, find a copy of *Our American Cousin*, the play Abraham Lincoln was watching when he was assassinated. Get together with friends or siblings and produce it. | DR- 50 H - 1 BE- 1 |

| 05A33. | Draw pictures of field trips in this unit. | VA - 2 ea. |

| 05A34. | Use drawing, painting and graphic arts to create displays and make posters as called for in this study. | Parent's discretion |

| 05A35. | Illustrate one or more of the poems you studied or memorized for this unit. | VA - 1 each |

| 05A36. | Set one or more of this unit's poems to music, using an original or existing tune. | MC - 2 each |

| 05A37. | Set one or more of the Scripture verses in this unit to music, using a tune you wrote for the purpose. | MC - 2 each |

UNIT 6

She considers a field and buys it;
with the fruit of her hands, she plants a vineyard.
Proverbs 31:16

Introduction to Unit 6

In this unit we see the ideal wife as an industrious gardener and real estate owner. In this context, you will look at Biblical principles for buying, selling and owning property. You will study God's demands concerning land purchases, boundaries, and property ownership in both the Old and New Testaments. You will also examine parables and teachings of the Lord concerning vines and vineyards. You will study all aspects of gardening, vineyards, and the growing of crops, concentrating primarily on vegetables, since fruit is covered in Unit 20.

This will lead into a full section on agriculture, including methods and equipment, both modern and historical. This will involve both corporate and private farms and those who work them, not only in your own country, but throughout the world. You will also study some of the environmental concerns of agriculture and the advantages or disadvantages of certain crops and/or procedures.

You will become familiar with laws regarding real estate and the processes involved in buying or selling it. This includes a study of such concepts as appraisal, mortgage insurance, title search, abstract of property, and equity. The opportunity is afforded for further study in real estate law on a local, federal, and state level.

In the context of farming and agriculture, we will study the Westward expansion of the United States. You will learn how and why people traveled West and settled there. You will see what they saw when they arrived and learn about how they lived. You will also study the Original Americans, known to us as Indians, and the impact on them of the Westward Expansion of white settlers.

Mini-Units

Mini-Units contained in this unit are:

    A. Gardening and Plant Propagation

    B. Farming and Agriculture

    C. The Real Estate Business

    D. Westward Ho!

    E. The First Americans

Mini-Units

Each thematic mini-unit is described and designated with a letter of the alphabet in the following paragraphs. Individual activities designed for use in one particular mini-unit will be marked with those letters. (For further help with this, please refer to the explanation of mini-units in the Guidelines section of this unit study guide.)

A. Gardening and Plant Propagation

In this mini-unit, you will study the life processes that occur in growing plants, and what materials are needed to further growth. Here you will learn how and where various crops grow best and how to improve growing conditions for plants of your choice. This will include examination of a wide variety of plant propagation and growth methods, learning which plants respond best to what.

This unit examines several parables and other teachings of Scripture related to gardening. The first garden, Eden, will be examined as well, to understand man's relationship and responsibility to the Earth and to Creation.

You will have a chance to try your hand at growing a wide variety of produce, both edible and ornamental and learning to harvest and use them. You will learn a variety of uses for the products you grow and how to make the most of each. You will use plants for beauty as well as utility and learn to develop an attractive landscape. There will also be suggestions on ways to make money from your crops.

B. Farming and Agriculture

As with the mini-unit on gardening, you will begin your study with a look at the agriculture of Bible times and the uses of farming and agriculture in Biblical symbolism, especially concentrating on the parables that relate to it. We will study the wide variety of Spiritual references to farms, vineyards, crops, harvests, etc., trying to minimize duplication between the two mini-units.

You will study farming and agriculture in various parts of the world and take a look at the diversity of crops grown and the nations that produce each. This mini-unit examines the economic impact of various crops on specific locales and on national and world economies as a whole. We will look at the major agricultural imports and exports of various nations and at the impact on the economy of each. You will also study the various laws that relate to agriculture and the agencies that regulate it.

We will study various farming practices through the ages and around the world, with an eye toward the best ways of doing each type of farming. You will learn how large, corporate farms work and why they seem to be taking over an ever-increasing share of the agricultural market. We will also look at nonfood farm products, agriculture outside the farm, the self-sufficient family farm, truck farming and sharecropping.

You will learn about types of soil and how to test it, as well as the products needed to improve a particular type of soil for various plants. You will study soil erosion and its prevention, as well as pest control, crop rotation, irrigation and other environmental issues related to farming. You will be able to compare organic and chemically-enhanced gardening to see the pros and cons of each.

Mini-Units

C. The Real Estate Business

This mini-unit will teach you the ins and outs of buying selling, and financing a home or other real estate. You will learn about various kinds of deeds and the laws regarding them. This will include zoning and deed restrictions that limit how a piece of property may be used. We have tried to give you ample opportunity to investigate various types of property and the kinds of loans available on them. This will include learning about amortization, payoffs, interest, points, discounts, and other factors that go into borrowing money for a mortgage.

You will investigate the world of the renters, those who do not own their own home. You will study what is involved in locating and renting an apartment, a house, or other property and how to relate to the owner and/or his/her representative. This will include an analysis of typical rental contracts and leases and an understanding of what they involve and how to interpret them. You will also learn what to look for in rental property and/or a rental contract.

This mini-unit will also cover various aspects of real estate insurance. You will learn about fire insurance, liability and hazard insurance and the more common comprehensive homeowner's policies. You will also study credit life policies and title insurance, as well as renters' insurance to cover the property of those not living in their own homes. You will learn about escrow accounts for paying insurance, taxes and other annual assessments on your property. You may also enjoy learning what these various taxes and assessments are and how they are computed and levied.

D. Westward Ho!

In a unit on agriculture and real estate, it seems only natural to include the study of the American West, an area of immense size and value, which has been heavily agricultural for much of its history. You will study the "western" states of the U. S. and the adjacent Canadian Provinces and territories. This study will include the geography and economy of the area but is mostly concerned with the history of its settlement.

In this context, you will study the expedition headed by Meriwether Lewis and Rogers Clark, who first explored much of this vast area, and the brave mountain men and pioneers who followed their lead into the territory. You will learn about the Oregon and Santa Fe Trails and the many branches off them as well as the wagon trains and stagecoaches that traveled along them. The settlements made by these pioneers and the forts built to house troops assigned to protect them will also be part of your studies here as will the life-styles of the settlers in various parts of the West.

We have broadened this study to include many of the important people and events which had a part in the development of the Great American West. This will span nearly 100 years and most of the continent as you travel West with fur traders, missionaries, early settlers, and gold prospectors. In this endeavor, you will read original writings of those involved as well as fiction and nonfiction books about the period to learn how they brought peace and prosperity to this wild land while building an economic foundation of strength for an entire continent.

You will study the geographic features which either helped or hindered these settlers and the struggles of their journeys. Plants and animals of the region, which greatly influenced life there, will be a part of this study, as will the rivers, valleys, deserts and other natural features. A look at the everyday life of women in several different times and locations will round out the study. Videos, audios, and even various artwork of the period will be used to give more of the flavor of life in the West.

Mini-Units

E. The Original Americans and Their Way of Life

In this unit, you will learn all about the first people to inhabit the Americas, those Columbus named "Indians", and the way they lived long before he came and for three to four centuries afterward. You will see how much their lives were tied to the land, even in the case of groups that never owned land or settled anywhere. You'll learn how the coming of the white man affected them, and how time and other factors forced most of them into a new life-style.

You will discover the names of some of the hundreds of nations represented on the shores of the Western Hemisphere before the nations of Europe knew of their existence. You will compare these nations, and tribes within each, to one another and the those nations of their day that were considered 'civilized'. You may be surprised to see how 'civilized' and highly developed some of these cultures were, and disappointed to discover that so few vestiges of those cultures survive today. You will discover what it was that led to the demise of the `Indian' cultures and how and where they live today.

In examining the historic way of life of these early peoples, you will look at nomadic tribes from as far back as Bible times to see what traits all nomads had in common. This will lead us to a comparison of the various nomadic American "nations" to one another and to those who were not nomads. You will also investigate how these people first came to live in the Western Hemisphere and what part a nomadic life-style played in that. Their origins and mode of travel to the 'New World' has provided substance for many a lively discussion over the centuries since they were found here, but few real conclusions have been reached. You will study all these theories and try to come to an answer with which you feel comfortable.

BIBLE AND CHRISTIAN CHARACTER

06B01.A	Study the creation of the Garden of Eden and God's command to Adam to have dominion over it as told in Genesis chapters 1 and 2.	B-4
06B02.A	Study the Genesis 3 account of the Fall and God's cursing of the ground, which caused weeds and other blights to affect the growing of our gardens and vineyards.	B-3
06B03.A	Study and compare the three versions of the parable of the sower in Matthew 13, Mark 4, and Luke 8.	B-5
06B04.A	Study and analyze the meaning of the Biblical phrase, "You reap what you sow".	B-2
06B05.A	Read other parables about planting and growing vineyards or gardens.	B-5
06B06.A	Copy for handwriting practice and/or dictation, memorize, and explain the literal and spiritual meaning of Jesus' words in John 12:24.	B-2
06B07.A	Look up and study other parables of our Lord that deal with plants or gardens.	B-1

BIBLE AND CHRISTIAN CHARACTER

06B08.A	Study Biblical harvest festivals in Exodus 9:32 and 34:22, and Leviticus 23:15-17 and 26: 5.	B-2
06B09.B	Use a concordance to look up and study Bible passages about farmers or farming.	B-1
06B10.B	Study the lives of the Old Testament prophets who were farmers when the Lord called them.	B-1
06B11.B	Study the parable of the wicked vine-growers in Matthew 21:33-41. Compare to the account of the same parable in Mark 12 and Luke 20.	B-2
06B12.B	Study the parable of the wheat and the tares in Matthew 13.	B-1
06B13.B	Study the concept of gleaning and the commands of God to His people regarding it (Leviticus 19 and other passages). Discuss with others how modern-day agricultural corporations could institute that practice in their operations.	B-2
06B14.B	Study other Biblical commands for man to have dominion and exercise stewardship over Earth. Explain how this relates to agriculture.	13-2
06B15.B	Read the account of crop failure and its resulting food shortage among Old Testament Israel as told in Deuteronomy 28, and determine the causes of poor harvests.	B-2
06B16.C	Study God's rules for the Hebrews about the sale and/or redemption of land as given in Leviticus 25:15-33 and 27:17-24.	B-2
06B17.C	Read God's instructions to Jeremiah on the buying and selling of land as recorded in Jeremiah 32:7-44.	B-1
06B18.C	Use a concordance to study Biblical teachings with regard to true and false land boundaries and honest measure.	B-1
06B19.C	Read about the first recorded instance of the conveyance of land ownership through written deed, told in Genesis 23:3-20.	B-1
06B20.C	Study Ruth 4 to understand another aspects of God's law (and Hebrew civil law) about the owning and distribution of real property.	B-2
06B21.C	Study your concordance to find out what the Bible has to say about leasing property.	B-2
06B22.C	Investigate the right of Old Testament women to own property. Beginning with Ruth 4:3-9 and Numbers 27 and 36, look for other passages in concordance.	B-2
06B23.C	Study all references to the year of Jubilee to find out what was to happen to the land then.	B-2

BIBLE AND CHRISTIAN CHARACTER

06B24.C	Study the Lord's reference to his own lack of ownership of any real property and analyze what it may mean for His followers.	B-2
06B25.C	Study the Lord's parable in Luke 12 about the man who owned land and attempted to hoard and build on it without consulting the Lord for guidance.	B-2
06826.D*	Study the major teachings of the Mormons, (LDS Church) who had an important role in the settling of what is now the U. S. state of Utah. Refute or support each of these teachings from the Old or New Testament only, using a concordance to find verses on each topic.	B-2
06B27.D	Study Matthew 6:19-21, and explain how it could have been a warning to those who participated in any of the 'gold rushes" that brought such large numbers of people into the U. S. & Canadian West looking to get rich quick.	B-2
06B28.D	Study Luke 12:31-34, and compare it to the verses above and relate them to the California and/or Pike's Peak Gold Rush.	B-2
06B29.D	Find and study other Scriptures that warn of undue love of money or material treasures.	B-2
06B30.D	Listen to and discuss with your family each of the devotions from history on "Little Bear" Wheeler's tape about the Old West.	B-3
06B31.D	Study the last few verses of Matthew 28, often known as the "Great Commission", and relate it to the settling of the American West by those who hoped to bring the gospel to the natives.	B-3
06B32.E	Read Genesis 4 to learn the origins of the first nomads and why they were often looked down on in later years, even though all of Cain's descendants had been destroyed by the Flood.	B-3
06B33.E	Study Ishmael and his descendants, the Ishmaelites, who were primarily nomads throughout the Old Testament.	B-1
06B34.E	Study the Rechabites, in Jeremiah 35:1-11, and how their nomadic ways saved them from the captivity that took others from their homeland in the days of Nebuchadnezzar.	B-2
06B35.E	Use *People of the Bible and How They Lived, Baker's Bible Atlas,* and/or other Old Testament references to help you study all Bible passages about nomadic groups, including the time periods when God's people lived as nomads before claiming Canaan as their promised land.	B-3

BIBLE AND CHRISTIAN CHARACTER

06B36.E There are many Christians who believe that the 'American Indians' are the descendants of the 'lost tribes' of Israel, who never returned to Judea after their captivity under the Babylonians and Persians. Read the books of Ezra and Nehemiah to learn which tribes these were and what clues, if any, are given as to what happened to them. B-4

06B37.E Read Isaiah 11:6-14 and discuss whether this is prophesying the return of the Children of Israel from the captivity in Babylon or the gathering of God's people at the final judgment or something else entirely. Whichever interpretation you take, try to determine to which lands or nations the 'islands' of the sea might refer, as this has never been clearly identified. Many believed that this means the then-undiscovered lands of the world, including the Western Hemisphere. 8-3

06B38.E Study Isaiah 42:1-13. Many believe that the word translated here as 'isles' (or alternately, `coastlands') refers to the lands now known as America and the people we call 'Indians' or `Native Americans, who had to wait until arrival of the Europeans on their shores to learn of the true God and His Son Jesus. This passage is what spurred some of the early explorers to bring missionaries come to the New World and set up extensive ministries to these people. What evidences, Biblical or otherwise, can you find to support or refute that belief? B-3

06B39.E Read the judgment of God on all the disobedient of the Earth, as prophesied in Jeremiah 25. Note the many references to those 'across the seas' or 'afar off, and application of this to 'all the Earth'. As you study the lives of the earliest inhabitants of the Americas, look for things in their ways of life and cultures that could be manifestations of the judgment of God in which they were included, though the prophet who foretold it did not know of their existence. B-3

06B40. E* Using the list (made in the Cultural Studies section) of the attributes revered by American 'Indian' nations in the 'gods' and created things they worshipped, find Scripture passages that extol each of these in Jehovah, the true God. Do you think this shows that the ancestors of these people brought some knowledge of the true God with them when they migrated to North America, thereby giving more credence to one of the above theories. Discuss the idea with your parents. B-3

06B41.E Read Psalm 19:1-4 as another explanation for the same phenomenon observed in the previous activity. B-1

06B42.E Read and study Romans 1 for a more thorough discussion of the same concept as above. B-1

06B43. Memorize one or more of the passages studied in the unit. B - 1per 4 verses

BIBLE AND CHRISTIAN CHARACTER

06B44.	Read through the book of Proverbs each month, reading the chapter to coincide with each date.	B- 2 per week
06B45.	Continue reading through the Bible at a rate of 1-5 chapters per day. If you use *The Daily Bible* or some other version designed for that purpose, following their assigned daily readings will take you through the entire Bible in one year. You may follow a pattern of your own at a different rate if you like.	B- 1 credit when finished

CULTURAL STUDIES

06C01.A	Visit your county agricultural extension office and discuss how they can help you as a home gardener. Learn about this federal government agency and its duties.	CG-2
06C02.A	Study a geological survey map of your area to learn about its topography, soil condition and other factors that could affect your garden.	SE-2
06C03.A	Study climate charts for the plants you wish to grow and determine which ones will grow well in your climate.	PA-2
06C04.A	Contact your state's land grant college (usually has "A & M" or "Tech" in its name) and find out what type of information and/ or services they can offer to the small home gardener.	CG-2
06C05.A	Study the history of the Hanging Gardens of Babylon to discover who created and planted them, when they were planted, and when and how they were destroyed.	H-3
06C06.A	Study the landscaped, formal, ornamental gardens that used to be popular in England and some parts of the United States and Canada. To what would you attribute their decline in popularity.	PA-3
06C07.A	Through videos, travel brochures, and/or books, study oriental gardens and the plants most often used in them.	G-2
06C08.A	Through videos, field trips, brochures or books, learn about the cactus gardens grown in deserts and other arid areas.	G-2
06C09.A	Using *Life and Customs of Bible Times*, or any other book on that topic, study the tools and methods used for home gardening in Old and New Testament times.	H-2
06C10.A	Trace the development of home gardening through the ages, studying the changes in tools, methods, and crops.	H-2
06C11.A	Contact and interview the director of the agency charged with the care of your city's public parks, botanical gardens, and/or other landscaped areas. Learn about his job and any special tips he can give you.	PA-3

CULTURAL STUDIES

06C12.A	Locate on a map the likely site of the Garden of Gethsemane, where Jesus was betrayed and later buried. Study its history and its present condition and ownership.	G-2
06C13.B	Talk with local officials and/or commercial farmers to learn about pollution laws and regulations in your area that affect the agricultural community.	CG-2
06C14.B	Use encyclopedias, books, Internet sites, or information available from your state's agriculture department to study the economic impact of agriculture on your state. Pay attention to major products, areas in which they grow, and other agribusiness industries.	CE-4
06C15.B	Mark on a map of your country all regions, states, provinces, or territories whose primary economic life is agricultural. Designate with some symbol what types of crops or products each produces.	G-1
06C16.B	Mark on a world map, designating as you did in the activity above, all nations whose primary exports are agricultural.	G-1
06C17.B	Investigate any agribusiness companies that may be located in your local area. Find out about their corporate makeup, their financial status, and where and how they do business.	CE-3
06C18.B	Study the U. S. Department of Agriculture or its counterpart in your own country. Discover its duties, sources of funding and regulatory laws and agencies.	CG-3
06C19.B	Study the U. S. Forestry Service and interview one or more Forestry Service workers on the answers to the following questions: What government department is over the Forestry Service? Why is it placed there? What is the Forestry Service's job? Do you consider trees and forests agricultural products? If so, why? Be prepared to discuss their answers with your parents.	CG-3
06C20.B	Learn about all laws in your country, state, province, or local area with regard to clear-cutting, reforestation, use or lease of public lands or other aspects of timber harvesting.	CL-2
06C21.B	Study and/or tour the Sand Hills National Forest in Nebraska, the only public forestry area in the world known to have been cultivated by mankind mostly for recreational purposes.	SE-2
06C22.B	Study the Civilian Conservation Corps (CCC) Camps of the U.S., in which depression-era young men were paid to create and care for national forests, parks, and recreation lands.	H-2
06C23.B	Study, locate on a map, and/or tour other National Forests in your country.	SE-2 CS-2

CULTURAL STUDIES

| 06C24.B | Study the impact of the forest products industry on the economy of your nation, state/province and local area. Learn what forest products are produced, where and how they are processed and marketed, how many people the companies employ, and how their products affect the area. | CE-3 |

| 06C25.B | Study all other governmental agencies connected in any way with agriculture and/or agribusiness. Prepare a chart or other display showing the jobs of each of these agencies and the relationships between them. | CG-3 |

| 06C26.B | From the above agencies, determine and locate sources and producers of any other non-farming industries that may be considered agriculture or agribusiness in state or province. | CE-3 |

| 06C27.B | Study each of those industries, if any, in your local area that fall into the category of agribusiness. Visit one of more of them and learn what they do. | CE-3 |

| 06C28.B | Study and compare the collective farming systems employed in various socialist and/or communist countries. | CS-1 |

| 06C29.C | Interview real estate, property tax, and/or insurance appraisers about the purpose and methods used for each type of appraisal. List the factors each has to consider in property appraisal. | CE-2 |

| 06C30.C | Study the real estate laws of your state and any additional ordinances your local area may have on that topic. | CL-1 |

| 06C31.C | Study zoning laws in general and the specific ones that apply in your area, Discuss with a knowledgeable adult how this affects the sale or purchase of real estate. | CL-2 |

| 06C32.C | Study building and fire codes in your area and how they affect the building or remodeling of a home or other building. | CL-1 |

| 06C33.C | Learn what deed restrictions are and how they affect property ownership, property value, the rights of the property owner and the ability to resell the real estate on which the restriction is placed. | CL-1 |

| 06C34.C | Examine the property tax rules for your area to learn who pays the tax, how it is calculated and assessed, and when and where it is to be paid. | CL-2 |

| 06C35.C | Examine a real estate contract, title abstract, surveyor's report, and/or real estate appraisal. Get a lawyer, real estate broker or similar knowledgeable person to explain each document. | CL-1 |

| 06C36.C | Study the inheritance laws of your state/province or other governmental entity, looking especially at the laws covering the inheritance of real property. | CL-2 |

CULTURAL STUDIES

06C37.C	Interview a mortgage loan officer to find out what (s)he does in relation to granting a loan and how (s)he decides who to grant a mortgage.	CE-2
06C38.C	Learn what is involved in applying for a mortgage and the factors considered when it is granted or refused. Learn about different types of real estate loans, including second mortgages, equity loans, adjustable rate mortgages, and home refinancing. Learn when loans are or are not assumable.	CL-1
06C39.C	Interview a real estate lawyer to find out how appraisals, surveys and title searches are used in the real estate business and why each is necessary.	CS-2
06C40.C	Talk with a real estate agent about his/her job and learn how (s)he helps clients to purchase homes and other property.	CG-3
06C41.C	From talking with your local office's staff and/or other resources, learn about the Federal Housing Authority and the Farmers' Home Administration, both set up to provide mortgage money for certain classes of buyers to purchase homes. List on some type of chart, their differences and similarities and the requirements for getting a loan from each.	CG-1
06C42.C	Learn what kind of permits needed by home builders in your area and what is required to get them.	H-2 each tape
06C43.D	Listen to and take notes on the Western expansion tapes from the *America: The First 350 Years* audio series.	H-2
06C44.D	From the above tape set, Carson's *Basic History of the United States*, Marshall's *The Light and the Glory*, or other U. S. history books from a Christian perspective, study the early Spanish and French explorers who first discovered parts of what is now the Western U. S. long before the U. S existed.	H-1
06C45.D	From the above books and/or other sources, study the lives of some of the early Christian missionaries to the "Indian" nations of the American West.	H-5
06C46.D	Study the Louisiana Purchase, which first opened the West for settlement by U. S. citizens.	HG-10
06C47.D	Study the geography, topography, history and forms of government of all the states that were originally part of the Louisiana Purchase and others that make up what is considered the West.	H-12
06C48.D	Study all original documents in the "Jackdaws" portfolio on the Lewis and Clark Expedition and at least one Christian history text to study this first attempt by Americans to explore the huge expanse of territory that made up the Louisiana Purchase, bought from France in 1803.	H-6

CULTURAL STUDIES

06C49.D	Study the life and term of Thomas Jefferson, the President in whose term the Louisiana Purchase was made. Make timeline entries for his term of office and all major events that took place during it.	H -5
06C50.D	Use *The Light and the Glory* and *From Sea to Shining Sea* or other Christian United States history books to study the doctrine of Manifest Destiny and how it influenced the settling of the West.	H-4
06C51.D	On a U. S. map, trace the Oregon and Santa Fe Trails of the wagon trains and each of their branches, the Butterfield and Overland stage routes, and the route used by the riders of the Pony Express.	H-2
06C52.D	Study the "Jackdaws" portfolio on The California Gold Rush to learn, from the original documents, how the discovery of gold in California in 1849 impacted the settlement of the Western U. S.	H-8
06C53.D	Study the Homestead Act and how it affected the settling of the West.	CG-1
06C54.D	Study the history of the U. S. Army in the West, from archive records wherever possible. Compare it to the record of the Northwest Mounted Police (now Royal Canadian Mounted Police) in Canada. Notice especially incidents of violence, prevalence of outlaws, and the 'Indian problem'. Mind map and/or discuss with parents major similarities and differences.	H-6
06C55.D	Study the life of Theodore Roosevelt and all that he did to encourage Westward Expansion in the U. S and the conservation of its natural resources.	H-5
06C56.D	Study the history of Texas, considered by many to be the quintessential Western state. Use the Jackdaws portfolio on that subject or other resource(s) of your choice.	H-5
06C57.D	Study the early history of any other state in what is considered the West.	H-5
06C58.D	Use any of the books suggested here or in the Reading and Literature section to study other people and events that helped settle the West.	H-8
06C59.E	Study the variety of theories, found in books listed in Reading and Literature or other sources, about how the 'first Americans' came to be on that continent.	H-6
06C60. E*	Watch the History Channel video *500 Nations* to get a real understanding of the immense diversity among 'Indian' nations in North America and why their members resent being grouped together as just 'Indians' or even 'Native Americans'.	H-5

CULTURAL STUDIES

06C61.E *	As you watch *500 Nations* or read about the religions of the original American nations in other studies for this unit, list all the qualities they worshiped in their various "gods'. Compare this list to the attributes of God as directed in the Bible and Christian Character section of this mini-unit.	H-6
06C62.E	Study and compare the culture of those Native nations that cultivated crops to the nomads of the Great Plains who did not.	H-4
06C63.E	Study the history of the Cherokee, Iroquois, and other Woodlands Nations of the Eastern U. S.	H-2
06C64.E	Watch the *Trail of Tears* video from the Real West series or study it another way.	H-3
06C65.E	Read the writings of John Ross and/or other Christian leaders of the Cherokee nation at the time of removal to Oklahoma.	H-4
06C66.E	Study the history of the Mayas, Aztecs and other nations who once occupied the area now known as Central America.	H-6
06C67.E	Study the history of the Dakota (also called the Sioux), Cheyenne, Shoshone, Blackfoot, and other original nations of the American Great Plains. Learn how they lived and what effect the coming of the White Man had on them.	11-6
06C68.E	Study the history of the state of Oklahoma, which was once known as "Indian Territory" and guaranteed by the U. S. government to these displaced nations and their descendants forever, yet another promise not to be kept.	H-4
06C69.E	Study the lifestyles and history of the Navajo, Hopi, and other Indian nations who made their homes in the inhospitable deserts of the Southwestern United States, and were never forced to leave entirely, due primarily to the undesirability of their homelands.	H-4
06C70.E	Study the French and Indian War from several sources, including *The Light and the Glory* or another one from a Christian perspective.	H-3
06C71.E	Study Prince Philip's War from some Christian resource and its impact on American settlement. To what do you attribute its cause?	H-4
06C72.E	Study the Indian Wars of the 1860's and 70's in the U. S. West, trying to look at both sides, weighing atrocities by Indians ans against harm done to them by whites, both intentional and not.	H-4

CULTURAL STUDIES

06C73.E	Study the rise and fall of the Indian nations on the Plains, paying special attention to the "battles" of Bent's Fort, Sand Creek, Washita, and Little Big Horn.	H-3
06C74. E	Compare the history of the Native Americans in Canada with that of those in the United States. Discuss and/or mind map and be prepared to write about what factors you think made the difference.	H-4
06C75.E	Study the history of the original nations that occupied your home state or province, if they were not included in other activities in this unit.	H-4
06C76.E	Study the lives, duties, and treatment of women among various 'Indian' nations and compare them on a chart or display.	H-1
06C77.	Make timeline entries for the major events in the lives of each of the authors, inventors, or artists mentioned or read in this mini-unit.	H-2
06C78.	Make timeline entries for each person, movement and/or event studied in this mini-unit.	H-3
06C79.	Use material studied for this mini-unit as well as Usborne's *World History Dates, The Kingfisher History Encyclopedia,* and/or other reference books to find the information needed for making timeline entries for all the people, movements, and events studied in this mini-unit.	H-3
06C80.	Use Usborne's *World History Dates* to identify and make timeline entries for other important events during each time period studied in this mini-unit.	H-3
06C81.	Make timeline entries for all inventions and/or discoveries studied in this mini-unit and all major events in the lives of their inventors.	G-1
06C82.	Use encyclopedias or other references to study all countries mentioned in any context within this mini-unit.	G-2
06C83.	Locate on a map or globe each country studied in this mini-unit.	G-1
06C34.	Locate on a map and study the geography of all municipalities you studied in this mini-unit.	G-2
06C85.	Locate on a U. S. map all states mentioned or studied in this unit.	G-1
06C86.	Study the geography of the home country of each author, inventor, or artist whose works were used or studied in this mini-unit.	G - 1 each

CULTURAL STUDIES

READING AND LITERATURE

06R01.A	Read *Square-Foot Gardening*.	PA-3
06R02.A	Read a biography of Luther Burbank, whose work with potatoes and other plants greatly affected the whole realm of gardening.	H-5
06R03.A	Read a biography of Gregor Mendel, the Father of Genetics, whose works were primarily done with common garden vegetables.	H-5
06R04.A	Read biographies of Robert Hooke, Stephen Hale, Hugo von Mohl and others who made astounding discoveries and/or did important work in the area of plant propagation and growth.	H-5
06R05.A	Read *A Gardener Looks at the Fruits* by Philip Keller, who was a farmer and gardener.	L-4
06R06.A	Read the pastoral poetry of John Donne and his British contemporaries.	L - 2
06R07.A	Memorize 50 - 70 lines of English pastoral poetry.	L - 12
06R08.A*	Read *The Secret Garden*. (Though done in an innocent, non-occult manner this book does include a form of magic, which some Christian parents may find offensive.)	L - 5
06R09.A	Read all parts of *The Hidden Art of Homemaking* that relate to gardening, landscaping, flowers, or similar topics.	LH - 2
06R10.A	Read one or more how-to books on vegetable gardening.	PA-3
06R11.A	Read one or more how-to manuals on flowers or other plants used for ornamental gardening, landscaping and horticulture.	LH-2
06R12.A	Read one or more guides to growing house plants.	LH-1
06R13.B	Read novels or biographies about migrant farm workers in the United States or Canada.	L-5
06R14.B	Read *Sounder* or other novels about sharecroppers.	L-5
06R15.B	Read *The Grapes of Wrath*, the story of a farm family in the Great Depression.	L-8
06R16.B	Read novels or other books set in countries known to be major exporters of agricultural products.	L-5 each
06R17.B	Read novels in which farms, orchards, vineyards, or crops figure importantly.	L-5 each

CULTURAL STUDIES

06R18.B	Read biographies of Cyrus McCormick, John Deere, and/ or other inventors whose inventions made major changes in farming and agriculture.	H-5 each
06R19.B	Read *Spring and Summer in the North Carolina Forest*, and/or *Fall and Winter in the North Carolina Forest* or similar books about forests.	L-5
06R20.B	Read *Girl of the Limberlost* or other novels about forests.	L-5 each
06R21.B	Read any or all four of the books in Janette Oke's "Seasons of the Heart" series which follows a farm family from the late nineteenth century to the CCC camps of the Great Depression.	L-5 each
06R22.B	Read novels about or set in the rice patties of Southeast Asia.	L-5 each
06R23.B	Read *Green Mansions*, a classic novel set among the lush, green, over-arching, 'mansions' of the rain forests of South America.	L-6
06R24.C	Read the section on "Land: Buying It — Building on It" in the book *Back to Basics*.	L-2
06R25.C	Read Virgil's *Poetry Ecologues* (in the original or an English translation), written in the wake of having lost his lands through confiscation.	L -4
06R26.C	Read any training manual for those who wish to become real estate agents or brokers.	CE - 3
06R27.C	Read a guide for first time home buyers.	CE-2
06R28.C	Read one or more novels in which the sale or purchase of a home or other property figures prominently.	L - 5
06R29.C	Read *The Good Earth* by Pearl Buck.	L - 6
06R30.C	Read *Spencer's Mountain*, a novel about a close-knit, loving family whose lives were closely intertwined with the land they owned and loved.	L-6
06R31.D	Read *Frontier Living* for an overall look at life in the West, beginning when "the West" was Kentucky, Michigan, and Indiana, and moving west with the nation's expansion.	H-5
06R32.D	Read biographies of Meriwether Lewis and/or George Rogers Clark.	H-4
06R33.D	Read *The Pony Express*, an authentic account of what is commonly considered one of the most exciting episodes of American history.	H-5

READING AND LITERATURE

06R34.D	Read *Buffalo Bill: Army Scout*, a biography of a man whose name has become synonymous with the Wild West.	H-5
06R35.D	For a fact-based novel about this period, read *On to Oregon*, about seven orphans who made the trip by wagon train.	LH-5
06R36.D	Read *The Holy Warrior, The Reluctant Bridegroom*, and any other appropriate volumes of the House of Winslow fiction series by Gilbert Morris.	LH-5
06R37.D*	Read any or all books from the "Canadian West Series". (These do contain an element of romance, so some parents may not want their girls to read them.)	LH-4
06R38.D*	Read any or all of the books in the "Women of the West Series". (These do contain an element of romance, so some parents may not want their girls to read them.)	LH-4
06R39.D	Read any or all of the "Little House" books by Laura Ingalls Wilder, sharing them with a younger sibling or friend.	L-5
06R40.D	Read *Caddie Woodlawn*, and share it with a young sibling or friend.	L-5
06R41.D	Read all three books in the "Orphan Train West" series, about three young orphaned girls who went West by train to find adoptive families and start new lives.	L-15
06R42.D	Read biographies of Narcissa Whitman and other godly women who accompanied their husbands into the West as missionaries to the Indians and helped blaze a trail for many more white settlers to follow.	H-5
06R43.D	Read *Streams to the River, River to the Sea*, a novel based on the life of Sacajawea, a squaw who traveled with Lewis and Clark.	L or H-5
06R44.E	Read a true biography of Pocahontas, which is not at all like the Disney movie.	H-5
06R45.E	Read a Christian biography of Squanto, the first known believer among his people.	H-5
06R46.E	Read biographies (from a Christian perspective, if possible) of famous Native American leaders such as, Massasoit, William Weatherford, (aka Red Eagle), Powhatan, Tecumseh, and John Ross.	H-4 each
06R47.E	Read all sections on the original Americans in *The Light and the Glory* or another Christian American history book.	H-10
06R48.E	Read *The Last of the Mohicans*.	L-7

READING AND LITERATURE

06R49.E	Read *Custer and Crazy Horse*.	H-5
06R50.E	Read biographies of Sitting Bull, Crazy Horse, Geronimo, Quanah Parker, Cochise and other 'Indian' war chiefs or military leaders.	H-4 each
06R51.E*	Read one or more of the mysteries by Navajo writer Tony Hillerman, all of which are set on the modern-day Navajo Reservation of Arizona and New Mexico. (While these books give a very good look at modern reservation life, they may contain references to superstitions, beliefs, and/or practices of the ancient Navajo religion.)	L-5 Each
06R52.E	Read biographies of Jim Thorpe, Ira Hayes and/or other 'Native Americans' who have made a name for themselves in the 20th century.	H-4 each
06R53.E*	Read *Bury My Heart at Wounded Knee* by Sioux author Dee Brown.	L-5
06R54.E*	Read the Dorling-Kindersley book *Native American Peoples*.	L-5
06R55.	Read one or more historical novels set in one of the time periods studied in this unit.	H-5 each
06R56.	Read at least one book per week over and above those you are doing as assignments in this or other sections of this study. Choose from those listed here or in the resource list, or use any book your parents approve.	L-4 each
06R57.	Read any other appropriate books on the subject of the mini-unit you are studying.	L-5 each
06R58.	Read biographies of people in this mini-unit.	H-3 each

COMPOSITION

06W01.A	Write an essay (1-2 pages) on what it means to 'have dominion over the Earth', giving specific examples in the area of horticulture and/or gardening.	PA-10
06W02.A	Look up any available gardening information from the following sources or any others that may seem appropriate: 1. Smithsonian Institute 2. U. S. Environmental Protection Agency 3. Consumer Information Services 4. Library of Congress	EC-1 Each
06W03A	Write a symbolic poem using horticultural terms to describe a person or object totally unrelated to that subject.	EC-3

COMPOSITION

06W04.A	Write a short (2-3 paragraph) essay analyzing the Biblical statement "you reap what you sow", explaining it in the literal, agricultural sense and as a Spiritual principle.	EC-1 PA-1 B-1

06W04.A   Write a short (2-3 paragraph) essay analyzing the Biblical statement "you reap what you sow", explaining it in the literal, agricultural sense and as a Spiritual principle.   EC-1 PA-1 B-1

06W05.A   Write a 'parable' of your own, using gardens, plants, or some gardening concept to teach a Spiritual lesson.   EC-1 PA-1 B-1

06W06.A   Write an informational brochure, letting other know about the services available to the home gardener from the Agricultural Extension Office and/or your state's land grant college.   EC-4 PA-2

06W07.A   Write a research paper on "The Home Garden Through the Ages" in which you cover this topic thoroughly. Use *Writers Inc., Guide to Writing the Term Paper* or another guide book for writers to help you do this in formal, 'term-paper' style.   EC-2

06W08.A   Paraphrasing and combining tips and information you have collected in this unit, write a how-to guide (15 - 20 page minimum) for the beginning gardener. Include both vegetable and ornamental gardens.   PA-3 EC-5

06W09.A   Write a paper explaining the differences between organic gardening and the kind most people do and giving the pros and cons of each.   EC-1 PA-1

06W10.A   Write a pastoral poem, mimicking the style of John Donne and his contemporaries and extolling the virtues of gardens or gardening.   PA-1 EC-2

06W11.B   Write an investigative report on your national agricultural agency. Share as much as you understand of what they do, how they operate, who is in charge, and how it is funded. Draw a conclusion as to whether or not you believe it's a legitimate use of government funds and your reasons for your decision.   PA-1 EC-2

06W12.B   Rewrite the parable of the wicked vine-growers, applying the same principles to a situation more common in our modern society.   EC-2

06W13.B   Write a report on forestry in your state or province, including various types of trees grown in your state, products harvested or made from them, names of companies engaging in this type of business in your area, and government agencies assigned to regulate it.   EC-3

06W14.B   Write a comprehensive article (as if for a periodical) on agribusiness in your area.   EC-2

06W15.B   Write a persuasive speech, designed to encourage a large agricultural firm to make provisions in its operations for gleaning by the poor. Provide some actual ideas of how this could be done as well as evidences as to why it should be.   EC-3

COMPOSITION

06W16.B   Write a report in which you examine and compare various examples of the principle of 'gleaning' in your own culture today. Stretch your definition of 'gleaning' to include non-agricultural pursuits. You may wish to mind map on this topic first.

EC-2
PA-1

06W17.B   Write a short story about sharecroppers or a poor farmer and his family. Show how their faith in the Lord helps them handle the problems that are a normal part of their life, just like the Lord helps others of us in very different circumstances.

EC-20

06W18.B   Write a journal with 25-30 entries, covering a full year in the life of a migrant farm worker who is also a mother. Use your knowledge of various crops and where and when they grow to envision where the family goes and the crops they harvest. Add a human touch by including such things as concern that her children have to move so much, missing extended family who did not travel with them, worries over weather, health or other variables that could affect the job.

EC-15

06W19.B   Write a research paper (8-10 typed pgs.) entitled "Farmers and the Environment". Show why taking care of the environment is important to farmers and how farmers can help in that effort. Use *Writing a Research Paper* or *Writing for College* as a guide. Include citations and a bibliography.

SE-20
Or
EC-20

06W20.B   Write a newspaper report on the life and living conditions of migrant farm workers in your state or province. If possible, interview an actual migrant family.

EC-3

06W21.C   In reading contracts, leases, and other legal papers related to the buying, selling, and/or renting of real estate, copy all the words that are unfamiliar to you into your vocabulary notebook. Define them and mark syllabication and pronunciation.

EG-1

06W22.C   Write a brief report on the jobs of real estate agents, brokers, and attorneys. Compare and contrast their educational requirements, job descriptions, pay rate, and the amount of real expertise needed.

EC-3

06W23.C   Write an essay on the Old Testament institutions of the seventh-year Sabbath of the land, and the Jubilee Year. Explain how each of these affected land owners and real estate deals.

EC-2

06W24.C   Write an investigative report on "Land Ownership Rights for Women" beginning with the principles concerning this that are established in Scripture and following this issue through various time periods to the present day. Explain God's plan in this regard as you understand it.

B-1
H-1
EC-2

06W25.C   Write an essay explaining the inheritance laws of your state with regard to real estate. Make a special point of explaining what happens to the property of someone who dies without a will.

EC-2

COMPOSITION

06W26.C	Write a sample legal brief explaining some your state's real estate laws. Use as many actual legal terms as possible.	EC - 2
06W27.C	Write a paper contrasting and comparing various types of mortgages, showing the advantages and disadvantages of each.	EC -1
06W28.C	Write a simple how-to guide (tract or pamphlet size) showing and explaining each step in the process of buying a home. Be careful to define all terms and include all necessary information for each step.	EC - 3
06W29.C	Write a paper (Consumer Reports style) comparing various types of building materials, grading them for various uses.	EC - 1
06W30.C	Write a news report on GPS (see Science section) tracking and its use for surveying.	SP - 2
06W31.D	Keep a diary as if by a woman or young girl heading West on the Oregon Trail. Write at least ten entries, including both everyday life and special events, and discussing sights along the trail as well.	EC - 5
06W32.D	Write both sides of a correspondence (6-8 letters) between a pioneer woman and her family back East, as if written at a time when letters were carried by the Pony Express. Write about her hopes, dreams, and concerns, loneliness, and the affairs of everyday life on the Prairie.	EC - 3
06W33.D	Pretend you are a journalist traveling with Lewis and Clark. Write a series of articles about their travels, highlighting important discoveries or events, but also sharing the everyday sights and sounds of the prairies and the mountains as they crossed them.	EC - 5
06W34. D	Write an essay as if to be published in the early 1800's explaining Manifest Destiny and why you agree or disagree with it.	EC - 2
06W35.D	Write a one-two page advertisement designed to attract new settlers to join a wagon train headed West. Include success stories and provide the answers to common questions.	EC-1 each
06W36.D	Write a brief (one-page) report on each of the states that make up what we now consider the West.	EC-2
06W37.D	Write a report (1-3 pages) comparing life for those settling the Western U. S. with their counterparts in Canada. Take into account the climate, terrain, attitude and availability of help from their respective governments and the U. S. Army or the Canadian Mounted Police.	EC-2

COMPOSITION

06W38.D   After researching life in cattle towns, gold fields, and logging camps as compared to more stable family settlements, write a paper explaining the statement: "In a very real sense, it was women — wives and mothers — who tamed the Wild, Wild West." Tell whether you agree or disagree with it.   EC-5

06W39.D   Write a skit or play about the founding of one of the western states.   EC-10+

06W40. D   Write a news report as might have been done by the first discoverers of the Grand Canyon, Pikes Peak, Old Faithful, Garden of The Gods, or some other natural wonder of the western U. S.   EC-2

06W41.D   Write a travel guide of advice for those traversing the deserts of the American Southwest, both in the days of covered wagons and today.   EC-15

06W42.E   Define 'aboriginal', usually shortened to 'aborigine', into your vocabulary notebook. From this definition, do you believe this term is an appropriate one for the peoples included in this mini-unit? Why do you suppose no one wants to use that name to describe them?   H- 10
EC - 50

06W43.E   Write a paper explaining what you consider to be the appropriate name for these early Americans. You may choose 'Indian', given to them by Columbus; the currently popular 'Native American'; Original American', which we use here; or one that you think of yourself. Bear in mind that these people have always preferred to be called by their specific 'national' name (Dakota. Hopi, Cheyenne, Cherokee, Navajo etc.), but we need some term to use in grouping them all together.   H- 1
each

06W44. E   Prepare a notebook on The Original Americans. For your first entries, write reports on each of the major groups within these nations: Woodlands Nations, Plains Nations, Mound Builders, Cave (or Pueblo) Dwellers, Coastal tribes, Aleuts and other groups of the far North, and the highly developed nations of Central and South America. For each group, include main occupation (means of obtaining food), primary dietary habits, tribal and family structure, style and construction of homes, religious beliefs, area in which they lived, relations with whites, and some of the nations included.   H - 10

06W45.E   Write a brief report (1-2 pages) on one nation in each of the major Native groups above to add to your notebook.   EG - 1

06W46.E   Write a play or skit about one of the major events of Native American history.   EC - 20

06W47.E   Prepare both sides of a debate on: "The 'Indians' Are Descended from the Lost Tribes of Israel."   EC - 20

COMPOSITION

06W48. E	Write a report on the destruction of the buffalo herds from the standpoint of the Cheyenne, Sioux, or other original Americans who relied on them for survival.	EC - 1
06W49.E	Write questions you would ask in an interview with Sitting Bull or Crazy Horse, and answer as you think they would.	EC - 5
06W50. E	Write a short story of life with one of the nations studied here.	EC - 25
06W51.E	Write reports for your notebook on Jim Thorpe, Ira Hayes, or other 'Native Americans' who have become well known during the 20th century, even outside their own communities.	EC- 2 each
06W52.	Using *Writers Inc., the College English Handbook*, or similar reference, proofread and correct all written work for this unit.	EG - 1 per 4 pages
06W53.	Use a good dictionary to proofread all written work in this unit and correct it for errors in spelling.	EG - 1 per 4 pages
06W54.	Keep a journal of each day's school activities through this entire curriculum. If done well, this journal can serve as documentation of your school year.	EC - 2 per week
06W55.	As you listen to any of the suggested audios in this unit, take notes on what you hear.	EC- 2 each
06W56.	Use your notes to outline, summarize, and/or discuss the tapes as requested.	EC- 2 each
06W57.	As an alternative to cursive writing, try Italic or Spencerian calligraphy using books in the resource list.	VA - 1 per complete course or 1 per hour
06W58.	Outline one or more of the nonfiction books used in this unit.	EG- 3 ea.
06W59.	Instead of, or in addition to, outlining the books studied or read in this unit, write reviews of some of them, writing as if you planned to be published in a periodical.	EC- 1 each
06W60.	Use any Scripture passage, poem or other material you are memorizing to copy for handwriting practice.	EG - 1 per hour
06W61.	Use the same material to write from dictation, being careful about spelling, punctuation, etc. Have someone read the passage to you slowly while you write it.	EG - 1 per hour
06W62.	Write a brief report on any one or more of the important people about whom you read books or studied in this unit.	EC - 2 each
06W63.	Write a news article on each of the field trips you took in this unit.	EC-1 each

COMPOSITION

06W64.   Write a thank you note to the organizer, supervisor, and/or   EC - 1 each
          guide of any field trip you took for this unit.

06W65.   Write summaries of any or all of the books read in this unit.   EC - 1 ea.

06W66.   Write reports on any or all of the women studied in the unit.   EC -1 each

06W67.   Write a book report on one book each week, choosing books   EC - 2 each
          listed in this unit or others approved by your parents. Use a
          variety of approaches to the report, including any of those listed
          in the Appendix article entitled "Twenty-Five Ways to Have Fun
          with Book Reports"

06W68.   Define and put into your vocabulary notebook ten new words   EG   1 per
          per week, using first those you encountered in your studies.   week
          Write definitions and pronunciations.

06W69.   Learn to spell all the words in your vocabulary notebook for   EG - 2 per
          this unit.   week

MATHEMATICS AND PERSONAL FINANCE

06M01.A   Measure the spot you plan to use for your garden and calculate   M- 1
          the area contained in it. Using information on your seed
          packages, determine how many rows or plants of each type
          you will be able to have in your garden space.

06M02.A   Using the information that comes on seed packages and/or   PA - 1
          with bedding plants, calculate the approximate germination
          and harvest dates for each of the plants you plan to grow in
          your garden.

06M03.A   Prepare and keep a spreadsheet of your garden, showing how   M - 1
          much of each thing you planted, how much it yielded, cost of   BE - 2
          plants, seeds, and supplies, and the market value of the harvest.

06M04.A   From your records of planting and harvest amounts, calculate   M - 2
          the total yield for each crop and for all of them together, the
          percentage of increase from your starting quantities (overall and
          for each crop) and the average yield of each plant of each
          type.

06M05.A   Draw an appropriate graph to show the information collected   M - 5
          in the above activities.

06M06.A   Use information from your gardening records referred to above   M - 2
          to create word problems for practice with fractions, decimals,
          per cents, ratios and proportion.

06M07.A   Learn all axioms, theorems, and formulae used with parallel   M - 3
          and perpendicular rows, as you will plant in your garden.

MATHEMATICS AND PERSONAL FINANCE

06M08.B	Use your study of grain elevators and silos to learn the geometry formulae for cylinders and cones and to practice using those formulae to find the volume of containers in each of those shapes.	M - 4
06M09.B	After investigating the commodities market, try your hand with a mock account ONLY. Check prices daily, choose investments; follow them for several weeks to see how you much money you might have made or lost. (DO NOT GET INTO THE REAL COMMODITIES MARKET UNLESS YOU CAN AFFORD TO LOSE IT ALL.)	M - 2 CE - 2
06M10.B	Keep track of your commodities account on an ongoing line graph. Then calculate minimum, maximum and average daily, weekly, and total fluctuations.	M - 5
06M11.B	Learn to measure bushels, pecks, and other common measures used to compute yields of crops and how to convert each of these to their metric equivalents.	M- 1
06M12.B	Measure the amount of seed planted, the amount of produce harvested, and/or any amount wasted. Compute the percentage of increase in yield of a particular field of wheat or other grain crop.	M- 1
06M13.B	Using the above figures and the current market value of the product, determine the value of your harvested crop. Deduct all of your expenses in growing, preparing, transporting, and marketing, and determine the profit made from that field.	M-1
06M14.B	Learn to measure acreage and to convert acres to whole and partial square miles.	M - 1
06M15.C	Study an amortization chart for a real mortgage. Use it to find what percentage of each of several selected payments will go toward interest and/or principal.	M - 2 each time max. of 20
06M16.C	Use the above chart to set up several different prepayment plans to complete the loan payoff in fewer years than the original contract.	M - 5
06M17.C	From an amortization chart, compute the amount of each payment if the buyer paid double principal payments each month. Bear in mind that each advance payment will be a different amount.	M - 5
06M18.C	Examine and learn to complete capital gains tax forms for the sale of actual or imagined real estate.	M - 3
06M19.C	Learn and use appropriate formulae to figure interest, APR, total payment and the portion of each payment that is principal on several different loans, given each other piece of information on each.	M - 3

MATHEMATICS AND PERSONAL FINANCE

06M20. C   Study geometric shapes and measurements commonly used   M- 5
in real estate and learn to use appropriate formulae to find
area and perimeter of each shape.

06M21.C   Use geometry formulae to find perimeter and area of your   M - 2
family's home, land, and other real estate, including all of the
rooms in the home.

06M22.C   This is the time to take a geometry course if you and your   M - 1
parents have planned that as part of your high school credits   credit
and you did not do it in Unit 1.

06M23.C   Determine the equity your family has in its home based on   M - 2
actual principal payments, repairs, and improvements. Compare
those figures to the total arrived at by deducting payoff
value from market value.

06M24.D   Using census figures for several successive decades, plot a   M - 5
line or bar graph showing rate of population growth (or
decline) in various Western states or provinces.

06M25.D   Compute these same census figures in percents and ratios.   M - 2

06M26.D   Play level 2 or 3 of the computer game, Oregon Trail, which   M - 2 each
requires both math and strategy. Choose a different occupation   time
and change other variables each time to see how each   max. of 20
affects the outcome.

06M27.D   Chart on a graph the following for each round of Oregon Trail: M - 5
distance completed, time taken, number of survivors for entire
trip, money and goods left at arrival. Use this to measure your
ongoing progress.

06M28.D   Collect data on the sizes (in both area and population) of the   M - 3
states considered to make up the West (from the Great Plains
westward) in the U. S. or the Western provinces in Canada. Use
this data to compute relative population density of each state and
show on some type of graph the relationship be-tween them all.

06M29.E   Research numbering systems used by the Aztecs, Incas and   M - 7
other original nations. Learn to count and/or calculate using each
one.

06M30.E   Research the systems and units of measure used by the peoples   H - 3
studied in this unit, and compare them to your own.

06M31.E   Study census reports to find the 'Native American' population   M - 1
of the U.S. and of different states at various times in history.
Prepare a bar graph to compare these.

06M32.E   Insofar as possible, break down the population figures gathered   M - 5
above by 'nation' (or tribe) and prepare a graph to show
the relative sizes of the major nations and confederations.

MATHEMATICS AND PERSONAL FINANCE

06M33. E   Using any appropriate books and maps of the time period, calculate the maximum area ever occupied by each of the major 'native' groups and compare it to the size of the reservations on which they were eventually forced to live.   M - 3

06M34.   Continue to brush up on basic math as needed.   M - 2

06M35.   Use data from any of the graphs you make or study in this mini-unit to practice calculating per cent, ratio and proportion.   M - 2

SCIENCE

06S01.A   Through interviews or books and magazines, learn about organic gardening and why people prefer it.   PA - 1

06S02.A   Tour an organic garden and observe the methods used to enrich soil, eliminate weeds, and control pests without chemicals.   PA - 2

06S03.A   Investigate the pros and cons of chemical fertilizers, herbicides, and insecticides to make an informed decision about them.   PA - 1

06S04.A   Learn how organic refuse turns into compost and how compost improves soil.   PA - 1

06S05.A   Learn the value of mulching garden vegetables and ornamentals and its primary purposes.   PA - 1

06S06.A   Use Plant and Soil Science material from 4-H to study and prepare a display or exhibit on various methods of plant propagation. Be sure to include: seeds, sprouting stems in water, rooting in soil, runners, tubers, bulbs, and any others you can discover.   PA - 10+

06S07.A   Read through a number of seed and/or nursery catalogs to learn about different varieties of the fruits, vegetables, and ornamentals you might be able to grow in your climate and soil.   PA - 3

06S08.A   Prepare an exhibit on seeds, showing the plant from which each comes, where each grows, and how each is scattered.   SB - 5

06S09.A   Watch the Moody Science Video, *Journey of Life*, which shows the various ways God created for seeds to travel and spread themselves   SB - 2

06S10.A   Prepare a chart, exhibit, or written report on germination of different plants, showing requirements and the effects of different conditions on speed of germination and rate of produce using each method for each type of plant.   SB - 10

SCIENCE

06S11.A   Use *Backyard Scientist* or any science text to study and perform   SB - 2
experiments about photosynthesis, transpiration, and other
processes in green plants.

06S12.A   Do this project to demonstrate the plant processes studied   SB - 2
elsewhere in this mini-unit: Plant a green plant in a mixture of
sand and peat moss in a large jar or bottle. Add one-two pieces of
charcoal, water well, and seal the container. Watch and record the
plant's growth. Prepare an exhibit and a report to show the results
of this experiment and an explanation of the processes involved
and how they can continue in this closed environment. Be sure to
tell where the plant gets its food and the carbon dioxide it needs to
perform photosynthesis and produce oxygen.

06S13.A   Study the parts of various types of plants and make charts   SB - 1
labeling parts on common plants.   each

06S14.A   Study various forms of fertilizer and learn the appropriate use   PA - 1
of each in commercial and home applications.

06S15.B   Learn about different methods of pollination and cross-pollination   PA - 1
and techniques used by farmers to encourage or prevent it.

06S16.B   Contact your nearest land grant college and arrange to tour   PA - 2+
one of their experimental or training farms. On your tour, learn
about different projects they have there and the purposes of each.

06S17.B   Study plant genetics and crossbreeding and how these are   SB - 2
used to reproduce specific traits or breed out others.

06S18.B   Learn from a seed grower or distributor how hybrid seeds are   PA - 3
created and grown and how their purity is protected.

06S19.B   Learn the benefits of crop rotation and crops that should be   PA - 2
used together.

S0620.B   Use material from your county extension service or soil conservation   PA - 2
office to study types of soil and soil testing. What do they show?
Why are they helpful?

S0621.B   Study the insects, fungi, and other pests which threaten fruit   PA - 2
and vegetable crops in your area. Find out what protective
measures are taken by community agencies and/or commercial
growers and how you can protect your own plants.

80622.B   Study ladybugs and other insects that are helpful for plants   SB - 1
in general or specific kinds.

S0623.B   Use a Christian biology text supplemented by materials from   SB - 20+
a library, 4-H, or county extension office for a thorough study   max 1/2
of entomology, if this is of interest to you.   credit

SCIENCE

S0624.B	Investigate the pros and cons of chemical fertilizers, herbicides, and insecticides as opposed to the strict organic method of farming to make an informed decision about them. Explain why it is difficult for commercial farmers to use fully organic methods.	PA - 2
S0625.B	Work with a county agent or a commercial farmer to list and learn about various types of equipment used in large-scale agriculture. Learn how each operates, what it does, and when it would be used.	PA - 2
S0626.B	Tour and study a grain processing plant, paying special attention to how the grain elevators work.	PA - 2
S0627.B	Tour a national and/or state forest and learn how they are preserved and protected. Find out if any part of it is leased, and if so, to whom and for what purpose.	SB - 3
06S28.B	Study about the products that come from trees and the processes used to produce them. Be sure to include paper products as well as the more obvious ones.	SB - 1
06S29.B	Tour a sawmill or lumber mill.	SP - 2
06S30.B	Tour a paper products manufacturing plant and follow the entire process from a living tree to the finished paper products.	SP - 2
06S31.C	Study the tools of surveying and how they are built, calibrated, and used. Learn how computer technology changed surveying.	SP - 2
06S32.C	Investigate (GPS) Geographic Positioning Satellite technology and how it is used. Learn and be able to explain how it could be applied to surveying, as it someday will.	SP - 2
06S33.C	Study the various kinds of soil and topography and which ones need what kind of special treatment to build a home on them.	SE - 2
06S34.C	Study the various treatments needed for wood to make it hold up to various weather conditions.	SP 1
06S35.C	Study the use of vinyl and other types of siding to protect the wood of homes. Compare qualities of each that make them more or less desirable for this purpose.	SP - 1
06S36.C	Study various roofing materials and compare them for desirability in particular circumstances.	SP - 1
06S37.C	Study the materials commonly used for supports or infrastructure on various types of buildings. Compare the various qualities of each.	SP - 1

SCIENCE

06S38. C   Investigate soil mechanics, the branch of civil engineering that relates to the soil and those things contained beneath it and within it. Try to determine why this is so important in the business of real estate.   SE - 2

06S39.C   Study the nature and instance of oil and/or other kinds of subterranean minerals and the processes by which they can be recovered. This will help you understand why most real estate sales in many parts of the world don't include mineral rights   SP - 1   SC - 1

06S40. C   Learn about the methods used at various times in history to find the water table on a piece of real estate. Then compare all of those to how it is done today.   H - 1   SP - 1

06S41.C   By talking to civil engineers, builders, or your county agent or from books on one or more of those topics, learn how variables in the water table can affect the type of buildings one can erect and the methods that might be used to build them.   SP - 2

06S42.C   From current engineering books or periodicals, learn how the technique of satellite imaging is used to locate and determine the depth of the water table in a particular area.   SP - 1   SE - 1

06S43.D   Watch the video *Grand Canyon: Monument to the Flood* by Master Books. If you substitute other videos on this subject, beware that most others are not from a Creationist perspective.   SE - 2

06S44.D   Tour Black Hills National Park, Yellowstone National Park or another mountainous area in the U. S. or Canadian West. Imagine the hardships of trying to travel through such areas with ox-drawn wagons or the obstacles to trying to settle and build homes there. What modern inventions or engineering techniques make life there more bearable today?   SE - 3   H - 1

06S45.D   Study the canyons, mountains, and other land formations of the Western U. S and Canada and the hardships they caused for the early settlers in that area.   SE - 2

06S46.D   Tour the Grand Canyon or another canyon or cavern in the area covered in this unit.   SE - 3+

06S47.D   As you take a drive through the Painted Desert or some other desert area of the Western United States, try to imagine the hardships of traveling or living in such an area without such modern conveniences as air conditioning, easily accessible water, protection from the Sun, etc.   SE - 2   H - 1

06S48.D   Tour the Petrified Forest of Arizona and attend one or more of their classes on the composition and history of petrified wood.   SE - 3

06S49.D   If you did not cover it in Unit One, study gold and silver as elements as well as instruments of monetary exchange.   SE - 1   SC - 1

SCIENCE

06S50.D	Learn how gold is extracted from ore and how assayers test ore samples for gold content.	SE - 1 SC - 1
06S51.D	Study copper, tin, boron, and other elements that are mined in abundance in the Western United States and only in few other places.	SE - 1
06S52.D	Study gold mining as it was done in the "Old West" and how it is done today in places that still have gold mines.	SC - 1 SE - 1
06S53.D	Study the topography and geology of the desert areas of the American Southwest.	SE - 3
06S54.D	Use field guides by Peterson, Audubon or others to identify and study as many as possible of the birds and animals that live in the deserts of the U. S. Make a chart to classify them by traditional taxonomy and the Biblical system you looked at in Unit 3.	SB - 2
06S55.D	Study the plant life indigenous to desert areas like those of the Western U. S. and catalog in keeping with plant taxonomy.	SB - 2
06S56. D	Study various methods of irrigation, which finally made life in desert areas more bearable. Make charts or diagrams of various types of irrigation systems, itemizing the components, configuration and operation of each. Determine which would work best in what kind of areas and under what conditions.	SP - 2
06S57.D	If you did not do so in Unit Four, study the early locomotive, the invention that may well have made the biggest single impact on settlement of the West.	SP-2
06S58.E	Study the buffalo and the many and varied uses for its assorted parts, all of which were used in one way or another by the Plains 'Indians'.	SB-1 H-1
06S59.E	Study the processes used by early Natives of the Great Plains for tanning buffalo hides. Compare to methods used to tan and cure leather today.	SC-1
06S60.E	Study the processes used by the Pueblo or 'Cave-Dwelling' American originals to dig and hollow out their homes on mesas and the sides of cliffs.	SP-1
06S61.E	Study the housing materials used by each of the other indigenous American groups. Considering the location and environment in which each lived, determine why they each used what they did.	SP-2
06S62.E	Study the fishing methods used by the various coastal 'tribes' and others who made fish a large part of their diets. How does this differ from the methods used today?	SP-1 PA-1

SCIENCE

06S63. E	Investigate the various rocks, minerals and other items used by the original Americans for making arrowheads. Compare desirable and undesirable qualities of each material for that purpose.	SP-1 SE-1
06S64.E	Study the aerodynamics of the bow & arrow and why it is so effective.	SP-1

HEALTH AND FITNESS

06H01.A	Study and chart the nutritive value and calorie count of several common vine-grown fruits and vegetables.	FN - 1
06H02.A	Study and add to the chart above, nutritional data on other fruits or vegetables commonly grown in home gardens in your area.	FN - 4
06H03.A	Learn about the nutritional and medicinal value of herbs, many of which can be easily grown in a home garden.	FN - 5
06H04.A	Study common pollen allergies and the plants most often responsible for them.	HE - 2
06H05.A	Study first aid for blisters, backaches, sunburn, muscle cramps, insect bites, and other ailments that affect gardening.	HE- 2
06H06 B	Study the harmful effects of widespread pesticide spraying on people's health and on the environment.	SE - 1
06H07. B	Learn first aid procedures for someone overcome by pesticide sprays.	HE- 1
06H08.B	Study assorted data on the health effects of residual chemicals sometimes found in agricultural products sold as foods. Find ways to safeguard your family from this?	HE- 1
06H09.C	Study the problem of underground deposits of toxic waste seeping into homes built on the site of waste dumps (like in the case of Love Canal) or other unsafe locations.	SE - 2
06H10.C	Study procedures by which a prospective real estate purchase could be checked for contaminants like those mentioned above.	SE - 2
06H11.C	Study procedures available for correcting problems of underground contamination allowing the land to become useful. again.	SE - 2
06H12.C	Examine ground water for contaminants and learn about various methods for purifying it.	SE - 2

HEALTH AND FITNESS

06H13.D	Study cholera, a disease that devastated whole communities and struck fear in people's hearts throughout the Western frontier. Determine the causes of this disease and why we rarely see it today.	HE - 3
06H14.D	Study smallpox, another frightening disease common to the American West during the mid-1800's, but which is almost nonexistent today.	HE - 2
06H15.D	Study vaccinations, which were first put into widespread use against smallpox and have since nearly eradicated it and some other diseases.	HE - 2
06H16.D	Study the side effects of all common vaccinations and the people or conditions for which each type is contraindicated. Discuss why some Christians refuse to give routine vaccinations for their children.	HE- 2
06H17.D	Study anthrax, rabies, hoof-and-mouth disease, and other diseases which ravaged livestock and work animals on various parts of the frontier.	HE - 2
06H18.D	Study methods used to combat the above diseases during the time studied in this mini-unit.	HE - 2
06H19.D	Investigate how the discovery of penicillin changed the treatment of any of the above diseases and others that were so often fatal as to be highly dreaded.	HE - 2
06H20.E	Learn to play "Chunky" or another active game or sport invented by the "Native Americans", and play it for exercise.	PE - 5 +
06H21.E	Study the ravages caused to the population of the Original American nations due to diseases imported by whites in the 19th century. Which of these diseases could be expected to be lighter in someone with natural immunities to them?	HE - 2
06H22.E	Study each of the diseases above to learn its cause, symptoms, and treatment.	HE - 6

PRACTICAL ARTS

06P01.A	Grow at least one type of fruit or berry that makes a vine.	PA - 10
06P02.A	Plant and grow a garden of several other edible plants, doing everything from ground preparation to harvesting on your own. Use plants that are propagated by different methods.	PA- 20 +
06P03.A	Grow a garden, planter box, or flower bed of flowers or other ornamentals, using a variety of propagation methods.	LH - 3

PRACTICAL ARTS

06P04.A	Learn to mix fertilizers, peat, topsoil, and other plant foods to make whatever type of mixture a particular plant needs in your particular soil.	PA - 1
06P05.A	Prepare a compost heap, and use the compost in your garden or flower bed.	PA 1
06P06.A	Learn to mulch the different types of plants you are growing, using a variety of methods.	PA - 1
06P07.A	Plan and execute one or more new landscape arrangements for your home.	LH - 3
06P08.A	Care for your lawn regularly, including mowing, edging, weeding and pruning.	LH - 50 per year
06P09.A	Learn several ways to keep birds and/or other animals from raiding your fruits or vegetables.	PA - 2
06P10.A	Make a scarecrow from readily-available materials and set it up in your garden.	CR - 5
06P11.A	Create attractive floral arrangements from plants you have grown.	CR - 1 each
06P12.A	Cook a meal using only vegetables or fruits you grew in your own garden.	FN - 3
06P13.A	Sell some of your produce at a farmer's market, flea market or roadside stand.	EC - 2 PA - 1
06P14.A	Learn to use a tiller or other garden tools.	PA - 1
06P15.B	Test several soil samples and learn the necessary steps to enrich each for growing various types of plants.	PA - 2
06P16.B	Learn to drive a tractor.	PA- 5 +
06P17.B	Learn how to mount, use, and remove all the attachments that go to the tractor you learned to drive.	PA - 2
06138.B	Learn to maintain the tractor and all of its attachments.	PA- 5
06P19.B	Learn to sharpen blades on tractor cutting attachments and how to know when they need to have it done.	PA - 3
06P20.B	Learn to drive and use other farm equipment.	PA - 5 +
06P21.B	Through 4-H or your county extension office, take a course in farm equipment safety.	PS - 3
06P22.B	Participate as an employee or volunteer in a commercial fruit or vegetable harvest.	PA- 1 per hour up to 40

PRACTICAL ARTS

06P23.B	Ride in the plane with a crop duster and learn how he does his job.	PA - 2
06P24.B	After studying insecticide and herbicides and what to use for what purpose, mix the exact proportions of appropriate products for specific crops and learn to distribute it.	PA - 2
06P25.B	Observe the filling of silos and grain elevators and learn how to operate the equipment used to fill them.	PA - 2
06P26.B	Learn to operate a grain elevator to release grain in appropriate amounts.	PA - 2
06P27.B	Learn when and how grain elevators and silos are cleaned.	PA- 2
06P28.B	Learn to use and maintain the type of irrigation system that your family uses or that is common in your area.	PA - 2
06P29.C	Learn to read appraisals on real property and to explain them to someone else.	BE - 1
06P30.C	Learn to read and interpret survey reports on real estate.	BE - 1
06P31.C	Read the abstract on your family's home or other real property and summarize it for someone who is not knowledgeable about such things.	CE - 2
06P32.C	Learn where and how to file the deed on your real estate with the proper government authorities.	CL - 1
06P33.C	Arrange with a real estate broker or lawyer to sit in on a closing in order to learn what is involved there.	CE - 3
06P34.C	Prepare an accurate amortization schedule for your family's home or some other piece of real property.	M- 3
06P35.C	Learn how and where to apply for a homestead exemption and how to know if your property is eligible.	EC - 1
06P36.C	Help your family paint the interior or exterior of your home.	IA - 1 per hour
06P37.C	Help your family do other repairs or remodeling to improve the value of your home.	IA - 1 per hour
06P38.C	Attend a meeting of your community's planning or zoning board (if applicable) to learn how one files a protest or requests a waiver or variance.	CL - 2
06P39.C	Learn where and how to apply for a mortgage loan and the factors taken into account by the lender in deciding whether to grant it.	CE- 2

PRACTICAL ARTS

06P40.D	Use Usborne's *How to Draw Maps and Charts* to make your own maps of areas you have traveled, duplicating the process used by Lewis and Clark in mapping out the Louisiana Purchase.	G- 5
06P41.D	Learn to use the surveying tools available to Lewis and Clark.	IA - 2
06P42.D	Learn Morse Code and send messages similar to those sent across the Great West shortly after the telegraph first linked the United States from coast to coast, making Western settlement even more attractive.	H - 2
06P43.D	Learn to saddle and otherwise outfit a horse for riding.	2
06P44,D	Learn the techniques of properly grooming a horse.	PA- 2
06P45.D	Take horseback riding lessons or learn to ride in some other way.	RE - 1 per hour
06P46.D	Complete the 4-H project book on Horsemanship.	RE - 25
06P47.D	Try your hand at panning for gold at one of the many tourist attractions that offer that.	CR - 1
06P48.D	Cook a full meal for your family using only cast iron or pewter pots hung over the fireplace or heated on a hearth, the most common method of cooking available to Western pioneer women.	FN - 3
06P49.D	Try washing your family's clothing on a scrub board as pioneer women had to do, drawing water from a well if you want to be even more authentic.	HM- 2 H 1
06P50.D	Use the *Foxfire* books or *Back to Basics* to learn about and try other skills, crafts, or chores as they were performed by pioneer women.	Parents' discretion
06P51.E	Make a dugout canoe from a felled tree like the ones used by the Woodland Indians, coating with pitch as they did.	WW - 15
06P52.E	Make appropriate oars for your canoe.	WW- 2
06P53.E	Take your canoe out on a river or lake, but only after testing it carefully for watertightness.	RE - 3
06P54.E	If you cannot carve a full-size canoe, make a miniature one from a tree limb and sail it in a tub or pool.	WW- 5
06P55.E	Make a tipi (teepee) like those used by the Plains Indians.	CR - 10

PRACTICAL ARTS

06P56.E	Go on an overnight camping trip with at least one other person and live off the land as the original Americans did. Sleep in the tipi you made or rent one. Eat only foods that you and your companions gather or kill, and do all preparation and cooking on an open fire, without benefit of electricity or other modern conveniences.	RE - 25
06P57.E	If you have not done so in another unit, learn to tell directions by the location of sun, moon, and/or star formations as early Americans did.	SE - 2
06P58.E	Construct a bow & arrows, working carefully to choose the right materials and form the shafts and heads correctly.	WW - 2
06P59.E	Learn to weave baskets using dried grasses and twigs as the Woodlands natives did.	CR - 4
06P60.E	Learn to tan hides in the way of the Sioux and Cheyenne and the scientific principles that make it work.	SC - 3
06P61.E	Make one or more pieces of pottery for decoration or other use in your home. Use only natural clay and the methods available to the Indians, not an electric wheel or any modern devices or supplies.	VA - 2 each
06P62.E	Learn to shoot a long bow.	PE - 5
06P63.E	Study the laws governing bow hunting in your state, province, or local area.	CG - 1
06P64.	Type any or all papers written during the study of this unit.	BE - 1 per paper
06P65.	Make your own puppets for any puppet show you do in this unit.	CR - 5+
06P66.	Design and sew your own costumes for any play you present in this unit.	CC - 5 each
06P67.	Use a variety of lettering styles to make the posters required for various exhibits elsewhere in this unit.	VA - 1 each
06P68.	Use your computer to make posters, signs or other graphics for your exhibits or displays.	CO - 1 each

DECORATIVE AND PERFORMING ARTS

06A01.A	Make a pottery or ceramic flowerpot or vase to use with the ornamental plants you will grow.	CR - 2
06A02.A	Draw landscapes featuring a variety of plant life, natural and/or cultivated.	VA - 2 each

DECORATIVE AND PERFORMING ARTS

06A03.A	Sketch a detailed plan for your vegetable or flower garden.	VA - 2
06A04.A	Use flowers, fruits, or vegetables from your garden to make attractive centerpieces for your table or other place in your home. (If you grow all three, try one of each.)	VA - 2 each
06A05.A	Press cut flowers and make a picture or collage from them, mounting on wood, metal, card stock, poster board or any other flat surface of your choosing that will lend itself to hanging on a wall.	VA - 2
06A06.A	Dry flowers and other plant products from your garden and use them in floral arrangements or other decorations.	VA - 2
06A07.A	Tour an exhibition of landscape art and notice each of these: ornamental gardens, vegetable/herb gardens cultivated fields, forests, and other areas.	AA - 2
06A08.B	Learn to sing several folk songs about farming or an agrarian life-style.	VM - 5
06A09.B	Draw a farm scene suitable to illustrate one of the pastoral poems read in this unit.	VA - 3
06A10.B	Instead of drawing a farm scene, paint it using watercolors, oils, or acrylics.	VA - 5 +
06A11. B	Design and perform a skit or play about a day on a farm. Use an original script.	DR - 20
06A12.B	Set one of this mini-unit's 'pastoral' poems to music composed by you.	MC - 3
06A13.B	Listen to a "pastoral" symphony and discuss why it is called that.	MA - 3
06A14.B	Using your artistic talents, create posters to promote soil and/ or water conservation, wise use of pesticides, and other environmentally-sound practices	VA— 1 each
06A15.C	Draw or paint a picture of your family's home, trying to be as precise as possible with even the smallest details.	VA - 3
06A16.C	Listen to the old Tennessee Ernie Ford song, "This Old House", and discuss or be able to write an essay on its spiritual significance and symbolism.	MA - 1
06A17.C	Learn to sing "This Old House" and sing it for an audience.	VM - 2
06A18.C	While listening to "This Old House", "My Old Kentucky Home" or other songs about houses or homes sketch a picture of the house you envision.	MA - 1 VA - 2

DECORATIVE AND PERFORMING ARTS

06A19.C	Draw blueprints (floor plans) and an artist's rendition of the finished product for your own personal dream house that you would like to own someday.	VA - 10
06A20.C	Use humorous, cartoon drawings to illustrate the how-to booklet you made on buying and selling real estate.	VA - 2
06A21.D	Study the Western art of Frederic Remington and learn to identify his common pieces that are often reproduced.	AA - 3
06A22.D	Study the Western art of the Wyeth family and learn to recognize the works of each of them by their own distinctive styles.	AA 5
06A23.D	Study the drawings of birds and other wildlife of the Western U. S., which first made John James Audubon famous. Compare these drawings to photos of the same birds or animals to see how accurate he was in his attention to detail.	AA - 3+ SB - 2
06A24.D	Listen to and discuss the songs on the audios, "Songs of America", "Westward Ho!" or any other collection of folk songs of the Old West.	MA - 2
06A25.D	Listen to several modern country/western songs and compare to Old West folk songs.	MA - 3
06A26.D	Learn to sing one or more songs from the early days of Western U. S. settlement.	VM - 2 each
06A27.D	As guitars, fiddles, harmonicas, and banjos were popular instruments during this period, this mini-unit would be a good place to begin or continue lessons on one of those instruments.	IM - 1 per hour
06A2S.D	Learn to play one or more of the songs studied in this mini-unit, using whatever instrument you play best.	IM - 2 ea.
06A29.E	Learn to sing one or more Native songs.	VM - 2 ea.
06A30.E	Learn to play one or more Native American tunes, preferably on instruments like those created by the Native peoples themselves.	IM - 2 ea.
06A31.E	View and discuss an exhibit of Native American folk art, preferably featuring pieces from different nations and locations.	AA - 1 H - 1
06A32.E	Create artwork featuring the symbols or patterns common to the works of Native Americans.	VA - 2 +
06A33.E	Create sand paintings using colored sand or cornmeal on a glass or clear plastic pane and designs or symbols of Native American folklore. Frame with underside showing.	VA - 2
06A34.E	Build a replica of an early village of one particular nation of Native Americans.	VA - 5

DECORATIVE AND PERFORMING ARTS

| 06A35.E | Draw or paint a picture of one or more famous Native Americans in traditional dress of their own nation. | VA - 2 |

| 06A36. | Draw pictures of any field trips you took. | VA - 1 ea. |

| 06A37. | Use drawing, painting and graphic arts to create displays and make posters as called for in this study. | VA - 1 ea. |

| 06A38. | Illustrate one or more of the poems you studied or memorized for this unit. | VA - 1 ea. |

| 06A39. | Set one or more of this unit's poems to music, using an original or existing tune. | MC - 3 ea. |

| 06A40. | Set one or more of the Scripture passages in this unit to music, using a tune you wrote for the purpose. | MC - 3 ea. |

UNIT 7

She girds herself with strength
and strengthens her arm.
Proverbs 31:17

Overview

This verse is an obvious reminder of the need for a woman to "keep up her strength" and to care for her health. However, we believe it is much more than that. The phrase, 'girds herself with strength' can have a much broader connotation than physical health, and this unit treats it that way. You will study health, fitness, and strength in their physical, spiritual, and emotional realms. This begins with the study of God's commands to his people regarding the care of the body and will then include spiritual health as well. Therefore, while you will study your physical body and how God expects you to care for it, you will also investigate other meanings of 'strength'.

Other mini-units involve the study of organized sports and fitness activities and the ways in which they have affected history. This naturally leads to a study of the Olympics and the ancient Greeks who invented it. You will look into sports and athletic traditions of many countries and other periods of history. You will study the history and political significance of the Olympic Games now and in Ancient times and investigate the ancient cultures in which they originated.

For ease of organization, the Roman Empire, also a nation obsessed with strength, is studied here as well. You will use many resources and projects to learn about the people of this great Empire and the time in which they lived.

Mini-Units

Mini-Units contained in this unit are:

A. All Kinds of Strength

B. Olympics and Sports

C. Ancient Greeks: Founders of the Olympics

D. Ancient Rome: Warriors of Great Strength

Each thematic mini-unit is described and designated with a letter of the alphabet in the following paragraphs. Individual activities designed for use in one particular mini-unit will be marked with those letters. (For further help with this, please refer to the explanation of mini-units in the Guidelines section of this unit study guide.)

Mini-Units

A. All Kinds of Strength

In this mini-unit, you will discover all the possible meanings of the words strength and strengthen and the various ways that can apply to our lives. You will look at physical strength and health, concentrating on musculature, nutrition, and fitness. Spiritual strength and the processes by which it is increased will be the topic of your Bible lessons in this mini-unit. We will also look at strength as it relates to nations and groups as well as how it can be measured and developed.

Another aspect of this mini-unit will involve a look at Scripture passages that liken the Christian life to some type of physical contest or challenge, thus equating strength with the spiritual as well as the physical part of our lives. You will do a thorough examination of the "whole armor of God" and what it means to each individual Christian.

You will learn how your body's skeletal and muscular framework operates and how best to care for it. This will include exercise, nutrition and general fitness, not just of these parts but of the whole body. One goal of this mini-unit will be to improve your own general health and your awareness of your body's needs. For that reason, you' will study human anatomy, physiology, and health in general, including the value of a good fitness program. To that end, you will be encouraged to start on a personal fitness program to meet your individual health needs, whatever they may be. This unit will also involve learning and practicing basic skills needed for a variety of team and individual sports. The emphasis is on helping you get yourself in better physical condition not turning you into a great athlete.

Practical arts for this mini-unit will include various health and first aid skills, including a complete class in CPR. You will have a chance to investigate careers in medicine, health care and physical therapy. Art activities explore the full realm of active recreational and fitness programs, including musical movement and dance of various kinds.

B. Olympics and Sports

Flowing naturally from the previous mini-unit, this one will cover the Olympic games and other major national and international sporting attractions, amateur and professional. You will learn about all the various sports that are part of the Summer and Winter Olympic games and how each is played. You have an opportunity to learn to play any that interest you, or you may study them only as a spectator, if you prefer.

You will also study the history of the Olympics, learning when, why and where they began. In the process of this investigation, you will look at the political issues that have affected the Olympics in various years and how each was handled. Also included here will be other international sporting events and the effects they have on relationships between peoples and countries. You will look at God's instructions regarding sports and athletics and will study the opportunities for such that were available during Bible times.

Science and practical arts activities for this mini-unit will have you building and using various types of fitness and sports equipment and/or learning how they work. These items will include the trampoline, a variety of gymnastics items, various types of bats and balls, and several different kinds of winter sports equipment as well as clothing and protective gear worn by the individual Olympian.

This unit is best done during a broadcast of the Olympics, preferably the summer games. Then you will be able to watch some of the contests and keep a day by day list of the gold, silver and bronze medal winners and their homelands. If this does not fit your schedule, try to record some of the televised events of an upcoming Olympics to watch when you do tackle this mini-unit

Mini-Units

C. Ancient Greeks: Founders of the Olympics

The mini-unit on the Olympic Games leads naturally into a study, Greece, of the nation and culture that developed them. You will study the ancient Greeks in history, as well as how they influenced those cultures that came later. This includes biographies of famous Greeks, samples of Greek philosophy, literature and other period documents. This mini-unit does include mythology, so parents should be cautious here.

You will learn much in this unit about the scientific, mathematical, and cultural discoveries of the Greeks and how they are still present in our world today. You will enumerate and pay special attention to the things we have inherited from them. This applies not only to material, scientific inventions or discoveries, but includes cultural and artistic creations and models as well. You will be able to experience Greek drama, music, art, and language to whatever extent you and your parents wish to pursue it. This can include learning the ancient Greek language in which the New Testament was first written.

D. Ancient Rome: Warriors of Great Strength

Like the Greeks, the Romans prided themselves on their strength, individually and as a nation. For this reason, we will study them here in this context, looking at their armies, their physical prowess, and their penchant for contests of skill and strength.

You will also study the history of the Roman Empire and its place in world history. This is done through biographies, original writings, scholarly studies, and historical fiction of the time period. You will see the world in the time of the Romans and how their territory expanded and then shrank. This history study will also include the beginnings of the Roman Catholic Church and its impact on the history of the world as a whole.

You will learn about the culture of the Romans, taking a special look at those elements of our own culture that came from them. This will give you a chance to learn about the music, drama, literature and other arts of these people. You may also wish to study Latin in this context.

BIBLE AND CHRISTIAN CHARACTER

07B01.A	Use concordance and/or Bible dictionary to find various uses of the word translated in this verse as "girds" and its actual meaning in each use.	B-1
07B02.A	Study and/or memorize Ephesians 6: 13-17 and relate it to the verse under discussion in this unit.	B-2
07B03.A	For an in-depth look at the above passage, read *The Christian in Complete Armor* and discuss with a parent how this relates to Proverbs 31:17.	B-10
07B04.A	Use a concordance and other resources to study other Scripture passages that teach the need for perseverance and endurance in the Christian life.	B-4
07B05.A	Study and memorize Ecclesiastes 9:11, and discuss with your parents how this relates to the other passages studied in this mini-unit.	B-2

BIBLE AND CHRISTIAN CHARACTER

07B06.A   Read II Corinthians 12:7-10 and memorize verse 9 as a reminder   B-2
of the source of our real strength.

07B07.A   Read the story of Samson in Judges 13-16 to see an example   B-3
of physical strength that did not profit its possessor until he
added to it the strength of a godly spirit.

07B08.A   Look up in a concordance and study each passage using the   B-3
word 'strength' or one of its synonyms you found in the related
Composition activity of this mini-unit. List all verse references,
paraphrase their meanings and tell to what type of strength
each refers. Save this list to use for later activities in
Composition.

07B09.B   Study II Timothy 2:3-16 and discuss how these verses relate   B-2
to the readiness, perseverance and alertness needed for an
Olympic athlete.

07B10.B   Study and memorize Hebrews 12:1-3, noticing its appropriateness   B-2
for a Christian athlete.

07B11.B   Read, study, and discuss with parents, I Corinthians 9:24-27,   B-2
and memorize verses 24 and 25, which could become a creed
for a Christian competing in the Olympics or other sports
contests.

07B12.B   Use a concordance to find and study all other Scripture passages   B-4
related to racing or other sports.

07B13. B   Use your concordance to find and study other Scripture passages   B-4
that compare the dedication, hard work and/or commitment of
top athletes to that demanded of the Christian life.

07B14.B   Use your concordance to look up and study two to four Scripture   B-5
verses dealing with each of the goals of the Olympic games as
you researched and defined them in the Composition section of
this mini-unit.

07B15.B   Look up in the concordance and study passages of Scripture   B-3
that teach the value of endurance, striving for excellence, and
other qualities of what we call good sportsmanship, all of which
can be learned through Olympic or other serious sports
competition.

07B16.C   Study carefully and discuss with your parents Paul's Sermon   B-2
at the Areopagus in Athens, as recounted in Acts 17:16-34.
Notice how Paul met the Athenians where they were, using
their own religious beliefs to point them to Christ. Mind map or
discuss with parents what implications this might have in your
own life.

07B17.C   Study Paul's ministry among Greek cities, as told in Acts   B-2
17-20. You may wish to refer to two or more commentaries for
historical background information.

BIBLE AND CHRISTIAN CHARACTER

07B18.C	Read the books of I and II Corinthians, written to one of the most important cities of what had recently been the glory of Greece.	B-6
07B19.C	Determine from your history study what other epistles of the New Testament were written to cities that were considered Greek. Read each of them and take note of things within them that reflect the Greek mindset or culture of the day.	B-10
07B20.C	Use the concordance to find and read all New Testament passages sages that use the word "Greek". Determine and catalog on as list the ones that actually refer to nationality and those that are simply designating the person as a Gentile. Discuss why this word was used for all Gentiles, regardless of actual ethnicity.	B-4
07B21.C	Read *Developing a Biblical Worldview* by C. Fred Smith and compare this viewpoint taught here with the humanism of the Greek philosophers whose writings you read in this unit.	PH - 10 or B - 10
07B22.C	To complete your study of comparative worldviews, study the entire course *Understanding the Times*.	PH - 1/2 credit
07B23.D	Reread the Gospels, looking specifically for times when the Roman government and its officials or laws were used by God to bring about His plan for Salvation, fulfill prophecy, and/or spread the Gospel. List these to use in other subject areas. A few are: Luke 2; Mark 15; John 18. See how many more you can find.	B - 20
07B24.D	As you read the gospels, list all references to Roman soldiers, rulers, or officials. Save the list for use later in Cultural Stud ies.	H - 3
07B25.D	Study the later life and ministry of Paul as told in Acts 22-28, paying special attention to the effect his Roman citizenship had on his trial, judgment, and sentencing and the part this played in determining the location and scope of his ministry for his last years. Make notes on this to use in other activities related to it.	B - 3
07B26. D	Study the entire book of Acts to find and list ways in which the size and uniformity of laws within the Roman Empire helped the disciples in spreading the Gospel "unto all the Earth".	B - 10
07B27.D	Read the Book of Romans, written by Paul to believers in the Empire's capital city long before his travels took him there. Take careful note of all passages that relate directly to elements of their government or culture.	B- 10
07B28.D	Research evangelism training literature to learn about the 'Roman road to salvation' method of witnessing with passages from Romans. Memorize the verses involved and learn to use them to share Christ.	B- 10

BIBLE AND CHRISTIAN CHARACTER

07B29.D	Study the New Testament books of Galatians, Ephesians, Philippians, and Colossians, all letters of the Apostle Paul to churches in Roman provinces.	B- 10
07B30.D	Study Jesus' command and instructions to Peter in Matthew 16:13-19. Discuss with parents the meaning of this passage, which forms the basis of the Roman Catholic papacy, as they believe this made Peter the first Pope. Determine from the passage itself and related Scriptures if you agree or disagree with this teaching.	B - 2
07B31.	Meditate on and memorize one or more of the passages studied in the mini-unit.	B - I per 3 verses
07B32.	Read through the book of Proverbs each month, reading each day the chapter that coincides with that day's date.	B - 3 per week
07B33.	Continue reading through the Bible at a rate of 1-5 chapters per day. If you use *The Daily Bible* or some other version designed specifically for that purpose, their daily readings will take you through the entire Bible in one year. You may follow a pattern of your own at a different rate if you like. Using a chronologically arranged Bible puts your reading in perspective as to time.	B- 1 credit when completed
07B34.	Keep a prayer journal, listing each day (or as the Lord brings to mind) prayer requests, needs in your spiritual life and things God is teaching you. Continue this throughout all units.	B - 2 per week

CULTURAL STUDIES

07C01.A	Study the history of the "fitness culture" in your own country.	H-4
07C02.A	Study the origin and history of physical education and sports in the government-funded schools of your area.	H-3
07C03.A	Investigate the economic impact of the sports industry in your nation, state or province, and/or locality.	CE-3
07C04.A	Study the economic impact of the recreation and fitness industry in your nation, state/province, and locality.	CE-2
07C05.A	Examine fitness and sports programs open to the public in your area. For each, learn: sponsors, who may participate, how it is funded, and its primary purpose.	CS - 2
07C06.A	Examine government funding of public recreation programs in light of the Bible's teaching on the role of government, the guidelines laid out in your nation's Constitution, and the laws of your own state/province or locality. Discuss with your parents the appropriateness of this use of tax revenues.	CG - 1 CE - 2

CULTURAL STUDIES

07C07.A	Study government funding of health care and health-related research in your nation, state/province, and/or locality. Determine which programs are primarily curative and which preventative.	CE - 1 HE - 1
07C08.A	Study various government agencies and programs in your country, state/province or locality that are primarily concerned with preventive health care and the promotion of healthy lifestyles.	CG - 1 CS - 1
07C09.A	Study private foundations, or groups in your country, state/province or locality that are mainly concerned with preventive health care and the promotion of healthy life-styles. Compare cost and effectiveness of these with similar government agencies.	CS - 2
07C10.A	Study the foreign policy concept of 'arguing from a position of strength', especially favored during the 'Cold War' of the middle and late 20th century. Discuss with parents what it means, how it has been manifest in various nations and whether your country subscribes to it at this time.	CG - 1 H - 1
07C11.B	Study the history of the Olympic games, tracing them back to ancient Greece. Learn why they were started, who took part in them, and how they were played. Compare and contrast the first games with those of today.	H - 5
07C12.B	Identify and mark on a world map all countries and the cities within them that have ever hosted the Olympic Games, summer or winter.	G - 3
07C13.B	Use a *World Almanac* or other form of synoptic reference to study each country that has ever hosted the Olympics.	G- 2 each
07C14.B	If possible, watch the opening ceremony of the Olympics, jotting down the names of all countries participating, relative sizes of their teams and the costumes/uniforms their members choose to wear.	G - 3
07C15.B	Locate and mark on a world map all nations who have teams in the current (or most recent) Olympics. As medals are awarded, mark on the map in gold, silver or bronze the winners of each event.	G - 3
07C16.B	Study the lives of Olympic athletes who (before or after the Games) distinguished themselves in other fields as well.	H - 5
07C17.B	Take a look at political issues that have affected various Olympic games and decide whether you feel they were handled in the best possible way to achieve the Olympic goals of international unity, peace, and goodwill. Pay special attention to the Berlin games of 1936, the 1976 Munich games, 1980's Moscow games, and the 1984 games in Los Angeles.	H - 5 CG - 10

CULTURAL STUDIES

07C18.B	Study how various nations fund their Olympic teams and support those who are training for them. Do you consider any of these methods to constitute athletes playing for pay, which is forbidden by Olympic rules? If so, how do you think that can be justified in what is supposed to be an all-amateur contest? Discuss this issue with your parents or other knowledgeable adults.	CS - 5
07C19.B	Study the geography and culture of all nations whose athletes won medals in the most recent Olympics.	G - 1 each
07C20.B	Study the makeup of the Olympic committees and their functions.	CS - 1
07C21.C	Read *Famous Men of Greece* and discuss with your parents each of the people there and the major contributions they made to their society and our own.	H - 5
07C22.C	Choose and do any activities you wish from *Greenleaf's Guide to Famous Men of Greece*.	Parent's Discretion
07C23.C	Use *Streams of Civilization* or another Christian history book to study the Greek Empire.	H - 1
07C24.C	Use materials of your choice to further study the lives of Alexander the Great and other Famous Greeks.	H - 1+ each
07C25.C	Use *Baker's Bible Atlas* or a similar book to find and mark on a map cities of the Bible that were located in what is now Greece. Designate in another way those that were part of the Greek Empire at the height of its size and power.	G 1
07C26.C	Study each of the cities from this mini-unit as they were in the days of the Greek Empire and during the time of the New Testament.	H - 1 each
07C27.C	Use the works of Josephus and/or other historical writings and timeline books such as *Timetables of History* to trace the history of the Greeks and that of the Hebrews during the same time period. Add major events of both and the events in which the two intersected onto your timeline.	H - 5
07C28.C	Use *The Ancient City: Life in Classical Athens & Rome* by Peter Connolly and Hazel Dodge, or any other resources listed in the Reading and Literature section or the Appendix to study everyday life in Ancient Greece, including the military, government and social structure, as well as the clothing, foods, homes, and general life-style of the people (especially women). Compare to Old Testament Hebrew life and culture as studied in Unit 1.	H- 10
07C29.C	Research various aspects of ancient Greece using Microsoft's interactive CD program *Ancient Lands* or a similar resource.	H- 10

CULTURAL STUDIES

07C30.C	To further investigate the government, culture, and arts of the ancient Greeks, especially areas in which their culture influenced your own, do an online search for appropriate resources.	H - 10
07C31.D	Read *Famous Men of Rome* and discuss with your parents each of the men included there.	H - 5
07C32.D	Choose and do activities as you wish from *Greenleaf's Guide to Famous Men of Rome*.	Parent's Discretion
07C33.D	Use *Streams of Civilization* or a similar Christian book to study the history of the Roman Empire.	H - 1
07C34.D	Use materials of your choice to further study the lives of famous Romans.	H - 5 each
07C35.D	Use *The Ancient City: Life in Classical Athens & Rome* by Peter Connolly and Hazel Dodge, or any other resources herein or others of your choice to study everyday life in Ancient Rome, including military, government and social structure, as well as the clothing, food, homes, and general lifestyle of the people.	H - 10
07C36.D	Use *Baker's Bible Atlas* to study and mark on a map the extent of the Roman Empire at the time of Jesus' birth, the time of his death/ resurrection, and at the destruction of Jerusalem in 70 AD.	G - 1 H - 1
07C37.D	Trace the history of the Roman Empire and note on timeline entries what events within it parallel events and time periods in the New Testament.	H - 5
07C38.D	Investigate the Roman occupation of Palestine, to include: how and when it began, the rulers involved, the system of government in Judea under Rome, the living conditions of its people, how the Romans influenced the life and culture of the Hebrews during that period. List ways in which Roman rule increased the spread of the Gospel after the ascension of Jesus.	H - 5
07C39.D	Study living conditions and governmental structure in all other conquered provinces of the Roman Empire during the same time period as in the above activity. Compare and contrast to that of the Hebrews in their native land.	H - 5
07C40.D	Research various aspects of ancient Rome using Microsoft's interactive CD program *Ancient Lands* or a similar resource.	H - 10
07C41.D	Study the development of the Roman Catholic Church and the Greek Orthodox Church and the struggle between them in the waning days of the Roman Empire.	H - 5
07C42.D	Study the history of the Byzantine Empire and its rise from that of Rome.	H - 5

CULTURAL STUDIES

07C43.D	Study the Holy Roman Empire of the early Middle Ages and trace its actual connection to Rome. (This could also be done in the unit on the Middle Ages.)	G	1 each
07C44.	Use encyclopedias or other references to study all countries mentioned in this unit.	G - 1	
07C45.	Locate on a map or globe all countries studied or mentioned in this unit.	G - 1	
07C46.	Locate on a map and study the geography of all cities or municipalities studied in this unit.	G - 1	
07C47.	Locate on a U. S. map all states studied in this unit.	G - 1	
07C48.	Study the homeland of each author, inventor, or artist whose works were used or studied in this mini-unit.	G	1 each
07C49.	Use books listed elsewhere in this unit, Usborne's *World History Dates, The Kingfisher History Encyclopedia,* or any other reference books to make timeline entries for all people, movements, and/or events you studied in this mini-unit.	No additional points	
07C50.	Make timeline entries for all inventions and/or discoveries studied here and major events in the lives of their inventors.	VA -1 per 10 H -1 per 10	
07C51.	Make timeline cards for all other major events and/or people mentioned in books read or studied in this mini-unit.	VA -1 per 10 H - 1 per 10	
07C52.	Make timeline entries for major events in the lives of each of the authors whose works were read in this mini-unit.	VA -1 per 10 H - 1 per 10	
07C53.	Make timeline entries for other famous people who lived in this time period.	VA -1 per 10 H 1 per 10	

READING AND LITERATURE

07R01.A	Read biographies of well-known Christians in professional sports.	H - 5 each	
07R02.A	Read novels or stories about sporting events or athletics or the people who play them.	L - 5 each	
07R03.A	Memorize a minimum of 50 lines of poetry related to the subject of strength in any of its forms.	L - 10	
07R04.A	Read a biography of Joni Eareckson Tada and the source of her strength even in the midst of suffering and paralysis.	H - 5	
07R05.A	Read Chuck Swindon's *Strengthen Your Grip.*	13 - 5	

READING AND LITERATURE

07R06.A	Read biographies of "strong men" from various sports and other walks of life.	H - 5 each
07R07.A	Read a biography of any professional trainer, coach, or fitness expert.	H - 5 each
07R08.A	Read one or more novels in which fitness and/or athletic prowess play a major role.	PE - 5 each
07R09.A	Read one or more manuals on how to play the sports that particularly interest you.	PE - 5 each
07R10.A	Read and study *Sportworks*.	PE - 5
07R11.A	Read *You and Your Fitness and Health*.	HE - 4
07R12.A	Read one or more of the popular how-to fitness books for women.	HE - 5 each
07R13.B	Read *Chariots of Fire* or any other biography of missionary Eric Liddel, who was also an Olympic athlete.	H - 5
07R14.B	Read a biography of Jesse Owens.	H - 5
07R15.B	Read a biography of Jim Thorpe, who won gold medals and then had to forfeit them, due to a technicality in Olympics rules.	H - 5
07R16.B	Read biographies of Peggy Fleming, Nancy Keragin, or other female Winter Olympics medalists.	H - 5 each
07R17.B	Read a biography of Olga Korbut, MaryLou Retton, Nadia Comaneche, or any other female gymnastics medalists.	H - 5
07R18.B	Read *The Los Angeles Times Book of the 1984 Olympic Games*, or *16 Days of Glory - The 1984 Summer Olympics* for a look at the U.S.A.'s most spectacular Olympic performance ever.	H - 5 each
07R19.B	Read the highlights of the Olympics record book of the most recent games.	H - 5
07R20.B	Read *100 Memorable Moments in the Olympics*.	H 5
07R21.B	Read any other book on the history of the Olympic Games.	H - 5
07R22.B	Read how-to manuals on any sport that is featured in Summer or Winter Olympics.	HE - 5
07R23.B	Read one or more books written by or about Olympic athletes or their coaches.	L - 5 each
07R24.C	Read Usborne's *The Greeks*.	H - 4

READING AND LITERATURE

07R25.C*	Read an anthology of the writings of Plato, Aristotle and/or other Greek philosophers. Compare the worldview found in these writings to the Christian worldview taught in the audios and books in this and/or other sections of this mini-unit.	L - 7
07R26.C*	Read *The Humanist Manifesto*, a modern document that had its basis in the philosophy of ancient Greece. Discuss it with your parents and find Scripture verses to refute each part of it.	PH - 3
07R27.C	Read *The Iliad* by Homer, using a full unabridged translation if possible.	L - 10
07R28.C	Read Homer's *The Odyssey* in an unabridged adult translation.	L - 10
07R29.C	If you prefer, read The Iliad and The Odyssey from *The Child's Homer.*	CG - 4
07R30.C	Read Usborne's *Greek Myths and Legends* or any other collection of Greek mythology.	L - 3
07R31.C	Read *Black Ships before Troy*, and other novels written about or set in ancient Greece.	L - 5
07R32.C	Read *Clothes & Crafts in Ancient Greece* by Philip Steele.	H - 5
07R33.C	Read *The Family in Greek History* by Cynthia B. Patterson	H - 5
07R34.C	Read *Archimedes and the Door of Science*.	H - 3 & SP - 2
07R35.C	Read a collection of *Aesop's Fables*, which originated with the ancient Greeks.	L - 3
07R36.C	Read "The Greeks and Greek Civilization" by Jacob Burckhardt.	H - 7
07R37.C	Read *Antigone* and/or other plays by ancient Greek playwrights.	L - 3 each
07R38.C	Read Shakespeare's *A Midsummer Night's Dream*, which is set in ancient Greece and incorporates much of their mythology.	L-5
07R39.D	Read a biography of one or more Roman Caesars.	H - 5
07R40.D	Read biographies of one or more of the rulers of the Holy Roman Empire after the demise of Rome but before the church and the civil government separated.	H - 5 each
07R41.D	Read biographies of any other men featured in *Famous Men of Rome*.	H - 5 each
07R42.D	Read any collection of Roman mythology. Compare their 'gods' and 'goddesses' to those of the Greeks.	H -5 or L- 5

READING AND LITERATURE

07R43.D	Read Usborne's *The Romans*.	H - 3
07R44.D	Read *Ben Hur,* a novel set in the Roman Empire of Jesus' day.	L - 5
07R45.D	Read or watch a video of *The Robe,* set in the post-crucifixion Roman Empire.	L - 5
07R46.D	Read Shakepeare's *Julius Caesar.*	L - 3
07R47.D	Read biographies of Polycarp and/or other Christian martyrs during the time of the Roman Empire.	L - 5
07R48.D	Read original works of Ovid, Virgil or other Roman philosophers in Latin or their English translations. Compare their teachings to those of the Greeks as studied in the previous mini-unit.	L - 7 each book
07R49.	Read wholesome novels set in the time period under study in this unit.	L - 5 each
07R50.	Read novels set in any of the countries or cultures studied in this mini-unit.	L - 5
07R51.	Read short stories written in or by people from one or more of the countries you have studied in this mini-unit.	L - 1 each
07R52.	Read works by any authors studied in this mini-unit.	L - 10 per book length work

COMPOSITION

07W01.A	Use a thesaurus to find all possible synonyms for "gird" and "strength" and add all of them to your vocabulary notebook, carefully defining each to differentiate them. Include all possible definitions of 'strength' and all other words with multiple meanings.	EG - 2
07W02.A	Write a paper explaining each type of strength mentioned in the Bible and how each would be important for a godly wife and/or mother.	EC - 3
07W03.A	After much prayerful consideration, write self-analysis, describing what you see as your own spiritual, physical, academic, or other strengths and weaknesses. Begin now to pray for the Lord to help you use and increase your strengths while building up your weaknesses.	EC - 1
07W04.A	Write a scholarly exegesis of Ephesians 6:13-17, explaining how it relates to Proverbs 31:17.	EC - 5
07W05.A	Write a brief paper (one to two pages) on the economic impact of athletics and fitness on your nation, state/province, and/or locality.	EC - 2

COMPOSITION

07W06.A   Write reports (one page each) comparing aerobics, jazzercise,   EC - 2
calisthenics, strength training, weightlifting and other types of
organized exercise. For each, give its purpose, a brief description
of the method, the muscles or other areas of the body on which it
concentrates and the type of people who benefit most from it.

07W07.A   Write arguments for either side of a debate on: "Resolved: Fitness   EC - 25
and health are so important as to justify all government
expenditures for that purpose." Interview experts in the field
and/or refer to appropriate Scripture verses as well as to your
nation's Constitution and other legal documents.

07W08.A   Write a report (one to three pages), giving the history of athletics   EC - 1
in your area.   each

07W09.A   Choose one of the health care entities studied in the Cultural   EC - 50
Studies section of this unit as a topic for a major term paper. Use
*Writing the Research or Term Paper, The College English
Handbook, Writer's, Inc.*, or a similar reference for information on
the mechanics of writing such a paper. You should include note
cards, outline, and bibliography, following instructions in your
chosen reference manual.

07W10.A   Write a short story in which physical strength was a major   EC - 15
factor in allowing someone to accomplish something important
or worthwhile.

07W11.A   Write diary entries for Samson as he might have written them   EC - 1 per
after his capture by the Philistines. Share what you believe   5 entries
were his deepest thoughts of regret and remorse as he sought the
Lord for the strength he had squandered.

07W12.A   Write reports (2-3 pages each) for your HUMAN BODY notebook   HA- 10
on the skeletal system, its most common disorders or
malfunctions and appropriate treatment for each. You will add this
notebook throughout this course of study.

07W13.A   Write reports (1-3 pages each) for your HUMAN BODY notebook   HA- 10
on the muscular (including major muscles and connective tissue)
and its most common disorders or malfunctions and proper care
or treatment for each. You will add this notebook throughout this
course of study.

07W14.A   If you have not done so in a previous unit, write reports (1-2   HA- 10
pages each) for your HUMAN BODY notebook on the brain and
nervous system and the most common ailments and disorders
affecting either as well as treatment and preventive care for each.
You will add this notebook throughout this course of study.

07W15.A   After researching it, write a paper (2+ pages) on the importance   EC - 2
of maintaining one's proper weight and the place of exercise
in that. You may wish to add this to your HUMAN BODY
notebook.

COMPOSITION

07W16.A	Write a report (two to three pages) on the other health benefits of various kinds of exercise. You may wish to add this to your HUMAN BODY notebook.	EC - 2
07W17.B	Write a brief report on each nation that has ever hosted the Olympic games. Put into your GEOGRAPHY notebook any that are not already there.	G - 1 each
07W18.B	Write a brief description (1 - 3 pages) of each sport featured in the Olympics, including how to play it, its objective, and where it is popular.	EC - 1 each
07W19.B	Add to your geography booklet reports on the countries that won gold medals in the current or most recent Olympics.	G - 1 each
07W20.B	Write a letter of encouragement to a Christian competing in the Olympics. Include Scripture verses and other admonitions to giving his all and to good sportsmanship.	EC-1
07W21.B	Compile all the verses used in the Bible and Christian Character section of this mini-unit and use them to write an essay on "Running the Race for the Crown of Christ".	EC-2
07W22.B	From your reading about the Olympic games, list their stated goals and write a paper (3 -5 pages) explaining and giving examples of how you believe they are or are not being achieved.	EC-3
07W23.B	Write a news report as if you were covering a real terrorist attack on the Olympic games and their participants.	EC-2
07W24. B	Write an extensive editorial on the politicizing of the Olympic games by boycotts and other disturbances over international issues such as apartheid, civil rights violations, invasions, etc. Give your opinion as to whether this is a valid use of these games.	EC-5
07W25.B	Write a how to manual to instruct an absolute beginner on how to play and compete in any Olympic sport of your choice. Include a list and description of all equipment, basic skills needed and how to learn them, an appropriate fitness regimen, the rules of play, and each step needed toward improving beyond the basics. Illustrate with drawings, charts, and or diagrams as needed.	EC-10
07W26.B	From your studies and/or reading, write a brief character sketch (1-2 pages) of any or all of the Olympic medalists mentioned in this mini-unit.	EC-2 each
07W27.B	Write a journal as might be kept by an athlete in training for the Olympics. Make at least ten entries, sharing the training regimen, what the athlete is giving up (time with friends, dating, a job, etc.) for this, his/her hopes, frustrations, fears, and the progress (s)he is making toward the goal.	EC- 5

COMPOSITION

07W28.B	Write a pamphlet on the common sports injuries incurred by Olympians and other athletes and the recommended methods of prevention and treatment for each.	EC-2 HE-1
07W29.B	Write a short story that takes place at or is centered around the Olympic games.	EC - 10 +
07W30.B	Write an imaginary letter to the International Olympic Committee on behalf or your city (or a large one near you) as the site of the next Olympic games. Extol the city's virtues and try to convince them that it can meet their needs better than any other place.	EC - 2
07W31.B	Write questions and answers for an imaginary interview with an Olympic gold medalist of your choice. Ask both personal and Olympic-related questions and research the correct answers.	EC-10
07W32.B	Write a recruiting brochure to encourage young citizens of your nation to practice and tryout for your country's Olympic teams.	EC - 2
07W33.B	Write a play, skit, monologue, or puppet show in some way related to the modern or ancient Olympic Games.	EC-15
07W34.C	Write a critique of the apostle Paul's sermon at the Areopagus, explaining how he used their own culture to get the people's attention and to meet them where they were. Try to explain why so few came to know Christ in response to this sermon.	EC - 2 B - 1
07W35.C	Take notes on the Christian worldview tapes and use them to outline the series.	EC-5
07W36.C	Write a brief exegesis (2-4 pages) on each New Testament epistle to a Greek city.	EC - 2 each
07W37.C	After reading several of the writings of one of the Greek philosophers mentioned elsewhere in this mini-unit, develop a Biblical refutation of his beliefs and write a treatise explaining it.	EC - 5
07W38.C	After reading *The Iliad* and *The Odyssey,* write a character sketch of Ulysses' wife, Penelope. Show ways in which she behaved as a godly wife should even though she didn't know the true God.	EC-2
07W39.C	Write an epic poem in the style of Homer telling the adventures of a person or group from today.	EC-5
07W40.C	Write a short story about a woman living in ancient Greece. Demonstrate your knowledge of their customs and culture.	EC - 15

COMPOSITION

07W41.C	Write a diary or journal as you believe Penelope, wife of Ulysses, might have kept during her long years of waiting for her husband's return. Write at least 20 entries from a variety of times during their separation. Include facts about her life at home, how she misses her husband and awaits his return, their son's growth to manhood, even the mundane affairs of her daily life. You may "make up" activities to include as long as they are not impossible for the time, out of character for her, or contradictory to the original story.	EC-10
07W42.C	Write an article for an imaginary magazine for godly women living in ancient Greece. Discuss timeless Biblical truths in the context of their culture and life-style.	EC-5
07W43.C	Write an extensive term paper on the mathematical, scientific, mathematical or architectural accomplishments of the Ancient Greeks. Tell which have proven to be true and continue today and which, if any, have been disproved. Use *Writers Inc.* or other grammar/writing handbook for guide-lines on this kind of paper.	EC - 50 +
07W44.C	Write an essay examining and critiquing the culture, philosophy and worldview of the ancient Greeks from the perspective of Scripture.	EC-5
07W45.C	Write a play set in or based on events in ancient Greece and patterned after the style of Sophocles and other early Greeks.	EC-25
07W46.C	Write a critical review of any early Greek play as if done by a theater critic at a live performance.	EC-5
07W47.C	Write a screenplay based on one of the Greek plays studied in this unit.	EC-20
07W48.C	After reading Aesop's Fables, write one of your own, mimicking his style but teaching Biblical character lessons.	EC-15
07W49.C	Write reports on any or all of the men featured in *Famous Men of Greece*.	EC-2 each
07W50.C	Copy the Hippocratic Oath carefully several times to practice your handwriting or calligraphy.	EG or VA - 1 each time
07W51.D	Write a short story set in ancient Rome. Draw heavily on your knowledge of the customs and culture of the time.	EC - 25
07W52.D	Write a brief exegesis (2-4 pages) on each Epistle written to a city of the Roman Empire listed in the Bible and Christian Character section of this mini-unit.	EC - 6
07W53.D	Write a travel brochure, circa 100 AD extolling the virtues of the city of Rome and its Empire and urging those from other parts of the world to visit or to relocate there.	EC - 10

COMPOSITION

07W54.D	Write a letter from a Christian woman in ancient Rome to her daughter or another younger woman at the time of her marriage. Share God's timeless Biblical truths in the context of their culture and life-style.	EC - 3
07W55.D	Write a news report as if you were covering any of the major events in the history of ancient Rome.	EC - 5
07W56.D	Write an imaginary interview with one or more of the men featured in *Famous Men of Rome*, giving both questions and the appropriate answers.	EC - 3
07W57.D	Write an essay examining the culture, philosophy and worldview of the Romans from the perspective of Scripture and show where and how they differ from it.	EC - 5
07W58.D	Write a short story or play about a woman living in ancient Rome or one of its provinces. Draw heavily upon your knowledge of the customs and culture of the time.	EC - 2
07W59.D	From your study of ancient Rome, prepare a paper detailing philosophical, artistic, scientific and other contributions they made to later cultures, including yours.	EC - 5
07W60.D	Write a brief report (two to three pages) on each of the men in *Famous Men of Rome*, drawing from there and other references as well. Do not copy or draw entirely from any one source.	EC - 2 each
07W61.D	Write a technical report on the engineering skills of the ancient Romans as evidenced by their roads.	EC - 5
07W62.D	Write an essay explaining the saying "all roads lead to Rome" from a historical perspective. (Hint: It has to do with the road building skills of the Romans and the size of their Empire.)	EC-2
07W63.D	Write a technical report on the engineering feats involved in the planning and construction of the Roman aqueducts.	EC-5
07W64.D	Outline the book of Romans.	EG-5
07W65.D	Have someone read aloud portions of one or more chapters of the New Testament book of Romans for you to copy for practice in your dictation skills.	EC-10
07W66.D	Write an extensive biographical sketch (5 or more pages) of one of the men you studied in *Famous Men of Rome*.	EC-20
07W67.D	Instead of a report or biographical sketch of any famous Roman, write a play or puppet show about his life. Perform it with friends and/or siblings or video tape it, playing all the parts.	EG-1 each
07W68.D	Rewrite in the form of a play or screenplay any sections of *The Histories* originally written by Tacitus or Pliny.	EC-20

COMPOSITION

07W69.D	Many people have compared Rome at its greatest to the U. S. in the Twentieth Century and at various other times in history. Write a paper tracing the cultural history of the Romans and comparing or contrasting it to that of the USA.	EC-10
07W70.	Write a brief (1-2 page) report on each country studied in this unit. Put each of them into your geography notebook.	G - 1 each
07W71.	As you read the Bible each day, keep a spiritual journal, taking notes on your readings and their applications in your life. Add prayer requests and answers as well as insights God may give you.	EG - 2 per week
07W72.	Use the Scripture passages in this mini-unit to practice dictation. Have someone else read them aloud for you to write, word for word with exact punctuation. If your beliefs allow, you may want to use a modern Bible translation for this exercise.	EG - 3 per 5 times
07W73.	Write a report on one or more of the people you studied in this unit.	EC - 2 each
07W74.	As you attend worship services or hear them on radio, TV, or recordings, take notes on the sermons.	EG - 2 each
07W75.	As you watch videos and/or listen to audios recommended in this unit, take notes on them.	EG - 2 each
07W76.	Use your notes to write a synopsis or summary of each audio and/or video used in this mini-unit.	EC - 1 each
07W77.	Write reviews of any or all of the videos in this unit, as if done by a movie critic.	EC - 1+each
07W78.	Write a character sketch of one or more of the men and women studied in this unit.	EG - 3 each
07W79.	Write a report on each field trip taken in this unit.	EC - 1 each
07W80.	Write thank you notes to field trip guides, people you interviewed, and others who helped in any way with this unit.	EC - 1
07W81.	Add one page to your school journal each day as explained in the guidelines in the front of the unit study.	EC - 3 per week
07W82.	Write book reports on any or all the novels or biographies in this unit.	EC - 2 each
07W83.	Outline one or more of the nonfiction books read in this unit.	EG - 4 each
07W84.	Write summaries and/or synopses of any of the books read in this unit.	EC - 2 each
07W85.	Write a thorough exegesis of any of the Bible chapters studied in this unit.	EC - 1 each

COMPOSITION

07W86.   Put ten or more new words from your studies each week into your vocabulary notebook. Add definitions, pronunciation marks, and syllables.   EG - 1 per week

07W87.   Learn to spell all new words added to your vocabulary note book in this unit, testing on them each week.   EG - 2 each week

07W88.   Use any good dictionary to proofread and correct spelling errors in all written work for this unit. (No points for use of an automatic spell checker!)   EG - 1 each paper

07W89.   Using *Writers Inc., The College English Handbook*, or a similar grammatical reference, proofread and correct grammar and mechanics in all written work done for this mini-unit.   EG - 1 each paper

07W90.   Write a review of each movie or play you watched or read for this unit.   EC - 1 each

MATHEMATICS AND PERSONAL FINANCE

07M01.A   Use established methods to find the ratio of fat to muscle in your own body and those of family members. Chart these on a bar (or other) graph, comparing them with averages and ideals from published charts as well.   M - 5

07M02.A   Use a weight chart available from a doctor, weight control program or the American Heart Association, determine out how much the weight of each member of your family fluctuates from the published 'norm' and use that data to calculate the percentage by which any member of your family is overweight or underweight. Show this comparison of real weights with ideal ones for each family member's age, height and body type on a bar graph.   M - 5

07M03.A   Using the same sources as above, find the number of calories burned by various fitness and exercise activities. Use these figures to determine how much of what kinds of food you need to eat to reach and/or maintain your goal weight while pursuing the fitness program you created for yourself in the Health and Physical Fitness section of this mini-unit.   M - 2

07M04.A   Prepare a line graph to track the number of calories you and family members consume and burn each day for two or more weeks.   M - 5

07M05.A   Use "Clever Catch Ball" with friends or siblings to practice and review math or algebra concepts while engaging in physical activity.   M - 2 per time

07M06.A   Play any appropriate level of "Math Chase" to hone mathematics skills.   M - 1 per time

MATHEMATICS AND PERSONAL FINANCE

07M07. B   Find out from your local school district and any nearby community or state-supported colleges what percentage of the budget of each goes into athletics. Prepare a chart to illustrate this data for various programs at each school.
    M- 3

07M08.B   Use data from the *World Almanac* or an Olympics record book to find how many countries entering the games in each year have won gold, silver, and bronze medals. Express these figures in terms of percent, ratio and proportion.
    M - 3

07M09.B   Present the above data for the most recent year and any others of your choice in the form of a set of pie graphs, one for each level of medal.
    M - 5 each

07M10.B   Using data for as many years as possible, compute the total number of medals of each type were won by each winning nation. Prepare a pictograph to show this information.
    M - 5

07M11.B   Using the above figures, determine the average number of winning nations in each of the years for which you have data and the average number of medals each would have won, if they had been distributed evenly.
    M - 2

07M12.B   Use the same figures to calculate the percentage of each country's total medals (for a specific year and overall) that were gold, silver and bronze.
    M - 2

07M13.B   Practice performing ratios and proportions with the data in any or all of the above graphs and/or calculations as your parents determine you need.
    M - 2

07M14.C   Study the mathematical discoveries of Archimedes and how they are used today.
    M - 2

07M15.C   Study the mathematical discoveries of Euclid and how they are used today.
    M - 2

07M16.C   Play the mathematical shape game "Oh Euclid" with parents, siblings, or friends.
    M - 1 each time

07M17.C   Study, memorize and practice working with the Pythagorean theorem in geometry, created by a Greek
    M - 2

07M18.C   This study of ancient Greece provides a good chance to study analytic geometry, created by a Greek. (This incorporates most of the previous four activities.)
    M - 1 Credit for complete course

07M19.D   Complete an extensive study of Roman numerals using material of your choice.
    M - 2

07M20.D   The calendar used by the Western World was given to us by the ancient Romans. Study other calendars, including Hebrew and Chinese, comparing the starting point and the length of months, years, etc.
    CS - 1   M - 1

MATHEMATICS AND PERSONAL FINANCE

07M21.D	From historical sources, compile data on the area and population of the Roman Empire and each of its regions, at various times in history. Express the relative sizes in a variety of mathematical equations.	M - 2
07M22.D	Prepare a graph to illustrate the data compiled in the previous exercise.	M - 5
07M23.D	Study mathematical skills needed for use in civil engineering and apply them in your efforts to duplicate Roman construction.	M - 2
07M24.	Use data from any or all of the above graphs to practice making and solving problems using percent, ratio, and proportion.	M - 1
07M25.	Continue to brush up on basic math as needed.	M - 1

SCIENCE

07S01.A	Use software, *Gray's Anatomy* or any other anatomy book to study muscles, tendons and ligaments, learning where they are located, what each does, and the names of major ones.	HA-2
07S02.A	Use Bodyworks software, *Gray's Anatomy* and/or any other good anatomy book to study the human skeletal system, learning the names and locations of the major bones.	HA-2
07S03.A	Study the nervous system with special attention to the parts that control movement and coordination.	HA-2
07S04.A	Examine the respiratory system, which also needs physical exercise, and the organs that comprise it.	HA-2
07S05.A	Study the heart and circulatory system and the vital part exercise plays in their health.	HA-2
07S06.A	Put together a plastic model of the human skeleton.	HA-3
07S07.A	Put together a complete model of the human body such as "The Visible Man" or "Visible Woman" model kits.	HA-3
07S08.A	Study Usborne's *How Your Body Works.*	HE-3
07S09.A	Study strength testing of building materials and the ratings of different ones.	SP-1
07S10.A	Study various types and sources of 'strength' in humans and animals.	SB - 1+

SCIENCE

07S11.B	Study the Olympic specifications for each court, track, rink, stadium or other facility used in the games. These should include sizes, shapes, type of surface, make up and location of permanently-installed equipment and/or fixtures. Learn the reasons behind each requirement and how such factors affect athletes' performances.	SP-4
07S12.B	Study the tools and equipment used for various Winter Olympic games. Discover how each is constructed, what materials are used, how they have changed other the years and how they are used. Include the differences between types of skates, skis, etc. and why different ones are needed for different contests.	SP-4
07S13.B	Study the tools and equipment used in Olympic gymnastics. Discover how each is constructed, what materials are used, how they have changed over the years, and how each is used.	SP-4
07S14.B	Study the tools and equipment used in Olympic track and field events. Discover how each is constructed, what materials are used, how they have changed other the years and how they are used.	SP-4
07S15.B	Study the tools and equipment used in various Olympic team sports. Discover how each is constructed, what materials are used, how this has changed other the years and how each is used.	SP-2
07S16.B	Study weather-related problems that might affect the Olympics and methods used to control them. Pay special attention to the effect of unseasonably way weather on the Winter Games or the effect of extreme heat on athletes in the summer.	SE-2
07S17.B	Study a variety of sportswear styles and fabrics to determine the effect each has on performance in various athletic events.	SP-1
07S18.B	Examine various styles and types of shoes to learn which are best for which type of sport.	SP-1
07S19.B	Study the environmental impact the Olympic games have had on the areas that have hosted them.	SE-1
07S20.C	In reading the story of the Trojan horse, try to determine how it was built, using only tools, materials and knowhow from that day.	HE-1
07S21.C	Study *How We Learned the Earth is Round* to learn how the ancient Greeks discovered that the Earth is round, long before the time of Columbus.	SP-3
07S22.C	Study the composition and construction of homes and other buildings in Ancient Greece.	SE-4
07S23.C	Study the shipbuilding techniques and materials of the ancient Greeks and the ships they built.	SP-2

SCIENCE

| 07S24.C | Study the navigational techniques used by the ancient Greek seafarers. | SP-2 |

| 07S25.C | Study the engineering and construction techniques that went into building the Areopagus, Parthenon, and other architectural masterpieces of the ancient Greeks. | SP-1 |

| 07526.C | After reading biographies or other books on Archimedes to discover the impact this Greek made on science, chart his discoveries and follow them through to their modern day results and uses. | SP-1 |

| 07S27.C | If not done in Unit 3, study the animal and plant taxonomy system devised by Linnaeus, a Greek. Prepare a chart or other display showing the various phyla and a representative sample of each. | SP-2 |

| 07S28.C | Investigate the various human anatomy discoveries made by first Archimedes and other ancient Greeks and how each of those led to further discoveries in health, anatomy, and medicine. | SP-2 |

| 07S29.C | If you wish, you may build upon this introduction to anatomy to undertake a complete course in human anatomy and physiology, using *Gray's Anatomy* or any other complete source. | SP-2 |

| 07S30.D | Study the techniques of civil engineering as employed by the Romans in their road building. | SP-2 |

| 07S31.D | Compare the strength of stone roads as built by the Romans to those of concrete and/or steel reinforced concrete. | SP-1 |

| 07S32.D | Compare the strength, load-bearing capabilities and limitations of the arch and double arch bridges of the ancient Romans with cantilevered, suspension and other bridges used today. | SP-1 |

| 07S33.D | Investigate the engineering techniques, equipment, and construction that went into the development and building of the Roman aqueducts. | SP-2 |

| 07S34.D | Study siphon and siphoning as the basis for the Romans' gravity-fed aqueducts. | SP-2 |

| 07S35.D | Study the materials and techniques used by the Romans in building the various weapons used by their armies. | SP-2 |

| 07S36.D | Examine the weapons of the ancient Romans. | SP-1 |

| 07S37.D | Study the homes of ancient Rome and compare them with those of the Greeks and other ancient civilizations. | SP-1 |

| 07S38.D | Examine architectural and engineering principles that went into building the Colosseum and other famous Roman structures. | SP-3 |

HEALTH AND PHYSICAL FITNESS

07H01.A	Learn the effects of proper and improper exercise on each of the systems and organs studied above.	HE-1
07H02.A	Study common health problems that affect one or more of the systems or organs studied in this mini-unit.	HE-3
07H03.A	Examine different types of exercise and fitness machines and try your hand at several of them. Learn what each one does for your body.	PE-2
07H04.A	Try a variety of different exercise or fitness programs, such as aerobics, dance, calisthenics, sports, and/or weight training, trying each for at least a week.	PE-1 each hour Max. 1 credit
07H05.A	Attend an aerobics class or exercise using an aerobics video for at least 30 minutes twice a week.	PE-2 per week Max. 1 credit
07H06.A	Walk or jog for 30 minutes or more at least three times a week, alternating days with the aerobics class.	PE-2 per week
07H07.A	Work with a personal trainer or fitness teacher to plan the right fitness program for you. Follow it diligently for a minimum of six weeks.	PE-30
07H08.A	Participate in an organized team or individual sport for a minimum of one hour at least twice each week.	PE-1 per week
07H09.A	Join a health club, YMCA, or other fitness group and participate in their fitness program regularly instead of trying to plan one of your own.	PE-30 per 6 weeks
07H 10.A	Choose and follow a nutritious diet designed to fulfill your caloric needs and help control any weight or other nutritional problems you may have.	HE-2
07H11.A	Join and participate in a Weigh Down Workshop, attending all sessions and completing all assignments. This is not only for those who are overweight, but also helps anorexics and others inordinately concerned about food or weight.	PE-3
07H12.B	Study the Usborne how-to guides or similar ones on any Olympic team sport you would like to play.	PE-3
07H13.B	Study Usborne's how-to guide or similar book for any individual Olympic sport you would like to learn.	PE-1/2 credit per semester
07H14.B	Join a team or class to learn to play one of the Team sports featured in the summer Olympics. Attend and practice faithfully for a minimum of six weeks.	PE -1/2 credit

HEALTH AND PHYSICAL FITNESS

07H15.B	Take a class or private lessons to learn one of the individual sports in the summer Olympics. Continue for at least six weeks.	PE-1 credit
07H16.B	Play on a team in one of the Olympic sports for at least one full season. This should include regular practice and at least 8-10 games, meets, or other competitions against other teams	1-1/2 credits
07H17.B	Take lessons in skiing, ice skating, or another Winter Olympic sport for at least six weeks.	1/2 credit
07H18.B	Compete in one of the individual Olympic sports for at least three major tourneys or contests.	PE-15
07H19.B	Learn all you can about the rules and scoring standards for one individual Olympic sport and become a judge for it. You must judge at least one complete tournament or competition to get these points.	PE-10
07H20.B	Learn the rules to any Olympic team sports and become a referee or judge. To earn these points, you must actually referee at least one complete game or contest.	HA - 2
07H21.B	Study the group of drugs known as steroids, their legitimate uses and side effects and why Olympic athletes must not use them.	HA - 2
07H22.C	Study the Greek model of human anatomy and physiology as investigated by Archimedes.	H-1 HA - 1
07H23.C	Determine where the Greeks were right and wrong about how the body works.	HE - 1 H - 1
07H24.C	Study the work of Hippocrates, the Father of Medicine and the health care discoveries he made.	H - 1 HE - 1
07H25.C	Compare Hippocrates' methods for the diagnosis and treatment of various diseases with the same ones today.	H - 1 HE - 1
07H26.C	Study uses commonly made of the word "Spartan" in relation to health and explain its origin.	EC - 1 HE - 1
07H27.C	Study the dietary and fitness regimens of Sparta and other Greek city-states. Compare these to what is considered healthy today.	H - 1
07H28.C	Investigate the normal diet of the Greeks of today and analyze several typical recipes for sodium, sugar, cholesterol, and other fat content.	HE - 2
07H29.D	Study the health effects of the lead eating and drinking vessels widely used by the Romans.	HE - 1

HEALTH AND PHYSICAL FITNESS

07H30.D	Study Caesarean section, which was first used in the Roman Empire. Learn how and when they are used today.	HE - 2
07H31.D	Study other surgical procedures that were invented or heavily used by the Romans.	HE - 2
07H32.D	Study the health effects of communal bath houses, common among the men of Rome and the diseases that are now known to be spread by such practices.	HE- 1
07H33.D	Study the venereal diseases that were widespread in the Roman Empire and the treatment methods that were available in those days.	HE - 2
07H34.D	Study other Roman medical and hygiene practices.	H - 1

PRACTICAL ARTS

07P01.A	Shop for and select appropriate clothing for the fitness program gram you intend to pursue. Get advice from sportswear professionals or someone active in the sport or activity as to style, fit, and fabric that will work best.	LS - 2
07P02.A	Shop for good walking or exercise shoes, studying health data beforehand to decide what qualities to look for in finding the right shoes for your purposes.	LS - 1
07P03.A	Use your sewing and needlework skills to create one or more pieces of your fitness wardrobe.	CC - 3 +
07P04.A	Study various pieces of equipment for use in your fitness program and shop for the ones best suited to your purposes.	PE - 2
07P05.A	For a fitness regimen that fills another useful function, take a course in karate, tae-kwon-do, or other martial arts to learn discipline, control, and self-defense. If possible, use a teacher from the Christian Martial Arts Federation as they teach with a distinctively Christian worldview.	PE - 1/2 credit
07P06.A	Organize and teach aerobics, calisthenics or other fitness classes (10-12 weeks duration) to one or more younger children.	TE - 1/2 credit per semester
07P07.A	Serve as a spotter for gymnastics or trampoline activities under a coach or teacher.	PE - 2 each time 30 Max
07P08.A	Build your own 'step' for step aerobics, sanding it down carefully and [painting it any color of your choice.	WW - 2

PRACTICAL ARTS

07P09.B	Learn to choose proper equipment for use in playing your favorite team sport, comparing all possible types and determining the best for your purposes.	PE - 2
07P10.B	Make your own equipment to use in pursuing your favorite individual sport.	IA - 3
07P11.B	Study the site of the next Olympics and determine where and how would be the best way to purchase tickets for it. Plan your entire trip as if you were going to attend, even if you cannot do so.	LS- 1
07P12.B	Plan and prepare all aspects of a party for your family or friends to watch some particular event of the next Olympics.	HM - 5
07P13.B	Design and construct (full size or for a child or doll) a costume you feel would represent your nation well in the Olympics parade of nations.	CC - 5
07P14.B	Design and construct a prototype of a modest, utilitarian, and attractive uniform to be used by your nation's team in an Olympic sport of your choice. Be sure to include something indicative of the nation into your design.	CC - 5
07P15.B	Coach some team sport for a group of younger children. This should include at least one (one hour or more) session per week for a minimum of 12 weeks, with games and skills practice.	TE or PE 1/2 credit
07P16.B	Serve as a referee, umpire, judge, scorekeeper, etc. for a children's game or tournament in a sport you play well.	PE - 5
07P17.C	Sew a simple tunic style garment like those made by the Greeks.	CC - 4
07P18.C	Weave a vine garland like those used by the ancient Greeks to wear in your hair or use for other decorative purposes.	CR - 2
07P19.C	Make a pair of leather sandals like those worn by the Greeks.	CR - 5
07P20.C	Construct models of one example of each animal phylum as categorized by Linnaeus and display them in some appropriate manner for a science fair or other exhibit.	SB - 10
07P21.C	Learn to perform dissections on animal specimens as begun by the Greeks to learn about anatomy.	SB — 2 each
07P22.C	Construct a model of the Trojan horse, trying to be as near to scale as possible.	CR - 5
07P23.C	Take a class of correspondence course in New Testament Greek, or teach it to yourself, using any available materials.	1 credit for complete Course

PRACTICAL ARTS

07P24.C	Use any available resources to learn the language spoken and written in Greece today. Compare it to the older form used for writing the New Testament.	1 credit for complete course
07P25.D	Learn to use a siphon, first invented by the Romans, for appropriate purposes. Use both manual and motorized types.	SP - 1
07P26.D	Follow the techniques used by the Romans to create a gravity-fed aqueduct at least ten feet in length. Use this for irrigation purposes of some type if possible.	IA - 20
07P27.D	Following the road building techniques of the Romans, build a stone pathway in your family's yard or garden using stones found in your local area.	IA-10
07P28.D	Create your own stepping stones with plaster or concrete and use them to build a walkway.	CR-10
07P29.D	Design and sew a toga for yourself or someone else.	CC - 5
07P30.D	Use *Artes Latinae* or any other materials of your choice to study Latin.	1 credit for complete course
07P31.D	Examine various styles of Roman architecture and use one or more to design a miniature (or full-sized) building.	AA - 3 VA - 5+
07P32.	If you don't already know how to create and use a computer database, you may wish to learn in this mini-unit so you can use the skill in later units of this study.	CO - 5
07P33.	Create and maintain a database to assist you as appropriate in this mini-unit.	CO - 2
07P34.	Type all written work using either a typewriter or computer. If you cannot type, now is the time to learn.	CO - 1 each paper
07P35.	If needed, take a class, follow a computerized, written or video tutorial, or a correspondence course in typing, keyboarding, and/or word processing.	CO - 1/2 credit for complete course
07P36.	Create a computer website to display what you have learned in this mini-unit.	CO - 2
07P37.	Frame and/or mat one or more of the pictures or posters you drew or created in the Decorative and Performing Arts section of this mini-unit.	CR - 2
07P38.	Make your own costumes for any performances done in the Decorative and Performing Arts section or plays written in the Composition section.	CC - 5 each

DECORATIVE AND PERFORMING ARTS

07A01.A	Color the appropriate sections of *Gray's Anatomy Coloring Book*.	VA-1 each
07A02.A	Use markers and highlighter pens to draw transparencies (for overhead projector) of all organs and systems studied in this unit.	VA-3
07A03.A	Create a life-sized poster of the human body by following these simple directions: Draw around the body of someone lying on the floor or have someone draw around yours. Fill in the various organs where they should fit in the outline, drawing on another sheet and overlapping as needed.	VA-2
07A04.A	Draw or paint still life pictures of arrangements containing sports and/or fitness equipment.	VA-2+
07A05.A	Use your creativity and any appropriate medium to decorate your personal exercise equipment.	VA-2+
07A06.A	Paint or otherwise decorate a sweatsuit or other clothing to use in your exercise program.	VA-2
07A07.A	Study movement exploration exercises as used in dance or drama. (A good course manual in either should have some.)	PE - 1/2 credit per semester
07A08.A	Enroll in and successfully complete a dance class. Choose from ballet, tap, jazz, or modern dance as you and your parents deem appropriate.	1 credit in PE or dance
07A09.A	Use your own drawings, cutouts, or photographs to illustrate the how-to sports manuals you wrote in the Composition section of this unit.	VA-2
07A10.A	Use this subject to learn to draw movement. You may do this through a class, a book or some other method.	VA- 2 +
07A11.B	Draw a cartoon centering on some event or idea relating to a recent Olympics.	VA - 3
07A12.B	Design a logo for a real or imaginary sports team.	VA - 2
07A13.B	Prepare and perform a humorous skit or monologue relating to the Olympic Games.	DR - 10
07A14.B	Listen to and compare the fight songs of several college or pro sports teams.	MA - 2
07A15.B	Learn to play and sing some of the above tunes.	VM - 1 each

DECORATIVE AND PERFORMING ARTS

07A16.B	Design and paint a logo for the next Olympic Games. Include the five circles of their international logo and something indicative of the host city.	IM - 1 each VA - 2
07A17.B	Choreograph a synchronization or other musical routine in swimming, gymnastics, or ice skating.	MC - 2
07A18.B	Compose a piece of music suitable to be used in synchronized swimming, rhythm gymnastics, or another Olympic sport performed to music.	MC - 5
07A19.C	Attend a performance or watch a video of *Antigone* or some other Ancient Greek play.	CR-3
07A20.C	Perform in or direct a production of *Antigone* or another Greek play.	DR-25+
07A21.C	Write a piece of music to accompany a scene in the Greek play you have chosen to produce.	MC-3
07A22.C	Listen to a live or taped performance on the pan flute and/or lute, musical instruments of ancient Greece.	MA-1
07A23.C	Learn to play a flute or another wind instrument that developed from "the pipes of Pan' of ancient Greece.	IM-1 credit for full school year
07A24.C	Prepare and present a dramatic recitation of a section from one of Homer's epics as it would have been done in the theater of their day.	DR-10
07A25.C	Use your calligraphy and drawing talents to produce a poster/ plaque of the Hippocratic oath suitable for hanging.	VA-2
07A26.C	Draw your own illustrations for *Aesop's Fables* or fables you wrote yourself.	VA-2
07A27.C	Draw a mural of a street scene in an ancient Greek city-state.	VA-2
07A28.D	Build Usborne's *Make this Roman Villa*.	VA-2
07A29.D	Complete Usborne's *Make this Roman Temple*.	VA-2
07A30.D	Complete a similar cutout model of the Roman Colosseum.	VA-2
07A31.D	Prepare and present a puppet show on ancient Rome, using the models you built and your own homemade stick puppets.	DR-10+
07A32.D	Draw a mural of a Roman street scene.	VA-2
07A33.D	Prepare a room box, diorama, or other 3-D display of the inside of a "typical" Roman home.	VA-3+

DECORATIVE AND PERFORMING ARTS

07A34.D	Watch a live performance or BBC theater video of *Julius Caesar*.	DR-3
07A35.D	Perform, direct, or otherwise help produce a live performance of *Julius Caesar*.	DR-50
07A36.	Draw pictures of any field trips you took in this unit.	VA - 2
07A37.	Use drawing, painting and graphic arts to create displays and make posters as called for in this study.	VA- 1
07A38.	Illustrate one or more of the poems you studied or memorized for this unit.	VA 1 each
07A39.	Set one or more of this unit's poems to music, using an original or existing tune.	DR - 50
07A40.	Set one or more of the Scripture verses in this unit to music, using a tune you wrote for the purpose.	MC - 5

UNIT 8

She perceives that her merchandise is good; her candle goes not out by night.
Proverbs 31:18

Introduction to Unit 8

This unit is based on what may be one of the least understood verses in all of Proverbs 31. Though many people interpret the phrase 'her light does not go out by night' to mean that she works long hours and is up all night, that is not the emphasis of the passage.

Certainly, it is clear from several verses of Proverb 31, that this woman is diligent and hard-working, but this passage does not address that. Instead, it relates to the Christian character traits of preparedness, readiness, and attentiveness to duty. It is because she is careful to plan ahead that the fire with which she lights (and heats) her home does not go out at night, causing her to have to seek some source for lighting it again later. You will study the importance of this in the culture of the day and its relation to Christian character.

Here you will study the parable of the 10 virgins and other Scriptural teachings on the need for vigilance and readiness. You will also look at Biblical references to lamps and light, both realistic and figurative.

This unit will provide our basis for studying light, various types and sources of light and vision, in all of its meanings. Since other units deal with appraisals and with self- evaluation, the two processes by which this woman "sees that her merchandise is good", we will not include those topics here.

Outgrowths from this topic include light, vision, the eyes and other related topics, all implied by this unit's verse.

Mini-Units

Mini-Units contained in this unit are:

A. Being Prepared for Whatever Comes

B. Light and Energy

C. Vision and Optics

Each thematic mini-unit is described and designated with a letter of the alphabet in the following paragraphs. Individual activities designed for use in one particular mini-unit will be marked with those letters. (For further help with this, please refer to the explanation of mini-units in the Guidelines section of this unit study guide.)

Mini-Units

A. Being Prepared for Whatever Comes

In this mini-unit, you will investigate many areas in which a careful wife and mother will prepare beforehand. This may range from simple, day-to-day organization and scheduling to preparation for major disasters or life changes. Some of these latter are discussed in detail in Unit 15, so there will be some overlapping of activities. As usual when that occurs, use the activities in either place but not both.

You will learn about preparedness on a national, state and local scale for such things as enemy attack, military endeavors, and natural disasters. You will study the history of these events and the organizations or agencies that are designed to cope with them. You will be given a chance to analyze such efforts in specific situations and to become a part of such a ministry as the occasion arises in your area.

You will study supplies and equipment used for various kinds of 'preparedness ' and how they operate. You may even learn to use some of these things yourself.

B. Light and Energy

Even a quick look at this verse leads us into the study of light, both natural and artificial, and its various sources. In this context, you will study animal and vegetable oils once used for heat and/or light, petroleum products, and natural gas as well as the industries that developed around them. You will also study electricity and electric lighting.

You will learn about some of the important people in the various fields related to light and energy. You will study the discovery and progress of electricity and the various ways it is used and produced. We will look briefly at the solar system and the universe in this mini-unit, though it is also studied in Unit 11.

We hope that in this course, you will be able to become very familiar with lots of lamps and lights from various periods of history. You will have the opportunity to make, use, and experiment with many different models, using a variety of fuels. You may delve deeply into, or just touch on, the scientific principles behind the various fuels and other types of energy that has been used to provide lighting over the centuries.

C. Vision and Optics

In this mini-unit, you will study vision and the organs that make it possible. This will include a through examination of the eye and how it works as well as ailments and diseases of the eye. You will be encouraged to pursue information on treatment and prevention of these diseases or disorders. You will learn about the causes of blindness, and how they can be prevented or treated before the sight is lost.

You will see how blind people can overcome their problem, and the lives of some famous blind people who did overcome it, living full lives without their sight. You will also learn about technology and equipment available to help blind people perform their daily tasks with ease and precision in spite of their disability.

This unit also deals with optical illusions, the spectrum of light and fiber optics. Some of this actually overlaps that in the previous mini-unit. When activities could apply either place, we chose one or the other rather than listing it twice. You may, of course, use it either place.

BIBLE & CHRISTIAN CHARACTER

08B01.A	Study the parable of the ten virgins in Matthew 25.	B - 1
08B02.A	Explain in discussion or a mind map the importance to people of Bible times of not letting one's light go out.	B - 2
08B03.A	Study the ministry of John the Baptist, whose job it was to 'prepare the way of the Lord'.	B - 2
08B04.A	Study Matthew 24:42-43, Matthew 25:13, and Mark 13:33, in which Jesus warned His followers to "watch" for something as a way of being prepared for it. Explain what this was and why it is important to be prepared when it comes.	B - 1
08B05.A	Read and discuss Paul's instructions on readiness in II Timothy 2.	B - 1
08B06.A	Study and discuss with parents the type of readiness described in 1 Peter 3:15 and what it means in your life.	B - 1
08B07.A	Use concordance or topical Bible to find and study other verses teaching attentiveness and readiness. (Include those that use the word "watch" as used above as well as other key words.)	B - 2+
08B08.B	Study the account of the poor widow and her oil in II Kings 4:1-7.	B - 1
08B09.B	Memorize Psalm 119:105.	B - 1
08B10.B	Study and explain the prophecy of Christ in Isaiah 9:2.	B - 1
08B11.B	Study and memorize John1:1-9 and explain the symbolic meaning of it.	B - 3
08B12.B	Study and memorize Christ's teaching in Matthew 5: 14-16.	B - 1
08B13.B	Use concordance to look up all other Bible verses about light or lamps. Read each to determine its meaning and prepare a chart to show which were referring to literal 'lights' of some type and which were using the term symbolically.	B - 2
08B14.B	Look up in concordance and study the verses that refer to Satan as an 'angel of light'. Discuss this with your parents and/or study it in commentaries (Always use at least two different ones.) to learn what is meant by that phrase and why it is used.	B - 2
08B15.C	Read, discuss with parents and memorize Proverbs 29:18	B - 1
08B16.C	Find in concordance, look up, and list all occurrences of `visions' in the Old Testament. For each, tell: Who had the vision? Where and/or under what conditions? What was seen? What was its meaning?	B - 3

BIBLE & CHRISTIAN CHARACTER

08B17.C	Read Hebrews 1:1 and discuss with your parents why God may have chosen to cease giving visions once Christ came and returned to Heaven.	B - 1
08B18.C	Study the temporary blindness and subsequent healing of Paul as told in Acts 8-10. Discuss with parents what purpose his blindness served.	B - 2
08B19.C	Study the healing of the man born blind as told in John 9.	B - 1
08B20.C	Look up in concordance and study other healings of the blind recorded in the New Testament.	B - 2
08B21.	Meditate on and memorize one or more of the passages studied in the unit.	B 1 per 3 verses
08B22.	Read through the book of Proverbs each month, reading the chapter to coincide with each date.	B - 3 per week
08B23.	Continue (or begin) to keep your prayer journal, listing each day (or as the Lord brings to mind) prayer requests, needs in your spiritual life and things God is teaching you. Continue this in all units.	B - 3 per week
08B24.	Continue reading through the Bible. If you use *The Daily Bible* or another version designed for that purpose, their daily readings will take you through the entire Bible in one year. You may follow a pattern of your own at a different rate if you like. Using a chronologically arranged Bible offers the added benefit of putting your reading in perspective as to time frame.	B - 1 credit when completed; no partial credit

CULTURAL STUDIES

08C01.A	Study the history of your country's early warning, radar tracking and/or other preemptive military systems and how they are used to achieve military preparedness.	H Z1 CG -1
08C02.A	Study your nation's philosophy of military preparedness and how the ideas in the last activity coincide with this philosophy.	CG -1 CS -1
08C03.A	Study the history of the "Cold War" between major world powers during the 1950's, 60's, 70's and 80's. Learn what part preparedness played in that whole scenario and why it was important.	H -1 CG -1
08C04.A	Through books or magazines of the time period, learn about the social and economic effects of the 'bomb shelter' craze in the U. S. of the 1960's, which arose from the Cold War.	CE 11 CS 1
08C05.A	Study the National Guard (or similar program if outside U. S.), whose purpose is to boost military strength in wartime or aid in disaster relief in times of peace. Learn how they stay prepared for both.	CS CG

CULTURAL STUDIES

08C06.A	Study the disaster preparedness program of your city, county or municipality.	SA - 1
08C07.A	Study your local, state, and/or national Civil Defense agencies and the U. S. Department of Homeland Security and related agencies.	CG - 1
08C08.A	Contact local radio or TV stations to learn about your area's Emergency Broadcast System. Learn how it works, when it is activated and its purpose.	SA- 1
08C09.A	Locate and learn about local evacuation routes in the case of snowstorms, hurricanes, wildfire, or other natural disasters that may make it necessary to leave your home.	SA - 1
08C10.A	Learn about the Red Cross and other disaster relief agencies and how they maintain readiness for such events.	SA - 1 CS - 1
08C11.A	Study the 'survivalist' craze of the 1980's when many Americans were preparing for a projected societal collapse which they believed would take out most basic services. (Writings by James Jordan, Gary North and others address this from the standpoint of the Christians involved in it.) Investigate the renewed interest in 'survivalism' in the 21ˢᵗ century. Compare and contrast the two.	H - 1 CS - 1
08C12.A	Read articles from Christian magazines and other sources (referred to in the next section) to learn about the preparations made by many who expected serious societal breakdown of computer systems at the beginning of the year 2000. Consult more modern sources to determine why this never happened.	H - 2 CS - 1
08C13.A	Use sources mentioned in the Reading and Literature section to study the work done by those in the computer industry to circumvent the potential problems with the year 2000 (Y2K).	H - 1
08C14.B	Study the history of lamps and other forms of artificial light, making a chart or poster of the ones used during various time periods. Instead of a poster, you may put together a collection of lamps and lights from different time periods, either actual, restored pieces or replicas.	H - 3
08C15.B	Use *Celebrating Jesus in the Biblical Feasts: Discovering Their Significance to You as a Christian* to study Hanukkah, the Feast of Lights.	H - 1 CS - 1
08C16.B	Study the life of Benjamin Franklin and his contribution to electric lighting.	H - 1
08C17.B	Study the life of Thomas Edison, including how and when he created the first successful incandescent bulb.	H - 1
08C18.B	Study the lives of other inventors and scientists who made major contributions to the development of modern lighting.	H 1 each
08C19.B	Study and prepare a chart or display of the various oils and other fuels that have been commonly used in lamps.	H - 3

CULTURAL STUDIES

08C20.B	Study the whaling industry and the ships used in it.	H - 1
08C21.B	Study the life-style of the men who were involved in the enterprise of whaling.	H - 1
08C22.B	Study and chart the history of the use of kerosene and other petroleum products for the production of light.	H - 1
08C23.B	Identify and trace on a map all major petroleum exporting nations.	G 1
08C24.B	Study the history of the oil and gas industry in the United States.	H - 1
08C25.B	Study the lives of important figures in the history of the oil and gas industry.	H - 1 each
08C26.B	Study laws, regulations and regulatory agencies governing the petroleum and natural gas industries in your nation and state or province.	CL - 1 CG-
08C27.C	Study the provisions made for vision care by the insurance policy covering your family.	CE - 1
08C28.C	Survey other families and/or contact your state's insurance board, to learn what percentage of insurance companies in your area provide coverage for vision care and what percentage of the people have it,	CE - 1
08C29.C	Investigate the vision requirements for drivers in your state and how and when their vision is tested.	C L - 1
08C30.C	Study the regulations of OSHA and other health and safety agencies with regard to on-the-job vision protection.	CG - 1
08C31. C	Study all provisions of the Americans with Disabilities Act that apply to the blind.	CL - 1
08C32.C	Tour your state's school for the blind and learn how students go to school there and what type of help they get getting jobs or going on to college when they finish.	CS - 3+
08C33. C	Tour a sheltered workshop or other training facility where blind adults are given job skills and work opportunities.	CS - 2+
08C34.C	Investigate colleges that offer specialized educational opportunities for blind or vision-impaired students.	CS - 1+
08C35. C	Study the life of Louis Braille and the alphabet he invented.	H - I
08C36.C	Study the life of Helen Keller, who was not only blind but also deaf.	H - 1
08C37.C	Tour the childhood home of Helen Keller in Tuscumbia, Alabama, or historic sites involving the lives of other well-known blind people.	H 2+

CULTURAL STUDIES

08C38.C	Study the lives of other well-known and successful blind people.	H - 1 each
08C39.C	Investigate agencies that train and furnish guide dogs for the blind. Learn how clients apply and are accepted, what is required to get and keep a dog, and what it costs.	CS - 1
08C40.	Use Usborne's *World History Dates, The Kingfisher History Encyclopedia,* or *Timetables of History* to find dates and prepare timeline entries for important people and events in this unit.	VA- 1 per 10 H -1 per 10
08C41.	Make timeline entries for all authors, inventors, artists, composers or others whose works were used during this unit.	VA- 1 per 10 H -113E2-10
08C42.	Make timeline entries for people or events mentioned in the books or videos used here but not already in your timeline	VA- 1 per 10 H -1 per 10
08C43.	Locate on a map or globe all countries studied or mentioned in this unit.	G 1
08C44.	Locate on a map and study the geography of all cities or municipalities and states or provinces studied in this unit.	G - 1
08C45.	Use an encyclopedia or similar reference to study the geography and culture of each country mentioned in this unit that you have not studied previously. Take notes on your studies so you can write a brief report (1-2 pages) on each of them in the Composition section.	G - 1 each

READING AND LITERATURE

08R01.A	Read books written in the 1970's or early 1980's by Gary North, David Chilton, or other Christian economists dealing with the economic problems they saw coming and learn how they advised people to prepare for them. (These books are out of print but can probably by found in public libraries and/or used bookstores.)	H - 6 each
08R02.A	Read Larry Burkett's *The Coming Economic Earthquake*. Investigate and determine whether or not the situation discussed here ever occurred and if the preparations urged in this book had any effect on the result. Discuss your findings with our parents and/or other Christian adults who may remember some of the events of that time.	EC - 6
08R03.A	Read, and discuss with someone who remembers the time period, *The Fifty-Year War: Conflict and Strategy in the Cold War* by Norman Friedman.	H - 6
08R04.A	Read *The Cold War: A Military History* by David Miller.	H - 6
08R05.A	Read one or more books written by military leaders of the U.S. or the Soviet Union during the Cold War.	H - 6
08R06.A	Read *Arms Control and Military Preparedness from Truman to Bush* (American University Studies Series).	H - 6

READING AND LITERATURE

08R07.A	Read one or more of the "preparation manuals" designed to help people make it through the widely-predicted Y2K crisis at the beginning of the year 2000. (These books are no longer printed, but many are available in libraries can be purchased from used bookstores or online sites.)	H - 4 each
08R08.A	As an alternative to books about Y2K survival, read 6-8 magazine articles from the late 1990's on that topic, using your library's periodical guide or online searches to find them.	H - I each
08R09.A	Read *Disaster Preparedness: Simple Steps for Businesses* by Julie Freestone and Rudi Raab.	SA - 5
08R10.B	Read *Brief History of Light and Those That Lit the Way*, one of the Series in Popular Science books.	H - 5
08R11.B	Read biographies of one or more of the people mentioned in the above book.	H - 5 each
08R12.B	Read a book on the history and 'how-to' of candlemaking and/or the use of whale oil for lamps.	H - 5
08R13.B	Read *Oil Lamps: The Kerosene Era in North America* or another book on this topic.	H - 5
08R14.B	Read books on the petroleum industry in your country or world-wide.	H - 5 each
08R15.B	Read biographies of men or women who made an impact on petroleum industry.	H - 5 each
08R16.B	Read Usborne's *Electricity* or a similar simple explanation of this topic.	SP- 3
08R17.B	Read biographies of one or more of the scientists, inventors or others involved in the discovery and use of electricity.	H - 5 each
08R18.B	Read the original, unabridged version of "Aladdin and the Wonderful Lamp" from *1001 Arabian Nights*. (This is not a kiddy story, nor is it the Disney version that was made into a cartoon. The story contains much magic and mysticism, which some parents may find inappropriate.)	L - 4
08R19.B	Read *Moby Dick*, a classic whaling tale.	L - 5
08R20.C	Read *The Miracle Worker*.	L or H - 4
08R21.C	Read a complete biography of Helen Keller.	H - 4
08R22.C	Read a biography of Helen Keller's teacher, Anne Sullivan.	H - 4
08R23.C	Read a biography of Louis Braille.	H - 4
08R24.C	Read a biography of blind hymn writer Fanny Crosby.	H - 4

READING AND LITERATURE

08R25.C	Read biographies of other well-known blind people and/or people who helped them.	H - 4 each
08R26.C	Read one or more Christian novels about or featuring a blind person.	L- 5 each
08R27.C	Read one or more medical or scientific books about blindness and its causes.	HE - 5+ each
08R28.	Read Christian or other wholesome novels set in any of the time periods under study in any particular mini-unit of this unit.	L 5 each
08R29.	Read other works by any authors studied in this unit.	L - 5 each

COMPOSITION

08W01.A	Write an essay on the Biblical principle of 'preparedness' as presented in the passages in this mini-unit.	EC - 2
08W02.A	Write a biographical sketch of John the Baptist, using all facts given in the Bible and filling in missing details from your imagination and knowledge of the times.	B - 2 EC - 2
08W03.A	Write an investigative report on some particular aspect of your nation's military preparedness. Expose some lack of preparation or explain the measures taken to be ready.	EC - 2
08W04.A	Write arguments for either side of a debate on the topic, "Resolved: The Country That is Best Prepared for War is Least Likely to Face it."	EC - 2 CS - 3
08W05.A	Write an imaginary advertisement (about one-page) for a fallout shelter like those sold during the Cold War. extolling its virtues in case of nuclear attack.	EC - 1
08W06.A	Write a first person story about someone who was able to leave East Berlin for the first time when the Berlin Wall came down in 1989. Share the joy of finding long-lost relatives and the strangeness of being able to come and go more freely.	EG - 10
08W07.A	Write an analysis of the causes of the Cold War and its outcome, including why you think it ended and who 'won'.	EC - 2
08W08.A	Write a thorough term paper (700-1000 words) on some aspect of the Cold War. Use Writer's Inc. or a similar reference book for help in how to do this.	EC - 50
08W09.A	Write an analysis of the projected Y2K problem and the preparations within the computer industry that prevented it.	EC - 2
08W10.A	Write an essay or letter praising the efforts of the computer specialists whose preparations prevented the predicted Y2K computer disaster.	EC - 1

COMPOSITION

08W11.B	Write a paper explaining the importance of not letting one's light go out during Bible times.	EC - I
08W12.B	Write five-to-ten journal or diary entries about life on a whaling ship of the 18th or 19th century.	H - 3
08W13.B	Write a paper describing the processes involved in coal mining.	EC - 2
08W14.B	Write a newspaper report on the invention of the incandescent light bulb, as if you were there when it happened.	EC - 2
08W15.B	Write a paper on the importance of the electric light bulb to our modern way of life.	EC - 4
08W16.B	Write a scholarly analysis of the economic impact of the oil and gas industry in your nation, state/province, or local area.	EC - 2
08W17.B	Write brief reports on any or all of the inventors, scientists or others who were instrumental in the development of modern lighting systems.	EC - 2 each
08W18.B	Write a poem about light, used in a natural or symbolic sense.	EC - 2+
08W19.C	Write a first-person story as if written by the blind man healed by Jesus in John 9.	EC- 10
08W20.C	Write a news report of the blinding of Saul and the subsequent events, as if written by a reporter of the day.	EC - 3
08W21.C	Write a Biblical analysis of Hebrews 1:1, explaining its meaning for your day.	EC - 1 B 1
08W22.C	Write a letter to your insurance company, asking for clarification of their vision coverage or asking them to consider including it, if they do not.	EC - 1
08W23.C	Write reports on Helen Keller, Louis Braille, and/or other well-known blind people.	EC -1 each
08W24.C	Write a first-aid manual on caring for injuries to the eyes.	EC-2AHE-3
08W25.C	Write a handbook on vision care for parents of young children. Include such things as how and when to have vision tests, protecting eyes from bright light and other hazards, using proper lighting for reading, and writing, etc.	EC - 4 HE - 6
08W26.C	Write a short story about a seeing-eye dog and the person with whom it works.	EC - 10
08W27.	As you read the Bible each day, keep a spiritual journal, taking notes on your readings and their applications in your life. Add prayer requests and answers as well as insights God may give you.	EC - 3 per week

COMPOSITION

08W28.	Define and put into your vocabulary notebook 10 new words per week, using first those you encountered in your studies. For each, write all common definitions and pronunciations.	EG - 1 per week
08W29.	Learn to spell all the words in your vocabulary notebook for this unit.	EG - 2 per 10 words
08W30.	Using *Writers Inc., the College English Handbook*, or another grammar reference, proofread and correct all written work for this unit.	EG- 1 per 5 pages
08W31.	Use a good dictionary to proofread all written work in this unit and correct it for errors in spelling.	EG - 1 per 5 pages
08W32.	Keep a journal of each day's school projects throughout the entire curriculum. If done well, this journal can serve as official documentation of your school year to meet legal requirements in many states.	EG - 2 per week
08W33.	Keep a journal of each day's school projects throughout the entire curriculum. If done well, this journal can serve as official documentation of your school year to meet legal requirements in many states.	EG - 2 per week
08W34.	As you attend worship services or hear them on radio, TV, or audio recordings, take notes on the sermons.	EG - 1 each
08W35.	As you watch videos and/or listen to audios take notes on them.	EG - 1 each
08W36.	Use your notes to outline, summarize, and/or discuss the sermons as requested.	EC or EG - 1 each
08W37.	Use your notes to write a synopsis or summary of each audio and/or video used in this mini-unit.	EC - 1 each
08W38.	Outline one or more of the nonfiction books used in this unit.	EG - 5 each
08W39.	Instead of, or in addition to, outlining the books studied here, write reviews of them, as might be published in a periodical of some type.	EC 1 each
08W40.	Use any Scripture passage, poem or other material you are memorizing to copy for handwriting practice.	EG - 1 per hour
08W41.	Use the Scripture verses, poems and other material you are trying to memorize to write from dictation. Have someone read the passage to you slowly while you write it, being careful about correct spelling, punctuation, etc. If your beliefs allow, you may want to use a modern Bible translation for this exercise.	EG - 1 per hour
08W42.	As an alternative to cursive writing, try Italic or Spencerian calligraphy, using books in the resource list.	VA- 1 per hour

COMPOSITION

08W43.   Write a news article on each of the field trips you took in this unit.   EC - 2 each

08W44.   Write a thank you note to the organizer, supervisor, and/or guide of any field trip you took for this unit.   EC - 1 each

08W45.   Write summaries or synopses of any or all of the books read in this unit.   EC - 1 each

08W46.   Write a report on one or more of the people you studied in this unit.   EC - 1 each

08W47.   Write one book report per week on a book included in this unit or another approved by parents. Use a variety of approaches, including any or all of those listed in the Appendix.   EC   1 each

08W48.   Write a brief (1-2 pages) report on each country studied in this unit. Put each of them into your geography notebook.   G - 1 each

08W49.   Write reviews of any or all of the videos in this unit, as if done by a movie critic.   EC - 1 each

08W50.   Write a character sketch of one or more of the men and women studied in this unit.   EC - 1 each

08W51.   Write a thorough exegesis of any of the Bible chapters studied in this unit.   EC - 1 each

08W52.   Write a review of each play you watched or read for this unit.   EC   1 each

MATHEMATICS AND PERSONAL FINANCE

08M01.A   Calculate and compare the military budgets of the U. S. and U. S. S. R. during several years of the Cold War.   M - 1

08M02.A   Using publications from the time, gather and compile on a graph average GNP and per capita income figures for the U. S and U. S. S. R. in each decade of the Cold War.   M - 5

08M03.A   Prepare a graph to show the population of each country of Eastern Europe when the Cold War ended and the Iron Curtain came down in 1989.   M - 5

08M04.A   Compute the original area of the Soviet Union and the relative sizes of each of the countries carved from it.   M - 2

08M05.A   Compute the population of each of the above countries when they were first established and today. Calculate the rate of growth of each.   M - 2

08M06.B   Use the study of light to learn the measurement of a light year and the use of scientific notation for writing very large amounts.   M - 1

MATHEMATICS AND PERSONAL FINANCE

08M07.B	Prepare a graph to compare the wattage output per dollar and/ or per hour of the various types of power plants.	M - 3
08M08.B	Learn the various units of measure connected with electricity, what each one means, and how they relate to each other.	M - 1
08M09.B	Prepare a graph to compare the energy efficiency ratings of various electrical appliances.	M - 4
08M10.B	Compute your own (or another) electric bill given the cost per kilowatt hour and the total usage.	M- 1
08M11.C	Study the numbers used to measure vision as a ratio between two numbers. Explain what both numbers mean and how the ratio is reached.	M - 1
08M12.C	Determine the monthly, yearly, and lifetime costs (average lifespan of different breeds) of owning a seeing-eye dog. Be sure to include all the initial costs relating to obtaining and training the dog.	A - 1
08M13.C	Calculate the amount of money your family spends on vision care and related services per year and how much money you save (or would save) by having insurance to cover this.	A - 1
08M14.C	Compare prices on several different types of eyewear at various places and prepare a graph to show the results.	CE - 3
08M15.	Use data from any of the graphs in this unit to practice making and solving problems using percent, ratio, and proportion.	M - 1 per hour
08M16.	Continue to review basic math as needed.	M - 1 per hour

SCIENCE

08S01.A	Study the GPS tracking system and its use as an early warning of military action anywhere in the world. Compare that to the uses most of us have for it today.	ST - 1
08S02.A	Study the U. S. defensive preparation known as NORAD. Learn what it is, when and why it was put into place, and how it works.	SP - 1 H - 1
08S03.A	Study the Strategic Defense Initiative (SDI), also known as the Star Wars Defense. Learn what it is, when and why it was put into place, and how it works.	ST - 1
08S04.A	Study other early-warning defense systems that operate on the premise that advance preparation is the best defense.	ST - 3
08S05.A	Tour one or more military installations involved in some type of 'early warning' or defense preparedness endeavor. Be aware that many parts and functions of such a facility will be 'classified' and not open to the public. Do not push to see closed areas or get answers to ignored questions.	ST - 2

SCIENCE

08S06.A	Study the atomic bomb, the primary object of all the above defenses.	ST - 1
08S07.A	Study the hydrogen bomb and the difference between the two types.	ST - 1
08508.A	Tour the museum areas of Los Alamos or another installation used at one time for production or testing of atomic weapons and/or defenses against them.	ST- 1 H - 1
08S09.A	Study the various types of missiles that could be used to deliver bombs from one place to another, making war much less personal and more global.	ST - 1
08S10.A	Study the make up and construction of 'fallout' shelters and the research that led to their creation as a defense against nuclear war.	SP - 1
08S11.A	If possible, tour one of the 'fallout' shelters left over from the Cold War. (Though they have not been sold or used in many years, most of those originally installed are still in place in yards of American homes and businesses. They are being used as storm shelter, storage facilities, or even office space, or are left unused completely.)	SP - 2
08S12.A	Study the 'early-warning' equipment used by meteorologists to help predict oncoming hurricanes, tornadoes and other severe weather in time to prepare for it.	ST - 1
08S13.A	Study the sirens, PA systems and other equipment used to broadcast' warnings of dangerous weather.	ST - 1
08514.A	Tour the local Civil Defense or Red Cross disaster preparedness headquarters. Pay special attention to the equipment they use and learn how it works.	SP- 1 SA - 1
08S15.A	Study the ways in which various animals prepare for the changing of seasons.	SB - 2
08S16.B	Study sun, moon, and stars and the ways in which they affect our Earth, particularly as regards length of days and nights and the provision of light.	SE - 2+
08517.B	Study the constellations common in your part of the world and learn to identify them in the night sky.	SE - 1
08S18.B	Study the chemical makeup of various substances used for candle making (now and in earlier times) and the differences in the quality and quantity of light produced.	SC - 2
08519.B	Study the sources, chemical properties and light production of each type of 'oil' used for lamps before the wide availability of petroleum products.	SC - 2

SCIENCE

08S20.B	Study the sources, production, and properties of coal, petroleum, and other fossil fuels. Make a chart comparing them to each other.	SC - 3
08S21.B	Study the recovery, refining, and delivery processes that make fossil fuels readily available in our homes.	SP - 2
08S22.B	Study natural gas and its uses for light and heat, both as a direct source and to power electric generators.	SC - 2
08S23.B	Tour a coal mining establishment.	SP - 2
08S24.B	Tour an oil-drilling rig, offshore or otherwise.	ST - 3
08S25.B	Study environmental dangers posed by oil and gas drilling and/or coal mining. Try to ease them without limiting the fuel supply.	SE - 3
08S26.B	Study the production of electricity and various sources of fuel used.	SP - 2
08527.B	Tour a hydroelectric power plant.	SP - 2+
08S28.B	Tour a coal-powered electric power plant.	SP - 2+
08S29.B	Tour a solar energy facility and learn how the sun is harnessed for our use.	SP - 2
08S30.B	Tour a nuclear power plant.	SP - 2+
08531.B	Study all five volumes (or any portion you wish) of *Basic Electricity: Complete Course*, or a similar basic electricity course.	1 credit in Electricity if completed
08S32.B	Learn about amps, volts, watts, and ohms and the equipment and procedures used to measure them.	SP - 2
08S33.B	Investigate the environmental hazards of each common method of electricity production and ways to minimize each.	SE - 1
08S34.C	Study the light spectrum and how a prism (or water) divides the light.	SE - 1
08S35.C	Study how various colors are produced and how our eyes see them.	SE - 1 HA - 1
08S36.C	Study fiber optics and how it works.	SP - 2
08S37.C	Study lasers and their many functions.	SP - 1
08S38.C	Study mirages and other types of optical illusions and how they occur.	SP - 1
08S39.C	Study the anatomy of the human eye.	HA - 2

SCIENCE

08S40.C   Dissect a cow or pig eyeball (these are available at animal   SB - 2
slaughterhouses), which is very similar to our own. Using a   HA - 2
schematic of the human eye (available from eye doctors,
educational resource companies. or medical supply firms), find
and examine each of the following parts: lens, iris, retina, optic
nerve, sclera and choroid layers, and aqueous and vitreous humors.
If you prefer, this can be done virtually online.

08S41.C   Study the functions of each part of the eye listed above.   HA - 2

08S42.C   Study the following eye accessories and their purpose in   HA - 2
producing an/or protecting our vision: eyelids, eyebrows,
lacrimal glands, eye sockets, eye muscles.

08S43.C   Study the materials and processes involved in the production   SP - 3
of various types of lenses for vision enhancement and/or
correction.

08S44.C   Study concave and convex lenses and the purposes of each.   SP - 1

08S45.C   Study materials and processes used to create and implant false   HE - 2
eyes for those who lose eyeballs to disease or accident.

08346.C   Study the uses of lenses in different types of cameras and how   SP - 2
they work.

08S47.C   Study the use of various types, sizes and strengths of telescopes,   SP - 2
microscopes and other magnifying devices and how
the different types of these items work.

08S48.C   Study mirrors and the reflection of light.   SP - 2

08S49.C   Visit a planetarium and learn how the optical equipment there   SP - 2
is used to produce the effects of a moving night sky.

08S50.C   Tour an optical laboratory and learn how eyeglasses and contact   SF - 2
lenses are made.

08S51.C   Tour one or more factories that make other types of lenses or   ST - 2
products in which they are used.

08S52.C   Tour a facility that makes artificial eyes and see how it is done.   ST - 2

HEALTH AND PHYSICAL FITNESS

08H01.A   Study hypothermia and other ill effects from extremely cold   HE - 1
weather and how proper preparation can prevent them.

08H02.A   Study sunburn, dehydration, heat stroke, and other ill health   HE - 1
effects of severe heat and or arid weather conditions and how
proper preparation can prevent them.

HEALTH AND PHYSICAL FITNESS

08H03.A	Study radiation sickness and its treatment.	HE - 1
08H04.A	Study the use of radiation therapy for cancer and other illnesses.	HE - 1
08H05.A	Study the negative effects sometimes experienced by radiation therapy patients.	HE - 1
08H06.A	Study nuclear medicine and the various uses of it.	HE - 2
08H07.A	Study epidemiology and how doctors can predict and prepare for outbreaks of contagious disease.	HE - 2
08H08.A	Study childhood immunizations, often considered the best preparation to prevent illnesses. Study the shots or vaccinations available, the diseases they prevent, their rate of effectiveness, and the possible side effects of them. Weigh the evidence to determine which immunizations are worth giving to your children and which are not.	HE - 2+
08H09.A	Study the objections many parents have to required immunizations for all children. Learn about some of the situations that contraindicate immunizations and the negative reactions some children have to them.	HE - 2
08H10.B	Study the health effects of vitamin E, found naturally in sunlight.	HE - 1
08H11.B	Study the effects of ultraviolet light on the skin and ways to protect against damage.	HE - 1
08H12.B	Study skin cancer (melanoma), which can be caused by exposure to sunlight.	HE - 1
08H13.B	Study the negative and positive health effects of tanning lights.	HE - 1
08H14.B	Study the use of infrared light for medical purposes.	HE - 1
08H15.B	Study laser surgery and how it has streamlined the removal and treatment of so many growths, tissues, and organs.	HE - 1
08H16.B	Study and mind map about other medical uses of lasers.	HE - 2
08H17.B	Study the medical uses of ultraviolet light.	HE - 1
08H18.C	Study the difference between the jobs of optician, optometrist and opthamologist.	HE - 2
08H19.C	Study cataracts, their common causes and how they can be treated.	HE - 1
08H20.C	Study glaucoma, its causes and how it can be treated.	HE - 1

HEALTH AND PHYSICAL FITNESS

08H21.C	Study nearsightedness and farsightedness and learn their correct medical names. Learn how the eyeball is shaped in each instance and how glasses or contacts work to correct each type of problem.	HE - 1
08H22.C	Study astigmatism and how lenses can be used to correct it.	HE - 1
08H23.C	Study all other vision disorders and how each can be prevented and/or treated.	HE - 1 each
08H24.C	Learn how a doctor administers a complete eye exam and what condition each part of the test is designed to diagnose.	HE - 1
08H25.C	Learn and practice safety rules for protecting your eyes from accidental injury or damage.	HE - 1
08H26.C	Learn basic first aid for various types of injuries to the eye.	HE - 1+
08H27.C	Study the modern trend in vision correction through surgery. Be especially aware of any dangers or hazards to this.	HE - 1

PRACTICAL ARTS

08P01.A	Review your family's health and life insurance policies to see just how well prepared you are financially in case of some emergency that would end your parents' earning power.	HM - I
08P02.A	In order to be prepared in the event of fire, theft, or other damage to your home, complete a household asset inventory. In a ledger or notebook, record all valuable belongings with their current appraisal or estimated market value. Include serial numbers whenever possible. Keep these records in a safe deposit box or other waterproof and fireproof storage.	HM - 1
08P03.A	Take pictures to go with your inventory to prove you actually owned the items and to show what they looked like.	VA- 1
08P04.A	Videotape your household inventory, describing items in words as you film them. Store it with the written list.	VA - 1
08P05.A	For extra protection from the unexpected, copy the video tape of your household inventory and give the second one to a friend or relative for safekeeping.	ST 1
08P06.A	Take a Red Cross disaster preparedness course.	SA - 1/2 credit
08P07.A	Volunteer to work in a Red Cross or Civil Defense disaster relief team and learn how to stay prepared for mobilization on a moment's notice.	SA - 1/2 credit per disaster worked (max. 2 credits)

PRACTICAL ARTS

08P08.A   Prepare an emergency preparedness kit for your family, choosing   HM - 3
an appropriate container and products to put in it. Plan for power
outages, storms, accidents, illnesses, and other types of
emergencies. Decide with your parents where it will be stored to be
safe from little ones and still readily accessible for the adults.

08P09.A   Assist your parents to shop for and install smoke detectors   HM - 1
and other household alarm systems.

08P10.A   Learn to operate, test and maintain fire extinguishers, smoke   HM - 1+
detectors, alarm systems and other emergency equipment used
in your home.

08P11.B   Learn to clean, fill, and trim the wicks of all oil and gas lamps   HM - 1
used in your home.

08P12.B   Make several types of molded and dipped candles, using mod-   CR - 1
em and folk methods.   each type

08P13.B   Make one or more attractive candleholders from common   CR- 1
household materials.   each

08P14.B   Create a working electric lamp from a glass jar or bottle or an   CR - 2+
odd-shaped log or piece of driftwood.

08P15.B   Wire two sets of lights, one each in parallel circuit and series.   IA - 2+
Be able to explain the difference.

08P16.B   Learn to replace broken electric sockets and light switches in   HM - 1
your home.

08P17.B   Learn to fix broken electric cords and to replace plugs on them.   HM - 1

08P18.B   Using directions in the "Electricity" article in *World Book*   CR - 2
Encyclopedia, Science Experiments on File, or online resources,
make a primitive battery from zinc and copper plates.

08P19.B   Using directions in the "Electricity" article in *World Book*   CR - 2
Encyclopedia, Science Experiments on File, or online resources,
make a small, crude electric generator.

08P20.B   Wire an electric light bulb to run off the homemade battery.   IA- 1
and/or generator you built in the last two activities.

08P21.B   Hang decorative lights in or around your home for Christmas   HM - 1
or another holiday season.   per hour

08P22.B   Learn to check strands of lights wired in series circuitry to   HM   1
determine which individual bulbs are out and replace them.

08P23.B   Build a model of a planetarium, following directions from   CR- 2
Science Projects on File or an online resource.

PRACTICAL ARTS

08P24.C	Make a simple telescope. (Instructions are available online, and in many books about science projects and/or astronomy.)	CR - 2+
08P25.C	Use instructions from any of the resources listed above or others to create a working model of a microscope.	CR - 2+
08P26.C	Use instructions from any of the resources listed above or others to create a simple, working model of a camera.	CR - 2+
08P27.C	Use your knowledge of mirrors, optics and telescopes to build a kaleidoscope to share with a younger child.	CR - 2+
08P28.C	Using one of the available kits from science teaching suppliers, build a fiber optic lamp.	CR - 2+
08P29.C	Learn to use various types of telescopes and study the stars with each one.	SE- 1
08P30.C	Learn how to use various types of microscopes, using each type to examine the same specimens and comparing them.	SB - 1
08P31.C	Learn how to load, unload and use a variety of different cameras.	RE - 1
08P32.C	Take a course (or do a scout or similar club project) in photography.	1/2 credit in Photography
08P33.C	Learn to develop your own photos.	SP - 2
08P34.C	Learn to read and write in Braille well enough to communicate that way.	'/2 credit
08P35.C	Learn to use Braille-to-English and/or English-to-Braille typewriter or keyboard.	BE - 2
08P36.	If you don't already know how to create and use a computer database, you may wish to learn in preparation for later units.	CO - 6
08P37.	Create and maintain a database to assist you as appropriate in this mini-unit.	CO - 2+
08P38.	Type all written work with a typewriter or word processor. If you do not know how to type, now is the time to learn.	BE - 1 per 4 pages
08P39.	If needed, take a class, follow a computerized, written or video tutorial, or a correspondence course in typing, keyboarding, and/or word processing.	1/2 credit in Typing or Keyboarding
08P40.	Frame and mat one or more of the pictures or posters you drew or created in the Decorative and Performing Arts section of this mini-unit.	CR - 2+ each

PRACTICAL ARTS

08P41.	Make your own costumes for any performances you chose to do in the Decorative and Performing Arts section of this mini-unit or plays you wrote in the Composition section.	CC - 5+ each
08P42.	Create a computer website to display what you have learned in this unit.	CO - 2+

DECORATIVE AND PERFORMING ARTS

08A01.A	Using calligraphy and art skills, draw an attractive but accurate diagram of the appropriate evacuation route to be taken by your family in the event of a major storm demanding such action.	VA- 1 SA - 1
08A02.A	Draw a mural or create a collage showing things for which families should prepare, but which may give little or no warning.	VA- 1+
08A03.A	Tour an art or photography exhibit related to storms, earthquakes, volcanoes, or other "natural disasters". Discuss how each artist achieves the sense of realism or emotion appropriate to the piece.	AA - 2+
08A04.A	Using your own pictures, make a photo journal of a natural disaster. Show examples of those who were prepared and those who were not.	VA - 2+
08A05.A	Prepare a poster, banner or other wall hanging featuring a Scripture verse extolling preparation. Write it in calligraphy or paint it in block or script letters and use appropriate art media to illustrate it.	VA - 1+
08A06.B	Make a collage or drawing of a wide variety of light sources.	VA- 1+
08A07.B	Assemble an attractive display of lamps used throughout history and paint or draw them.	VA - 3
08A08.B	Copy Psalm 119:105 in good calligraphy or stenciled lettering to make a poster or a caption for the picture in #08A06.	VA - 1
08A09.B	Learn to make shadow pictures and create a 'skit' using them.	DR - 1
08A10.B	Create a decorative holiday light display for your home, using strings of lights to make words, pictures or patterns for a complete design or story.	VA - 2+
08A11.B	Study exhibits, websites, or books featuring the art of Thomas Kinkade, known as the painter of light. Notice and discuss how he uses light to create various effects and emotions in his paintings.	AA - 2+
08A12.C	Listen to a collection of hymns written by blind songwriter Fanny Crosby and critique them for Scriptural content, emotional appeal, and musical quality.	MA - 1

DECORATIVE AND PERFORMING ARTS

| 08A13.C | Learn to sing one or more Fanny Crosby songs well enough to perform in public. | VM - 3+ |

08A14.C   Tour an art exhibit and describe each picture as vividly as possible, as you would for a blind person. Plan how you could describe colors, brightness, clarity, objects drawn, setting, and various other elements. Discuss with a parent the effect this exercise has on your ability to understand and enjoy art.   AA - 3+

08A15.C   To learn more about how visual art and blindness, try drawing a picture of an object you can't see. Have someone else describe it without telling you what it is while you draw it without looking at either the object or the paper on which you are drawing. When completed, see how near your drawing came to the actual object.   VA- 1

08A16.C   Using materials of your own choice, create a textured picture that could be enjoyed by a blind person using the fingers.   CR - 3

08A17.C   View and study an exhibit or book of "hidden" 3-D pictures created by optical illusions. See if you can find the picture inside each picture.   AA- 2

08A18.   Draw pictures of any field trips you took in this mini-unit.   VA - 1+ each

08A19.   Use drawing, painting and graphic arts to create displays and make posters as called for in this study.   VA - I each

08A20.   Illustrate one or more of the poems you studied or memorized for this unit.   VA - 1 each

08A21.   Set one or more of this unit's poems to music, using an original or existing tune.   VA - 1 each

08A22.   Set one or more of the Scripture verses in this unit to music, using a tune you wrote for the purpose.   MC - 5 each

UNIT 9

She lays her hands to the spindle;
her hand holds the distaff.

Proverbs 31:19

Introduction to Unit 9

This unit deals with the diligence and creativity of the godly woman and her commitment to hard work. It also deals with handicrafts — sewing and needlework in particular, including examples in Scripture of women who put their time and skills to good use in sewing for their families and others. In addition, we emphasize here the importance of learning a skill well and doing a good job of whatever one sets about to do. This is, we believe, the theme of this verse of Proverbs 31.

This unit includes the study of the spindle, the distaff and other tools of sewing or cloth making used by women in Bible times. The unit traces these items throughout history to see the development of their modern counterparts. Here you will examine various types of simple machines and various uses and alterations of them. This has been expanded to include industries and the Industrial Revolution, as well as the history of the labor union movement. Math covered in this unit includes units of linear measurement in both English and metric systems.

This unit abounds in homemaking skills as you will learn many forms of sewing and other fabric crafts. You will also have opportunity to learn spinning, weaving, tatting and other crafts that we tend to relate to an earlier time. The unit even offers instructions for making your own weaving looms and similar equipment should you wish to do so. In all of this, however, it is not our goal simply to teach you how to do these things, but to encourage you to do them diligently, as unto the Lord.

Mini-Units

Mini-Units contained in this unit are:

A. A Woman of Diligence

B. Sewing and Needlework

C. Simple Machines: The Seedbed of Invention and Industry

D. Industrial Revolution

Each thematic mini-unit is described and designated with a letter of the alphabet in the following paragraphs. Individual activities designed for use in one particular mini-unit will be marked with those letters. (For further help with this, please refer to the explanation of mini-units in the Guidelines section of this unit study guide.)

Mini-Units

A. A Woman of Diligence

This mini-unit is designed to stress the importance of diligence, hard work and the perseverance needed to stick with a task until it is completed. Through Bible reading and other studies, you will see what is involved in acquiring these related traits and why they are so important. You will examine the lives of women who were diligent and some who were not. You will look at the impact on history of diligence in the right causes and places, and the consequences of sloth, Biblically and in the lives of real people in history.

You will study the "Puritan work ethic" and the impact it had on making the American worker the most productive in the world when it was prevalent in society. On the other side of that coin, you will see what has happened to the productivity of the American worker now that diligence and hard work are no longer so highly prized. You will attempt to find out when and why the difference occurred and what American workers could do to turn the tide again.

B. Sewing and Needlework

This mini-unit will cover both the theoretical and practical sides of sewing and needle-work. You will learn the history of various types of sewing, quilting, spinning and weaving, including the actual processes employed. This will be your chance to learn to sew, quilt, knit or do other types of needlework, trying your hand at a variety and choosing one in which to specialize.

You will learn how to choose, use, and care for various types of sewing and needlework equipment and which is best for what jobs. It is hoped that this mini-unit will allow you to develop skills in this area that will serve you and your family for many years, as you make clothing and other items for all of you.

You will also study the history of sewing and needlework, learning about the discoveries and inventions that have made life easier in this area over the years. You are encouraged to investigate and try your hand at spinning and weaving, as well as sewing, on equipment from various periods of history.

Much in this mini-unit meshes with the Textiles mini-unit in Unit 3. Some activities are repeated in both places but should only be done once for the designated points. You and your family may choose where you use them. Some families have also combined these two. mini-units. This often works well and is an exception to the rule of only doing one unit at a time.

C. Simple Machines: The Seedbed of Invention and Industry

This will be a study of machinery and its history, from the first wheel to the most modern manufacturing facility. You will learn about the five types of simple machines, in which all machinery, no matter how complex or intricate, has its roots. You will trace the history of mechanization and industry in your nation and others.

You will study inventions that changed the world and the men and women who created and built them. You will learn how to build, operate, and maintain a variety of machines and equipment in the home, office, farm, or factory. This can be very basic for the average homemaker, but we have allowed options for those of you who want to learn more. You may even study mechanics or engine repair within this mini-unit if you choose to do so.

Mini-Units

D. The Industrial Revolution

You will use many different activities to study the period in the history of the Western World known as the Industrial Revolution. You will also study all major surges and developments in manufacturing and industry throughout the world. You will trace the history of this development and its effects on society, both negative and positive.

You will study the lives of industrialists and others who were important to society during this time period. This will include some of the world's best known evangelists and social reformers who worked first among the laborers of the 'new' industries. Studies of their lives will include biographies, videos, news stories from their own time about them, and some of their own writings.

You will study the plight of the laborer during the Industrial Revolution and the rise of various moves designed to better it. These include labor unions, child labor laws, wage and hour restrictions, and occupational safety laws, all of which will be examined in much detail. Modern-day working conditions in various countries will also be examined and compared to those of the Industrial Revolution.

Though it is not a part of the primary topic, this mini-unit will also touch on the more recent technological advances of what could be called the Electronic Revolution. While there is no mini-unit covering this, material about it is interspersed in several units to give you at least a small understanding of it.

BIBLE AND CHRISTIAN CHARACTER

09B01.A	Read and memorize II Timothy 2:15 and Colossians 3:22-24. Bearing in mind that all believers are slaves of Christ, discuss with a parent how these passages apply to the work you are asked to do in your own life.	B- 2
09B02.A	Study and discuss with your parents Titus 2:1-5, which contains commands on how the believer should do her work.	B - 2
09B03.A	Look up in your concordance the word 'sloth', an antonym for diligence, and read all passages listed to understand God's attitude toward the slothful.	B - 2
09B04.A	Memorize Proverbs 6:6-11 to help you remember the importance of diligence.	B- 2
09B05.A	Using your concordance, find and read all passages relating to the sluggard, the opposite of a diligent person. Notice the Lord's attitude toward such a person and the consequences (s)he will reap in this life.	B- 2
09B06.A	Read chapters 2 - 6 of Nehemiah to see an example of diligence set by the man God chose to rebuild His temple after the return of the Jews from their Babylonian captivity.	B - 1
09B07.A	Use a concordance to find and read all other Scripture passages that praise or command diligence, hard work, and/or perseverance.	B- 3

BIBLE AND CHRISTIAN CHARACTER

09B08.A   Read and discuss with parents all sections of *Gaining Favor*   B - 1 each
           with God and Man that relate to diligent work.

09B09.A   Listen to and discuss with a Christian mother the audio   B - 3
           series *Mary vs. Martha* by Sono Harris.

09B10.A   With help from your parents or others, honestly analyze your   B - 2
           level of diligence in your daily life. Ask others where they see
           you falling short of God's ideal. Do not let negative feedback
           cause you to be defensive but use this as a chance to become
           more obedient to Christ. Thank God for the things you are
           doing well and ask for His help to improve in the others.

09B11.B   Use the Bible, Bible study guides, All the Women of the Bible,   B- 2
           Bible storybooks or Biblical fiction, and/or two or more
           commentaries to study the life of Hannah as told in I Kings. Pay
           special attention to her use of sewing skills for the glory of
           God in the life of her son. Compare all other sources to Scripture
           for accuracy.

09B12.B   Read about Dorcas from Acts 9 and see how she used her   B- 1
           needlework skills to bring joy into the lives of others. Study her
           further in AU the Women of the Bible, Bible storybooks and/or
           other resources.

09B13.B   Study all references in *Acts* or Paul's epistles to Priscilla and   B- 2
           Aquila, who were tentmakers in Ephesus. Research their sewing
           methods and be ready to present in some way the changes that
           modern sewing machinery would have made in their lives.

09B14.B   Use *Beggar to King: All the Occupations of the Bible* or a   B- 2
           similar resource to list all jobs from Bible times that involved
           sewing or other fabric arts. Look up all Scripture references to
           any of them and catalog in some way.

09B15.B   Using the above list of Bible times occupations and the verses   B - 2
           relating to them, look up in the Bible someone who held each
           occupation and study all references to him or her.

09B16.B   Use your concordance to find and list all other Bible verses   B- 2
           related to sewing and/or needlework. Read each passage and
           make a chart showing, for each reference, how the skill was
           used, by whom, and to what end.

09B17.B   Prayerfully consider your own talents in the area of needlework   B- 1
           and pray that the Lord will give you opportunities to use
           your skills for His glory.

09B18.C   Read the account of the woman at the well in John 4 and   B- 1
           discuss whether this may have been an artesian well or what
           type of pulley she may have used to draw water from it.

BIBLE AND CHRISTIAN CHARACTER

09B19.C   Study Genesis 4:16-22 and any other information you can   B- 2
find on the life of Tubal Cain, who seems to have been the first
inventor and machinist. Read at least two commentaries and
discuss with your parents what bearing, if any, his being a
descendant of Cain has upon the acceptability of technology
and invention for us as believers.

09B20.C   Lest the invention of tools and craftsmanship by Cain's   B- 1
descendant lead us to reject it as evil, study Exodus 31:1-11, in
which God specifically calls upon certain Israelites who have
abilities in these areas to use them for building the Tabernacle.
List all those skills that are specifically mentioned in the
passage.

09B21.C   In I Kings 5 and 6, study the building of the temple of Solomon.   B - 1
Keep track of the skills and tools used and the number of
people who worked on the project.

09B22.C   Read and memorize God's praise of skilled workmen in Exodus   B- 2
35 and discuss how this might apply to those who invented
various machines.

09B23.C   Use concordance to look up and read all passages relating to   B- 2
machines and tools used in Bible times. List all those found
and keep list for use in later activities. Include: anvil and
hammer, ax, cart, plow, thresher, wheel and any others you
find.

09B24.C   Read *People of Bible Times and how they Lived, Beggar to*   B- 5
King: All the Occupations of the Bible, or a similar book to find
all occupations that dealt with machines. Read about each in
the actual Scriptures.

09B25.D   Use the book *Beggar to King: All the Occupations of the*   B- 3
Bible and a concordance to find and list all Biblical references to
metallurgy, woodworking, carpentry, and other occupations or
industries that would be considered manufacturing.

09B26.D   In Exodus 30 and 31, read God's orders to Moses for building   B- 2
the tabernacle. Note various types of skilled labor required and
discuss with parents how this demonstrates the importance to
God of skilled craftsmen and other laborers using their
abilities in any way they can. Relate this to the emergence of
inventions and ideas that fueled the Industrial Revolution.

09827.D   Find and study passages in I Chronicles related to the use of   B- 2
skilled laborers in the building of the temple. Discuss with
parents what this tells us about God's attitude toward invention
and industry.

09B28.D   Study the New Testament guidelines for 'servants and masters'   B- 1
in Ephesians 6:5-9 and see how you feel it could also
relate to employees and bosses.

09B29.D	Study God's attitude toward the value of labor as shown in Matthew 10:10, Malachi 3:5, and James 5:4. Compare this with common attitudes toward and treatment of workers in factories during and since the Industrial Revolution.	B- 3	
09B30.D	Commit one or more of the passages in the above activity to memory and paraphrase it to apply a situation that might be common today.	B - 1 each	
09B31.D	Study Jesus' parable in Matthew 20:1-16 and discuss with a parent how this might relate to management-labor relations today. Investigate to determine how many strikes and other labor disputes result from an unwillingness to accept the principles taught here.	B- 2	
09B32.D	Obtain a copy of the policies of a labor union and large corporation and/or a contract between them. Compare the principles shown in both of these to God's standards for labor-management relations as set in the passages studied in this mini-unit.	B- 1 CL - 1	
09B33.	Memorize one or more of the passages studied in the unit.	B - 1 per 3 verses	
09B34.	Read through the book of Proverbs each month, reading the chapter to coincide with each date.	B - 2 per wk	
091335.	Continue reading through the Bible at a rate of 1-5 chapters per day. If you use *The Daily Bible* or some other version designed specifically for that purpose, their daily readings will take you through the entire Bible in one year. You may follow a pattern of your own at a different rate if you like.	B - 1 credit when completed	

CULTURAL STUDIES

09C01.A	Study the "Puritan work ethic" and the impact it made on society in the early years of the U. S.	H- 1	
09C02.A	Study employee handbooks from several different businesses and make a note of each reference to diligence or a similar trait. Discuss with your parents the conclusions you can draw from this data about the importance of diligence in the workplace.	CS - 2	
09C03.A	Interview five business owners or managers from different fields as to how each sees the importance of diligence and hard work for employees. Present this data in a chart or poster.	CS - 1	
09C04.A	Research and compare rate of worker productivity in various industries for several years to corporate profit, per capita income, GNP, and other measures of national prosperity. Find and discuss any correlations.	CE -	

CULTURAL STUDIES

09C05.A	Study the U. S. Civil Service Act or any similar law in your own country. Discuss with parents or others why you believe this was passed, what ills it was trying to address, and how it could be used to protect workers who are not diligent nor doing a good job. Compare this to any similar system that may be used in your state/province.	CL - 1
09C06.A	Compare average worker productivity in capitalist nations to those in economic systems that do not offer a worker the chance to rise above his current status or increase his income through better or more work.	CE - 1
09C07.B	Study various ways in which women have created and used fabrics during each period of history from Biblical times through today. Compare the skills and tools of each period.	H - 1 CC - 1
09C08.B	From encyclopedias or other references, study clothing construction in various parts of the world, emphasizing differences in technique, raw materials, and tools.	CC - 2
09C09.B	Use encyclopedias, history books, home economics texts, Usborne's *Invention and Discovery*, or other reference materials to study the history of sewing and the machines and other equipment used for it.	H - 1
09C10.B	Tour a living history museum and/or pioneer life exhibit to observe spinning, weaving, and other steps involved in making clothing at that time.	H - 2
09C11.B	Tour a sewing factory, if not done in another unit.	CC - 2
09C12.B	Examine and chart in some way the economic impact of the clothing industry on your nation, state or province, and/or local area.	CE - 2 -
09C13.C	Study the lives of Elias Howe, Eli Whitney, Thomas Edison, R. J. Letourneau, and other inventors of the machines studied in this unit.	H - 2 each
09C14.C	Study the history of mechanization in various industries and the economic impact it has had as it has displaced workers while increasing productivity.	CL - 1
09C15.C	Study patent laws in your country and the process for obtaining one.	H - 2 +
09C16.C	Study the history of computerization of industry over the last two decades. Notice and discuss how it has changed the nature of manufacturing, impacted the world economy, and affected the lives of families in your own nation and elsewhere.	CS 1 H - 1
09C17.C	Tour Greenfield Village, Menlo Park, or another museum of invention and industry.	H - 2 +

CULTURAL STUDIES

09C18.C   Study economic and social implications of the exportation of   CS   1
           jobs from the industrial giants to third world countries, noting
           how it has affected families in your own nation.

09C19. C   Add to your timeline, dates for all inventions studied in the   VA- 1
           Science section of this unit.   H- 1

09C20.D   Use Jackdaws portfolio, any good history text, and/or other   H   3
           resources to study the Industrial Revolution.

09C21.D   Examine living and working conditions of factory workers at   CS   1
           various times during and since the Industrial Revolution,
           including various reforms and the reasons for them.

09C22.D   Study the lives of Henry Ford, J. D. Rockefeller, the duPonts   H -1   each
           and other industrialists whose innovations in their own companies
           changed   the   face   of   manufacturing   and   business
           forever.

09C23.D   Study the history of labor unions, the abuses early unions   H-2
           sought to correct, and problems they created in the process.

09C24.D   Study the lives of some of the reformers of the Industrial Revolution.   H - 2
           Try   to   determine   their   motivation   for   getting   involved
           and their goals for their work.

09C25.D   Study the lives of some of the leaders of the labor union movement   H-2
           in your country and abroad.

09C26.D   Study current labor laws in your country and the history of   H- 1
           each. Include: when it was passed, the problem addressed   CL - 2
           and any new problems it may have created. Determine whether
           there was a better way to have solved the original problem.

09C27.   Make timeline entries for the major events in the lives of each   VA - 1 each
           of the authors, inventors, or artists mentioned or read in this   H-   1each
           unit.

09C28.   Make timeline entries for each person, movement and/or event   VA - 1 each
           studied in this unit.   H- 1each

09C29.   Use material studied for this unit as well as Usborne's *World*   No extra points
           History Dates, The Kingfisher History Encyclopedia, Time-   (see above for
           tables of History and/or other reference books to find the   points for time-
           information needed for making timeline entries for all the   line entries
           people, movements, and events studied in this unit.   themselves)

09C30.   Use Usborne's *World History Dates* or another source to identify   No extra points
           and make timeline entries for other important events during   (see above for
           ing each time period studied in this unit.   points for time-
                                                                                line entries)

09C31.   Make timeline entries for all inventions and/or discoveries studied
           in this unit and all major events in the lives of their inventors.   VA -1 each
                                                                                H - 1 each

CULTURAL STUDIES

09C32.	Use encyclopedias or other references to study all countries mentioned in any context within this unit.	G - 1 each
09C33.	Locate on a map or globe each country, state and/or municipality studied in this unit.	G - 2
09C36.	Study the geography of the home country of each author, inventor, or artist whose works were used or studied in this unit.	G - 1 each

READING AND LITERATURE

09R01.A	Read the Sower series book *Susanna Wesley*, or another biography of this diligent homemaker who raised 19 children for the glory of God.	H- 4
09R02.A	Read (or watch the video of) *Iron Will*, the true story of a young boy whose perseverance and diligence served him well, even in the wilds of Alaska.	B- 5
09R03.A	Read (or watch the video of) *The Miracle Worker*, the true story of a little girl and a teacher whose perseverance and diligence paid off in ways that changed their lives forever.	L- 5
09R04.A	Read and outline *What's a Smart Woman Like You Doing in a Place Like This* for more thought on how the diligent homemaker can and should make use of ALL her skills and talents, in whatever area they may fall.	HM - 5
09R05.A	Read *Christy*, a fact-based novel in which a young mission teacher's diligence to serve God changed her life and the lives of those around her.	L- 5
09R06.A	Read *Disciplines of a Beautiful Woman* to see the importance of self-discipline and organization to maintaining diligence in your work.	HM - 5
09R07.A	Read *More Hours in My Day, Sidetracked Home Executives* or another organizational manual for homemakers.	HM - 5 each
09R08.A	Read *Organizing from the Inside Out* for a slightly different take on this issue.	HM - 6
09R09.B	Read all chapters of *The Hidden Art of Homemaking* that apply to sewing or other needlework.	HM - 1
09R10.B	Read all sections of *The Foxfire Book* (any volume) that deal with spinning, weaving, sewing, knitting, or similar skills.	CC - 1
09R11.B	Read all sections of *Back to Basics* about sewing, spinning, weaving, knitting, or similar skills.	CC - 1

READING AND LITERATURE

09R12.B	Read a simple how-to guidebook on crocheting, knitting, or any other needlecraft.	CR - 3
09R13.B	Read *Threads of Love*, a Christian novel in which an estranged family is 'knit' together through an heirloom quilt.	L- 4
09R14.B	Read Lois Henderson's fictionalized biography of Priscilla and Aquila.	B - 4
09R15.B	Read *Lydia*, the fictionalized biography of this New Testament seamstress.	B - 4
09R16.B	Read all appropriate sections of *Training Our Daughters to Be Keepers at Home* for actual instructions on how to do any of the projects listed in Practical Arts for this mini-unit.	HM - 1 per chapter
09R17.C	Read *The Way Things Work*, concentrating on simple machines.	SP- 5
09R18.C	Read *Marbles, Roller Skates, Doorknobs: Simple Machines that are Really Wheels*.	SP- 3
09R19.C	Read *Seesaws, Nutcrackers, Brooms: Simple Machines that are Really Levers*.	SP - 3
09R20.C	Read any basic physics or engineering textbook or manual to learn more about how machines work.	SP - 6 +
09R21.C	Read the Sower series book *Isaac Newton* or some other biography of this early inventor.	H - 4
09R22.C	Read a biography of Leonardo DaVinci, possibly the world's most prolific inventor.	H 5
09R23.C	Read a biography of Benjamin Franklin, an inventor who may be better known for other reasons.	H - 5
09R24.C	Read *Mover of Mountains*, a biography of Christian engineer and inventor R. J. Letourneau.	H - 5
09R25.C	Read biographies of any of the other inventors whose inventions are studied in this unit.	H - 5 each
09R26.D	Read *David Copperfield, Oliver Twist, Hard Times, Nicholas Nickleby* or other Charles Dickens novels set in England during the Industrial Revolution.	L- 8 each
09R27.D	Read one or more of Horatio Alger's historical novels set during this period.	H - 5 each
09R28.D	Read other novels written and/or set during the Industrial Revolution.	H - 5 each

READING AND LITERATURE

09R29.D	Read biographies of J. D. Rockefeller, Henry Ford, Cornelius Vanderbilt, and/or other industrialists who made their fortunes during this time period.	H - 5 each
09R30.D	Read biographies of one or more labor union leaders.	H - 5 each
09R31.D	Read biographies of Jane Addams, D. L. Moody, Billy Sunday, and/or other social and spiritual reformers during the Industrial Revolution.	H - 5 each
09R32.D	Read biographies of inventors whose work helped create the mass production and industrialization that fueled the Industrial Revolution.	H - 5 each
09R33.	Read one or more other historical novels set in one of the time periods studied in this unit.	H - 5 each
09R34.	Read biographies of people in this unit.	H - 5 each
09R35.	Read at least one book per week beyond those you are doing as assignments. Choose from those listed here or in the resource list, or use any book your parents approve.	L - 5 each
09R36.	Read any other appropriate books on the subject of the mini-unit you are studying.	L - 5 each (or in subject area)

COMPOSITION

09W01.A	Write the following words into your vocabulary notebook with the exact definition: diligent, diligence, persevere, perseverance, endurance, effort, study, and conscientious. Also add these antonyms to the above words: sluggard, sloth, lazy, laziness, idleness.	EG - 1
09W02.A	Look up all the above words in your thesaurus and list, in vocabulary notebook, all synonyms of each. Define them all without using any of the synonyms in the definitions.	EG - 1
09W03.A	Write an analysis of your own life in light of the passages used for this mini-unit. Be sure to include plans for improving areas that fall short of God's standard.	EC - 1 B- 1
09W04.A	Write a report (3 - 5 pages) defining and explaining the "Puritan work ethic" and the impact it had on the economy and society in general in England, the U. S. and other countries influenced by it	EC - 2
09W05.A	Paraphrase and combine verses studied in this mini-unit to develop and write a brief (1-2 pages) exegesis of Biblical teaching on diligence and hard work.	EC - 1 B- 1

COMPOSITION

09W06.A   After studying his life in the books of Ezra and Nehemiah,   EC - 1
write a brief (1 - 2 page) character sketch of Nehemiah.

09W07.A   Write an essay on the meaning and importance of II Timothy   EC - 2
2:15 as it relates to activities other than studying. To help in
this, read the verse in various translations and/or look up 'study' in
the *Webster's 1828 Dictionary of the English Language.*

09W08.A   From your interviews with employers and the study of employee   EC - 1
handbooks in Cultural Studies, write a treatise for job seekers,
stressing the importance of diligence for getting and keeping a job.

09W09.A   Write arguments for either side of a debate on the topic, "Resolved: EC - 10
U. S. Civil Service and Other Merit Systems Encourage
Complacency of Employees."

09W10.A   Write a report (2 or more pages) on your findings with regard   EC - 1+
to productivity and diligence between employees in capitalist,
socialist, communist, and other economic systems.

09W11.A   Write a character sketch of any of the people whose biographies   EC- 1
you read (or watched on video) in the Reading and Literature
section of this mini-unit.

09W12.A   Write an announcement that might have been given to first   EC - 1
reveal the development of one of the modern conveniences that
make life easier for a diligent homemaker today.

09W13.A   Write a paper (2-3 pages) about fibromyalgia, chronic fatigue   EC - 2
syndrome, or one of the other ailments studied in Health and   HE- 1
Fitness for this mini-unit.

09W14.A   Write a letter to a young girl, stressing the importance of diligence   EC- 1
in chores and studies now and in all her duties as she grows
older.

09W15.A   Write a play or short story in which the diligence of a wife and   EC - 10 +
mother saved the day for her family and others as well.

09W16.B   Write five long, newsy letters (for five different years) that   EC - 4
Hannah might have left in the pocket of a coat she made for
Samuel each year. Make reference in each letter to his age at the
time and how long he has been gone from her. Use these letters
as a chance to explain her love for Samuel, why she left him with
Eli, her goals and desires for him, and her abiding faith in God.
You might also share news of his father and life at home in
terms understandable to a boy of each age. (Remember that
this is her only chance to communicate with him for a year;
take advantage of it.)

09W17.B   Write a play about the early life of Samuel, stressing the part   EC 15
played by his mother in making him who he was. Show the
yearly gift of a new coat as the very significant contact between
mother and son that is probably was.

COMPOSITION

09W18.B	Enlarge upon the little we know from the Bible about the life of Dorcas to write a biographical sketch (1-3 pages) about her.	EC - 1
09W19.B	Write a eulogy (about 1 page) for Dorcas as might have been given at her funeral by one of the many people she had helped over her lifetime.	EC - 1
09W20.B	From your study of Biblical occupations in the Bible and Christian Character section of this mini-unit, write a brief paragraph about each occupation related to sewing or other fabric crafts. Explain how each is done, then and now, and the common uses of each.	EC - 2
09W21.B	Write a 1-2 page report about the creation and use of various types of fabrics in each of these periods: Bible Times, Roman Empire, Middle Ages, Renaissance, American Colonies, 19th Century and 20th Century.	EC - 8
09W22.B	Write a step-by-step instructional manual to help a beginner learn some type of needlework or hand sewing.	EC - 5
09W23.B	Imagine you are a mother whose newly-married daughter is crossing the ocean or moving West on a wagon train to start her new life with her husband. Write a letter reminding her how to do the various kinds of needlework the two of you have worked on together at home over the years. Share a little of yourself in the letter as well.	EC - 1
09W24.B	Write a historical short story in which the needlecraft talents of the wife and mother had a prominent place.	EC - 15
09W25.B	Write a humorous play, puppet show, or skit related in some way to spinning, weaving, sewing, or other needlework.	EC - 10
09W26.B	Choose one of the cultures you studied in this mini-unit and write a magazine article about their choices in clothing styles, fabrics and construction.	EC - 1
09W27.B	Write copy for a TV or radio ad for an early version of any type of sewing equipment. Then write a similar ad for the most modern one, comparing it advantageously to all others.	EC - 1
09W28.B	Write a 3-5 minute persuasive speech stressing the importance of needlecraft skills even for a career woman.	EC - 3
09W29.C	Write an essay explaining why you believe God allowed machines and industry to be discovered by Cain's descendants and yet accepted and used by godly men, including Noah, before and after the flood.	EC - 2
09W30.C	Write a short story about the apostle Paul's life as a tentmaker. Set it in Bible times but allow for the use of modern equipment. Show in your story how different his life would have been.	EC - 10

COMPOSITION

09W31.C   Write a paragraph describing each Bible occupation that used   EC - 2 +
any type of machine you studied in the Cultural Studies section of
this mini-unit.

09W32.C   Write a scientific treatise on each of the simple machines and   EC - 3
the common variations on them. Explain how each works, what it
can do and how each variation enhances or changes it.

09W33.C   Write a detailed product explanation to accompany your patent   EC - 2
application for an invention that will significantly cut the
workload of full-time mothers.

09W34.C   Write a paper on the history of an industry of your choice,   EC - 10
showing how the invention or development of each new machine
changed the industry.

09W35.C   Write a biographical sketch of one of the inventors studied in   EC - 2
this mini-unit. Check *Writers Inc.* or other handbook for
information on this type of writing.

09W36.C   Write a detailed manual on the installation and/or assembly,   EC - 3+
care, maintenance, and use of any one of the inventions studied in
this mini-unit.

09W37.C   Write ads for three different versions of one machine, extolling   EC - 1
virtues of each.

09W38.C   Write a 7-10 page research paper on one of the inventions you   EC - 35
studied in this mini-unit. Use *Writer's Inc.'s* "Writing the Research
and Term Paper", or a similar reference to complete all steps in
this process, including notecards, outline, footnotes, and
bibliography.

09W39.C   Write a news report on one of the inventions in this mini-unit   EC - 1
as if done at the time of its first public unveiling.

09W40.C   Write a speech to encourage public acceptance of some 'new-   EC - 5
fangled' device that is being met with skepticism. This may be a
real item from history or one from your own imagination.

09W41.D   Write a skit or play about some important event of the Industrial   EC - 5 +
Revolution.

09W42.D   Write reports on one or more of the social reformers from the   EC - 1 each
time of the Industrial Revolution.

09W43.D   Write brief (1-2 pages) reports on each leader or other important   EC - 1 each
figure in the history of the labor union movement in your
country.

09W44.D   Write a news report of any event of the Industrial Revolution   EC - 1
as it might have been covered by the media of the day or by
today's media if they had existed.

COMPOSITION

09W45.D	Write at least ten diary entries for an immigrant factory worker during the Industrial Revolution. Write about the job, working conditions, home life, fellow workers, difficulties of adjusting to a new country, and the normal problems of life in that time and place.	EC - 2
09W46.D	Write a paper on the history and purposes of labor unions in your own country or another one of your choice.	EC - 3
09W47.D	Write a research paper on the history of one particular industry and its progress through the Industrial Revolution. Use *Writing the Term or Research Paper* or a similar guideline to include notecards, footnotes, bibliography, etc.	EC - 30
09W48.D	Write a speech that might be given to sway votes either way in a decision of whether to unionize the employees of a real or imaginary company.	EC 5
09W49.D	Write brief (1-2 pages) reports or biographical sketches on any or all of the industrialists studied in Cultural Studies of this mini-unit.	EC- 1
09W50.D	Write a paper explaining the Bible's stance on invention and skilled craftsmanship as studied in the Bible and Christian Character section of this mini-unit. Relate this to the apparent blessing of God upon the Industrial Revolution.	EC - 1 B- 1
09W51.D	Write an essay comparing the Industrial Revolution with the 'revolution' of the Electronic Age, which occurred in the last two decades of the 20th Century.	EC - 1
09W52.D	Write a first-person short story about a Christian family whose breadwinner lost his job due to the automation of his work place. Stress the strain of not having work, the difficulty of retraining for some other type work and the way a family must pull together to make it through the crisis.	EC- 5
09W53.D	Keep a diary (10 or more entries) for an immigrant to America who ends up working in a 'sweatshop'. Research to accurately compare this to the life (s)he left behind. Share the worker's dreams for a better life as well as the drudgery of the daily grind.	EC - 2+
09W54.	Define and put into your vocabulary notebook 10 new words per week, using first those you have encountered in your studies For each entry, write all possible definitions and pronunciations.	EG - 1 per week
09W55.	Learn to spell all the words in your vocabulary notebook for this unit.	EG - 2 per week
09W56.	Using *Writers Inc., College English Handbook*, or other grammar reference, proofread and correct all written work for this unit.	EG - 1 per 4 pages

COMPOSITION

09W57.   Use a good dictionary to proofread all written work in this unit and correct it for errors in spelling.   EG - 1 per 4 pages

09W58.   Keep a journal of each day's school activities throughout this curriculum. If done well, this journal can serve as documentation of your school year.   EC - 2 per week

09W59.   As you listen to any of the suggested audios in this unit, take notes.   EG-2 each

09W60.   Use your notes to outline, summarize, and/or discuss the audios as requested.   EC-1+each

09W61.   Outline one or more of the nonfiction books used in this unit.   EG-5 each

09W62.   Instead of, or in addition to, outlining the books studied here, write reviews of them, like those that might be published in a periodical of some type.   EC-1 each

09W63.   Write a brief report on any important person studied in this unit.   EC - 1 each

09W64.   Use any Scripture passage, poem or other material you are memorizing to copy for handwriting practice.   EG - 1 per hour

09W65.   Use the Scripture from this unit to practice writing from dictation, being careful about spelling, punctuation, etc.   EG - 1 per hour

09W66.   As an alternative to cursive writing, try Italic or Spencerian calligraphy using books in the resource list.   1 credit for Complete course

09W67.   Write a news article on each of the field trips you took in this unit.   EC-1 each

09W68.   Write a thank you note to the organizer, supervisor, and/or guide of any field trip you took for this unit.   EC-1 each

09W69.   Write summaries of any or all of the books read in this unit.   EC-1 each

09W70.   Write reports on any or all of the men or women studied in the unit.   EC-1 each

09W71.   Write one book report per week on a book related to this unit or another approved by parents. Use a variety of approaches, including any or all of those listed in the Appendix.   EC-1 each

MATHEMATICS AND PERSONAL FINANCE

09M01.A   Study and write an essay on the need for a woman to study math diligently and how its use can affect her ability to perform the basic skills of homemaking.   EC - 2

MATHEMATICS AND PERSONAL FINANCE

09M02.A   Using data available from the Chamber of Commerce, the   CE- 1
Business Council, Commerce Department or similar agencies,   M - 1
compute the relationship between productivity per man-
hour, Gross National Product (GNP), median salaries in
industry, and average per capita income across the board.

09M03.A   Graph the above information to show the relationships   M - 5
computed.

09M04.A   Practice your assigned supplementary math lessons diligently   M - 1 per
for at least 30 minutes each day.   hour

09M05.A   Brainstorm and mind map all uses of mathematics made by   HM - 1
the diligent homemaker in the course of a day.

09M06.B   Use the study of sewing to learn and memorize the various   M - 2
English and metric units of measure and the relationships
between them. Practice converting between metric and English
units of measure and memorize the formula for each conversion.

09M07.B   Learn to read and use size & measurement charts on the back   HM - 1
of pattern packages, working in both English and metric units.

09M08.B   Learn the correct way and place to take all of your body measurements   HE - 1
and the various tools available to do it. Practice taking your
own and someone else's.

09M09.B   Use your math skills to alter patterns that aren't the exact   M - 1
size for the person who will be wearing the garment.

09M10.C   Using data supplied by manufacturers, compare productivity   M - 6
levels of different brands of several types of machines or other
mechanical devices. Present this data on a graph of some type.

09M11.C   Compare prices and features on the machines priced in the   M - 3
above activity and do the necessary calculations to see which
of these would be the best buy for your family or company.

09M12.C   Use mathematical formulae to create scale models of any or   M- 1
all of the machines studied in this unit.   IA - 3

09M13.C   Compare horsepower (or other measure) of output to wattage   HM 1
of electricity usage on a variety of common household appliances   M - 1
and machines and do the necessary calculations to determine
fuel or energy efficiency for each.

09M14.C   Prepare a graph or statistical analysis of the fuel or energy   M- 5
efficiency of the above machines relative to one another.

09M15.D   Determine the cost of living in each decade during and since   M - 7
the Industrial Revolution by researching average prices on a
variety of common purchases. Compare this data to determine
the relative cost of living and record on some type of graph.

MATHEMATICS AND PERSONAL FINANCE

09M16.D	Compare and graph the average wage, average workweek, and average per capita income in each decade since the beginning of the Industrial Revolution.	M-5
09M17.D	After studying the history of the time, calculate the relative costs in man-hours at the going wage (then and now) of producing each of several common products by hand in small quantities and with the mass production made possible by the Industrial Revolution.	M - 2
09M18.D	Compare wholesale and retail prices for a number of printed or manufactured items in varying quantities and discuss with someone in the business why volume buying produces such discounts. Calculate the percentage saved at each larger quantity level.	CE - 1 M-1
09M19.	Continue to review basic math.	M-1 per hr.
09M20.	Use data from any of the graphs you make or study in this mini-unit to practice calculating per cent, ratio and proportion.	M - 1

SCIENCE

09S01.A	List the items in your home that make life easier for the diligent homemaker of today than it was in Bible times.	HM - 1
09S02.A	Determine and list all raw materials used to make each of the items listed in the previous activity.	SP 2
09S03.A	Study all of the materials and scientific processes used to produce each of the modern conveniences listed in #09S01. Include all possible options where available.	SP - 1 each
09S04.A	Study different power sources available for each of devices named above and determine which is best for each.	SP - 2
09S05.A	Study how each of the above machines operate and what they accomplish when used with diligence. Explain this in paragraph or diagram form for each.	SP 1 each
09S06.A	Use materials from County Extension Service or other sources to study ants and determine why Proverbs 6 tells us to learn of them and emulate them.	SB - 1
09S07.A	Study the Pulitzer Prize winning book, *Journey to the Ants: A Story of Scientific Exploration.*	SB - 3
09S08.A	Build an ant farm with a kit or directions from *Science Projects on File* or similar book. Watch and study the ants and their underground world and draw a diagram of their "building scheme. Notice how hard they work and how quickly the tunnels get built.	SB - 3

SCIENCE

09S09.B	Study the construction and use of the spindle and distaff in Bible times and compare to equipment used for the same purposes today.	SP- 1 H - 1
09S10.B	Study and compare the weaving loom of Bible times to the equipment used for commercial and family weaving today.	SP - 1 H - 1
09S11.B	Study the variety of sewing machines available today and compare the suitability of each for each specific task.	SP - 1 HM - 1
09S12.B	Study composition and construction of various kinds of sewing needles available today. Compare these to the limited variety available when they were made by hand by blacksmiths.	SP - 1
09S13.B	Study the tools and processes used at various times in history to produce needles and similar equipment.	SP - 1
09S14.B	Study the construction and operating principles of all other sewing or fabric construction equipment.	SP - 2
09S15.B	Study the differences in woven and knitted fabrics and the varieties of each. Determine the suitability of different fabrics for different purposes.	SP - 2
09S16.C	For an introduction to the ideas of this mini-unit, watch the video *Work, Power, and Energy* by Science Videos.	SP- 1
09S17.C	Use one or more of the books in the Reading and Literature section of this mini-unit or any similar resource to study the four types of simple machines: pulley, lever and fulcrum, inclined plane, and wheel and axle.	SP - 4
09S18.C	To approach this topic in another way, watch the video *Machines*, produced by Science Videos.	SP - 1
09S19.C	Examine all tools and appliances in your home to determine which of these simple machines is the basis for each.	SP- 3
09S20.C	Investigate these machines further with the interactive CD-ROM version of *The Way Things Work*.	SP - 2+
09S21.C	Use the book *Invention and Discovery* to find out when and by whom each of the above pieces of household equipment was first invented as well as all improvements that led to the form in which we use it today.	H - 2
09S22.C	Tour a manufacturing facility and make a note of all the machines used there.	SP - 2
09S23.C	Make a chart of all machines used in the factory you toured showing which simple machine is the basis for each.	SP - 1

SCIENCE

09S24.C	Using *How Things Work* or a similar resource, study all the machines used in the factory you toured to learn how each is made and how it works.	SP- 1+
09S25.C	In *Forces and Motion* from the Dr. Liem's Science Book series, complete the units on: torque, friction, simple machines, inertia, and Newton's Laws.	SP - 3
09S26.D	Study the equipment and processes used to create the assembly line that first generated mass production.	SP- 1
09S27.D	Study the conveyor belt and how it is used in a assembly lines and other applications.	SP - 1
09S28.D	Study the steam engine and machinery powered by it now and in the past.	SP- 1+
09S29.D	Study changes in transportation due to the invention of the steam engine, and how this new source of power influenced the growth of factories.	H - 2
09S30. D	Study the construction of the electric motor and how it works to power devices. Compare uses and efficiency of this motor with muscle-driven and steam-powered engines of the past.	SP- 2
09S31.D	Study the design and construction of factories now and at the height of the Industrial Revolution. Determine what factors brought about the changes in modern plants.	H - 1 ST- 1
09S32.D	Study schematics and descriptions of all machines and equipment included in the Jackdaws portfolio on the Industrial Revolution.	ST - 2+
09S33.D	Read and discuss with a Christian adult, the book *God in the Machine*.	SP- 1+
09S34.D	Tour a large, modern factory and notice how many jobs are fully-automated and operated by computer, thereby cutting the work force needed to run the plant.	CS - SP-

HEALTH AND FITNESS

09H01.A	Study the importance of diligence in any fitness or exercise program.	HE- 1
09H02.A	Prepare or have a personal trainer prepare a fitness program just for you and arrange for some form of accountability to insure that you practice your program diligently.	PE - 1+

HEALTH AND FITNESS

09H03.A   Study in medical journals and learn the symptoms of chronic   HE - 1
fatigue syndrome, fibromyalgia, and other ailments that can
thwart efforts to be diligent.

09H04.A   Talk with people who have these ailments and list the major   HE - 1
drawbacks they mention to their own diligent work.

09H05.A   Learn correct treatment for each of the above diseases to allow   HE - 1+
for maximum diligent activity in spite of the illness.

09H06.A   Investigate the effect of emotions on physical health, and list   HE - 1
the positive health benefits of the satisfaction one gets from a job
well done.

09H07.A   Study psychosomatic ailments that could cause someone,   HE - 1
consciously or not, to be a less than diligent worker. Devise ways
to help those who suffer from these ailments to understand and
cope with them while still diligently pursuing their work.

09H08.B   Take tests to measure hand strength and grip, and hand-eye   HE - 1+
coordination, all of which affect the ability to do handicrafts.

09H09.B   Learn to administer and evaluate the above tests, giving them   HE-1 each
to at least one person correctly.

09H10.B   Learn and faithfully follow exercises and other activities to   PE   1 per
improve any deficiencies shown by the tests above.   hour

09H11.B   Study perception and visual acuity as they relate to the skills   HE - 1
needed for needlework.

09H12.B   Take a common test for identifying any perceptual problems   HE - 1
that might affect your ability to do needlework or similar crafts.

09H13.B   Study pamphlets and brochures from a doctor on the various types   HE - 1+
of arthritis, including carpal tunnel syndrome and brainstorm as to
how those would affect one's ability to do handicrafts.

09H14.B   Take an eye test to find any vision problems that might make   HE - 1
needlework hard for you to do.

09H15.B   Study hand dominance and the genetic and anatomical factors   HE- 1
that seem to determine or cause it.

09H16.C   Study the machines used in the diagnosis of disease. You   SP - 2+
should include x-ray, EEG, EKG, CAT scan, sonogram and MRI
equipment, as well as others you may discover.

09H17.C   Study the use of machines in preparing, preserving, and   SP- 1
distributing medicines and health products of various kinds.

09H18.C   Study other machines used by doctors and hospitals for   SP - 1
treatment of disease.

HEALTH AND FITNESS

09H19.C	Study the mechanisms of hospital beds and other appliances used to keep patients comfortable during illness but not directly related to treatment.	SP - 1
09H20.C	Study wheelchairs and other 'machines' that make life easier for the disabled.	SP- 1
09H21.C	Study the use of wheels, levers, pulleys, and other simple machines in physical therapy.	SP - I
09H22.C	Study physical therapy by taking an introductory course or studying a book.	1 credit for Complete course
09H23.D	Study consumption, now known TB or tuberculosis, which showed a dramatic increase in large cities during the Industrial Revolution. Explain why this was true.	HE - I
09H24.D	Study the various tests given to detect tuberculosis.	HE - 1
09H25.D	Study influenza, which first appeared in the early 20th Century among urban factory workers who were forced together in poorly ventilated buildings for long periods of time. Discuss how this environment bred this illness.	HE - 1
09H26.D	Study other airborne communicable diseases that spread quickly in crowded, closed quarters.	HE - 1
09H27.D	Study occupational health standards, including building codes, that have been passed to prevent the spread of diseases in the work place.	CG - 2
09H28.D	Study smog and other air pollutants emitted by modern factories and health problems associated with them	SE - I

PRACTICAL ARTS

09P01.A	Discuss with parents what household chores they wish you to do and how often each is to be done. Then, prepare a schedule to do them all in a consistent, diligent manner.	HM - 2
09P02.A	Read one or more of Don Aslett's cleaning manuals to learn the easiest way to do various homemaking chores and begin doing them that way. Discuss with your mother how knowing the best way to do something makes it easier to be diligent.	HM - 4
09P03.A	Learn to personalize and use Microsoft Outlook or some other computerized scheduler to remind you of chores and appointments, thus helping you to be more diligent in your work.	CO - 1
09P04.A	Purchase and set up a personal organizer to keep your appointments and other tasks organized so you can be more diligent. Fill in all daily and/or weekly tasks, regular classes, meetings and/or appointments, and your school schedule. Add to it regularly as other appointments and activities arise.	BE - I

PRACTICAL ARTS

09P05.A	Time yourself one morning as you complete all your daily chores. Then try using a timer each day for a week or two to see if you can improve your previous time without sacrificing quality in the work. You may be surprised to find how much time you have been wasting even when you thought you were being diligent.	HM- 1
09P06.A	Follow any or all other suggestions for organizing your home found in any of the books in the Reading and Literature section of this unit.	Parent's discretion
09P07.A	With your parents' permission, choose your own assignments throughout this unit and do them each week without reminders from your parents. Check each week to be sure you have the correct amount of work and that you have included all subjects required by your parents. Ask a parent for an evaluation of your work at the end of each week, and strive to improve any problem areas.	Parent's discretion
09P08.A	Diligently pursue all your chores for one month and have your parents critique your efforts. Discuss with them areas where you need to be more diligent, and ask God to help you do it.	HM - 1 per hour Worked
09P09. B	Spin thread from wool, flax, or cotton, using various types of equipment.	CC - 1
09P10.B	Make a weaving loom, using directions from *The Foxfire Book* or *Back to Basics*.	IA - 2+
09P11.B	Weave a piece of cloth large enough to make a garment for yourself.	CC - 5+
09P12.B	Analyze a large number of patterns from the books at your fabric center and choose one that you believe will look becoming to you. Find your pattern in the cupboard or drawer and determine your correct size from the measurements listed on back.	CC - 1
09P13.B	Examine a variety of fabrics to use for making the garment you selected. Take into account weight, texture, seasonal considerations, style of garment, nap or directional print, if any, and cost per yard. Find and read care instructions on the fabric bolt to decide if you can care for the finished garment properly. Choose your fabric and measure how much you need and what that will cost.	CC - 2
09P14.B	Read directions on a given pattern and decide which layout to use for which types and/or sizes of fabric and how to proceed for each pattern view shown. Study each step in the process from *Training Our Daughters to be Keepers at Home* or a similar book.	CC - 3+
09P15.B	Instead of the three previous activities, make a garment for yourself (from cloth you wove, if possible). Do all steps from start to finish.	CC - 10

PRACTICAL ARTS

09P16.B	If you are not making a garment at this time, observe all the steps in doing it by watching someone else. Ask questions as needed to learn what to do and why.	CC - 2
09P17.B	Learn to do a variety of mending tasks, by hand and with a machine. Include split straight seams, loose hems, lost buttons, and broken or jammed zippers, as well as others you would like to learn.	CC - 1 per hour to a maximum of 10
09P18.B	Decorate the garment you made or a bought one with smocking, tatting, or appliqué as appropriate to the item.	CC - 2+
09P19.B	Embroider, cross-stitch or needlepoint one pillow, pillowcase, or wall hanging.	HM - 4+
09P20.B	Learn to knit or crochet and make one simple item, such as a scarf, a table runner, coasters or a cozy.	HM - 4+
09P21.C	Design and build one device based on a lever and fulcrum that can be used to accomplish regular, mundane tasks in or around your home.	IA- 2+
09P22.C	Design and build one devise based on a wheel and axle that can perform some needed task in or around your home.	IA- 2+
09P23.C	Design and build one devise based on or utilizing a pulley that can perform some needed task in or around your home.	IA - 2+
09P24.C	Build a ramp (inclined plane) to make a church building, home, or other facility more accessible for the mobility-impaired.	IA- 5
09P25.C	Learn to use a variety of wheeled tools and devices for working around your home.	IA - 1 per hour
09P26.C	Learn to use screwdrivers and drills and try to determine which simple machine forms the basis for them.	IA - 1
09P27.C	Learn to use claw hammers, crowbars and other hand tools that are based on the lever.	IA- 1
09P28.C	Use Lego Technics, Construx, or similar materials to build a device using at least two of the simple machines and designed to perform some specific task in or around your home.	SP - 1 IA - 3
09P29.C	Build and learn to use the mechanical scale from the "Woodkrafter Kit" of that name.	IA - 3
09P30.C	Design a new invention based on some simple machine that will solve a problem or perform a task in your home or family business.	IA - 3+

PRACTICAL ARTS

09P31.D	Learn to clean a variety of the equipment used in the factory where you worked or observed. Be sure to take whatever measures are necessary to preserve your and others' safety and to maintain the machines in good working order.	IA or BE- 1 per hour
09P32.D	Volunteer or get a temporary job in a large manufacturing plant and learn as many of the jobs there as possible.	IA - 1 / hr. up to 5 / job
09P33.D	Contact your country's patent office to obtain and fill out a patent application for your invention.	CG- 1
09P34.D	Perform a safety inspection of your family's or a friend's business, using the occupational health and safety standards currently in use by your nation's health and safety agencies.	BE - 1
09P35.D	Obtain and complete an application for a work permit whether or not you actually have a job. (You should be the one to locate the form, pick it up, fill out all sections to be done by the student, and make arrangements for others to fill out their appropriate sections.) If you do not have a real job, have the sections filled out for practice.	BE - 1
09P36.D	Build a conveyor belt and learn to use it to make some household job easier.	IA- 1
09P37.D	Organize an assembly line of siblings or friends to make some multifaceted chore easier and faster. Complete the chore to get the points.	IA- 1 / hour of chore (min. of 1)
09P38.D	Shop for jewelry, clothing, and/or gifts in several different stores, comparing prices and quality between handmade items and those that were mass-produced in a factory. Discuss with parents if (or when) having an original one-of-a-kind item is important enough to pay the difference. Do not do this activity online as you cannot compare quality as well.	CE 1
09P39.	If you don't already know how to create and use a computer database, you may wish to learn in this unit so you can use the skill in later units of this study	CO - 6
09P40.	Create and maintain a database to assist you as appropriate in this unit.	CO - 2+
09P41.	Type all written work for this mini-unit. If you do not know how to type, now is the time to learn.	BE - 1 per 4 pages
09P42.	If needed, take a class, follow a computerized, written or video tutorial, or an online course in typing, keyboarding, and/or word processing.	1/2 credit in Typing or Keyboarding
09P43.	Create a computer website to display what you learned in this mini-unit.	CO - 1+

PRACTICAL ARTS

09P44.   Frame and/or mat one or more of the pictures or posters you   CR- 2
drew or created in the Decorative and Performing Arts section   each
of this mini-unit.

09P45.   Make your own costumes for any performances you chose to   CC - 5 +
do in the Decorative and Performing Arts section of this mini-   each
unit or plays you wrote in the Composition section.

DECORATIVE AND PERFORMING ARTS

09A01.A   Use clip art or magazine cutouts to create a collage or   VA - 2
montage of the work of a diligent homemaker.

09A02.A   Use calligraphy and/or original artwork to design a poster of   VA- 1
II Timothy 2:15.

09A03.A   Video a day in the life of your mother or another diligent   DR - 2+
homemaker, narrating as you go. Add captions, narration, music,
etc. to produce a documentary on the life of a keeper at home. Edit
as needed to produce a commercial-quality video to be shown to
your support group or other suitable audiences.

09A04.A   Attend a live performance or watch a video of the theatrical   DR - 2
version of *The Miracle Worker*.

09A05.A   Play a role, direct, or otherwise participate in a performance of   DR - 1/2
The Miracle Worker.   credit

09A06.A   Use the medium of your choice to create a mural of the life of   VA   1+
a diligent worker in the home.

09A07.B   Design an original pattern to use for embroidery or painting   CC - 2
on clothing or other items you made in this mini-unit.

09A08.B   Draw sketches of all of your completed needlework projects   VA- 1
from the Practical Arts section of this mini-unit. Keep these   each
in a portfolio for future reference.

09A09.B   Take your own pictures and create a photo montage of all the   VA - 2
garments and other items you made in the Practical Arts section
of this mini-unit.

09A10.B   Tour an exhibit of tapestry, crewel, or other fabric art.   AA - 2

09A11.B   Use airbrush, stamping, or other process to paint a picture or   VA- 2
design on one of the garments or other items you made in this
mini-unit.

09A12.C   Draw pictures of each of the simple machines you have studied   VA- 1
in this unit and enhance them with designs or embellishments   each
of your choice.

DECORATIVE AND PERFORMING ARTS

09A13.C	Use your art skills to illustrate the instruction booklet you wrote for the Composition section of this mini-unit.	VA - 4+
09A14.C	Complete the *Great Inventors and Inventions Coloring Book.*	VA-5 & H-5
09A15.C	Use stencils, sponge paint, or any other media to decorate one or more of the machines you built in the Practical Arts section of this mini-unit.	VA - 1 each
09A16.C	Draw a complete schematic for your invention, which could be sold as plans to those who might want to make one. (If you ever plan to patent your invention, be careful not to show or give this drawing to anyone who might copy it and/or use it without permission.)	VA- 1 CR - 1
09A17.C	Examine the various instruments used in a band or orchestra and determine which ones were based on one of the simple machines you studied in this mini-unit.	MA - 1 DR - 3
09A18.D	Watch a live or videotaped theatrical performance of *Oliver*, based loosely on *Oliver Twist*, a novel about life during the Industrial Revolution in England.	
09A19.D	Listen to 10-12 American folk songs from this period dealing with topics related to industry and commerce and discuss the purpose they served in the lives of the working men of that era. Some examples are: 'I've Been Working on the Railroad', `16 Tons', 'John Henry' The Erie Canal'. See if you can find and study others.	MA - 2 H - 1
09A20.D	Learn to sing all verses of one or more of the above folk songs well enough to perform for a group.	VM - 3 each
09A21.D	Learn to play one or more of the above songs on your instrument of choice.	IM - 3 each
09A22.D	Learn to sing one or more of the songs from the musical *Oliver*.	VM - 3 each
09A23.	Draw pictures of any field trips you took in this mini-unit.	VA- 1 each
09A24.	Use drawing, painting and graphic arts to create displays and make posters as called for in this study.	VA 1 each
09A25.	Illustrate one or more of the poems you studied or memorized for this unit.	VA 1 each
09A26.	Set one or more of this unit's poems to music, using an original or existing tune.	VA - 1 each
09A27.	Set one or more of the Scripture verses in this unit to music, using a tune you wrote for the purpose.	MC - 5 each

UNIT 10

She extends her hand to the poor.
Yes, she reaches out her hands to the needy.
Proverbs 31:20

Overview

The thrust of this verse is to emphasize the importance of charity and sharing with others. This verse praises the godly woman for a giving spirit and the willingness to follow through in helping others. This verses leads us to look at what the Bible says here and elsewhere about giving of both our substance and ourselves to the Lord and His people, with a special look at practical ways to help those in need around us. It is clear that this woman did that in her daily life. We will discuss the dual Biblical concepts of stewardship and tithing, which seems to go hand in hand with this topic.

The topic of this verse has been expanded to include a look at social programs, both public and private, which are designed to help people with special needs, those referred to by this passage as the needy'. It is our goal to train you to determine from Scripture whether a program is run according to God's standards and to differentiate between the correct realms of government, church, and family in administering help as God outlines it in His Word. You will also look at the Bible's guidelines with regard to who is entitled to such help and what they should be required to do to get it. You will then be asked to analyze programs available in your community by the above guidelines. All of this will help you in striving to emulate the `rubies' woman while not giving to an unworthy cause.

As with many Biblical character traits, one of the best ways to learn this is through examples, both positive and negative, from history. For this reason, this unit will lead you to look at the lives of some of the world's foremost philanthropists and social reformers (especially Christians) who made an impact among the needy of the world. To analyze the causes of poverty and find solutions to it, you will study unemployment, inflation, national debt, and other economic problems of families and nations as well as the life-styles of people in areas where poverty is rampant. You will also learn the history of successful and failed domestic and foreign aid and social services programs, many of which originated during the Great Depression of the 1930's. As this depression was sandwiched between and related to the two World Wars, we have included them in this unit. By understanding the causes and results of these wars, you should be better able to understand much of what is happening in the world today.

The true object of this unit is to encourage you, the student, to get involved in helping others. In addition to learning the Biblical reasons for kindness to the poor, and the actual make up of structures which do that, we recommend hands-on experience. In that vein, this unit suggests numerous opportunities for you to serve others, alone or with your family or homeschool group. All students are strongly encouraged to do this part of the curriculum by choosing and participating in one or more of the volunteer opportunities listed.

Mini-Units

Mini-Units contained in this unit are:

A. Poverty, Charity, and Welfare

B. The Great Depression

C. The War to End All Wars (WW I)

D. The Next Great War (WW II)

Each thematic mini-unit is described and designated with a letter of the alphabet in the following paragraphs. Individual activities designed for use in one particular mini-unit will be marked with those letters. (For further help with this, please refer to the explanation of mini-units in the Guidelines section of this unit study guide.)

A. Poverty, Charity, and Welfare

This mini-unit addresses the issue of poverty and how to alleviate it. You will look at the Bible's teaching on the topic, both in terms of whom we are to help and how we are to do it. In light of the Scripture passages you will study, you will examine a variety of church, government, and private antipoverty programs, to determine how each measures up to God's standards for charity. You will look at, not only the program itself, but how it is administered, how well it is working, and whether it is Biblical.

You will also study the major causes of poverty and programs aimed at correcting those at their roots. This will include looking at economic development efforts in third world countries, recovery of areas where the economy has been slow, literacy and training efforts in areas of widespread illiteracy, and similar 'bootstrap' programs. You will try to determine which areas need the most help and why, as well as most effective ways to offer this help. Another area of concern in this section will be the environmental problems often faced by very poor areas and ways they can be addressed.

You will study agencies, organizations and individuals devoted to the battle against poverty. In this context, you will learn about the laws of your nation with regard to assistance to the poor or those with specialized needs, and how well these laws are enforced. You will also look at government subsidies and entitlements, including the negative aspects of fraud and abuses within them.

This mini-unit will also look at the lives of many of the world's foremost philanthropists and social reformers and of Christians who have made an impact among the poor and needy of the world. In analyzing the causes of poverty, we look at unemployment, inflation, national debt, and other economic problems of families and nations. We will also try to examine the life-styles of people in countries where poverty is rampant, in an effort to find ways to help those people help themselves

You will study the history of domestic and foreign aid and social services programs, most of which originated during the Great Depression of the 1930's. As this depression was sandwiched between and related to the two World Wars, we have included them in this mini-unit. By understanding the causes and results of these wars, you should be better able to understand much of what is happening in the world today.

Mini-Units

This mini-unit offers many opportunities for you to be active in reaching out to the poor or other needy, through volunteer projects of various kinds. We highly recommend that all students take part in one or more of these activities or similar ones designed by you or your family. This will give you a chance to share God's love with others through material gifts and the ministry of helps.

B. The Great Depression

The Great Depression of the 1930's (mostly) affected the majority of the world and brought about many of the government welfare programs operating in most of the Western World today. For that reason, it is an important part of any study of poverty and antipoverty programs. You will learn which programs began then, what they were attempting to do, and how they measure up to God's standards for such things.

This unit will examine the conditions of the world economy prior to this Depression and the probable causes of it. In this context, you will learn about the economic indicators used to determine when an economy is in a depression, recession, or downturn. This will allow you to analyze your own nation's economic indicators and see if another depression might be looming on the horizon.

You will analyze the extent of the Great Depression in various nations of the world and various approaches taken to try to end it, all of which were, at best, only partially successful. This emphasis will include studying the ideas and efforts of heads of state of various nations during the time period before and during the Great Depression and those who advised or assisted them. Though concentrating on their handling of the depressed economy, you will learn about their lives and their beliefs on other issues as well. In addition, you will study the lives of social reformers and activists outside the government itself whose activities had a major impact on the society of this day.

C. The War to End All Wars

Since World War I was one of the events that brought about the Great Depression, this seems the logical place to study that war. It also seems logical to study the two World Wars together as they were closely related. However, due to size constraints and historical chronology, we have separated the two Wars into two mini-units. Your family may choose to do them together, which is certainly permissible. Throughout this study, you will be asked to make many comparisons between the two wars, which can be done as you go or added when both mini-units are finished.

Your study of this 'Great War' will include the actual battles and those who fought them, of course. Yet, it will be much more far-reaching than that. You will study the various nations involved, as they were when the War began, how their actions or conditions contributed to the onset of war, and how the War affected the size or condition of the nations.. This will include a look at the major political and military figures of this time period, relating how each contributed to the beginning arid/or end of the conflict.

You will examine the motives of those who entered this war on either side and the conviction many of them had that this war was necessary to make war obsolete from that point forward. In this context, you will examine plans for the League of Nations and the factors that kept it from succeeding.

Mini-Units

D. The Next Great War

You will see how God used the Second World War to end the Great Depression and bring stability to the world economy, in spite of the ravages of war on some parts of the world. This will include a look at the economic conditions of various nations leading up to and during this conflict and how those conditions influenced the drive toward war.

You will study political and military alliances and actions that contributed to the war and the direction it took. This will include a look at each warring nation and the military and political leaders of each as well as the governmental systems and ideologies that made them `tick'. This will include an investigation of the Holocaust and other evils connected with this war. Parents may wish to temper some of this for your own benefit. Please honor their wishes.

A major part of this study will be the actual battles and takeovers that occurred and the people involved in them. You will learn how various countries coped with being invaded or conquered and how those that never suffered either came to the aid of the beleaguered ones. This will include many examples of true heroism on various fronts.

The most important part of this study for you, the godly, young woman, is to look at life on the home front in your nation. You will see how women of your country participated in the war effort and how that changed their corporate lives forever. This will include war bonds, volunteer aid to soldiers and their families, women replacing men in the work force, rationing of household needs, and those women who served in various capacities alongside the men at the front. Your goal will be to develop a firm belief with regard to how a woman can and should serve her country.

BIBLE AND CHRISTIAN CHARACTER

10B01.A	Study all Old Testament verses dealing with charity or giving of alms.	B 2
10B02.A	Study I Corinthians 13 and relate it to the theme of this mini-unit.	B 1
10B03.A	Study the institution and function of deacons in the book of Acts.	B - 1
10B04.A	Study the poor tithe (tax) of Old Testament Israel and determine how this relates to Social Security and/or welfare today.	B - 1
10B05.A	Study all other Old Testament laws that relate to the poor and their relief.	B - 2
10B06.A	Study all New Testament commands with regard to the treatment of the poor.	B - 2
10B07.A	Compare your church's benevolence policy to the Scripture verses you have read on this topic.	B - 1

BIBLE AND CHRISTIAN CHARACTER

10B08.A	Take a look at the people with whom you come in contact daily and single out any who have special needs. Ask God to show you how you can serve each of them.	B - 1

10B09.B   Study and memorize Malachi 3:10-13 and discuss with your parents what bearing this may have had on the severity of the Great Depression in countries that called themselves 'Christians'.   B - 1

10B10.B   Use your concordance to look up and study famines of Biblical times. Compare each to the Great Depression and discuss whether you think they could have been similar punishments for similar reasons.   B- 3

10B11.B   Read the book of Jeremiah and compare the people of his day and nation with the overall life-style of the United States and other industrialized nations in the decade prior to the Great Depression. Discuss and decide if you believe that the Depression could have been a punishment on Western society like the one on Israel discussed in Jeremiah.   B- 4

10B12.B   In your study of New Deal agencies and programs as outlined in the Cultural Studies section of this mini-unit, compare each to Scriptural guidelines regarding poverty relief and working for your living. Determine what programs did or did not offer the acceptable kinds of help, according to God's Word.   CS-1

10B13.B   Study the above agencies in light of Scriptural teachings on the proper role of government to determine which ones are and are not valid.   CS-1

10B14.B   Study the Old Testament principle of the Sabbath year (one in seven) in which everything should lay fallow and unused. Many people believe that our unwillingness to honor God in that as a nation led to the Great Depression in which the Lord forced a whole economy to 'lay fallow'. After studying this concept, discuss it with your parents.   B-1

10B15.B   Study the Biblical farming guidelines in Leviticus 19 and 25 and analyze the situation in the Dust Bowl of the 1930's to see if following these 'laws' could have prevented what happened there.   B-2

10B16.C   Study the battle for Jericho as told in the book of Joshua, noting what God told the Israelites to do to the city's residents when it fell. Learn as much as you can about the residents of Jericho to learn why God made such a strong command. Do any of these reasons apply to the involvement of your country in WWI.   B-2

10B17.C   Study God's instructions to Gideon with regard to the Midianites and his battle against them in Judges 6-7. Discuss with your parents if this type of battle against oppression explains why your nation or any of the major combatants got involved in WWI.   B-1

BIBLE AND CHRISTIAN CHARACTER

10B18.C	Use your concordance to look up and study other passages in which God defends or commands war for His people. Compile a list of these for a later project.	B-2
10B19.C	Based on the above passages and others that talk of Christians as peacemakers, discuss with your parents when (or if) it would be acceptable (or even required) for a Christian to fight in a war.	13-2
10B20.C	Based on the passages studied in this mini-unit, determine and discuss with parents whether or not WWI was a 'just' war in which Christians should have been involved. Prepare to present your answer as a paper or in another format in a later activity.	B-2
10B21.D	Repeat 10B16. 10B17 and 10B20 with regard to WWII, and discuss with parents the validity of Christians getting involved in it, on either side.	B-2
10B22.D	Study and memorize Psalm 24:11-12, passages used by many Christians to justify their involvement on the side of the Allies in WWII. Discuss with your parents the validity of this belief.	B-1
10B23.D	Study all passages in Scripture that teach about the rite of circumcision, one of the things used to single out Jewish men during the Holocaust.	13-4
(10B24.D)	Many Christians rallied to fight the Nazis and help rescue Jews from persecution primarily from the belief that they (the Jews) were still God's chosen people. After reading chapters 2 through 8 of Romans, discuss and decide if this is a valid belief. Support all conclusions with quotes from specific Scripture passages.	B-8
10B25.D	Study, analyze and memorize Psalm 144: 1-2, in which we are told that God trains His people in warfare. Explain in light of all other passages discussed in this mini-unit and the previous one.	B-1
10B26.	Meditate on and memorize one or more of the passages studied in the mini-unit.	B-1 per 3 verses
(10B27.)	Read through the book of Proverbs each month, reading the chapter to coincide with each date.	B-3 per week
(10B28.)	Continue reading through the Bible at a rate of 1-5 chapters per day. If you use *The Daily Bible* or some other version designed specifically for that purpose, their daily readings will take you through the entire Bible in one year. You may follow a pattern of your own at a different rate if you like. Using a chronologically arranged Bible offers the added benefit of putting your reading in perspective as to time frame.	B-1 credit When completed

BIBLE AND CHRISTIAN CHARACTER

| 10B29. | Continue (or begin) to keep your prayer journal, listing each day (or as the Lord brings to mind) prayer requests, needs in your spiritual life and things God is teaching you. Continue this throughout all units. | B-2 per week |

CULTURAL STUDIES

| 10C01.A | Study chapters 9 and 10 of *God and Government,* and complete all activities. Answer all chapter questions in writing or discuss them with your parents. | CG-10 |

| 10C02.A | Study tithing as described in Scripture and your church's teaching on it. | B-1 |

| 10C03.A | Investigate your church's benevolence fund and how it is distributed. | CE-1 |

| 10C04.A | Interview two lawmakers on different sides of the question of governmental help for the poor. Analyze and summarize the views of each on: kind of help to be given, length of eligibility, eligibility criteria, private and church involvement, and sources of funding. Compare the views of each lawmaker with the Bible's teaching in this area. | CE-2 CG-2 |

| 10C05.A | Interview a social worker or agent of any public or private social services group. Find out about his/her duties, clients served, services offered, and guidelines for eligibility. | CS-2 |

| 10C06.A | Study the IRS Earned Income Credit as a form of government subsidy. Compare it to other forms of subsidy in relation to Biblical guidelines for such assistance. | CG-1 |

| 10C07.A | Compile and keep for later use a list of church, government, and private agencies that help the poor, the homeless, widows, the elderly, and/or other needy people in or near your community. | CS-1 |

| 10C08.A | Determine what kind of help each of the above groups gives, who they serve, and how services are administered. | CS-2 |

| 10C09.A | Learn about the U. S. Government's 'welfare to work' program and how successful it has been. | CS-1 |

| 10C10.A | Study CARE, Peace Corps, Christian Children's Fund, World Vision, and other government and private groups involved in relief efforts outside their home country. Prepare a chart comparing these as to: leadership and operating regulations, sources and amount of funding, goals, methods, and target populations. | CS-3 |

| 10C11.A | Study the plight of the poor at various times in different countries of the world and compare to the situation of those currently considered poor in your own country. | CS-2 H-1 |

CULTURAL STUDIES

10C12.A	In the above activity, try to identify the external and internal causes of extreme poverty in areas where it is particularly widespread and look at possible solutions to the problem.	CS-2
10C13.A	Study the foreign policy of your nation as it relates to aid to underdeveloped and poor countries. Look at the effects of this aid and discuss whether it is beneficial or not and to whom.	CS-1 CE-1 CO-1
10C14.B	Read about the Great Depression from The Welfare State volume of Clarence Carson's *Basic History of the United States* series.	CE-2
10C15.B	Study all the original documents contained in the Jackdaws portfolio on The Great Depression.	CE-2
10C16.B	Using the above materials or any others you choose, study the Great Depression and various New Deal programs that were implemented to fight the widespread poverty of the time. Prepare a chart to show laws passed and/or agencies formed during this time, along with the stated purposes and date enacted, signed, or created for each. Note on your list any that are still in operation today.	CE-2 H-1
10C17.B	Learn about what the 'leading economic' indicators in your nation are, how they are used and measured, and what signs indicate the probability of a depression.	CE-2
10C18.B	Study the U. S. Federal Reserve System and how it may have contributed to the Great Depression and/or its resolution.	H-1
10C19.B	Study the U. S. Social Security system and/or similar programs begun in other countries during the time of the Great Depression and compare them with Scriptural principles for care of the poor that you looked at elsewhere in this unit.	H-4
10C20.B	Study the stock market and how it affected the Great Depression.	H-3 CL-1 CS-1
10C21.B	Study inflation, recession and other economic conditions that can limit or erode the financial health of a nation but are not as serious as an actual depression.	CE-2
10C22.B	Study weather conditions, poor farming practices, and other problems that created the 'dust bowl' in the Central Plains area of the United States. Explain how this interacted with the generally depressed economy to wreak havoc in that area.	H-2
10C23.B	Study the life and administration of Herbert Hoover, President of the United States at the time of the Great Depression.	H-1
10C24.B	Study agriculture subsidies instituted by the U. S. Government during the Great Depression, noting which ones are still in place today. Discuss with parents or other knowledgeable adult the pros and cons of these programs.	CE-1

CULTURAL STUDIES

10C25.B	Using online sources or reference books, find and read interviews or first-person stories of those who survived the Great Depression.	H-3
10C26.B	For a poignant look at everyday life during the Great Depression, watch the movie *Places in the Heart*, the story of a Texas widow who struggles to keep her home and family together during this time of economic turmoil for her nation and the world.	H-2
10C27.C	Study World War I from at least three different sources, including one or more written from a Christian viewpoint. Make a chart listing all the countries involved on each side, major causes, important battles and conditions in the world when it ended. You may use any reference book or history text suggested here or elsewhere as well as other books in this mini-unit's Reading and Literature section.	H-5
10C28.C	Using the above sources or others, identify the ruler and form of government of each country involved in WWI. Explain how the leaders and governmental systems contributed to causing the war and to its ultimate resolution.	H-3
10C29.C	Using historical videos, history texts, biographies, and/or encyclopedias, study the administration and life of Woodrow Wilson, who was President of the United States during World War I.	H-1
10C30.C	Watch and discuss a video of the movie *Sergeant York*, based on the true life story a Christian pacifist who became one of the greatest heroes of his nation in WWI.	H-3
10C31.C	Using videos, biographies, and/or other sources, study the lives and careers of Eddie Rickenbacker, Baron Manfred von Richthoffen and other WWI aviators.	H-2 each
10C32.C	Study and trace on a timeline your own country's involvement in WWI.	H-1
10C33.C	Study the sinking of the Lusitania and the effect that had on the war effort in various countries.	H-1
10C34.C	After studying the changes in the boundaries and names of various nations made by WWI, draw and label a map of the world (or Europe only) as it was before and after the war.	H-10
10C35. C	Study the Treaty of Versailles that ended WWI. Discuss with parents and/or mind map what provisions of it might have created some of the conditions that led to WWII?	H-3
10C36.C	Study and list President Woodrow Wilson's 'Fourteen Points' designed to provide and maintain a lasting peace after WWI.	H-1

CULTURAL STUDIES

10C37.C	Study the League of Nations, established after WWI in hopes it could prevent future wars. Try to learn who created it, what its goals were and why it never worked.	H-2
10C38.C	Mind map the ways the world would be changed today if the League of Nations had succeeded.	H-2
10C39.C	Study the lives of American women during World War I and how they contributed to the war effort of their nation.	H-2
10C40.D	Study the plight of Jews, Catholics, Gypsies and others labeled undesirable under the Nazi rule in Europe before and during World War II.	H-1
10C41.D	Study the Holocaust perpetrated upon the Jews and others by the Nazi regime and the part that played in causing and spreading World War II.	H-2
10C42.D	Watch the video *Schindler's List* and/or *The Holocaust* to get a realistic picture of atrocities committed by the Nazis against Jews and others.	H-5 each
10C43.D	Tour one of the Holocaust museums and watch the video presentation.	H-3
10C44.D	Study the teachings and beliefs of church groups in Europe that caused Christians to allow the holocaust to happen with little protest. Why do you think churches got to that point? Could something similar happen in your country today?	H-2
10C45.D	Study other causes of World War II and especially the reasons why your own nation became involved.	H-3
10C46.D	Watch *Tora, Tora, Tora* or another video about the bombing of Pearl Harbor. Discuss with your parents the significance of that event. Do not use the video movie *Pearl Harbor*, as it is not realistic.	H-3
10C47.D	Trace the involvement of your nation in WWII on a timeline and/or map as appropriate.	H-1
10C48.D	Mark on a world map all major battles or turning points of the war.	H-1
10C49.D	Watch and take notes on one or more of the videos in the History Channel series *The World at War*.	H-1 each
10C50. D	Interview several men of the appropriate age about their service in WWII. Try to go beyond facts to get their opinions, feelings, and impressions about events and places that were new to them at that time.	H-3
10C51.D	From magazines or newsreels of the time, books on the topic, and/or interviews with people who lived it, learn about life on the home front during WWII in the United States, Canada and other countries who had troops involved in the war but saw little or no fighting on their own soil.	H-3

CULTURAL STUDIES

10C52.D	Using the same sources as above, learn whatever you can about life for women and other noncombatants in war-torn Europe or Eastern Asia.	H-3
10C53.D	Interview family members or others who lived it to learn about the role of women in the war effort in your own country and others. Include things like replacing men in the work force, civilian defense jobs, rationing of household goods, purchasing of war bonds, women in the armed services and anything else you can learn. Record and/or make notes of these conversations for posterity.	H-2
10C54.D	From personal interviews or first-person articles, study the plight of Japanese Americans living on the U. S. west Coast during WWII. Discuss why this happened and how it may have been avoided without jeopardizing security.	H-1
10C55.D	Identify on the world map all combatants and other nations involved in WWII, showing the boundaries of each before and after the war.	G-1 H-1
10C56.D	Study Nazi, Communist and Fascist belief systems to discover how these ideologies impacted the outcome of WWII and the lives of the people of Europe.	CE-3 CG-3 H-1
10C57.D	Study the lives of military and political leaders of the various nations involved in this war.	H-5
10C58.	Use Usborne's *World History Dates, The Kingfisher History Encyclopedia,* or other reference books listed here or elsewhere to make timeline entries for all people, movements, and/or events you studied in this unit.	No extra points
10C59.	Make timeline entries for major events in the lives of famous people studied herein.	VA-1 each H-1 each
10C60.	Make timeline entries for major events in the lives of each of the authors whose works were read in this unit.	VA-1 each H-1 each
10C61.	Make timeline entries for all inventions and/or discoveries studied in this unit and major events in the lives of their inventors.	VA-1 each H-1 each
10C62.	Make timeline cards for all major events and/or people mentioned in books read for this unit but not included elsewhere.	VA-1 each H-1 each
10C63.	Study the homeland of each author, inventor, or artist whose works were used or studied in this unit	G-1 each

READING AND LITERATURE

READING AND LITERATURE

10R01.A	Read biographies of Jane Addams, Amy Carmichael, Mother Teresa, and other women who devoted their lives to helping the needy.	H-5 each
10R02.A	Read a biography of William Booth and/or his wife Catherine, founders of the Salvation Army.	H-5
10R03.A	Read the biography or autobiography of George Mueller, founder of early Christian orphanages in England.	H-5
10R04.A	Read *In the Shadow of Plenty* and/or other Christian books on the subjects of poverty and homelessness.	CE-5
10R05.A	Read *Bringing in the Sheaves* and study its approach to Christian charity.	CE-5
10R06.A	To look at the lighter side of social agencies, read George Bernard Shaw's *Major Barbara*.	L-4
(10R07.A)	Read or see a performance of *Guys and Dolls*, a musical comedy about the Salvation Army.	L-4
10R08.A	Read sections in *Hidden Art of Homemaking* that apply to charity and care for others.	HM-1
(10R09.B)	Read *The Grapes of Wrath*, a novel about the Dust Bowl during the time of the Great Depression.	L-8
(10R10.B)	Read *Sounder,* which also takes place during the Great Depression.	L-4
(10R11.B)	Read *Where the Red Fern Grows*, an uplifting, heartwarming story in spite of being set during the Great Depression.	L-4 each
(10R12.B)	Read the *Seasons of the Heart* Christian novel series by Janette Oke, the last volume of which takes place during the Great Depression.	L-5
10R13.B	Read other American novels written or set during the Great Depression.	H-5 each
(10R14.B)	Read one or more biographies of Herbert Hoover or Franklin Roosevelt, both of whom served as President of the United States during the Great Depression.	H-5 each
10R15.B	Read biographies of others who were important in your nation during the Great Depression.	H-5 each
10R16.B	Read biographies of people who grew up during the Great Depression and later became famous in your nation.	H-5 each

READING AND LITERATURE

10R17.C	Read *The Illustrated Red Baron: The Life and Times of Manfred von Richthoffen* and or other biographies of any WWI aviators.	H-5
10R18.C	Read *The Sinking of the Lusitania* or another book about that tragedy.	H-4
10R19.C	Read biographies of Woodrow Wilson and other world leaders during WWI.	H-5 each
10R20.C	Read *War Game*, a fictionalized account of the true incident when opposing WWI armies ceased their hostilities and spent Christmas Day playing soccer and having fun together between the barbed wire and the trenches of the battlefield.	H-5
10R21.C	Read one or more historical novels about WWI or set during that time period.	H-5 each
10R22.C	Read one or more biographies of military leaders in WWI.	H-5 each
10R23.C	Read *War and Peace* or any other historical novel or documentary about the Bolshevik Revolution, which coincided with WWI.	L-20
10R24.C	Read and memorize "In Flanders Fields" or another poem written in honor of those killed in either of the World Wars.	L-5
10R25.D	Read *The Greatest Generation* by Tom Brokaw and discuss or mind map why this title may be true of the men it is meant to describe.	H-5
10R26.D	Read *Anne Frank: Diary of a Young Girl* or the play version, *The Diary of Anne Frank*.	H-4
10R27.D	Read *The Hiding Place* and other books by and/or about Corrie Ten Boom.	H-4
10R28.D	Read *Number the Stars*, a novel about two young girls living in Nazi-occupied Denmark.	H-4
10R29.D	Read any or all volumes of *World War II* by Winston Churchill.	H-7
10R30.D	For a fictional but accurate look at one aspect of WWII in America, read *The Red Signal*, by Grace Livingston Hill.	L-4
10R31.D	Read or watch a video of *The Guns of Navarone*, an adventure novel of WWII by British author Alistair Maclean.	H-4
10R32.D	Read one or more books or book-length documentaries of battles or campaigns in World War II.	H-5
10R33.D	Read *Never Give In*, the Leaders in Action series' biography of Winston Churchill.	H-5

READING AND LITERATURE

10R34.D	Read biographies of any other of the world's heads of state during World War II.	H-5 each
10R35. D	Read one or more biographies of military leaders WWII.	H-5 each
10R36.D	Read *White Cliffs of Dover*, the story of a courageous American woman living in Britain during both World Wars.	L-5
10R37.D	Read and discuss with someone who lived through it the book *America in the 40's: A Sentimental Journey*.	H-4
10R38.	Read Christian or other wholesome novels set in the time period under study in any particular mini-unit.	L-5 each
10R39.	Read novels set in any of the countries or cultures studied in this mini-unit.	L-5 each
10R40.	Read short stories written in or by people from one or more of the countries you have studied in this mini-unit.	L-5 each
10R41.	Read additional works by any authors studied in this mini-unit.	L-5 each

COMPOSITION

10W01.A	Prepare for either side (your choice) of a debate on "Who's Responsible to Care for the Needy — State or Church?" Support all arguments from Scripture.	EC-10
10W02.A	Write an informative speech on the topic of helping others from a Biblical perspective.	EC-10
10W03.A	Write a job description for New Testament deacon as given in the book of Acts.	EC-1 B-1
10W04.A	Prepare a proposal to present to your church with regard to a new project for helping others. Include what needs to be done, ideas for how to do it, who will be involved in it, who will be eligible for help, how funds will be raised, and any other information that seems appropriate.	EC-3
10W05.A	Write a speech designed to urge people to support the above proposal or some other volunteer effort.	EC-4
10W06.A	Write a news article on one of the programs that have been successful in fighting poverty in your own community. Include: who started it, who administers it, who it helps, what it does, how it is funded, how it can measure success. Some testimonials or case histories will add a nice touch, if they are available.	EC-2
10W07.A	Write a paper (1-2 pages) comparing and contrasting the average cost effectiveness of church, private, and governmental programs for administering material and financial assistance to those who need it.	EC-1

COMPOSITION

10W08.A	Using the Scriptures you studied in the Bible and Christian Character section of this mini-unit, write a paper to serve as a guideline for Christian agencies describing the type of person we should help.	EC-1 B-1
10W09.A	After your studies on these issues, write a bill to be presented in your state or national legislative body to put their dealings in the area of poverty, charity, or welfare more in line with Scripture's teaching on the subject, whether or not they willingly acknowledge that.	EC-2 B-1
10W10.A	Write a description of one of the U. S. Corps of Engineers projects you studied in this mini-unit that have helped alleviate flooding or other environmental problems, thereby decreasing the incidences of poverty in your own state or local area.	EC 1
10W11.A	Write a report on the problem of homelessness in your community and the agencies that work to alleviate it.	EC-2
10W12.A	Write a short story about a family who find their way out of poverty through hard work and the help of God's people.	EC-10+
10W13.A	Write a paper on the dangers of pollution caused by living conditions in areas populated by those of lower socioeconomic levels, encouraging those who live there to help fight it for themselves.	EC-2
10W14.A	Write an essay explaining the passage: "If a man will not work, neither let him eat," and how this should affect the programs we sponsor and/or support for helping the hungry.	EC-2
10W15.B	Write arguments for either side of a debate on the validity of the Social Security System as an option for Christians, supporting all statements from Scripture.	EC-10
10W16.B	Using the list of New Deal agencies and programs you compiled in the Cultural Studies section of this mini-unit, write a report (1 -2 paragraphs) on each. Include: telling what it was to do, whether or not it is still operating, who is/was in charge of it, who is/was helped by it, and how successful it is/was.	EC-1 each
10W17.B	Write a report in the form of an interview with someone who survived the Great Depression. Research the period in whatever way you wish.	EC-2
10W18.B	Write a large article (2 -3 pages) or a series of brief news reports analyzing each of the above New Deal agencies or programs from a Biblical perspective.	EC-2
10W19.B	Write an essay explaining, in the context of his day, the meaning of President Roosevelt's most famous quote from the Great Depression: "We have nothing to fear but fear itself."	EC-1

COMPOSITION

10W20.B	Write a detailed (8-12 pages) research or term paper on one of the agencies or services created by the New Deal. Use *Writers Inc.* or a similar reference from our resource list to assure the proper format and style.	EC-50
10W21.B	Write a fictional short story about a family or individual who lost everything in the stock market crash of 1929 but managed to come back and survive by hard work and determination.	EC-10+
10W22.B	Write 10-12 entries for a journal kept by a young man in the Civilian Conservation Corps during the Great Depression.	EC-3
10W23.B	Write an investigative report comparing living conditions in various parts of the world during the Great Depression. Include an analysis of what you think made the difference.	EC-3
10W24.B	Write a detailed (3-5 pages) biographical sketch of someone who grew to adulthood during the Great Depression and went on to become rich and famous in his/her own country.	EC-2
10W25.B	Define into your vocabulary notebook the words: 'depression', 'recession', 'inflation' and 'downturn' in relation to economics. Compare and contrast these in an essay.	EC-2
10W26.B	Write a newspaper ad or editorial to encourage Americans to start investing in their country's industries again after the Great Depression.	EC-1
10W27.C	Write a poem in memory of men who died fighting for your country in WWI.	EC-1
10W28.C	Write an essay explaining why WWI was called the 'war to end all wars'.	EC-2
10W29.C	Write a Bible study for women entitled "What God's Word Says about War". Use many different Scripture passages and interpret them in light of each other. Use inductive questions to get students to delve deeply into each passage.	EC-4 B-2
10W30.C	Based on the passages you studied in the Bible and Christian Character section of this mini-unit, write an essay defining what you believe the Bible teaches about lust' wars and explaining whether you believe WWI was one.	EC-3+
10W31.C	Write a series of letters home as if from one of the U. S. 'doughboys' serving abroad in WWI. Write at least one letter to each of the following: wife, parents, sibling, friend. Share not only what is happening where he is but how he feels about the war and other events around him. Try to explain why he felt the need to volunteer to fight in this war which did not directly involve his homeland.	EC-1
10W32.C	Write copy for a brochure that could have been used to recruit U. S. or Canadian citizens to serve overseas in WWI.	EC-2

COMPOSITION

10W33.C   Write a news report on one of the major battles or campaigns   EC-1
of WWI, as if by a correspondent on the scene writing to share
news with people back home.

10W34.C   Write biographical sketches of Manfred von Richthoffen (the   EC-4
Red Baron) and Eddie Richenbacher, comparing and contrasting
their lives, personalities and beliefs.

10W35.C   Write a piece for a scientific journal of the day extolling the virtues   EC-2
for military use of tanks, airplanes, the howitzer, or some other
weapon based on technology that was brand new during WWI.

10W36.C   Write an editorial using the sinking of the Lusitania as a rallying   EC-2
point to encourage British, Canadian and/or U. S. citizens to
fully back the war effort.

10W37.D   Write a speech that might have been given in the U. S. Congress   EC-5
in support or opposition for the 'lend lease ' policy of the
U. S. in the early years of WWII.

10W38.D   Define 'appeasement' into your vocabulary notebook and write   EC-2
an essay on the part it played in causing World War II.

10W39.D   Write a letter you might have sent to the U. S. Congress to help   EC-2
persuade them to go to war against Germany and their Allies
even before the bombing of Pearl Harbor. Explain reasons why
the U. S. should be involved in this largely European struggle.

10W40.D   Based on the passages you studied in the Bible and Christian   EC-2
Character section of this unit, write an essay defining what you
believe the Bible's teaching to be about a 'just' war and
explaining whether you believe WWII was one.

10W41.D   Write a 'Help Wanted' ad for one of the jobs done by women   EC-2
while the men were gone to war. Make it at least 3-5 sentences
in length and be specific as to duties and requirements.

10W42.D   Write a first-person short story about someone who was at   EC-20
Pearl Harbor when the December 7, 1941 bombing occurred.

10W43.D   Write a journal for someone living in France or another Nazi-   EC - 2 per
occupied country at that time. Discuss historical events as if   5 entries
they were happening as you wrote. Try to honestly portray the
feelings and attitudes of citizens of the area, including any
attempts at revolt, the underground movements, etc. Include the
day of takeover, the day of liberation by the Allies, a few days
of ordinary life under the Nazis and days when other important
events took place.

10W44.D   Write a series of letters both ways between a husband and   EC - 2 per
wife separated by his service in WWII. Don't make these into   5 letters
love letters but concentrate on sharing what is happening in
each of their lives at the time and how they feel about the war
and other events of the day.

COMPOSITION

10W45.D	Write the copy for a recruitment brochure that might have been used to draw young men into the armed services during WWII. Emphasize the need of the nation, the citizen's duty, and the call of the hero inside most of us.	EC-1
10W46.D	Write a letter of condolence to the family of an Allied soldier or sailor killed in action in World War II. Choose an actual battle and share in the letter some of its results, without being unnecessarily graphic. Offer the "heartfelt thanks of a grateful nation" for the family's "ultimate sacrifice".	EC-2
10W47.D	Write a speech to be presented at a ceremony in honor of WWII veterans.	EC-5
10W48. D	After reading *The Greatest Generation*, write an essay on whether or not you agree with the author's assessment of the men who fought WWII and why.	EC-3
10W49.D	Write a newspaper article (as if factual) telling what you believe happened to Raoul Wallenberg, rescuer of hundreds of Holocaust Jews.	EC-2
10W50.D	As if you were a citizen of a Nazi-occupied nation, write a psalm or poem of praise to God for deliverance from Nazi rule at the time of your nation's liberation.	EC-2
10W51.D	Prepare a skit to be performed with others later about some particular event in or during the time of WWII.	EC-5+
10W52.	As you read the Bible each day, keep a spiritual journal, taking notes on your readings and their applications in your life. Add prayer requests and answers as well as insights God may give you.	EC-3 per week
10W53.	Use the Scripture passages in this unit to practice dictation. Have someone else read them aloud for you to write, word for word with exact punctuation. If your beliefs allow, you may want to use a modern Bible translation for this exercise.	EG- 1 per hour
10W54.	Write a report on one or more of the people you studied in this unit.	EC-3
10W55.	Write a brief (1-2 page) report on each country studied in this unit. Put each of them into your geography notebook.	EC-1 each G-1 each
10W56.	As you attend worship services or hear them on radio, TV, or recordings, take notes on the sermons.	EC-1 each B-1 each
10W57.	As you watch videos and/or listen to audios recommended in this unit, take notes on them.	EC-1 each page
10W58.	Use your notes to write a synopsis or summary of each audio and/or video used in this mini-unit.	EC-2 each

COMPOSITION

10W59.	Write reviews of any or all of the videos in this unit, as if done by a movie critic.	EC-2 each DR-2 each
10W60.	Write a character sketch of one or more of the men and women studied in this unit.	EC-1 each
10W61.	Write a report on each field trip taken in this unit.	EC-2 each
10W62.	Write thank you notes to field trip guides, people you interviewed, and others who helped in any way with this unit.	EC-1 per 5 notes
10W63.	Add one page to your school journal each day as explained in the guidelines in the front of the unit study.	EC-1 each page
10W64.	Write book reports on any or all the novels or biographies in this unit.	EC-2
10W65.	Outline one or more of the nonfiction books read in this unit.	EC-1 each
10W66.	Write summaries and/or synopses of any of the books read in this unit.	EC-1 each
10W67.	Write a thorough exegesis of any of the Bible chapters studied in this unit.	B-2 each EC-2 each
10W68.	Put ten or more new words from your studies each week into your vocabulary notebook. Add definitions, pronunciation marks, and syllables.	EG-1 per 10
10W69.	Learn to spell all new words added to your vocabulary notebook in this unit, testing on them each week.	EG-1 per 10
10W70.	Use any good dictionary to proofread and correct spelling in all written work. (No pts. for use of an automatic spell checker.)	EC-3 per 3 paragraphs
10W71.	Using *Writers Inc., The College English Handbook,* or a similar grammatical reference, proofread and correct grammar and mechanics in all written work done for this mini-unit.	EG-3 or EC-3 per 3 para-graphs
10W72.	Write a review of each movie or play you watched or read for this unit.	DR-2 each

MATHEMATICS AND PERSONAL FINANCE

10M01.A	Calculate the percentage of your own congregation's budget that goes to benevolence and the ratios between that and other categories of spending. Prepare a graph to present this data and display it somewhere in the church building.	M-3

MATHEMATICS AND PERSONAL FINANCE

10M02.A   Determine the amount of your family's (and/or your own) tithe   M-2
           at 10% of actual earnings and compare it to the amount you
           actually give to the church and other worthy causes.

10M03.A   Use the information in the two previous activities to calculate   M-1
           the amount and percentage of income your family gave to
           benevolent causes in the previous year and so far this year.

10M04.A   Determine the official poverty level in your state and those   M-5
           surrounding it and make a graph to compare them. Investigate to
           learn what factors determine poverty levels and why they differ
           from state to state.

10M05.A   Fill out a tax return for an Earned Income Credit for an imaginary   M-2
           family at or near the income level determined in #10W01.

10M06.B   Find out how economic indicators are figured on a national   CE-3
           basis and monitor your nation's for a few months.

10M07.B   Keep up with figures on unemployment, consumer prices, GNP,   CE-10
           rate of inflation, and other economic indicators for a period or six
           months (or collect the data for the previous six months) and chart
           them on a line graph.

10M08.B   Obtain Social Security earning figures for your family and determine   M-2
           what your benefits would be in case of one or both parents being
           disabled or deceased.

10M09.B   Create a graph of stock market prices for several months before   M-5
           and after the crash of 1929.

10M10.C   Collect data on the number of troops sent into battle by each   M-5
           of the combatants in each year of WWI. Show and compare this
           data on a graph.

10M11.C   Compile statistics on number of war casualties suffered by   M-5
           each combatant in WWI. Prepare a bar graph or pictograph to
           compare this information.

10M12.C   Use the data in the above activity to calculate each nation's   M-2
           war casualties in relation to each other and to their total number of
           troops as ratios, proportions, and/or per cent.

10M13.C   Compile statistics and prepare a graph showing the percentage   M-5
           of each nation's war casualties who actually died from the infection
           of a wound or other noncombat causes.

10M14.C   Prepare a graph to show the relative populations of combatant   M-5
           and occupied nations at the start and end of WWI.

10M15.C   Perform the necessary calculations with parabolas to aim and   M-3
           properly fire a Howitzer in order to hit the intended target.

MATHEMATICS AND PERSONAL FINANCE

10M16.D	Collect data on the number of troops sent into battle by each of the combatants in each year of WWII. Show and compare this data on a graph.	M-5
10M17.D	Use the data in the above activity to calculate each nation's war casualties in relation to each other and to their total number of troops as ratios, proportions, and/or percentages.	M-5
10M18.D	Compile statistics and prepare a graph showing the percentage of each nation's war casualties who were civilians. Do not include victims of the Holocaust.	M-5
10M19.D	Prepare a graph to show the relative populations of combatant and occupied nations at the start and end of WWII.	M-3
10M20.D	Compile and analyze statistics on the number and percentages of deaths and injuries to those of each age group from the atomic bombs dropped on Japan. Show this on a chart in relation to all other war dead.	M-5
10M21.D	Using actual data from the time on the earnings of 'war' bonds or 'victory' bonds, calculate the initial cost of bonds of each denomination.	M-5
10M22.	Use data from any or all of the above graphs to practice making and solving problems using percent, ratio, and proportion.	M-7
10M23.	Continue to brush up on basic math as needed.	M-2

SCIENCE

10S01.A	Study the environmental problems such as poor sewage, unclean drinking water, insects, rodents, lack of adequate heat or cooling, and others that often go along with widespread poverty.	SE-4
10S02.A	Study various methods of water treatment and/or sewage disposal from the primitive to the modern, including things that can be done with minimal money and/or technology.	SE-3
10S03.A	Learn nonhazardous (to humans) methods for the extermination of household pests that flourish in poverty areas and may carry diseases.	B-1
10S04.A	Tour one of the laboratory farms of SIFAT or some other agricultural ministry that works to find ways of improving crop production and living standards in underdeveloped nations, using only the technology they have readily available.	SE-2 PA-2
10S05.A	Research and mind map solutions for any other environmental problems related to poverty as identified in #10S01.	SE-1 SP-1

SCIENCE

10S06.A	Study hybrids and other improved forms of grains and food crops and learn how each improves yield and/or nutritional value, thereby helping to fight poverty in the world as a whole.	SP-4
10S07.A	Study various types of farm equipment used to increase yields or ease production of food crops, thereby raising the level of food production to better feed the hungry of the world.	SE-2
10S08.A	Learn about the flood control projects of the U. S. Army Corps of Engineers that stopped erosion and brought prosperity to many very needy areas of that country.	SB-2
10S09.B	Study the work of Depression-era (CCC) Civilian Conservation Corps, which hired and paid many unemployed young adult U. S. citizens to work in the creation of national parks and forests and a variety of other projects aimed at conserving the nation's natural resources.	SP-2
10S10.B	Study the construction and operation of the Tennessee Valley Authority (TVA) and other electric power facilities built by the U. S. Government during the Great Depression using labor of the unemployed.	SP-2
10S11.B	Study other engineering and construction projects undertaken by the WPA or PWA, giving jobs to the unemployed during the Great Depression.	H-2
10S12.B	Study other scientific or technological breakthroughs that helped bring the U. S. and the rest of the world out of the Great Depression.	SP-3 H-1
10S13.B	Study the causes and effects of serious droughts like the one that turned the American Central Plains into the Dust Bowl during the Great Depression.	SE-1
10S14.B	Study various methods of irrigation that could have prevented the creation of the Dust Bowl had they been available then.	SP-4
10S15.B	Study crop rotation and other methods of preventing over-worked soil and erosion like what occurred in the Dust Bowl.	SE-2
10S16.C	Using *The New Way Things Work* or a similar resource, study the construction and operation of the tank, first used in warfare at this time.	SP-2
10S17.C	Study the technology that allowed the use of airplanes in battle in WWI and the differences that made in warfare.	SP-2
10S18.C	Study the construction and operation of the howitzer, used first in WWI.	SP-2
10S19.C	Compare the cannon and other ground artillery used in WWI with that used in previous and later wars.	SP-1

SCIENCE

10S20.C	Tour an aviation museum and examine WWI era planes.	SP-2
10S21.D	Study the development and use of the submarine as used by both sides in WWII.	SP-2
10S22.D	Learn about radar and sonar that allow submarines to work properly.	SP-3
10S23.D	Study the additional development and added uses of military aircraft in WWII as compared to WWI.	SP-1 H-1
10S24.D	Tour a military museum and study the variety of weapons and other equipment used in each of the two World Wars.	SP-2
10S25.D	Study the atomic bomb and the processes used to create it.	SP-2
10S26.D	Study nuclear power plants and other peacetime uses of atomic power.	SP-2
10527.D	Tour a nuclear power plant and learn how it works, using technology first created for this war.	SP-2

HEALTH AND FITNESS

10H01.A	Study dysentery and other diseases caused by poor sanitation and learn methods of prevention and/or treatment of each.	HE-1
10H02.A	Study the health hazards of roaches, flies mosquitoes, and other insects that are often uncontrolled in low income societies.	HE-1
10H03.A	Study diseases and other health hazards carried by rats and mice.	HE-1
10H04.A	Study other health hazards most common in truly poor areas and measures that could be taken to prevent or correct them.	HE-1
10H05.A	Study the basic needs of man as defined by medicine and psychology. Explain how and for whom a godly woman is able and expected to fill each of these needs.	HE-1 B-1
10H06.A	Look at the public health system in your country and catalog those services they make available to the truly poor.	CG-1
10H07.A	Visit a public or free private health clinic or hospital to see what services they offer and how they are administered.	CS-2
10H08.A	Study the symptoms and long-term effects on the body of severe malnutrition.	HE-1
10H09.B	Study dehydration and other health effects that might be caused by a drought like the one in the Dust Bowl in the 1930's.	HE-1

HEALTH AND FITNESS

10H10.B	Study other health care problems that ran rampant during the Great Depression.	HE-2
10H11.B	Study the effects of clinical depression, which was first diagnosed in large numbers during the Great Depression. Learn to determine when this is a real illness and when it is caused by fear or some other sinful emotion.	HE-1 B-1
10H12.B	Study antidepressants and the effects on the human body of their prolonged use.	HE-2
10H13.B	Study St. John's Wort and other herbs that help fight depression.	HE-1
10H14.B	Study other non-chemical treatments for depression and the effectiveness of each.	HE-1
10H15.B	Learn about the nutritional value of the commodity program established by the USDA during the Great Depression and its importance to many of America's poor during those years.	FN-1 H-1
10H16.C	Study the effects on the human respiratory system of exposure to mustard gas and chlorine, both used extensively as weapons during WWI.	HE-2
10H17.C	Study the ravages of gangrene and other infections on wounded soldiers in WWI. Mind map how different things would have been if penicillin and/or other antibiotics had been available at that time.	HE-2
10H18.C	Study the methods available for fighting infection prior to penicillin and the relative effectiveness of each.	HE-1
10H19.C	Study claustrophobia, which was found to plague many of those who were first assigned to tank duty in WWI.	HE-1
10H20.C	Study other possible health hazards from long periods of duty in the closed quarters of a tank, submarine, or similar vehicle.	HE-1
10H21.C	Study other ailments common to military troops during World War I and learn about the treatment of each then and now.	HE-2
10H22.D	Study the effects of radiation on the human body, first observable with the development of the atomic bomb in WWII.	HE-2
10H23.D	Study methods of diagnosis and treatment for various ailments caused by exposure to radioactive materials.	HE-2
10H24.D	Study the injuries most common from various types of bombs and land mines used in WWII. Compare to those from the previous war.	HE-3
10H25.D	Study other ailments common to military troops during World War II and learn about the treatment of each then and now.	HE-2

HEALTH AND FITNESS

10H26.D	Study the use of radiation in the form of x-rays and other diagnostic tools to improve health care.	HE-1
10H27.D	Study nuclear medicine and its uses, all of which derived from the research into the atomic bomb during World War II.	HE-2
10H28.D	Study sonograms and other medical uses of sonar technology, originally created for use in World War II submarines.	HE-1
10H29.D	Research to find out what other medical technologies created for the battlefield of WWII have since become commonplace in your country and saved many lives.	HE-2

PRACTICAL ARTS

10P01.A	Plan and supervise a fitness and/or recreation day for needy children.	TE-4
10P02.A	Prepare and serve at least one complete meal in a local soup kitchen, rescue mission, or homeless shelter.	FN-5
10P03.A	Participate in a group outing to clean, decorate, or otherwise help out at a nursing home, mission, or shelter.	Parents Discretion
10P04.A	Sew at least one article of clothing to be given to a needy child or adult.	CC-5
10P05.A	Organize a group to provide practical help for victims of a house fire, tornado, hurricane, or other disaster.	Parents Discretion
10P06.A	Volunteer to help in a clerical or patient-assistance position at your public health department or charity hospital.	BE-1 per hr Max. 1 credit
10P07.A	Plan and conduct a yard sale or collect and sell items for a thrift shop of which the proceeds go to help the needy.	BE-2
10P08.A	Provide free baby-sitting for a needy mother to look for work of take care of other necessary (!) business.	HM-1 per hour
10P09.A	Volunteer as a disaster aide with the Red Cross or similar association after any natural disaster hits your area.	CS-1 per hour
10P10.A	Help in an international relief effort for victims of war, oppression, or natural disaster in any way possible and acceptable with your family.	Parents Discretion
10P11.A	Do a shopping comparison to see how little money you can use in feeding a family of a given size fully balanced meals for one week. Prepare a chart showing low-cost sources for all required nutrients.	HM-3
10P12.A	Help build a house for a needy family through Habitat for Humanity.	IA-1 per hour

PRACTICAL ARTS

| 10P13.B | Practice filling out applications for a Social Security card and social security benefits. | BE-1 |

| 10P14.B | Contact the Social Security Administration and get a copy of your family's earning and benefits records. Use these for activities in the Mathematics section. | BE-1 |

| 10P15.B | Learn how to read stock market reports so you can follow the progress of your investments to prevent being caught in a depression that may come in the future. | BE-2 |

| 10P16.B | Study various types of investments to help make your family's income as `depression-proof as you possibly can. | CE-2 |

| 10P17.B | Organize a systematic stock-up program for your family to assure you have plenty of food and other essentials on hand in the event of a depression or recession. | HM-2 |

| 10P18.B | Discuss your family's current financial condition with your parents. Help them make contingency plans in case of a recession or depression. | CE-1 |

| 10P19.B | Investigate the safety of deposits in your bank or credit union. If your facility is not a member of FDIC or NCUA, find out how and by whom your money is insured and what would happen to it in the event of another 'crash' like the one in 1929. If you aren't satisfied that your deposits are safe, find a bank where they will be. | CE -1 |

| 10P20.B | Prepare an archive-quality audio or video of your interview with someone who remembers the Great Depression. | Parents Discretion |

| 10P21.B | Volunteer for at least 5 hours with some social service agency founded during the Great Depression. | 1 per hour in appropriate subject |

| 10P22.C | Volunteer to help maintain whatever WWI Memorial or monument your community may have. | IA or LH - 1 per hour |

| 10P23.C | If your community does not have a memorial to honor its WWI veterans, plan and help create one. | IA-3+ VA-3+ |

| 10P24.C | Design and sew a WWI uniform to be used for a reenactment or memorial ceremony. | CC-5 |

| 10P25.C | Build a model floating bridge like the one used to transport tanks across rivers in WWI. | IA-5+ |

| 10P26.C | Build a working model of any item of WWI military artillery. | IA-6+ each |

| 10P27.C | Build plastic or wooden models of WWI planes, tanks, or other military vehicles. | IA-6+ each |

| 10P28.C | Use the Internet to identify and trace in state and/or national archives any ancestors of yours who fought in WWI. | BE-3 |

PRACTICAL ARTS

10P29.D	Volunteer to help maintain whatever WWII Memorial or monument your community may have.	IA or LH - 1 per hour
10P30.D	Learn to fire any weapon similar to one used in World War II.	PS-5
10P31.D	"Adopt" a "grandparent" from among the elderly residents of a WWII veterans' home or hospital. Go to see him/her regularly and learn all you can about that time period while meeting his/her needs for friendship and personal assistance. Learn to push the wheelchair, feed the patient, or meet other personal needs. Make cards and small gifts to take along when you visit. Be sure to check on dietary and other restrictions that may affect what you can take to your friend.	Parent's discretion
10P32.D	Embroider or otherwise create a patch of his regimental insignia for your 'adopted' grandparent to wear on a cap or jacket.	HM-3
10P33.D	Learn to read and interpret radar and/or sonar screens.	Parent's discretion
10P34.D	Observe and/or help in the administration of one or more medical sonograms.	HE-1 per hour
10P35.D	Learn to administer and interpret x-rays and other medical data from sources originating in WWII.	HE-1 per hour
10P36.D	Build a working model of any item of WWII military artillery or hardware.	1A-10 each
10P37.D	Tour a WWII era battleship or cruiser and learn how the engines and other essential parts worked.	H-2
10P38.	If you don't already know how to create and use a computer database, you may wish to learn in this unit.	CO-1 per hour
10P39.	Create and maintain a database to assist you as appropriate in this mini-unit.	CO-1 per hour
10P40.	Type all and print out written work. If you do not know how to type, now is the time to learn.	BE – 1 per paper
10P41.	If needed, take a class, follow a computerized, written or video tutorial, or a correspondence course in typing, keyboarding, and/or word processing.	BE-1/2 credit
10P42.	Create a computer website to display what you have learned in this mini-unit.	CO-5
10P43.	Frame and/or mat one or more of the pictures or posters you drew or created in the Decorative and Performing Arts section of this mini-unit.	VA-2 each

PRACTICAL ARTS

10P44.	Make your own costumes for any performances you chose to do in the Decorative and Performing Arts section of this mini-unit or plays you wrote in the Composition section.	CC-5+ each

DECORATIVE AND PERFORMING ARTS

10A01.A	Make and mail valentines or other greeting cards to all widows, widowers, and others within your church family who live alone.	VA-3+
10A02.A	Perform a vocal or instrumental music concert alone or with a group for residents at a shelter, mission or similar facility	VM or IM-5
10A03.A	Sing, lead singing, or play an instrument in a worship service for a poor congregation or at a nursing home or similar facility.	VM or IM-2
10A04.A	Direct and/or perform in a Christian play or skit for shelter residents or other needy people.	DR-10
10A05.A	Draw pictures, murals, or banners to decorate and beautify a shelter or rescue mission.	VA-5 each
10A06.A	Make and distribute greeting cards at a rescue mission, homeless shelter, or soup kitchen.	VA-2+
10A07.B	Watch a live performance or video of the play (or movie) *Annie,* set during the Great Depression.	DR-3
10A08.B	Learn to sing one or more of the songs from *Annie.*	VM-3
10A09.B	Choreograph your own special dance number to one or more of the songs in *Annie.*	DR-5
10A10.B	Listen to a variety of songs written about or during the Great Depression, analyzing them as to theme and style.	MA-2+
10A11.B	Learn to sing one or more of the above songs.	VM-2 each
10Al2.C	Set your poem about WWI to music, using any tune you know.	MC-2
10A13.C	Write a composition of your own to be used with the lyrics of your poem.	MC-5
10A14.C	Draw a mural of one of the major battles of WWII, showing all aspects of the battle in as much detail as possible.	VA-2
10A15.C	Listen to several examples of the music that was popular in your country during WWI.	MA-2+
10A16.C	Draw several of the planes, tanks etc. used in WWI.	VA-1 each
10A17.C	Learn to sing some of the 'battle songs' sung by the soldiers in WWI.	VM-2+

DECORATIVE AND PERFORMING ARTS

10A18.D	Make a birthday card for a grandfather, "adopted grandfather" or someone else from the WWII/Korean War generation.	VA-2
10A19.D	Listen to and analyze several (10 —12) examples of the music popular during WWII.	MA-3
10A20.D	Design and create artwork for decorating the marker or other memorial your group is planning to build for WWII veterans.	VA-5
10A21.D	Use your artwork to illustrate the poem you wrote for the WWII memorial.	VA-1+
10A22.	Draw pictures of any field trips you took in this mini-unit.	VA-1 each
10A23.	Use drawing, painting and graphic arts to create displays and make posters as called for in this study.	VA-2 each
10A24.	Illustrate one or more of the poems you studied or memorized for this unit.	VA-1 each
10A25.	Set one or more of this unit's poems to music, using an original or existing tune.	MC-5 each
10A26.	Set one or more of the Scripture verses in this unit to music, using a tune you wrote for the purpose.	MC-5 each

Proverbs 31:10-31 KJV

❧

Who can find a virtuous woman? for her price is far above rubies.
The heart of her husband doth safely trust in her, so that he shall have no need of spoil.
She will do him good and not evil all the days of her life.
She seeketh wool, and flax, and worketh willingly with her hands.
She is like the merchants' ships; she bringeth her food from afar.
She riseth also while it is yet night, and giveth meat to her household, and a portion to her maidens.
She considereth a field, and buyeth it: with the fruit of her hands she planteth a vineyard.
She girdeth her loins with strength, and strengtheneth her arms.
She perceiveth that her merchandise is good: her candle goeth not out by night.
She layeth her hands to the spindle, and her hands hold the distaff.
She stretcheth out her hand to the poor; yea, she reacheth forth her hands to the needy.
She is not afraid of the snow for her household: for all her household are clothed with scarlet.
She maketh herself coverings of tapestry; her clothing is silk and purple.
Her husband is known in the gates, when he sitteth among the elders of the land.
She maketh fine linen, and selleth it; and delivereth girdles unto the merchant.
Strength and honour are her clothing; and she shall rejoice in time to come.
She openeth her mouth with wisdom; and in her tongue is the law of kindness.
She looketh well to the ways of her household, and eateth not the bread of idleness.
Her children arise up, and call her blessed; her husband also, and he praiseth her.
Many daughters have done virtuously, but thou excellest them all.
Favour is deceitful, and beauty is vain: but a woman that feareth the Lord, she shall be praised.
Give her of the fruit of her hands; and let her own works praise her in the gates.

❧

Far Above Rubies, Volume One
Appendix

Recommended Resources

Unit by Unit Resource Guide

CHRONOLOGICAL Cross-Reference with BITM

THEMATIC Cross-Reference with BITM

25 Ways to Have Fun with a Book Report

Recommended Resources

If your student is college bound you may need to supplement Far Above Rubies with upper level math and lab sciences. Some colleges and universities also require foreign languages. Many of these courses are recommended in certain units as follows.

Unit One -   Geometry

Counseling

Geology

Chemistry

Unit Two -   Accounting

Unit Three -   Zoology/Animal Biology

Unit Four -   Marine Biology

Foreign Languages

Unit Sixteen - Psychology

Neuroscience

Home Health Care/Pre-nursing

While we have offered some suggestions for teaching these in the appropriate units, this is in no way intended to be an exhaustive list. Here are some other resources that other families have used successfully.

Apologia High School Science

ABeka High School science

ABeka High School math courses

Math You See

Saxon Math

Rosetta Stone language series,

The Learnables language series

Artes Latinae

In an attempt to make locating resources as easy as possible, we have listed them in alphabetical order (excluding the initial word A or The in the title) within every unit in which they are used. When the activity suggests books by a certain author or in a series, but not by title, the resource listing will reflect that as well. Some resources that are not specifically designated in a particular unit, may be listed there due to their relevance to the subject of the unit.

As we are aware that more than one item may have the same title, we have added information on authors, publishers and websites whenever possible. While most of these items may be available from Amazon, Barnes and Noble and other large sites, we recommend purchasing from the actual publisher or sites known to be operated by Christians to support our brothers and sisters whenever possible. You should do whatever you feel is the best stewardship of the financial resources God has given you. Titles of older classic works that are no longer under copyright protection have often been reprinted by many different publishers. To avoid confusion, we have not listed any publisher on these, but have noted wide availability. We have also let you know when such books are likely to be in the public library.

We have researched these resources to be sure that all are currently available at the time of this publication and to alert you to any that are hard to find. However, things can change rapidly and these resources may not be available when you are using this unit study. Should you find that an item is unavailable or too hard to find, feel free to substitute a similar item from the same general perspective. If that is not possible, or if a given resource item does not agree with your personal Christian persuasion, please skip that activity rather than choose materials that might go against God's Word or our purposes here. Do be aware, however, that some items --- such as the writings of Darwin – that are definitely not Biblical are offered to help students understand the 'worldview' they are learning to counteract. If you do not wish for your student to know about these things, just skip them. No one activity is absolutely required, and there is much more work than any one student can do. (Refer to Guidelines for more about this.)

Reference books used on many occasions in different units are listed in each unit even if they are not specifically suggested in the activities of that unit. Use them as you see fit to complete any activity that includes studying something on a related topic. Many of these items can be found in public libraries, but if you expect to use them often, it may be wise to purchase them. Some other materials are also recommended in more than one unit, sometimes even used for basically the same activity. This is because the activity relates equally well to both topics and can fit either of the mini-units in which it is listed. In these cases, you should use the same exact activity only once and only count it in one of the units. Never give points in two places for the same activity or the same resource used in the same way.

For all units

America: The First 350 Years by Steven Wilkins, produced by Covenant Publications on CD–ROM or P3 format (will play on computer or MP3 compatible CD players, and DVD players, but not on traditional CD players) order from www.shekinahhomeschool.com/*america-the-first-350-years*

American Historical Documents, a collection of works by various authors, compiled by Dr. Charles Elliot as part of the 51-volume *Harvard Classics*, long out of-print, can be found at used booksellers, some public libraries and download, borrow, or read online at https://openlibrary.org/books/

American Original Documents (see *American Historical Documents*)

Anatomy of the Human Body by Henry Gray, available for sale from several retailers, but can be searched online at http://www.bartleby.com/107/

Baker's Bible Atlas by Charles F. Pfeiffer, edited by Ernest Leslie Carlson and Martin H. Scharlemann, available in print and ebook format from many retailers and libraries

Basic History of the United States, Vol. 3: The Sections and the Civil War 1826-1877 by Clarence B. Carson published in print by American Textbook Committee and on audio CD by Blackstone Audio; both can be ordered from www.exodusbooks.com/author.aspx?id=2496

Beggar to King: All the Occupations of Bible Times, by Walter Duckat published by Abingdon Press www.abingdonpress.com can be read online through www.librarything.com

The Biblical Feasts (see *Celebrating Jesus in the Biblical Feasts*)

Celebrating Jesus in the Biblical Feasts: Discovering Their Significance to You as a Christian by Dr. Richard Booker published by Destiny Image, www.destinyimage.com available in both print and e-book

(A) Christian Survey of World History audio set by R. J. Rushdooney, available in CD and MP3 format from http://chalcedon.edu/store/all/History/

The College English Handbook (see *Harbrace College Handbook)*

(The) Daily Bible by F. La Gard Smith published by and available from Harvest House, www.harvesthousepublishers.com

The Foxfire Book by Elliot Wigginton, published by Anchor, an imprint of Random House www.knopfdoubleday.com/imprint/anchor

From Sea to Shining Sea, by Peter Marshall and David Manuel, published by Baker Book House, www.bakerbookretail.com

Gaining Favor with God and Man, by William Thayer, published by Lionheart Publishing www.lionheartbooks.org

Gray's Anatomy (see Anatomy of the Human Body by Henry Gray

Gray's Anatomy Coloring Book, by Fred Stark, published by Running Press, available from www.hometrainingtools.com

Harbrace College Handbook, edited by John C. Rogers, published by Harcourt, Brace, Jovanovich, available anywhere college textbooks are sold. You may be able to rent one by the school year at www.chegg.com

The Hidden Art of Homemaking by Edith Schaeffer, published by Tyndale House. www.tyndale.com

Invention and Discovery published by Usborne Books, sold by independent distributors; find one or order online at www.ubam.com

Inventors and Inventions, published by Usborne Books, sold by independent distributors; find one or order online at www.ubam.com

Italic Handwriting Curriculum by Barbara Getty and Inga Dubay, published by Allport Editions, available from www.christianbook.com

The Kingfisher History Encyclopedia, edited and published by Houghton, Mifflin, Harcourt available through www.amazon.com and in many libraries

The Light and the Glory by Peter Marshall and David Manuel published by Baker Book House, www.bakerbookretail.com

Manners and Customs in the Bible, by Victor H. Matthews, published by Baker Academic, www.bakerretail.com

Portfolios of primary source documents, researched and translated by Jackdaw Publications, a division of Golden Owl Publishing, www.jackdaw.com

Science Projects on File, large reference book may still be found in many libraries but can also be replaced by online searches or resources

Sketches of Church History, by S. M. Houghton and Iain Murray, published by Banner of Truth, www.banneroftruth.org

Spencerian Penmanship developed by P. R. Spencer, published by Mott Media, www.mottmedia.com

Streams of Civilization, by Mary Stanton and Albert Hyma; published by Christian Liberty Press, www.shopchristianliberty.com

Timetables of History, by Bernard Grun, currently out-of-print but readily available through many used sources

Training Our Daughters to Be Keepers at Home by Ann Ward, published by Smiling Heart Press now available from www.shekinahhomeschool.com/page92.html

The Way Things Work or *New Way Things Work* by David Macaulay, published by Walter Lorraine Books, imprint of Houghton Mifflin   www.hmhco.com/at-home, may be in libraries

Webster's 1828 Dictionary published by Merriam –Webster, sold by many homeschool suppliers and a few general bookstores, can also be searched online at www.1828.mshaffer.com

What in the World is Going on Here? audio CD set by Diana Waring available from http://www.dianawaring.com/store/history-curriculum/what-in-the-world-1-track-titles

With Christ in the Biblical Feasts (see *Celebrating Jesus in the Biblical Feasts: Discovering Their Significance to You as a Christian*)

World Almanac, published annually by World Almanac Company, available in most bookstores and libraries. (You need not buy a new one every year, as the information you will be using from it will not change that often.)

World History: A Christian Survey (See *A Christian Survey of World History*)

World History Dates; published by Usborne Books, sold by independent distributors; find one or order online at www.ubam.com

Writer's Inc. published by The Write Source, www.thewritesource.com

Writing a Research Paper by Edward J. Shevan, published by Christian Liberty Press, available in both print and e-book versions from www.shopchristianliberty.com

Writing for College, published by and available from The Write Source www.thewritesource.com

UNIT 1
A virtuous wife, who can find?
Her value is far above rubies.
Proverbs 31: 10

Adam and His Kin: The Lost History of Their Lives written by Ruth Beechick, available through many homeschool vendors

Ah, Assyria: Studies in Assyrian and Ancient Near East History by Cogan, Mordechai, Eph'al, and Israel published by Magnes Press https://www.logos.com/product/30257/ah-assyria-studies-in-assyrian-history

Alabaster Doves: True Stories of Women Whose Lives Were Characterized by Strength and Gentleness written by Linda Holland, may be available in libraries or can be purchased online

All the Women of the Bible by Herbert Lockyer, published by Zondervan, www.zondervan.com

Almost Twelve by Kenneth N. Taylor, published by Tyndale House, available from many Christian book sellers and used books sites

(The) Amazing Story of Creation from Science and the Bible by Duane Gish, illustrated by Earl and Bonnie Snellenberger, published by Institute for Creation Research www.icr.com

Anatomy of the Human Body by Henry Gray, available for sale from several retailers, but can be searched online at http://www.bartleby.com/107/

(The) Ancient Engineers by L. Sprague DeCamp, published by Barnes and Noble publishers. www.barnesandnoble.com

(The) Ancient Near East by Amelie Kuhrt, and Eva Von Dassow, part of the *Routledge History of the Ancient World* series published by Routledge Taylor & Francis Group, available from www.routledge.com/books

Answers in Genesis DVD seminar, available at https://answersingenesis.org

Antiquities of the Jews; Flavius Josephus, available through most online sellers of used or reprinted Christian or history books

Atoms and Molecules by Usborne Books, sold by independent distributors; find one or order online at www.ubam.com

Baker's Bible Atlas by Charles F. Pfeiffer, edited by Ernest Leslie Carlson and Martin H. Scharlemann, available in print and ebook format.

Beautiful Girlhood original by Mabel Hale, or revised edition by Karen Andreola, published by Great Expectations Co. available from www.pumpkinseedpress.net

Beyond Beautiful Girlhood Plus Companion Guide by Shelley Noonan and Margaret Sangster published by Pumpkin Seed Press, available in print and Kindle format from www.pumpkinseedpress.net

(The) Biblical Basis for Modern Science by Henry Morris, published by Answers in Genesis, www.answersincenesis.org

Bones of Contention: A Creationist Assessment of Human Fossils by Marvin L. Lubenow published by Baker Books www.bakerpublishinggroup.com

Book of Virtues, by William J. Bennett, readily available in many bookstores, online sites and public libraries

The Care and Keeping of You (for girls entering puberty) compiled, edited and published by American Girl; http://www.americangirl.com/shop/bookstore/advice-library

The Care and Keeping of You 2: The Body Book for Older Girls compiled, edited and published by American Girl; http://www.americangirl.com/shop/bookstore/advice-library

Celebrating Jesus in the Biblical Feasts: Discovering Their Significance to You as a Christian by Dr. Richard Booker available in both print and ebook.

Children's Book of Virtues, by William J. Bennett, readily available in many bookstores, online sites and public libraries

Christian Character: A Course for Training Young People by Gary Maldaner from http://www.elwoodbiblebaptistchurch.com/garymaldaner.php

(A) Christian Survey of World History audio set by R. J. Rushdooney, available in CD and MP3 format from http://chalcedon.edu/store/all/History/

Chronology of the Bible by Frank R. Klassen, available from www.christianbook.com

(The) Companion Guide to Beautiful Girlhood by Shelley Noonan and Kimberly Zach published by Pumpkin Seed Press, in print and Kindle format www.pumpkinseedpress.net

Competent to Counsel by Dr. Jay Adams published by Zondervan, www.zondervan.com

Creation Facts of Life, by Gary Parker, published by and available from Institute for Creation Research www.icr.org

D is for Dinosaur, by Ken Hamm, published and sold by Answers in Genesis, www.answersingenesis.org

(The) Daily Bible by F. La Gard Smith published by and available from Harvest House www.harvesthousepublishers.com

Dear Princess: A Book for Girls, by Mary M. Landis, published by and available from Rod and Staff publishers, www.rodstaff.com

Dictionary of Chemistry published by Usborne Books, sold by independent distributors; find one or order online at www.ubam.com

Dinosaurs and the Bible, published by Institute for Creation Research, www.icr.org

Dinosaurs by Design by Duane Gish with illustrations by Earl and Bonnie Snellenberger, published by Institute for Creation Research, www.icr.org

Dinosaurs: Those Terrible Lizards by Duane T. Gish published by Institute for Creation Research, available from www.icr.org

Elsie Dinsmore series by Martha Finley, published by Mead-Dodd. Many of the original books are out of print but can still be found in many libraries or can be read online at Project Gutenberg or Internet Archive and/or downloaded in audio format at LibriVox as well as ordered in book form. Here is a complete list of all the Elsie Dinsmore titles: *Elsie Dinsmore, Elsie's Holidays at Roselands, Elsie's Girlhood, Elsie's Womanhood, Elsie's Motherhood, Elsie's Children, Elsie's Widowhood, Grandmother Elsie, Elsie's New Relations, Elsie at Nantucket, The Two Elsies, Elsie's Kith and Kin, Elsie's Friends at Woodburn, Christmas with Grandma Elsie, Elsie and the Raymonds, Elsie Yachting with the Raymonds, Elsie's Vacation, Elsie at Viamede, Elsie at Ion, Elsie at the World's Fair, Elsie's Journey on Inland Waters, Elsie at Home, Elsie on the Hudson, Elsie in the South, Elsie's Young Folks, Elsie's Winter Trip, Elsie and Her Loved Ones, Elsie and Her Namesakes*

(The Elsie Dinsmore series has also been redone *as Elsie Dinsmore Life of Faith*. The language has been modernized and some situations have been "updated". However, many of the characters, events, and situations have been excluded, which may have weakened the strong Christian perspective in the story line.)

Empires and Barbarians published by Usborne Books, sold by independent distributors; find one or order online at www.ubam.com

Essential Chemistry published by Usborne Books, sold by independent distributors; find one or order online at www.ubam.com

Esther: A Woman of Strength and Dignity, by Charles Swindoll, published by Thomas Nelson, www.thomasnelson.com

Evolution: Fact or Belief, a DVD by Eric Holmberg, produced by The Apologetics Group., available at www.theapologeticsgroup.com

(The) First Civilizations: History of Everyday Things, , by Usborne Books, sold by independent distributors, find one or order online at www.ubam.com

Friendly Chemistry, a complete lab course for the home or school, by Joey and Lisa Hajda, available from www.friendlychemistry.com

Gem Hunters' Kit by Tim Lutz, produced by Running Press, harder to find now, might need to look at used sources or find a similar kit in craft stores

Genesis: Finding Our Roots written by Ruth Beechick, available through many homeschool vendors

(The) Genesis Flood by Henry Morris, published by Institute for Creation Research, available from www.icr.org

Geometry: the beauty of numbers, produced by Old Fashioned Crafts, available at www.mugginsmath.com

God's Priceless Woman Bible study guide by Wanda Sanseri, published by Back Home Industries, available from homeschool or Christian book distributors.

Grand Canyon: Monument to Catastrophe by Dr. Steve Austin, published by Institute for Creation Research, available form www.icr.org

Gray's Anatomy, (see *Anatomy of the Human Body*)

(The) Great Dinosaur Mystery and the Bible by Paul S. Taylor, published by The Chariot Victor Publishing Group, www.christian-book-store.christiansunite.com/.../Chariot-Victor-Publishing

Greenleaf Guide to the Old Testament; published by Greenleaf Press http://greenleafpress.com

Harbrace College Handbook, edited by John C. Rogers, published by Harcourt, Brace, Jovanovich, available anywhere college textbooks are sold.

(The) Herbal Bible: A Family Guide to Herbal Home Remedies by Michael A. Weiner published by Quantum Books

History Begins at Sumer: Thirty-Nine Firsts in Man's Recorded History by Samuel Noah Kramer, published by University of Pennsylvania Press, available in most online bookstores

How Should We Then Live: multi-volume video series by Francis Schaeffer, no longer being produced but available through www.amazon.com

Italic Handwriting Curriculum by Barbara Getty and Inga Dubay, published by Allport Editions, available from www.christianbook.com

Jane Eyre by Charlotte Bronte`, readily available in public libraries

The Jewish Wars, by Flavius Josephus, widely available in used book stores or sites and may be in many libraries

Little Women -Treasury of Illustrated Classics Storybook Collection by Louisa Mae Alcott published by Modern Publishing, also available from other publishers in other formats including Kindle, found in most libraries

Manners and Customs of Bible Lands by Fred Wight; may be hard to find and can be replaced with *The New Manners and Customs of Bible Times* by Ralph Gower, available from online retailers

O! Euclid game, by Ampersand Press, available from https://boardgamegeek.com/boardgame/37293/o-euclid

On the Origin of Species by Charles Darwin, available in many libraries and secular college bookstores

Origins: How the World Came to Be by Dr. A. E. Wilder-Smith, produced by Films for Christ, and Eden Communications available from www.worldcat.org (individual titles: *Origins of the Universe; Earth, A Young Planet; The Origin of Life; The Origin of Species; The Origin of Mankind* and T*he Fossil Record*

Our Father Abraham: Jewish Roots of the Christian Faith by Marvin R. Wilson, published by Wm. B. Eerdmans Publishing Co. www.eerdmans.com

Preparing for Adolescence by James Dobson, published by Revell, a division of Baker Publishing Group www.bakerpublishinggroup.com/revell

The Ra*re Jewel of Christian Contentment* by Jeremiah Burroughs, part of the Puritan Paperbacks series, www.banneroftruth.org/us/store

Rocks and Minerals, by Usborne Books, sold by independent distributors, find one or order online at www.ubam.com

The Rodale Whole Foods Cookbook by Dara Demoelt, published by Rodale Books

Rubies and Sapphires by Fred Ward, part of Fred Ward Gem series, available in many libraries

Scientific Creationism by Dr. Henry M. Morris, published by and available from Institute for Creation Research www.icr.org

Sense and Sensibility by Jane Austen, readily available in libraries

Spencerian Penmanship developed by P. R. Spencer, published by Mott Media, www.mottmedia.com

Streams of Civilization V. I; by Mary Stanton, Albert Hyma; published by Christian Liberty Press, www.shopchristianliberty.com

Time-Life series entitled *Lost Civilizations* (includes all the following): *Unlocking the Mysteries of Creation* DVD or CD seminar by Dennis Peterson, produced by Creation Resource Foundation, can be purchased with or without companion textbook and workbook *Sumer: Cities of Eden; Mesopotamia: the Mighty Kings; Persians: Masters of the Empire,* available through Time-Life books and may be in some public libraries

Unlocking the Mystery of Creation by Dennis R. Peterson, published by Institute for Creation Research, available from *www.icr.org*

Webster's 1828 Dictionary published by Merriam –Webster, sold by many homeschool suppliers and a few general bookstores, can also be searched online at www.1828.mshaffer.com

What in the World is Going on Here? CD set by Diana Waring available from
http://www.dianawaring.com/store/history-curriculum/what-in-the-world-1-track-titles

What Really Happened to the Dinosaurs? By Henry Morris and Ken Hamm , published by Institute for
Creation Research, www.icr.org

The World that Perished by John C. Whitcomb

World Almanac, published annually by World Almanac Company. You need not buy a new one every
year, as the information you will be using from it will not change that often. These are sold in
most book stores or sites and can often be found in libraries

World History Dates; published by Usborne Books. www.usbornebooks.com available in many
bookstores and websites and through local representatives

Writer's Inc. published by The Write Source, www.thewritesource.com

Writing a Research Paper by Edward J. Shevan, published by Christian Liberty Press, available in both
print and e-book versions from www.shopchristianliberty.com

Writing for College, published by and available from The Write Source www.thewritesource.com

Wuthering Heights, by Emily Bronte`, readily available in public libraries

UNIT 2
The heart of her husband safely trusts in her;
He will have no lack of gain. She does him good and not evil all the days of her life.
Proverbs 31:11-12

Abigail: A Novel by Lois Henderson, published by Harper Collins, www.harpercollins.com

Accounting Made Simple by Mike Piper, CPA published by Simple Subjects Inc. now available only in Kindle format through www.amazon.com

(The) Art of Choosing Your Love by Jim West, CreateSpace Independent Publishing Platform, www.createspace.com

(The) Bare Facts: 39 Questions Your Parents Hope You Never Ask about Sex by Josh McDowell, published by Moody Publishers

Before You Meet Prince Charming by Sarah Mally, published by Tomorrow's Forefathers, www.tomorrowsforefathers.com

Big Ideas, Small Budget by Pat Wesolowski published by the author, currently available only used through Amazon Marketplace of other used vendors.

Boy Meets Girl: Say Hello to Courtship by Joshua Harris available from www.joshharris.com

(The) Challenges of Christian Womanhood interactive Bible Study series, produced by Tri-R Ministries and available from http://tri-r-ministries.com/

Choices and Consequences (out-of-print see: *What's the Big Deal*)

(The) Christian Family, by Larry Christenson published by Bethany House, www.bakerpublishinggroup.com/bethanyhouse

Christian Living in the Home By: Jay E. Adams P & R Publishing, www.prpbooks.com

Christy by Catherine Marshall, published by HarperCollins Publishers, available from www.goodreads,com

(The) Courtship of Sarah Mclean, by Stephen B. Castleberry, published by Castleberry Farms Press, www.castleberryfarms.com

Creative Counterpart: Becoming the Woman, Wife, and Mother You've Longed to Be by Linda Dillow, published by Thomas Nelson, www.thomasnelson.com

(The) *Daily Bible* by F. LaGard Smith published by Harvest House, available from www.harvesthousepublishers.com

Dating with Integrity by John Holzmann, published by Christian Publishers, available from www.harvesthousepublishers.com sold by www.sonlight.com

Facing the Facts: Truth about Sex and You from the *God's Design for Sex* series, by Stan and Brenna Jones, published by Nav Press, buy from http://www.christiansexed.com/books/

Financial Peace University, on DVD or in a live seminar featuring Dave Ramsey, www.daveramsey.com/store

(The) Fruitful Life by Jerry Bridges, published by Nav Press, www.navpress.com

Get a Grip on Your Money by Larry Burkett, published by Focus on the Family
www.focusonthefamily.com

God and Government by Gary Demar published by American Vision Press,
http://store.americanvision.org/products/god-and-government

(A) Good Man is Hard to Find- Unless You Ask God to be the Head of your Search Committee, by Jo Lynne Poole, published by Nelson Books, available from www.goodreads.com

Grace Livingston Hill books --- *The Works of Grace Livingston Hill* by Grace Livingston Hill (a collection of 11 of her most popular novels), and single volumes of her more than 100 novels, available for purchase at www.goodreads.com and in many public libraries

Gray's Anatomy, (correctly entitled *Anatomy of the Human Body*) by Henry Gray, available for sale from several retailers, but can be searched online at http://www.bartleby.com/107/

Gray's Anatomy Coloring Book by Fred Stark, published by Running Press, available from www.hometrainingtools.com

(The) Great Romance: The Ultimate Purpose by Jonathan Lindvall, available online at 'http://w.thelastdays.net/317-TheGreatRomance.mp3 Bible, Homeschooling, and the Law

Harbrace College Handbook, edited by John C. Rogers, published by Harcourt, Brace, Jovanovich, available anywhere college textbooks are sold, or may be rented for one school year at www.chegg.com

Her Hand in Marriage written by Douglas Wilson, published by Canon Press, available from www.goodreads.com/book/show/547276

How to Live on Practically Nothing and Have Plenty by Janet Chadwick, published by Knopf-Doubleday www.pantheonpress.com probably in many public libraries

I Kissed Dating Goodbye by Joshua Harris, available in both book and DVD format from www.joshharris.com

Italic Handwriting Curriculum by Barbara Getty and Inga Dubay, published by Allport Editions, available from www.christianbook.com

Janette Oke wrote four major series: *Love Comes Softly, Seasons of the Heart, Canadian West, Women of the West*, a few trilogies and many stand-alone books, all from a Christian perspective set in the pioneer West of North America when courtship, betrothal and parent involvement in youthful romance were the norm. For a list of all her books, see https://www.goodreads.com/author/list/4049.Janette_Oke. Many of these are in libraries

Jeff McLean: His Courtship, by Stephen B. Castleberry, published by Castleberry Farms Press, www.castleberryfarms.com

Letters to Karen by Charlie Shedd published by Abingdon Press www.abingdonpress.com

Macbeth by William Shakespeare, best seen as a live play but can be ordered or rented on video, available on DVD and Netflix

Miserly Moms by Jonni McCoy, self-published, now available as ebook only, from http://www.miserlymoms.com/jonnisbooks_updated.html

Moral Purity (audio); by Pastor Bill Lehman; published by Pilgrim Tape Ministry; free mp3 download; http://www.pastorbilllehman.org/index.php/sermons/serie/13-moral-purity

More than Enough by Dave Ramsey, published by Penguin Group available from www.daveramsey.com/store

Of Knights and Fair Maidens, by Jeff and Danielle Myers, published by Grace and Truth Books, www.graceandtruth.com

Passion and Purity by Elisabeth Elliott, published by Revell, a division of Baker Publishing Group, www.bakerpublishinggroup.com, available at www.graceandtruthbooks.com

Physician's Desk Reference (PDR) online at www.pdr.net,

Preparing for Adolescence by Dr. James Dobson, published by Focus on the Family, www.focusonthefamily.com

Priscilla and Aquila, a fictionalized by Lois Henderson, published by Harper Collins

www.harpercollins.com

Quest for Love: True Stories of Passion and Purity by Elisabeth Elliot, published by Revell, a division of Baker Publishing Group, www.bakerpublishinggroup.com available from www.graceandtruthbooks.com

Romeo and Juliet by William Shakespeare, best seen as a live play but can be ordered or rented on video, can be viewed as a movie on DVD and Netflix

Ron Blue Institute https://www.indwes.edu/ron-blue-institute/ offers books, videos, and complete courses in financial planning and long-range money management based on Biblical principles

(The) Shaping of the Christian Family, written by Elisabeth Elliott, published by Revell, available from www.graceandtruthbooks.com

Spencerian Penmanship developed by P. R. Spencer, published by Mott Media, www.mottmedia.com

Straight Talk to Men and Their Wives by James Dobson, published by Focus on the Family, www.focusonthefamily.com

Surviving the Money Jungle by Larry Burkett, published by Focus on the Family, www.focusonthefamily.com

(The) Taming of the Shrew by William Shakespeare, best seen as a live play but can be ordered or rented on video best seen as a live play but can be ordered or rented on video

Tightwad Gazette series -- *(The) Complete Tightwad Gazette. The Tightwad Gazette II* and *The Tightwad Gazette III* by Amy Dacyzyn, published by Villard, available from www.amazon.com

True Love Project DVD series with student workbook, by Clayton King, published by Lifeway Christian Resources, www.lifeway.com

Waiting for Her Isaac by Mr. and Mrs. Stephen B. Castleberry, published by Castleberry Farms Press, www.castleberryfarms.com

What Every Christian Should know about the AIDS Epidemic by Franklin E. Payne, published by Baker Publishing Group, available from http://www.alibris.com

Whatever Happened to Penny Candy? by Richard Maybury, published by Bluestocking Press www.bluestockingpress.com

What's the Big Deal from the *God's Design for Sex* series, by Stan and Brenna Jones, published by Nav Press, buy from http://www.christiansexed.com/books/

Why Wait? by Josh McDowell and DIck Day, published by Thomas Nelson, Inc. www.thomasnelson.com

Writer's Inc. published by The Write Source, www.thewritesource.com

Writing a Research Paper by Edward J. Shevan, published by Christian Liberty Press, available in both print and e-book versions from www.shopchristianliberty.com

Writing for College, published by and available from The Write Source www.thewritesource.com

UNIT 3
She seeks wool and flax and works with her hands in delight.
Proverbs 31:13

All Creatures Great and Small, by Dr. James Herriot DVM, to order or for a complete list of all his works, see http://www.jamesherriot.org/his-works/

All Things Bright and Beautiful, by Dr. James Herriot DVM, to order or for a complete list of all his works, see http://www.jamesherriot.org/his-works/

All Things Wise and Wonderful, by Dr. James Herriot DVM, to order or for a complete list of all his works, see http://www.jamesherriot.org/his-works/

All the People of the Bible by Richard R. Losch, published by Wm. B. Eerdmans Publishing Co, www.eerdmans.com

Anatomy of the Human Body by Henry Gray, available for sale from several retailers, but can be searched online at http://www.bartleby.com/107/

Bambi, vintage book by Felix Salten, published by Grossett and Dunlap in 1939. Other editions are available now, but for the authentic ones that are true to the original, visit www.stucco.com

Beggar to King: All the Occupations of Bible Times, by Walter Duckat published by Abingdon Press www.abingdonpress.com can be read online through www.librarything.com

The Biblical Feasts, (no longer available, see *Celebrating Jesus in the Biblical Feasts*)

Black Beauty by Anna Sewell, *published by* Dover Children's Thrift Classics, www.doverpublications.com

*The Black Stallion (*and other books in this series) *by* Walter Farley, published by Yearling, an imprint of Random House www.randomhousekids.com available in many libraries

Born Free, by Joy Adamson, published by Pantheon Books, a division of Grand Central -Doubleday www.pantheonpress.com. A DVD for this is also available but should not take the place of reading the book

Call of the Wild by Jack London, classic literature currently published in various editions by several companies, found in most libraries

Celebrating Jesus in the Biblical Feasts: Discovering Their Significance to You as a Christian by Dr. Richard Booker available in both print and e-book from major online retailers

Charlotte's Web by E. B. White, published by HarperCollins, www.harpercollinschildrens.com, probably available in many libraries

The Chronicles of Narnia series by C. S. Lis, available in many libraries in editions published by HarperCollins *www.harpercollinschildrens.com* and Scholastic Inc. www.scholastic.com

College English Handbook renamed *Harbrace College Handbook* and listed below

(The) *Daily Bible* by F. LaGard Smith published by Harvest House, available from www.harvesthousepublishers.com

David, A Man of Passion and Destiny, by Charles Swindoll, published by Thomas Nelson, www.thomasnelson.com

Gray's Anatomy, (see *Anatomy of the Human Body*)

Harbrace College Handbook, edited by John C. Rogers, published by Harcourt, Brace, Jovanovich, available anywhere college textbooks are sold, or may be rented for one school year at www.chegg.com

How to Draw Animals by Jack Hamm, published by Perigee Publishers www.penguin.com/meet/publishers/perigee

James Herriot's novels include: *All Things Bright and Beautiful, * All Creatures Great and Small, * All Things Wise and Wonderful*, and *The Lord God Made Them All*, all of which are listed separately with contact information in this list. He wrote many other novels which you may also read if you wish.

The Jungle Book classic literature by Rudyard Kipling, published in several forms by varied publishers, available on most libraries

The Kingfisher History Encyclopedia, edited and published by Houghton, Mifflin, Harcourt available through www.amazon.com and is n many libraries

Lad, A Dog written by Albert Payson Terhune, published by Townsend Press, www.townsendpress.com

Lassie Come Home, by Eric Knight and Marguerite Kimsey, published by Square Fish, available from many retailers and often in juvenile section of libraries

Lessons from a Sheep Dog, by Philip Keller, published by Zondervan, www.zondervan.com

The Lion the Witch and the Wardrobe, by C. S. Lewis, (part of *The Chronicles of Narnia*), published by HarperCollins *www.harpercollinschildrens.com* and Scholastic Inc. www.scholastic.com

Misty of Chincoteague by Marguerite Henry, published by Rand McNally & Company, www.randmcnally.com

National Velvet by Enid Bagnold, published by Dover Children's Classics, www.doverpublications.com

The New Way Things Work by David Macaulay, published by Houghton Mifflin/Walter Lorraine Books www.hmhco.com/at-home, widely available for purchase and in some libraries

A Shepherd Looks at the 23rd Psalm, by Philip Keller, published by Zondervan, www.zondervan.com

Spencerian Penmanship developed by P. R. Spencer, published by Mott Media, www.mottmedia.com

Timetables of History, by Bernard Grun, currently out-of-print but readily available through Amazon, e-bay and other used sources, ay substitute with *The Amazing Bible Timeline*,

Watership Down, by Richard Adams, published by Scribner, an imprint of Simon & Schuster, www.simonschuster.com

Webster's 1828 Dictionary published by Merriam –Webster, sold by many homeschool suppliers and a few general bookstores, can also be searched online at www.1828.mshaffer.com

Where the Red Fern Grows, by Wilson Rawls, published by Yearling, an imprint of Random House www.randomhousekids.com available in most libraries

White Fang, by Jack London, currently published in different versions by several companies, available in most libraries

World Almanac, published annually by World Almanac Company. You need not buy a new one every year, as the information you will be using from it will not change that often. These are sold in most book stores or sites and can often be found in libraries

World History Dates; published by Usborne Books. www.usborne.com available in many bookstores and websites and through local representatives

Writer's Inc. published by The Write Source, www.thewritesource.com

Writing a Research Paper by Edward J. Shevan, published by Christian Liberty Press, available in both print and e-book versions from www.shopchristianliberty.com

Writing for College, published by and available from The Write Source www.thewritesource.com

The Yearling by Marjorie Kinnan Rawlings, published by Aladdin Classics, www.aladdinbooks.com in most libraries

UNIT 4
She is like merchant ships,
she brings her food from afar.
Proverbs 31:14

1492: Conquest of Paradise, motion picture produced by Alain Goldman and Ridley Scott, available from www.netflix.com, and other online sources

America: The First 350 Years, by Steven Wilkins, produced by Covenant Publications CD–ROM or MP3 format (will play on computer or other MP3 compatible CD players, and DVD players, but not on traditional CD players) from www.shekinahhomeschool.com/*america-the-first-350-years*

American Historical Documents, a collection of works by various authors, compiled by Dr. Charles Elliot as part of the 51-volume *Harvard Classics*, out of-print, can be found at used booksellers, some public libraries and download, borrow, or read online at https://openlibrary.org/books/

American Original Documents (see *American Historical Documents*)

Anatomy of the Human Body by Henry Gray, available for sale from several retailers, but can be searched online at http://www.bartleby.com/107/

(The) Ancient Mariner (see *The Rime of the Ancient Mariner*)

Around the World in Eighty Days by Jules Verne, classic literature, available from many book vendors and most public libraries

Atlas of North American Exploration by William H. Goetzmann and Glyndwr Williams published by University of Oklahoma Press, sold by all major online retailers and may be in public libraries.

Back to Basics: A Complete Guide to Traditional Skills, edited by Abigail Gehring, published by Skyhorse Press, www.skyhorsepublishing.com

Baker's Bible Atlas by by Charles F. Pfeiffer, edited by Ernest Leslie Carlson and Martin H. Scharlemann, available in print and ebook format from many retailers, may be in some libraries

(The) Blue Nile, by Alan Moorhead, published by Harper Perennial, sold by most major bookstores and their websites

Christopher Columbus, by Bennie Rhodes, part of the Sower Series published Mott Media, www.mottmedia.com

Christopher Columbus: How He Did It, by Charlotte Yue, published by Houghton Mifflin, www.hmhco.com

Columbus and Cortez: Conquerors for Christ by Dr. John Eidsmoe, published by New Leaf Publishing Group, www.nlpg.com

Columbus and the Age of Explorers, a portfolio of primary source documents, translated by Jackdaw Publications, a division of Golden Owl Publishing, www.jackdaw.com

Columbus: the Last Crusader (see The *Last Crusader: Untold Story of Christopher Columbus*)

(The) Daily Bible by F. La Gard Smith published by and available from Harvest House www.harvesthousepublishers.com

David Livingstone by John Hudson Tiner, part of the Sower Series published Mott Media, www.mottmedia.com

Everything Kids Science Experiment Book, published by Adams Media, available from
    www.sciencemadesimole.com/store

Explorers of North America, a Good Apple History Packet, published by Good Apple, a division of Frank
    Schaffer publications, http://www.k12schoolsupplies.net/Frank-Schaffer-Publications-s/1299.htm

Explorers: From Columbus to Armstrong, by F. Everett, published by Turtleback Books, available only
    used or in libraries at this time

Gaining Favor with God and Man, by William Thayer, published by Mantle Ministries
    www.mantleministries.com

Global Pursuit board game, designed by Howard E. Paine, produced by National Geographic Society,
    www.nationalgeographic.com

Gray's Anatomy, (see *Anatomy of the Human Body* by Henry Gray)

Gray's Anatomy Coloring Book, by Fred Stark, published by Running Press, available from
    www.hometrainingtools.com

How to Draw Ships and Boats: Drawing Books for Beginners Volume 30,

How to Draw Maps and Charts by Pam Beasant and Alistair Smith, published by Usborne Books, sold by
    independent distributors find one or order online at www.ubam.com

Invention and Discovery published by Usborne Books, sold by independent distributors find one or order
    online at www.ubam.com

Jackdaws portfolio on Christopher Columbus (see *Columbus and the Age of Explorers*)

The Kingfisher History Encyclopedia, edited and published by Houghton, Mifflin, Harcourt available
    through www.amazon.com and in many libraries

Kidnapped, by Robert Louis Stevenson, classic literature published by various companies in assorted
    formats, in most public libraries

Kids Kit: Magnets produced by Usborne Books, sold by independent distributors find one or order online
    at www.ubam.com

Kon-Tiki: Across the Pacific in a Raft by Thor Heyerdahl , published by Simon & Schuster, Inc.,
    www.simonandschuster.com

Th*e Last Crusader: Untold Story of Christopher Columbus)* by George Grant, published by Crossway
    Books www.crossway.org/books

The Light and the Glory, by Peter Marshall and David Manuel, published by Baker Book House,
    www.bakerbookretail.com

Meeting the Whales, by Erich Hoyt, publisher Sagebrush, part of their Equinox Guides series,
    www.jacketflap.com

Moses: A Man of Selfless Dedication from the Great Lives Series by Charles R. Swindoll, published by
    Thomas Nelson, www.thomasnelson.com

The New Way Things Work by David Macaulay, published by Houghton Mifflin/Walter Lorraine Books
    www.hmhco.com/at-home, widely available at retailers and libraries

*Ocean Life, p*ublished by Usborne Books sold by independent distributors find one or order online at
    www.ubam.com

The Old Man and the Sea by Ernest Hemingway, classic literature, available in many bookstores and
    libraries

On Assignment, created and produced by National Geographic Society, www.nationalgeographic.com

Pirates and Plunder game created by Brian L. Bird, Richard T. Rowan, and Jerry Lee, with Print & Play Productions, available at www.mugginsmath.com

Riding with the Dolphins, by Erich Hoyt, publisher Sagebrush, part of their Equinox Guides series, www.jacketflap.com

The Rime of the Ancient Mariner an epic poem by Samuel Taylor Coleridge, found in many anthologies of classic poetry or literature textbooks, or can be read online at https://openlibrary.org/books/

The Ring of the Nebulung, by Richard Wagner, translated by Andrew Porter, an opera available in CD, DVD, book and MP3 formats from various web locations; the film version can be rented from Netflix.

The Sea Hawk, by Rafael Sabatini, published by Wild Side Press and others, freely available for sale new and used and often in libraries

Search for the Blue Nile, (See the Blue Nile)

The Sinking of the Titanic and Great Sea Disasters, by Bob Garner, published by The Vision Forum Inc, which is now closed; the book is still available from several major retailers.

Sketches of Church History, by S, M, Houghton and Iain Murray, published by Banner of Truth, www.banneroftruth.org

Spices of the World game, developed by Rex A. Martin, published by Avalon Hill, available from www.boardgamegeek.com

Streams of Civilization, V. 1, by Mary Stanton, Albert Hyma; published by Christian Liberty Press, www.shopchristianliberty.com

Timetables of History, by Bernard Grun, currently out-of-print but readily available through Amazon, e-bay and other used sources

Two Years before the Mast, by Richard Henry Dana, published many times --- most recently by CreateSpace Independent Publishing Platform www.createspace.com

Treasure Island, by Robert Louis Stevenson, classic literature published by various companies in assorted formats, in most public libraries

Where in the World? Developed by Aristoplay and currently marketed by Talicor hwww.beso.com/talicor-games

Where in the World is Carmen Sandiego? Computer games can be played online at http://www.letsplaysnes.com/play-where-in-the-world-is-carmen-sandiego-online/

World Almanac, published annually by World Almanac Company. You need not buy a new one every year, as the information you will be using from it will not change that often. These are sold in most book stores or sites and can often be found in libraries

World History Dates; published by Usborne Books. www.usbornebooks.com available in many bookstores and websites and through local representatives

(The) Wright Brothers, by Charles Ludwig, part of the Sower Series published Mott Media, www.mottmedia.com

Writer's Inc. published by The Write Source, www.thewritesource.com

Writing a Research Paper by Edward J. Shevan, published by Christian Liberty Press, available in both print and e-book versions from www.shopchristianliberty.com

UNIT 5
She rises while it is yet night and gives food to her family and a portion for her maidens.
Proverbs 31:15

America: The First 350 Years, lectures by Steven Wilkins, produced by Covenant Publications CD–ROM or MP3 format (will play on computer or other MP3 compatible CD players, and DVD players, but not on traditional CD players) from www.shekinahhomeschool.com/*america-the-first-350-years*

American Historical Documents, a collection of works by various authors, compiled by Dr. Charles Elliot as part of the 51-volume *Harvard Classics*, long out of-print, can be found at used booksellers, some public libraries and download, borrow, or read online at https://openlibrary.org/books/

American Original Documents (see *American Historical Documents*)

Anatomy of the Human Body by Henry Gray, available for sale from several retailers, but can be searched online at http://www.bartleby.com/107/

Ancient Egypt: A DK Eyewitness Book by George Hart, published by Dorling-Kindersley www.dk.com

Ancient Egypt Explorer's Kit, by Denise M. Doxey Ph.D., published by Running Press Book Publishers, www.runningpress.com

Ancient Egypt Treasure Chest, by James Putnam, published by Hodder Children's *Books,* www.hoddereducation.co.uk

Archaeology, published by Usborne Books, sold by independent distributors, find one or order online at www.ubam.com

Backyard Scientist Series One: 25 Experiments That Kids Can Perform Using Things Found around the House, written by Jane Hoffmann, published by Backyard Scientist www.backyardscientist.com

Baker's Bible Atlas by Charles F. Pfeiffer, edited by Ernest Leslie Carlson and Martin H. Scharlemann, available in print and e-3book format from many retailers, and libraries

Basic History of the United States, Vol. 3: The Sections and the Civil War 1826-1877 by Clarence B. Carson published in print by American Textbook Committee and on audio CD by Blackstone Audio; both can be ordered from www.exodusbooks.com/author.aspx?id=2496

Before Freedom: When I Just Can Remember: Twenty-Seven Oral Histories of Former South Carolina Slaves by Belinda Hurmence published by John F. Blair, www.blairpub.com

Black Confederates by Charles Kelly Barrow and J. H. Segars, published by Pelican, www.pelicanpub.com

Cakes and Cookies for Beginners (A Child's Cookbook) by Usborne Books, sold by independent distributors, find one or order online at www.ubam.com

The Cat of Bubastes by G. A. Henty, published in print by Robinson Books, www.robinsonbooks.com also available in audio book format from Jim Hodges Audio Books, www.jimhodgesaudiobooks.com

Christ in the Camp, by J. William Jones published by The Vision Forum, which is now closed, book is still available from several major retailers.

(A) Christian Survey of World History audio set by R. J. Rushdooney, available in CD and MP3 format from http://chalcedon.edu/store/all/History/

Civil War Game produced by Educational Materials Associates, available from www.donsgamecloset.com

The Civil War mini-series, produced by PBS, available on DVD from www.pbs.org

The Civil War portfolio or *War Between the States: Civil War* portfolio of primary source documents, researched and translated by Jackdaw Publications, a division of Golden Owl Publishing, www.jackdaw.com

Clarence Carson's U. S. History series (see *A Basic History of the United States*)

Cooking for Beginners, by Usborne Books, sold by independent distributors, find one or order online at www.ubam.com

DK Ancient Egyptians (see *Ancient Egypt: A DK Eyewitness Book*)

(The) *Daily Bible* by F. LaGard Smith published by and available from Harvest House, www.harvesthousepublishers.com

Devil on the Deck, a Stirring Adventure about John Newton's Discovery of Amazing Grace, by Lois Hoadley Dick published by F. H. Revell, a division of Baker Publishing Group bakerpublishinggroup.com/revell

Eat Well, Live Well, by Pamela M. Smith, published by Thomas Nelson, www.thomasnelson.

The Egyptians, by Usborne Books, sold by independent distributors, find one or order online at www.ubam.com

T*he Egyptian Echo,* by Usborne Books, sold by independent distributors; find one or order online at www.ubam.com

Egyptian Treasure Chest (see Ancient Egypt Treasure Chest)

Egyptian Funeral Boat (Make Your Own Cut-out Model), by Allan Cole, published by The British Museum, www.britishmuseum.org

Facts the Historians Leave Out by John S. Tilley, published by The Confederate Reprint Company, www.confederatereprint.com

Food, Fitness, and Health published by Usborne Books sold by independent distributors, find one or order online at www.ubam.com

From Calabar to Carter's Grove, by Lorena S. Walsh, published by University of Virginia Press, www.upress.virginia.edu

Fun with Hieroglyphs, by Usborne Books, sold by independent distributors, find one or order online at www.ubam.com

Gods and Generals by Michael Shaara, published by McKay Publishing, contact them at www.jacketflap.com available from many retailers and in most libraries

The Golden Goblet by Eloise Jarvis McGraw, published by Puffin Books as part of their Newberry Library, www.puffin.co.uk

Gone with the Wind, written by Margaret Mitchell, most recent edition published by Pocket Books, an imprint of Simon & Schuster, www.simonandschuster.com

Gray's Anatomy Coloring Book, Gray's Anatomy Coloring Book, by Fred Stark, published by Running Press, available from www.hometrainingtools.com

Greenleaf's Guide to Ancient Egypt published by Greenleaf Press http://www.greenleafpress.com

Hagar, a fictionalized biography, by Lois Henderson, published by Harper Collins www.harpercollins.com

Harbrace College Handbook, edited by John C. Rogers, published by Harcourt, Brace, Jovanovich, available where college textbooks are sold and may be able rented by the school year at www.chegg.com

Hearth and Home, written and published by Karey Swann, available only as digital downloads from http://mbpdf.abhappybooks.com/book/978-1929125067

The Hidden Art of Homemaking by Edith Schaeffer, published by Tyndale House www.tyndale.com

Homemade Health, by Anke Bialis, published by Natator Publishing, www.herbologyathome.com

How They Lived in Bible Times written by Graham Jones, published by Scripture Union, available to purchase or borrow from https//openlibrary.org

How to Live on Practically Nothing and Have Plenty, by Janet Chadwick, published by Knopf, available from many major book sellers and public libraries

Into the Mummy's Tomb (A Time Quest Book) by Nicholas Reeves, published by Scholastic www.scholastic.com

*Italic Handwriting c*urriculum by Barbara Getty and Inga Dubay, published by Allport Editions, available from www.christianbook.com

Jackdaws portfolio of The Civil War (see *The Civil War* from Jackdaws)

John Brown's Body book-length poem, by Stephen Vincent Benet,

Joseph: A Man of Integrity and Forgiveness by Charles Swindoll, published by Thomas Nelson, www.thomasnelson.com

Killer Angels, by Michael Shaara, published by McKay Publishing, contact them at www.jacketflap.com available from many retailers and in most libraries

The Kingfisher History Encyclopedia, edited and published by Houghton, Mifflin, Harcourt available through www.amazon.com and in many libraries

Little Dorritt, classic literature by Charles Dickens, available at most general bookstores and public libraries

Make History: Ancient Egypt by Nancy Fister and Charlene Olexiewicz published by Lowell House, find them at www.jacketflap.com

Make it Work: Ancient Egypt by Andrew Haslam, published by Cooper Square Publishing, find them at www.jacketflap.com

Make this Egyptian Temple published by Usborne Books, sold by independent distributors; find one or order online at www.ubam.com

Make this Egyptian Mummy published by Usborne Books, sold by independent distributors; find one or order online at www.ubam.com

Manners and Customs of Bible Lands by Fred Wight; may be hard to find and can be replaced with *The New Manners and Customs of Bible Times* by Ralph Gower, available from well-known online sellers

Miriam, a fictionalized biography, by Lois Henderson, published by and available from Harper Collins, www.harpercollins.com

Moses video produced by the Genesis Project (DO NOT SUBSTITUTE ANY OTHER VIDEO OF THAT TITLE.) This one may be hard to find.

Mrs. Robert E. Lee, by Rose Mortimer Ellzey MacDonald, published by R. B. Poisal, out-of-print but possibly available through used book sources

My Folks Don't Want Me to Talk about Slavery: Twenty-One Oral Histories of Former North Carolina Slaves, by Belinda Hurmence published by John F. Blair, www.blairpub.com

Once a Month Cooking, by Mary Beth Lagerborg and Mimi Wilson, published by St. Martin's Griffin, an imprint of Macmillan *http//:us.macmillan.com/smp*

Pasta and Pizza for Beginners published by Usborne Books sold by independent distributors; find one or order online at www.ubam.com

Pharaohs and Kings: A Biblical Quest by David Rohl, published by Three Rivers Press, www.crownpublishing.com/imprint/three-rivers-press

Pharaohs and Pyramids, published by Usborne Books, sold by independent distributors; find one or order online at www.ubam.com

Prince of Egypt animated movie, directed by Brenda Chapman, Steve Hickner, and Simon Wells, produced by Penney Finkelman Cox, available on Netflix, www.netflix.com and from many retailers

The Pyramid Explorer's Kit, published by Running Press Book Publishers, www.runningpress.com

Queen Nefertiti coloring book by Bellerophon Books, www.bellerophonbooks.com

Red Badge of Courage, by Stephen Crane, classic literature available at most major book retailers and many libraries

Roots: Saga of an American Family, by Alex Haley, published by Vanguard Press, www.vanguardpressbooks.com, *also made into a movie available on DVD and Netflix,* www.netflix.com

Slavery in the United States, by Gary Barr, published by Heinemann-Raintree, www.heinemannraintree.com

Spencerian Penmanship developed by P. R. Spencer, published by Mott Media, www.mottmedia.com

Streams of Civilization, V. 1, by Mary Stanton, Albert Hyma; published by Christian Liberty Press, www.shopchristianliberty.com

The Ten Commandments, a Paramount Pictures movie, directed by Cecile B. DeMille, available on DVD and through Netflix, www.netflix.com

Timetables of History, by Bernard Grun, currently out-of-print but readily available through many used sources

Twice Freed, by Patricia St. John, published byCF4Kids, www.cf4kids.com

Uncle Tom's Cabin, by Harriet Beecher Stowe, classic literature widely available in bookstores and libraries

Up from Slavery, autobiography of Booker T. Washington, published by Dover Publications www.doverpublications.com and available to read online at www.bartleby.com

Vegetarian Cooking for Beginners, published by Usborne Books, sold by independent distributors; find one or order online at www.ubam.com

Webster's 1828 Dictionary published by Merriam –Webster, sold by many homeschool suppliers and a few general bookstores, can also be searched online at www.1828.mshaffer.com

The (Rodale) Whole Foods Cookbook by Dara Demoelt, published by Rodale Books, www.rodaleinc.com

World History: A Christian Survey (See *A Christian Survey of World History*)

World Almanac, published annually by World Almanac Company. You won't need a new one every year, as the information you will be using will not change that often. Sold by most book stores or sites and often found in libraries

World History Dates; published by Usborne Books, sold by independent distributors; find one or order online at www.ubam.com

Writer's Inc. published by The Write Source, www.thewritesource.com

Writing a Research Paper by Edward J. Shevan, published by Christian Liberty Press, available in both print and e-book versions from www.shopchristianliberty.com

Writing for College, published by and available from The Write Source www.thewritesource.com

UNIT 6
She considers a field and buys it;
with the fruit of her hands, she plants a vineyard.
Proverbs 31:16

500 Nations (eight-part video documentary), directed by Jack Leustig, produced by Kevin Costner for Warner Home Video, available from Netflix and many other sources

American Historical Documents, a collection of works by various authors, compiled by Dr. Charles Elliot as part of the 51-volume *Harvard Classics*, long out of-print, can be found at used booksellers, some public libraries and download, borrow, or read online at https://openlibrary.org/books/

American Original Documents (see *American Historical Documents*)

Anatomy of the Human Body by Henry Gray, available for sale from several retailers, but can be searched online at http://www.bartleby.com/107/

Back to Basics: A Complete Guide to Traditional Skills, edited by Abigail Gehring, published by Skyhorse Press, www.skyhorsepublishing.com

Backyard Scientist Series One: 25 Experiments That Kids Can Perform Using Things Found around the House, written by Jane Hoffmann, published by Backyard Scientist www.backyardscientist.com

Baker's Bible Atlas by Charles F. Pfeiffer, edited by Ernest Leslie Carlson and Martin H. Scharlemann, available in print and ebook format from many retailers, may be in some libraries

Basic History of the United States, Vol. 4: The Growth of America by Clarence B. Carson published in print by American Textbook Committee and on audio CD by Blackstone Audio; both can be ordered from www.exodusbooks.com/author.aspx?id=2496

The Bible Almanac: A Comprehensive Handbook of the People of the Bible and How They Lived, by J. I. Packer, Merrill C. Tenney and William White Jr. published by Thomas Nelson, www.thomasnelson.com

Buffalo Bill: The Last Great Scout, by Helen Cody Wetmore, currently available only as a Kindle edition from www.amazon.com, but may be found in print in some libraries

Bury My Heart at Wounded Knee by Sioux author Dee Brown, published by Holt, Rinehart & Winston, find them on www.jacketflap.com

Caddie Woodlawn, classic literature, available from some general bookstores and many public libraries

California Gold Rush 1849, portfolio of primary source documents, researched and compiled by Jackdaw Publications, a division of Golden Owl Publishing, www.jackdaw.com

Canadian West Series containing six books by Janette Oke, published by Bethany House, www.bakerpublishinggroup.com/bethanyhouse

College English Handbook, (see *Harbrace College Handbook*)

Crazy Horse and Custer: The Parallel Lives of Two American Warriors by Stephen E. Ambrose, published by Anchor Books, an imprint of Random House www.knopfdoubleday.com/imprint/anchor

The Curious Life of Robert Hooke: The Man Who Measured London by Lisa Jardine published by Harper Millennial, *www.harpercollins.com*

(The) Daily Bible by F. La Gard Smith published by and available from Harvest House,
    www.harvesthousepublishers.com

The Ecologues of Virgil, translated by H. R. Fairclough, volumes 63 and 64 of the   H. R. Loeb Classical
    Library Volumes 63 & 64. Cambridge, MA. Harvard University Press,
    http://www.theoi.com/Text/VirgilEclogues.html

Fall and Winter in the North Carolina Forest, published by Rod and Staff Publishers,
    www.milestonebooks.com

From Sea to Shining Sea, by Peter Marshall and David Manuel, published by Baker Book House,
    www.bakerbookretail.com

Frontier Living by Edwin Tunis, published by Lyons Press, www.lyonspress.com

A Gardener Looks at the Fruits of the Spirit by Philip Keller, published by Word Books,
    www.wordbooks.com

A Girl of the Limberlost, by Gene Stratton-Porter, published by Norilana Books, www.norilana.com

The Good Earth by Pearl Buck, published by Washington Square Press (imprint of Atria Books)
    www.imprints.simonandschuster.biz/atria widely available and in most libraries

Grand Canyon: Monument to the Flood DVD by Master Books, found at New Leaf publishing,
    www.nlpg.com

The Grapes of Wrath, by John Steinbeck, classic literature widely available for purchase and in many
    libraries

Green Mansions, by W. H. Hudson, classic literature, available at most major book sellers and in many
    libraries

Gregor Mendel and the Roots of Genetics (Oxford Portraits in Science), by Edward Edelson, published by
    Oxford University Press, www.ox.ac.uk

Harbrace College Handbook, edited by John C. Rogers, published by Harcourt, Brace, Jovanovich,
    available anywhere college textbooks are sold. You may be able to rent one by the school year at
    www.chegg.com

The Hidden Art of Homemaking by Edith Schaeffer, published by Tyndale House, www.tyndale.com

The Holy Warrior by Gilbert Morris, published by Bethany House, a division of Baker
    www.bakerpublishinggroup.com/bethanyhouse

How to Draw Maps and Charts by Usborne Books, sold by independent distributors; find one or order
    online at www.ubam.com

Italic Handwriting Curriculum by Barbara Getty and Inga Dubay, published by
    Allport Editions, www.allport.com

Jackdaws" portfolio on The California Gold Rush (see *California Gold Rush 1849*)
Jackdaws' portfolio on the Lewis and Clark Expedition (see *Lewis and Clark Expedition*)

Journey of Life produced by Moody Science Videos, www.moodypublishers.com watch online at
    www.youtube.com/watch?v=czMwurMFlKY

The Last of the Mohicans, by James Fenimore Cooper, classic literature reprinted several times and
    available in many bookstores and libraries

Lewis and Clark Expedition 1804-1806, Portfolio of primary source documents, compiled by Jackdaw
    Publications, a division of Golden Owl Publishing, www.jackdaw.com

Life and Customs of Bible Times (see *Manners and Customs in the Bible*)

The Light and the Glory, by Peter Marshall and David Manuel, published by Baker Book House,
www.bakerbookretail.com

Little House books by Laura Ingalls Wilder, several books --- all beginning with the words 'Little House
--- published in multiple editions by different companies, found in most libraries

Luther Burbank, by Elbert Hubbard, published by Kessinger Publishing LLC. www.kessinger.net

Manners and Customs in the Bible, by Victor H. Matthews, published by Baker Academic,
www.bakerretail.com

Native American Peoples, part of the Dorling-Kindersley Home Library collection, published by Dorling-
Kindersley, www.dk.com

On to Oregon, by Honore Morrow, published by and available from Harper Collins, available
www.harpercollins.com

Oregon Trail, a classic simulation video game that can be played online for free,
www.free*game*empire.com/*games*/*Oregon-Trail*

Orphan Train West series by Jane Peart, published by F. H. Revell, a division of Baker Publishing,
www.bakerpublishinggroup.com/revell

People of the Bible and How They Lived (see *The Bible Almanac: A Comprehensive Handbook of the
People of the Bible and How They Lived*)

Poetry Ecologues, (see *The Ecologues of Virgil*)

The Pony Express: The History and Legacy of America's Most Famous Mail Service, by <u>Charles River</u>
published by CreateSpace Independent Publishing Platform, an Amazon Company
www.createspace.com

The Reluctant Bridegroom, by Gilbert Morris, published by Bethany House, a division of Baker
www.bakerpublishinggroup.com/bethanyhouse

Seasons of the Heart, four-book series by Janette Oke, published by Bethany House,
www.bakerpublishinggroup.com/bethanyhouse

The Secret Garden, by Frances Hodgson Burnett, published by CreateSpace Independent Publishing
Platform, www.createspace.com

Sounder by William H. Armstrong, published by Harper Collins children's division,
www.harpercollinschildrens.com

Spencerian Penmanship developed by P. R. Spencer, published by Mott Media, www.mottmedia.com

Spencer's Mountain, by Earl Hamner, published by Dell, available in ebook and audiobook from online
sources, print version probably in most libraries

Spring and Summer in the North Carolina Forest, published by Rod and Staff Publishers,
www.milestonebooks.com

Square-Foot Gardening Second Edition: The Revolutionary Way to Grow More In Less Space by Mel
Bartholomew, published by Cool Springs Press www.coolspringspress.com

Streams to the River, River to the Sea, a novel by Scott O'dell, published by HMH Books for Young
Readers, available in many retail outlets and libraries

Trail of Tears: A Native American Documentary Collection, DVD produced by Mill Creek Entertainment,
available in most major retail outlets and Netflix

Women of the West Series by Janette Oke, published by Bethany House, www.bakerpublishinggroup.com/bethanyhouse

Webster's 1828 Dictionary published by Merriam –Webster, sold by many homeschool suppliers and a few general bookstores, can also be searched online at www.1828.mshaffer.com

World Almanac, published annually by World Almanac Company, available in most bookstores and libraries. (You need not buy a new one every year, as the information you will be using from it will not change that often.)

World History Dates; published by Usborne Books, sold by independent distributors; find one or order online at www.ubam.com

World History: A Christian Survey (See *A Christian Survey of World History*)

Writer's Inc. published by The Write Source, www.thewritesource.com

Writing a Research Paper by Edward J. Shevan, published by Christian Liberty Press, available in both print and e-book versions from www.shopchristianliberty.com

Writing for College, published by and available from The Write Source www.thewritesource.com

UNIT 7
She girds herself with strength
and strengthens her arm.
Proverbs 31:17

16 Days of Glory: The 1984 Sumer Olympics, documentary originally shown on HBO, now available on DVD produced by Delta Studios

100 Greatest Moments in Olympic History, compiled and written by Bud Greenspan, www.abebooks.com/100-Greatest-Moments-Olympic-History

Aesop's Fables, ancient classical literature translated by Don Daily, published in book form by Running Press, www.runningpress.com or can be read online at www.aesopsfables.com

Anatomy of the Human Body by Henry Gray, available for sale from several retailers, but can be searched online at http://www.bartleby.com/107/

The Ancient City: Life in Classical Athens & Rome by Peter Connolly and Hazel Dodge published by Oxford University Press, www.ox.co.uk

Ancient Lands Microsoft interactive online program to learn about the ancient world, www.worldcat.org/title/microsoft-ancient-lands/oclc/31854133

Antigone, by Sophocles, ancient book that has been translated and published many times, now most readily available at www.RareBookClub.com

Archimedes and the Door of Science, by Jeanne Bendick, published by Bethlehem Books, www.bethlehembooks.com ,

Artes Latinae Level I and II Bolchazy-Carducci publishers

Baker's Bible Atlas by Charles F. Pfeiffer, edited by Ernest Leslie Carlson and Martin H. Scharlemann, available in print and ebook format from many retailers, may be in some libraries

Ben Hur, by Lew Wallace, classic literature available in many retail outlets, used bookstores, and public libraries

Black Ships before Troy: The Story of the Iliad, by Rosemary Sutcliffe, reprinted by Laurel Leaf www.laurel-leaf.stuccu.com

Chariots of Fire, by W. J. Weatherby, published by Dell Publishing Company *www.*biglittlebooks.com/*dell*.html

The Children's Homer by Padraic Colum, published by Aladdin Books www.aladdinbooks.com

The Christian in Complete Armor, three volumes by William Gunall, published by Hendrickson Publications, www.hendrickson.com

(A) Christian Survey of World History audio set by R. J. Rushdooney, available in CD and MP3 format from http://chalcedon.edu/store/all/History/

Clothes & Crafts in Ancient Greece by Philip Steele, published by Gareth Stevens Publishing, www.garethstevens.com

The College English Handbook (see *Harbrace College Handbook*)

(The) Daily Bible by F. La Gard Smith published by and available from Harvest House, www.harvesthousepublishers.com

Developing a Biblical Worldview, by C. Fred Smith, published by B & H Academic, www.bhacademic.com

The Family in Greek History by Cynthia B. Patterson, published by Harvard University Press, www.hup.harvard.edu

Famous Men of Greece, published by Greenleaf Press http://greenleafpress.com

Famous Men of Rome, published by Greenleaf Press http://greenleafpress.com

Gray's Anatomy (see Anatomy of the Human Body)

Gray's Anatomy Coloring Book, by Fred Stark, published by Running Press, available from www.hometrainingtools.com

Greek Myths and Legends, published by Usborne Books, sold by independent distributors; find one or order online at www.ubam.com

The Greeks, published by Usborne Books, sold by independent distributors; find one or order online at www.ubam.com

The Greeks and Greek Civilization by Jacob Burckhardt, published by St. Martin's Griffin, an imprint of Macmillan *http//:us.macmillan.com/smp*

Greenleaf's Guide to Famous Men of Greece, published by Greenleaf Press http://greenleafpress.com

Greenleaf's Guide to Famous Men of Rome, published by Greenleaf Press http://greenleafpress.com

Harbrace College Handbook, edited by John C. Rogers, published by Harcourt, Brace, Jovanovich, available anywhere college textbooks are sold. You may be able to rent one by the school year at www.chegg.com

How We Found out the Earth is Round, by Isaac Asimov, published by Walker and Company, available through www.jacketflap.com

How Your Body Works, published by Usborne Books, sold by independent distributors; find one or order online at www.ubam.com

The Humanist Manifesto, by Karl Marx, probably available in most public libraries

The Iliad by Homer, classic literature, English translations available in many versions, should be in most libraries

Italic Handwriting Curriculum by Barbara Getty and Inga Dubay, published by Allport Editions, available from www.christianbook.com

Jesse Owens: A Biography, by Jacqueline Edmondson Ph.D., published by Greenwood Publishing Group, www.greenwood.com

Julius Caesar by William Shakespeare, best seen as a live play but can be ordered or rented on video, excellent to watch as a live play if possible but also available on DVD from various online sources

The Kingfisher History Encyclopedia, edited and published by Houghton, Mifflin, Harcourt available throughwww.amazon.com and in many libraries

The Los Angeles Times Book of the 1984 Olympic Games, published by *The Los Angeles Times,* store.latimes.com/books.html, may be in some libraries

Make this Roman Villa, published by Usborne Books, sold by independent distributors; find one or order online at www.ubam.com

Make this Roman Temple, published by Usborne Books, sold by independent distributors; find one or order online at www.ubam.com

A Midsummer Night's Dream, by William Shakespeare, best seen as a live play but can be ordered or rented on video, excellent to watch as a live play if possible but also available on DVD from various online sources

The Odyssey by Homer, classic literature, English translations available in many versions, should be in most libraries

O! Euclid game, produced by Ampersand Press, available from https://boardgamegeek.com/boardgame/37293/o-euclid

The Robe, written by Lloyd C. Douglas, published by Mariner Books, an imprint of Houghton Mifflin, www.hmhco.com available at many retailers and most libraries

The Romans, published by Usborne Books, sold by independent distributors; find one or order online at www.ubam.com

Spencerian Penmanship developed by P. R. Spencer, published by Mott Media, www.mottmedia.com

Sportworks, by Ontario Science Centre, published by agreement with De Capo Press, www.ontariosciencecentre.ca

Streams of Civilization, V. 1, by Mary Stanton, Albert Hyma; published by Christian Liberty Press, www.shopchristianliberty.com

Strengthening Your Grip by Charles Swindoll, published by Worthy Publishing, www.worthypublishing.com

Timetables of History, by Bernard Grun, currently out-of-print but readily available through many used sources

Understanding the Times and its optional student guide, by David Noebel, published by Summit Press, www.summit.org

Weigh Down Workshop Exodus out of Egypt, audio CDs and workbook, by Gwen Shamblin, www.weighdown.com

World Almanac, published annually by World Almanac Company, available in most bookstores and libraries. (You need not buy a new one every year.)

World History Dates; published by Usborne Books, sold by independent distributors; find one or order online at www.ubam.com

World History: A Christian Survey (See *A Christian Survey of World History*)

Writer's Inc. published by The Write Source, www.thewritesource.com

Writing a Research Paper by Edward J. Shevan, published by Christian Liberty Press, available in both print and e-book versions from www.shopchristianliberty.com

Writing for College, published by and available from The Write Source www.thewritesource.com

UNIT 8
She perceives that her merchandise is good;
her candle goes not out by night.
Proverbs 31:18

Aladdin and the Wonderful Lamp from 1001 Arabian Nights, classic literature available in many bookstores and libraries

Anatomy of the Human Body by Henry Gray, available for sale from several retailers, can be searched online at http://www.bartleby.com/107/

Anne Sullivan Macy: The Story behind Helen Keller, by Nella Braddy Henney, published by Doubleday, Doran & Co. www.randomhouse.com/doubleday

Arms Control and Military Preparedness from Truman to Bush (American University Studies Series), by Martin Goldstein, published by Peter Lang International Publishers, www.peterlang.com

Basic Electricity: Complete Course, by Van Valkenburgh, Nooger, and Neville, published by Prompt Publications; sold with college textbooks or can be rented from www.chegg.com

Benjamin Franklin: An American Life, by Walter Isaacson, published by Simon & Schuster, www.simonandschuster.com; also available in ebook and audio format

The Biblical Feasts (see *Celebrating Jesus in the Biblical Feasts: Discovering Their Significance to You as a Christian*)

Brief History of Light and Those That Lit the Way (Popular Science Volume 1), written by Richard Weiss, published by World Scientific Publishing Company, www.wspc.com

Celebrating Jesus in the Biblical Feasts: Discovering Their Significance to You as a Christian by Dr. Richard Booker, published by Destiny Image, www.destinyimage.com available in both print and e-book format

The Cold War: A Military History by David Miller, Stephen Ambrose, Caleb Carr, and Robert Cowley, published by Random House, www.randomhouse.com

The College English Handbook (see *Harbrace College Handbook*)

The Coming Economic Earthquake, by Larry Burkett, published by Moody Press, www.moodypublishers.com

(The) Daily Bible by F. La Gard Smith published by and available from Harvest House, www.harvesthousepublishers.com

Disaster Preparedness: Simple Steps for Businesses by Julie Freestone and Rudi Raab, published by Crisp Publications, www.mycrisp.com/publications/index.html

Electricity, published by Usborne Books, sold by independent distributors, find one or order online at www.ubam.com

Fanny Crosby, Queen of Gospel Songs, by Rebecca Davis, published by Potter's Wheel Books, www.hiddenheroesmissionarystories.com

The Fifty-Year War: Conflict and Strategy in the Cold War by Norman Friedman, published by the U. S. Naval Institute Press, www.usni.org/navalinstitutepress

George Westinghouse: Gentle Genius, by Quentin Skrabec, published by Algora Press, www.algora.com

Gray's Anatomy (see Anatomy of the Human Body by Henry Gray

Gray's Anatomy Coloring Book, by Fred Stark, published by Running Press, available from www.hometrainingtools.com

Harbrace College Handbook, edited by John C. Rogers, published by Harcourt, Brace, Jovanovich, available anywhere college textbooks are sold. You may be able to rent one by the school year at www.chegg.com

Helen Keller: The Story of my Life, by Helen Keller and Candace Ward, published by Dover Classics, www.doverpublications.com

Inventors and Inventions, published by Usborne Books, sold by independent distributors; find one or order online at www.ubam.com

Italic Handwriting Curriculum by Barbara Getty and Inga Dubay, published by Allport Editions, available from www.christianbook.com

The Kingfisher History Encyclopedia, edited and published by Houghton, Mifflin, Harcourt available through www.amazon.com and in many libraries

Louis Braille: A Touch of Genius by C. Michael Mellor published by National Braille Press www.nbp.org

The Miracle Worker by William Gibson, published in paperback by Pocket Books an imprint of Simon & Schuster www.simonandschuster.com, also available in e-book format from other sources

Moby Dick by Herman Melville, classic literature available at many retailers, used book stores and libraries

Nikolas Tesla biography (see *Wizard: The Life and Times of Nikola Tesla: Biography of a Genius)*

Oil Lamps: The Kerosene Era in North America, by Catherine Thuro, published by Wallace-Homestead Wallace-Homestead, now closed, order from www.worldcat.org

Science Experiments on File, large reference book may still be found in many libraries but can also be replaced by online searches or resources

Science Projects on File large reference book may still be found in many libraries but can also be replaced by online searches or resources

Spencerian Penmanship developed by P. R. Spencer, published by Mott Media, www.mottmedia.com

Streams of Civilization, V. 1, by Mary Stanton, Albert Hyma; published by Christian Liberty Press, www.shopchristianliberty.com

Thomas Edison: A DK Biography by Jan Adkins, published by Dorling-Kindersley, www.dk.com/us

Timetables of History, by Bernard Grun, currently out-of-print but readily available through many used sources

Webster's 1828 Dictionary published by Merriam –Webster, sold by many homeschool suppliers and a few general bookstores, can also be searched online at www.1828.mshaffer.com

With Christ in the Biblical Feasts (see *Celebrating Jesus in the Biblical Feasts: Discovering Their Significance to You as a Christian)*

Wizard: The Life and Times of Nikola Tesla: Biography of a Genius, by Marc Seifer, published by Citadel Press www.thecitadel.bncollege.com

World Almanac, published annually by World Almanac Company, available in most bookstores and libraries. (You need not buy a new one every year, as the information you will be using from it will not change that often.)

World Book Encyclopedia, published by Field Enterprises, available in most libraries and now searchable online

World History Dates; published by Usborne Books, sold by independent distributors; find one or order online at www.ubam.com

World History: A Christian Survey (See *A Christian Survey of World History*)

Writer's Inc. published by The Write Source, www.thewritesource.com

Writing a Research Paper by Edward J. Shevan, published by Christian Liberty Press, available in both print and e-book versions from www.shopchristianliberty.com

Writing for College, published by and available from The Write Source www.thewritesource.com

UNIT 9
She lays her hands to the spindle;
her hand holds the distaff.
Proverbs 31:19

All the Women of the Bible by Herbert Lockyer, published by Zondervan, www.zondervan.com

American Historical Documents, a collection of works by various authors, compiled by Dr. Charles Elliot as part of the 51-volume *Harvard Classics*, long out of-print, can be found at used booksellers, some public libraries and download, borrow, or read online at https://openlibrary.org/books/

American Original Documents (see *American Historical Documents*)

Anatomy of the Human Body by Henry Gray, available for sale from several retailers, but can be searched online at http://www.bartleby.com/107/

Back to Basics: A Complete Guide to Traditional Skills, edited by Abigail Gehring, published by Skyhorse Press, www.skyhorsepublishing.com

Baker's Bible Atlas by Charles F. Pfeiffer, edited by Ernest Leslie Carlson and Martin H. Scharlemann, available in print and ebook format from many retailers and National Braille Press libraries

Basic Machines and How They Work by Naval Education And Training Program , published by Dover Publications, www.doverpublications.com

Beggar to King: All the Occupations of Bible Times, by Walter Duckat published by Abingdon Press www.abingdonpress.com can be read online through www.librarything.com

Bible Manners and Customs: How the People of the Bible Really Lived, by Dr. Howard F. Vos, published by Thomas Nelson, www.thomasnelson.com

(A) Christian Survey of World History audio set by R. J. Rushdooney, available in CD and MP3 format from http://chalcedon.edu/store/all/History/

Christy, by Catherine Marshall, published by HarperCollins Publishers, available from www.goodreads,com

The College English Handbook (see *Harbrace College Handbook*)

(The) Daily Bible by F. La Gard Smith published by and available from Harvest House, www.harvesthousepublishers.com

David Copperfield by Charles Dickens, classic literature can be found in many bookstores and libraries and is also available in DVD which really captures the actual story

Disciplines of a Beautiful Woman, by Anne Ortlund, published by Word Books,

Forces and Motion, written by Rand Casey, published by Heinemann-Raintree

The Foxfire Book, by Elliot Wigginton, published by Anchor Books, an imprint of Random House www.knopfdoubleday.com/imprint/anchor

Gaining Favor with God and Man, by William Thayer, published by Lionheart Publishing www.lionheartbooks.org

God in the Machine: Video Games as Spiritual Pursuit, by Liel Leibovitz, published by Templeton Press, www.templetonpress.org

Gray's Anatomy (see Anatomy of the Human Body by Henry Gray

Gray's Anatomy Coloring Book, by Fred Stark, published by Running Press, available from www.hometrainingtools.com

Great Inventors and Inventions Coloring Book by Bruce LaFontaine, published by Dover Publications www.doverpublications.com

Harbrace College Handbook, edited by John C. Rogers, published by Harcourt, Brace, Jovanovich, available anywhere college textbooks are sold. You may be able to rent one by the school year at www.chegg.com

Hard Times, by Charles Dickens, classic literature, can be found in many bookstores and libraries and may be found in an abridged version using modern vocabulary and easier to read

The Hidden Art of Homemaking by Edith Schaeffer, published by Tyndale www.tyndale.com

How Things Work: The Physics of Everyday Life, by Louis Bloomfield, published by John Wiley & Sons, www.wiley.com as a college textbook, available for rent one semester at a time from www.chegg.com

How Things Work Encyclopedia (for young people and less technical than the above), published by Dorling-Kindersley, www.dk.com

The Industrial Revolution, portfolio of primary source documents, researched and compiled by Jackdaw Publications, a division of Golden Owl Publishing, www.jackdaw.com

Inventors and Inventions, published by Usborne Books, sold by independent distributors; find one or order online at www.ubam.com

Iron Will, by Orison S. Marden, published by Wilder Publications www.wilderpublications.com

Isaac Newton, by John Hudson Tiner, part of the Sower Series published by Mott Media, www.mottmedia.com

Italic Handwriting Curriculum by Barbara Getty and Inga Dubay, published by Allport Editions, available from www.christianbook.com

Journey to the Ants: A Story of Scientific Exploration, written by Bert Hölldobler and Edward O. Wilson, published by W. W. Norton & Company, www.wwnorton.com

The Kingfisher History Encyclopedia, edited and published by Houghton, Mifflin, Harcourt available through www.amazon.com and in many libraries

Lydia, a fictionalized, Bible-based biography by Lois Henderson, published by Harper-Collins, www.harpercollins.com

Machines, produced *by Science Videos* (substitute *Basic Machines and How They Work*)

Marbles, Roller Skates, Doorknobs: Simple Machines that are Really Wheels by Christopher Lampton, published by Millbrook Press, an imprint of Lerner Publishing Group www.lernerbooks.com

Mary vs. Martha, inspiring audio/CD devotional message by Sono Sato Harris, Noble Publishing Associates/Noble Books; this company is out of business but the item is still available used through online sources

More Hours in My Day: Proven Ways to Organize Your Home, Your Family, and Yourself by Emilie Barnes, published by Harvest House, www.harvesthousepublishers.com

M*over of Men and Mountains, Autobiography of R. G. LeTourneau*, published by Prentice Hall, www.phschool.com

Nicholas Nickleby by Charles Dickens, classic literature, which can be found in many bookstores and libraries and may be found in an abridged version using modern vocabulary and easier to read

Oliver Twist, by Charles Dickens, classic literature, which can be found in many bookstores and libraries and may be found in an abridged version using modern vocabulary and easier to read. DO NOT SUBSTITUTE THE MOVIE *OLIVER*. It is NOT the same.

Organizing from the Inside Out, by Julie Morgenstern, published by Holt Paperbacks www.us.macmillan.com/HenryHolt.com

People of Bible Times and How They Lived (see *Bible Manners and Customs: How the People Of the Bible Really Lived*)

Priscilla and Aquila, fictionalized biography by Lois Henderson, published by Harper-Collins www.harpercollins.com

Science Projects on File large reference book may still be found in many libraries but can also be replaced by online searches or resources

Seesaws, Nutcrackers, Brooms: Simple Machines that are Really Levers by Christopher Lampton, published by Millbrook Press, an imprint of Lerner Publishing www.lernerbooks.com

Sidetracked Home Executives, by Pam Young and Peggy Jones, published by Grand Central Publishing, a division of Hachette www.hachettebookgroup.com
Sketches of Church History, by S. M. Houghton and Iain Murray, published by Banner of Truth, www.banneroftruth.org

Spencerian Penmanship developed by P. R. Spencer, published by Mott Media, www.mottmedia.com

Streams of Civilization, V. 2, by Mary Stanton, Albert Hyma; published by Christian Liberty Press, www.shopchristianliberty.com

Susanna Wesley, by Charles Ludwig, part of the Sower Series published by Mott Media, www.motmedia.com

Threads of Love by Susan Paige, published as part of the Patchwork Mysteries Series by Guideposts, www.guideposts.org

Timetables of History, by Bernard Grun, currently out-of-print but readily available through many used sources

Training Our Daughters to Be Keepers at Home by Ann Ward, published by Smiling Heart Press, www.shekinahhomeschool.com/page92.html

The Way *Things Work,* or *The New Way Things Work* by David Macaulay, published by Houghton Mifflin/Walter Lorraine Books, www.hmhco.com/at-home, may be in libraries also in video format on CD-rom

Webster's 1828 Dictionary published by Merriam –Webster, sold by many homeschool suppliers and a few general bookstores, can also be searched online at www.1828.mshaffer.com

What's a Smart Woman like You Doing in a Place like This? By Mary Ann Froehlich published by Woglemuth & Hyatt, available at www.worldcat.org

Work, Energy, and Power: An Introduction to Basic Energy Physics, by Sarah Allen, currently available in Kindle format only

Work, Power, and Energy (see *Work, Energy, and Power: An Introduction to Basic Energy Physics*)

World Almanac, published annually by World Almanac Company, available in most bookstores and libraries. (You need not buy a new one every year, as the information you will be using from it will not change that often.)

World History Dates; published by Usborne Books, sold by independent distributors; find one or order online at www.ubam.com

World History: A Christian Survey (See *A Christian Survey of World History*)

Writer's Inc. published by The Write Source, www.thewritesource.com

Writing a Research Paper by Edward J. Shevan, published by Christian Liberty Press, available in both print and e-book versions from www.shopchristianliberty.com

Writing for College, published by The Write Source www.thewritesource.com

UNIT 10
She extends her hand to the poor.
Yes, she reaches out her hands to the needy.
Proverbs 31:20

Adolf Hitler: The Definitive Biography by John Toland, published by Anchor Books, an imprint of Random House www.knopfdoubleday.com/imprint/anchor

All Quiet on the Western Front by Erich Maria Remarque and A W. Wheen published by Ballantine Books, imprint of Random House, www.randomhousebooks.com

America in the 40's: A Sentimental Journey published by Readers Digest, available in hard cover book, audio CD and VHS tape, DVD format coming soon

Amy Carmichael: Rescuer of Precious Gems, by Janet and Geoff Benge, published as part of the Christian Heroes: Then & Now by YWAM Publishing

Anatomy of the Human Body by Henry Gray, available for sale from several retailers, but can be searched online at http://www.bartleby.com/107/

Anne Frank: Diary of a Young Girl by Anne Frank and B.M. Mooyaart, published by Bantam Paperbacks an imprint of Random House www.randomhousebooks.com (Use only editions published earlier than 1994 as some later ones have added material not widely believed to have been in the original diary.)

Baker's Bible Atlas by Charles F. Pfeiffer, edited by Ernest Leslie Carlson and Martin H. Scharlemann, available in print and e-book format from many retailers and libraries

Basic History of the United States, Vol. 5: The Welfare State by Clarence B. Carson published in print by American Textbook Committee and on audio CD by Blackstone Audio; both can be ordered from www.exodusbooks.com/author.aspx?id=2496

Benito Mussolini: The First Fascist by Anthony L. Cardoza, published as part of Pearson's Library of World Biography Series, www.pearsonhighered.com/educator/series/Library-of-World-Biography/10492.page

The Biblical Feasts (see *Celebrating Jesus in the Biblical Feasts*)

Bringing in the Sheaves by George Grant published by Christian Liberty Press, www.shopchristianliberty.com

Celebrating Jesus in the Biblical Feasts: Discovering Their Significance to You as a Christian by Dr. Richard Booker published by Destiny Image, www.destinyimage.com available in both print and e-book

(A) Christian Survey of World History audio set by R. J. Rushdooney, available in CD and MP3 format from http://chalcedon.edu/store/all/History/

The College English Handbook (see *Harbrace College Handbook*)

Corrie ten Boom: Keeper of the Angels' Den by Janet Benge, published as part of the *Christian Heroes: Then & Now* series by YWAM www.ywampublishing.com

(The) Daily Bible by F. La Gard Smith published by and available from Harvest House, www.harvesthousepublishers.com

The Diary of Anne Frank: The Play, written from Anne Frank's diary by Francis Goodrich and Albert Hackett, published by Random House www.randomhouse.com

George Muller: The Guardian of Bristol's Orphans by Geoff Benge, published as part of the Christian Heroes: Then & Now series by YWAM www.ywampublishing.com

God and Government by Gary Demar published by American Vision Press, http://store.americanvision.org/products/god-and-government

The Grapes of Wrath by John Steinbeck, classic literature widely available for purchase and in many libraries

Gray's Anatomy (see Anatomy of the Human Body by Henry Gray)

Gray's Anatomy Coloring Book, by Fred Stark, published by Running Press, available from www.hometrainingtools.com

The Great Depression portfolio of primary source documents, researched and compiled by Jackdaw Publications, a division of Golden Owl Publishing, www.jackdaw.com

The Greatest Generation by Tom Brokaw, published in hardback, paperback, e-book and audiobook by Random House, www.randomhouse.com

The Guns of Navarone by Alistair MacLean published by Fawcett, available online and in libraries

Guys and Dolls, by Damon Runyon, the basis for a Broadway play by the same name, available in print and e-book and as a movie on DVD (WARNING TO PARENTS: This is a musical comedy set in the 1920's; some of the humor may be objectionable to some parents)

Harbrace College Handbook, edited by John C. Rogers, published by Harcourt, Brace, Jovanovich, available anywhere college textbooks are sold. You may be able to rent one by the school year at www.chegg.com

The Hiding Place by Corrie Ten Boom, published in print, e-book and audiobook by Chosen Books, an imprint of Baker Books www.bakerpublishinggroup.com/chosen

The Holocaust: A History of the Jews of Europe during the Second World War by Martin Gilbert, published by Holt Paperbacks, us.macmillan.com/HenryHolt

The Illustrated Red Baron: The Life and Times of Manfred von Richthoffen by Peter Kilduff, Cassell Books, now part of Orion Publishing Group www.orionbooks.co.uk

In the Shadow of Plenty, by George Grant, published by Christian Liberty Press, www.shopchristianliberty.com

Inventors and Inventions, published by Usborne Books, sold by independent distributors; find one or order online at www.ubam.com

Italic Handwriting Curriculum by Barbara Getty and Inga Dubay, published by Allport Editions, available from www.christianbook.com

Major Barbara, a stage play by George Bernard Shaw, published as a book by Penguin Classics www.penguin.com and may be available on DVD

Mein Kampf by Adolf Hitler, translated by James Murphy, published by CreateSpace Independent Publishing Platform www.createspace.com

Never Give In! The Best of Winston Churchill's Speeches by Winston Churchill, compiled by his grandson and published by Hachette www.hachettebookgroup.com

Number the Stars by Lois Lowry, published by HMH Books for Young Readers www.hmhco.com/at-home

Places in the Heart, movie written and directed by Robert Benton, produced by Sony Pictures Home Entertainment, www.sonypictures.com/movies available on DVD (Rated PG, some material may be objectionable)

The Red Signal, by Grace Livingston Hill, available for purchase at www.goodreads.com and other online sites, and may be in many public libraries

Schindler's List, produced and directed by Steven Spielberg in DVD, Blu-Ray and digital video for Universal Studios, can be purchased and rented from most common outlets (Rated R for graphic Holocaust scenes)

Seasons of the Heart, four-book series by Janette Oke, published by Bethany House, www.bakerpublishinggroup.com/bethanyhouse

The Second World War (six-volume set) by Sir Winston Churchill published by Mariner Books an imprint of Houghton Mifflin,   www.hmhco.com/popular-reading/reading-groups

Sergeant York, movie directed by Howard Hawks, produced by Warner Brothers, now available as DVD Blu-Ray, or digital video

The Sinking of the Lusitania by Patrick O'Sullivan, published by The Collins Press

www.collinspress.ie

Sketches of Church History, by S. M. Houghton and Iain Murray, published by Banner of Truth, www.banneroftruth.org

Sounder, by William H. Armstrong, published by Harper Collins children's division, www.harpercollinschildrens.com

Spencerian Penmanship developed by P. R. Spencer, published by Mott Media, www.mottmedia.com

Streams of Civilization, V. 2, by Mary Stanton, Albert Hyma; published by Christian Liberty Press, www.shopchristianliberty.com

Timetables of History, by Bernard Grun, currently out-of-print but readily available through many used sources

Tora, Tora, Tora video directed by Kinji Fukasaku, Richard Fleischer, Toshio Masuda, produced by Twentieth Century Fox, available to buy or rent in DVD or Blu-Ray

Training Our Daughters to Be Keepers at Home by Ann Ward, published by Smiling Heart Press now available from www.shekinahhomeschool.com/page92.html

War and Peace by Leo Tolstoy, translated by Richard Pevear and Larissa Volokhonsky, published by Vintage Classics www.vintage-books.co.uk/classics

War Game: Village Green to No-Man's-Land written by Michael Foreman from true stories of his uncles' experiences, published by Pavillion www.pavilionbooks.com (This book is written for younger children, but is fun reading for all.)

Webster's 1828 Dictionary published by Merriam –Webster, sold by many homeschool suppliers and a few general bookstores, can also be searched online at www.1828.mshaffer.com

Where the Red Fern Grows by Wilson Rawls, published by Yearling, an imprint of Random House www.randomhousekids.com available in most libraries

White Cliffs of Dover (Britain at War) by Jean Kathleen Allred, published by CreateSpace Independent Publishing Platform, www.createspace.com

With Christ in the Biblical Feasts (see *Celebrating Jesus in the Biblical Feasts: Discovering Their Significance to You as a Christian*)

World Almanac, published annually by World Almanac Company, available in most bookstores and libraries. (You need not buy a new one every year, as the information you will be using from it will not change that often.)

The World at War by Sir Winston Churchill (see *The Second World War* by Sir Winston Churchill)

The World at War video on DVD from The History Channel, www.shophistorystore.com

World History Dates; published by Usborne Books, sold by independent distributors; find one or order online at www.ubam.com

World History: A Christian Survey (See *A Christian Survey of World History*)

Writer's Inc. published by The Write Source, www.thewritesource.com

Writing a Research Paper by Edward J. Shevan, published by Christian Liberty Press, available in both print and e-book versions from www.shopchristianliberty.com

Writing for College, published by and available from The Write Source www.thewritesource.com

CHRONOLOGICAL Cross-Reference Guide for using
"Far Above Rubies" and "Blessed Is The Man" concurrently

Time Period	FAR Mini-Unit Title	BITM Mini-Unit Title	FAR Unit #	BITM Unit #
Creation	Creation and the Origin of the World We Know	Creation Versus Evolution	1	1
Old Testament	The World of the Old Testament	The Old Testament World	I	2
Ancient Egypt	Ancient Egypt	The Old Testament World	5	2
Ancient Greece	Ancient Greeks: Founders of the Olympics	New Testament Cultures	7	1
Ancient Rome	Ancient Rome: Warriors of Great Strength	New Testament Cultures	7	1
Middle Ages	The Middle Ages	The Middle Ages	14	3
Renaissance & Reformation	Renaissance & Reformation	Renaissance & Reformation	12	3
Explorers	Explorers and the Age of Exploration	Age of Exploration	4	3
Pre-Colonization	The First Americans		6	x
Colonial America	The Founding of America	Founding of the U.S.A.	13	4
American Revolution and Political System	The U. S. Constitution	War for American Independence	13	4
The War Between the States	The War Between the States and its Aftermath	The War Between the States	5	2
Westward Expansion	Westward Ho!	Westward Expansion	6	3
Industrial Revolution Revolution	The Industrial	Invention and Industry	9	3
World War I	The War to End All Wars (WWI)	The Holocaust and WWII	10	2
The Great Depression	The Great Depression	Poverty, Welfare, Depression	10	7
World War II	The Next Great War	The Holocaust and WWII	10	3
Late 20th Century	Scattered Throughout	Scattered Throughout		

THEMATIC Mini-Unit Cross-Reference Guide for using
"Far Above Rubies" and "Blessed Is The Man" concurrently

Thematic Unit	Unit and Mini-Unit in FAR	Unit and Mini-Unit in BITM
Agriculture	6-B	8-B
Animals	3-B & 3-C	6-D
Architecture	13-E	3-D
Arctic/Antarctic	11-A	6-F
Astronomy	11-C	1-D
Atmosphere	11-C	8-C
Banking	2-D	7-C
Beauty	19-B	n/a
Birds	3-C & 4-All	6-D
Botany	6-A & 12-D	6-E
Brain	16-B	1-A
Business	14-A	7-D
Charity	10-A	7-E
Child Training	16-C & 18-B	6-C
Childbirth	18-A	6-C
Civil War	5-D	2-C
College/Apprenticeship	20-C	1-A
Courtship/ Marriage	2-A	6-B
Creation	1-C	1-C
Digestive System	5-A	8-A
Diligence	9-A & 17-B	7-All
Diligent Work	3-All & 17-B	7-All
Early America	13-C	4-C & 5-E
Early Bible Times	1-D	2-A & 2-B
Economics	4-A	7-C & 7-D
Egypt, Ancient	5-C	2-A
Environment	11 Throughout	5-All
Exercise	7-A	Assorted
Explorers	4-C	3-C
Exterior Design	12-D	N/A
Eyes	8-C	7-A
Fabric/ Sewing	3-D & 9-B	N/A
Fashion	12-B	N/A
Federal Government	13-D	4-B & 4-D
Future	15-C	9-C
Gardening	6-A	6-E
Godly Wives	19-All	6-B
Government	2-C & 13 Throughout	4-B & 4-D
Graduation	20-C	9-D
Great Depression	10-B	7-E
Greece, Ancient	7-C	1-C
Health	5-A & 7-A	7-A
Heart/ Circulatory System	7-A & 16-B	7-A
Home Education	16-C	1-A
Home Industries	14-A	7-D
Homemaking	17-A & 17-D	Assorted
Human Body (general)	7-A	7-D & 2-E
Industrial Revolution	9-D	3-F
Insects	6-B	6-D
Interior Design	9-B & 12-C	N/A

Thematic Unit	Unit and Mini-Unit in FAR	Unit and Mini-Unit in BITM
Inventors	9-C	3-F
Light/ energy	8-B	Assorted
Local Government	17-C	Assorted
Machines	9-C	3-F
Marriage	13-A & 19-C	6-B
Medicine	15-13	Assorted
Middle Ages	14-C	3-B
Oceans	4-D	8-E
Parenting	18-B	6-C
Personal Economics	2-D	7-B
Politics	13-D	4-D
Prayer	Throughout	Throughout
Real Estate	6-C	7-B
Reformation	12-A	3-D
Renaissance	12-A	3-D
Reproduction	2-B	6-B
Respiratory System	11-Assorted	7-A
Rocks/ Minerals	1-B	2-B
Rome, Ancient	7-D	1-C
Sheep	3-A	6-D
Ships	4-B & 4-D	3-C
Skeletal/ Muscular System	7-A	7-A
Skin	19-B	7-A
Slavery	5-B	2-C
Space	11-C	1-D
Spiritual Fruit	20-A	6-A
Sports	7-B	Assorted
Textile Industry	3-D & 9-B	N/A
Travelers	4-B	N/A
Vikings	4-C	3-B
Virtue	1-A	Assorted
Weather	11-B	8-F
Westward Movement	6-D	3-E
Wisdom	16-A	1-A & 4-A
World War I	10-C	7-E
World War II	10-D	2-D

Twenty-Five Ways
to Have Fun with Book Reports

1. Write a straight summary of the story.

2. Write a three-to-five sentence synopsis of each chapter.

3. Write a character sketch of one or more of the people in the story.

4. Write diary and/or journal entries as they would have been done by one of the characters during the action of the book.

5. Write a review of the book telling why you did or did not like it. (To prepare for this, read book and/or movie reviews in the newspaper.)

6. Write a newspaper or magazine article as it might have been written by a reporter on the scene of one of the book's major events.

7. Write letters that might have been exchanged between two of the characters during or after the events in the book.

8. Write a poem or song to summarize the plot of the story or to extol the virtues of one of its characters.

9. If the book is organized in such a way that it is possible, outline it.

10. If your book does not have chapter titles, write them, naming each chapter according to the action or other information in it. Use titles that will add suspense or interest for the reader.

11. Write an alternate ending to the book.

12. Write and/or draw a newspaper ad extolling the virtues of why a person should read this book.

13. Folding a large piece of drawing paper in half, make a jacket for your book with an appropriate picture on the front and some juicy tidbits to attract the reader's interest on the back.

14. Draw a mural of several scenes showing the main flow of action in the book.

15. Draw a chart showing the relationship between various characters in the book. (This could be a family tree or any other type of chart as appropriate.)

16. Draw and cut out paper dolls to look like the characters in the book. Provide appropriate clothing and accessories and use these to act out scenes from the story.

17. Draw pictures of events from the story and arrange in order to make a picture book. Add very short captions as needed to tell the main plot of the story to a younger child.

18. Draw a poster or bulletin board display that you believe would entice someone to read the story, featuring something actually happening in the story.

19. Make a diorama or shadowbox depicting an important scene in the book.

20. Make cloth, paper bag, or finger puppets and use them to act out the story.

21. Conduct an 'interview' with a character from the book as it might have been done on radio or TV as the book's action was taking place or immediately afterward. (This can be done live by having a parent or sibling ask pre-written questions or can be taped with the child doing both parts.)

22. Prepare a costume and give an oral report about the events in the book as one of the characters to whom they happened.

23. Plan and perform a short skit illustrating one of the main events of the book. (Call on siblings or friends to help you with the performance.)

24. Do the above skit as a radio play on audio cassette with the reader playing all parts.

25. Give a live or taped 'newscast' (TV or radio) of one or more events from the book as if you were reporting directly from the scene.

These companion volumes are also available from homeschool curriculum providers or Amazon.com:

FAR ABOVE RUBIES, Volume II (Units 11 – 20)
by Lynda Coats

BLESSED IS THE MAN (VOLUMES I & II)
by Lauren & Lynda Coats

and you will also want to see

THE GIRL'S GUIDE TO HOME SKILLS
by Martha Greene, Jan Drexler & Rebekah Wilson

THE BOY'S GUIDE TO HOME SKILLS
by Martha Greene & Gail Kappenman

Visit us at
www.TheHomemakersMentor.com
or
www.HomeschoolFreebieOfTheDay.com

Made in the USA
Columbia, SC
18 March 2020